Philip Royston
8.15.09

GENTLEMEN FROM HELL

GENTLEMEN FROM HELL:
Men of the 487th Bomb Group

Leaders of the Largest
Eighth Air Force Mission
of World War II

By C.C. Neal
and
487th Veterans
in their own words

Turner
PUBLISHING COMPANY
NASHVILLE, TENNESSEE • PADUCAH, KENTUCKY

TURNER PUBLISHING COMPANY
412 Broadway • P.O. Box 3101
Paducah, KY 42002-3101
(270) 443-0121
www.turnerpublishing.com

Turner Publishing Company Staff
Randy Baumgardner, Editor
Frene Melton, Designer

Copyright © 2005: C.C. Neal
Publishing Rights: Turner Publishing Company
All rights reserved.

No part of this book may be reproduced or transmitted in any form or by any means, electronic or mechanical, including photocopying, recording, or by any information storage and retrieval system, without permission in writing from the publisher.

ISBN: 1-59652-197-X
Library of Congress Control No.: 2005928402

Printed in the United States of America.

0 9 8 7 6 5 4 3 2 1

Dedication

*To my father, Thomas William Craig,
who instilled in me the feelings of passion,
admiration and respect for my country,
flag and freedom.*

For those who never returned home.

Acknowledgments

This book has been put together as a tribute to the men of the 487th Bomb Group, as well as to all those who have served our country. It is full of personal accounts, in their own words, with vivid descriptions of their trials and tribulations during World War II.

To those who have supported and helped me with your enthusiasm and patience during this endeavor, I will be forever grateful.

Jonathan Foster, who was indispensable. His tireless work in assisting me and passion for the subject made continuing the project a joy - even during the frustrating times. I am in awe that he was able to juggle being my assistant, with all the tasks involved, while finishing his master's degree at UNC-Wilmington.

Peter Etters and Brendan Drury were encouraging, as well as patient as they literally taught me how to use the computer and transcribed the veterans' taped interviews for the book. Both of them were always so pleasant and willing to help at a moments notice.

Jake Austad and Randy Baumgardner at Turner Publishing Company have been absolutely the expert professionals. They're so knowledgeable about the business and have made publishing my book fun.

My girlfriends, Candy Raymer, Pru Patterson and Susie Karn, ask me almost every time I talk with them how the book is coming along. Mel Riegel, wife of one of the veterans in the book, kept me going with her many phone calls and notes of encouragement.

The members of my family were so helpful in seeing me start this project to its completion. My mom, Louise Craig, always said you could do anything well if you just put your mind to it. My husband, Larry, has seen me through laughter and happy times of getting to personally know these veterans better, as well as the tears when the news has come that one of them has passed away. He has read every chapter and taken many messages as well as a genuine interest in my project.

My cousin, Jeff Carpenter, who's really like a brother to me, thanks for your concern as well as emotional support. My lifelong confidant, Idella, you know I thank you.

Last but certainly not least, my daughter, Sherry Barrow, and her husband, Klay, and my son, Tommy Honey, and his wife Kate, have been my rock and inspiration during the three years of compiling these stories - they are literally the "sunshine of my life."

The veterans stories you will read were told to me in personal taped interviews or sent to me, in their own words. Their accounts are their own as each veteran remembers. Because of this, the factual information may seem to vary once in a while. To the men of the 487th who let me tell your story, I will be forever in your debt and honored to get your story out there, to go down in history and to be remembered forever.

TABLE OF CONTENTS

Dedication v
Acknowledgements vii
Introduction 1

836th Squadron 5
    Paul Tomney 7
    Bob Densmore 15
    John C. Broom 19
    Junior Gossell 25
    Jim Bradford 29
    Paul L. Biri 30
    Jim Erskine 32
    Jack Kohl 34
    Donald Frantz Partain 36
    Stanley E. Rolfes 41
    Duane Kaiser 47
    Neil F. Matz 51
    Karl Kandler 59
    Jim Wandless 67
    Joe Gaffney 83
    Jim Hyland 85

837th Squadron 91
    Jim Brooks 92
    George Phillips 96
    Leonard Davis 102
    George Battschinger 106
    Clark Yocum 111
    John Beeson 115
    Walter Zmud 120
    Julian Headley 124
    Tom Valentine 127
    Howard (Pete) M. Peterson 130
    Alan H. Wheasler 136
    David B. Dahlberg 141

838th Squadron 149
    Julian Messerly 151
    Thomas William Craig 158
    Richard Atkins 161
    Pete Riegel 164
    William Henry Hughey 169
    James Spurlock 173
    Roy Hon, Sr. 175
    Art Silva 180
    Isadore Lerner 188
    William Bowers 191
    Francis Eberhart 198
    Roy M. Levy 201
    William C. Rich 204
    Chuck Haskett 206
    Mike Quering 214
    Walter C. Moore 226
    Paul White 243

839th Squadron 247
    Kay Voss 248
    Walter Baker 255
    Donald Kilburg 262
    Al Rasof 267
    Gerald Obrecht 270
    Walter Wise 272
    Bobby Wayne Heard 274

669th Aero-Engineering Squadron 279
    William Michaels 280

Epilogue 291
Index 295

Introduction

On December 24, 1944, the "Mighty Eighth" Air Force sent 2,034 B-17 and B-24 bombers and 936 fighters over Germany. This was the single greatest force of airplanes ever dispatched in history, and the 487th Bomb Group was selected to lead the way. Bernie Lay, a member of the 487th, and author of *Twelve Oaks High* had this to say about the group. "Every Bomb Group that flew to the United Kingdom in World War II began as a number. When the smoke of battle had cleared, and the weeds had begun to sprout in the cracks of the runways at Lavenham, the number '487' was no longer an impersonal set of digits. The number bespoke the highest peak of achievement of a lifetime for all the men who served at Lavenham, England. And in the cold, black and white figures at Headquarters, Eighth Air Force, which measured performance, the number '487' identified a group of airmen whose record in combat had been surpassed by none."

In the 487th Bomb Group, there were four squadrons - the 836th, 837th, 838th and 839th. The 487th Bomb Group was one of 46 bomb groups in the heavy division of the Eighth Air Force, which was one of several Air Force groups in the U.S. They were even rewarded with an imposing nickname. While in Alamogordo, New Mexico, waiting to fly to Europe, some British soldiers noted, "This place is hotter than Hell, and there's no place for a Gentleman here." To which one veteran replied, "We must be the Gentlemen from Hell." The name stuck as a nickname for the 487th.

The assignment of the "Mighty Eighth" Air Force was to defeat the German military which was under the Nazi regime that had conquered 27 countries. The Eighth received the name "Mighty Eighth" because it was the largest air armada ever assembled during World War II. In fact, the Eighth Air Force was so large it was the largest armada ever assembled in any war: over 350,000 served in the Eighth, 26,000 lost their lives, and another 28,000 became prisoners of war.

You will read an overview to some of the men's personal stories in the introduction to each of the four squadrons. Remember, these are their own stories - some personal interviews, and some written and sent to me, 60 years later. Their stories are verbatim as to how they told them to me during interviews, which began at the 487th Bomb Group Reunion in Omaha, Nebraska, on August 10, 2002. You'll read more about my travels during the last three years of putting this book together, the camaraderie I've developed with these veterans, and why I wanted to write this book in the Epilogue.

The last personal interview, which was taped in Omaha, Nebraska, is the only one not in a specific squadron. This is the story of William Michaels, who was in Aero Engineering and a squadron mechanic for all four squadrons of the 487th.

If this book does nothing else but make each reader want to thank the next veteran they see for all they did for our freedom, then my goal will have been met. I also have pledged 50 percent of the proceeds of my book, after expenses, to the 487th Bomb Group Treasury. It has been an honor and a privilege to compile the stories of some of the men of the 487th Bomb Group of which my father, Thomas W. Craig, was a member. He always told me that it was the ones that didn't make it home who were the supreme heroes. His friend and fellow 487th crew member, Julian Messerly, was one of those men. Also, there are accounts of five POWs, including Jim Hyland, George Phillips, Leonard Davis, Jim Brooks and Walter Moore.

My father passed away seven years ago, and after deciding to do this book, I went to his bedroom and went through his WWII books about the 8th Air Force, 487th Bomb Group, to see if there were any clues that would help me with pulling his chapter together. There were enough notes written by him in the margins for me to tell his story.

Each man's story is intriguing, fascinating and also grueling. After reading their individual stories, you will have a deeper understanding about what they endured and survived for our freedom. These men are getting older. They are dying at a rate of more than 1,000 a day, and it's of utmost importance to have their experiences recorded in history and never forgotten.

836TH SQUADRON INTRODUCTION

In reading first-hand accounts of their World War II years, you'll marvel at the unbelievable memories of these veterans. It's amazing how, 60 years later, these men each can recall how high they were flying on certain missions and details of each one. As you read their stories, you'll discover that they recall very specific moments in their military history. The memories of war are permanently etched in their minds.

First is the account of Paul Tomney, who trained as a flight engineer. Read Tomney's account of missions in December 1944 and you'll discover why this notice was sent to their base: "For their glorious record in the month of December, the men of the 487th Bombardier Group were commended with great enthusiasm by General Arnold, Lt. General Spatz, and Gen. Eisenhower and Major Gen. Patridge, Commanding General of the 3rd Air Division." Tomney also flew with the next man interviewed, Bob Densmore. The chapter by Densmore is a pilot's riveting account of one horrible mission.

The next account is from John Broom, who flew as Bombardier on a B-17 and gives a description of his plane being destroyed with him inside before bailing out! The American soldiers on the ground where he had landed had been told that he was a German pilot who had been shot down. Read his story to see how he convinced them that he was an American. Junior Gossell's description of a bomb hung up in the bomb-bay makes the reader feel as if he's on the plane. Their frantic attempt at prying the bomb-bay open with a screwdriver is awesome. You'll read how the radio operator on that mission was out there without oxygen and nothing but a catwalk between him and the ground - 25,000 feet below.

The next story is that of Jim Bradford, whose good friend Bob Densmore was his co-pilot. Paul Biri tells, in his account, of how his group was selected to lead the 8th Air Force on December 24, 1944 - the largest bombing mission in history, with the target being Babenhausen, Germany. You'll read how his plane caught fire and his first pilot, Robert Harriman, gave orders to "bail out." Five out of his 10 crewmembers were killed that day, yet he chose to stay in the Air Force for 22 years.

Jim Erskine tells of his experience of flying 16 missions with 14 different crews, and how after 50 years had passed, he met up with Jack Kohl, who was co-pilot with Erskine's original crew. Kohl's story follows Erskine's. Don Partain makes reference to the idea that the group became known as the "Gentlemen from Hell" in Alamogordo, New Mexico. Stanley Rolfes' chapter recalls in vivid detail a few "close calls" he remembers that will make your hair stand on end. He did 28 missions on his first tour and 16 on his second tour.

Gentlemen From Hell

Duane Kaiser tells of his first four days of combat. They were so unbelievable that he ends his chapter saying, "So I had many long nights to twist and turn in bed, wondering how we could possibly finish 30 or so more missions out, considering what had happened to us on our first four days of combat." Kaiser was forced to parachute from his plane and justify his identity as an American citizen.

Neil Matz is deceased, and his information was sent to me by his family. He ends his chapter with, "Each year, there are fewer of us left to reminisce. At least now, my family knows what happened during the war."

Karl Kandler died in 1994, and his chapter was sent in by his son, Karl Kandler Jr. His son put together his dad's chapter by contacting other surviving crew members and locating original documents. You'll read excerpts from Kandler's pocket diary in the war from June 20, 1944 through December 1944. Jim Wandless tells of how the German crews were sending up "our captured B-17's to fly in formation with the 8th Air Force."

Joe Gaffney tells the account of an October 1944 mission: Target Cologne, when one of his crew was hit by flak and his oxygen mask was dangling loose at 27,500 feet.

Prisoner of War Jim Hyland's chapter is the last story in the squadron, and his story speaks for itself. The stories of the Prisoners of War are about as spellbinding as you can imagine. Hyland says, "Upon my return to the States, I made a point to visit the parents of each of the men in my crew who were killed and the pilot's wife. Two things sustained me during the ordeal: the power of prayer and a strong knowledge that God answers prayers." These are the men of the 836th Squadron and their youthful lives.

PAUL TOMNEY

LEFT: *Tomney served the 487th Bomb Group as a gunner from July 4, 1944 to February 8, 1945. Tomney's crew was prepared to ditch during an assignment on December 24, 1944 - the Battle of the Bulge - when the nose of the plane filled with smoke after taking damage, but the smoke cleared and the crew returned to base.* RIGHT: *Tomney in his library at his home.*

Let me introduce myself. I'm Paul Tomney. I was a Staff Sergeant and a gunner on a B-17 in the 487th Squadron, stationed at Lavenham field, from July 4, 1944 to February 8, 1945. To begin with, I would like to give you a synopsis of my military experience prior to arriving at my base in England.

My first actual experience with the war in Europe was during my high school years in Winchester, Virginia. Three students from Winchester, England sister city to Winchester, Virginia, were transferred to Handley High School because of the bombing of English cities.

After graduating in 1942, I went to work at Glenn L. Martin Aircraft Plant in Middle River, Maryland, building the PMB-3 flying boat. I worked there until the end of 1942. I decided to join up instead of being drafted. I tried to get into the Navy Flying School but at this time they were not taking volunteers - the schools were filled. I had my draft number moved up, and on January 14, 1943, I was ordered to report for my physical. My induction was on February 17 - I was 18 years old. Arrived at Camp Lee, Virginia, on February 24 and made it into the Army Air Corp.

My basic training was at Miami Beach, Florida, arriving there March 3. We stayed in the hotels on the beach and one of the golf courses was our drill field. Basic training lasted 56 days, after which I made PFC (Private First Class).

Gentlemen From Hell

On June 3, I shipped out to Keesler Field, Biloxi, Mississippi, where I completed airplane mechanic training for the B-24. The courses included hydraulic, electrical and fuel systems and airplane structure, engines, engine operations, instruments and propellers. Here, each student is getting a $2,500 course that used to take four years, in four months. Schools were held in three shifts around the clock.

Upon completion of the airplane mechanics course, I was sent to Harlingen Army Gunnery School, Harlingen, Texas. There, I had my first experience with high altitude and night vision testing. We had to field strip the .50 caliber machine gun in two minutes, blindfolded. We also had to detail strip the gun in 35 minutes. It only took me 29 minutes to complete this. There were 50 parts to handle in taking it apart and then putting the same 50 parts back together. We had to know the names of 110 parts. December 14. I was assigned to specialize in the Martin turret, which is the top turret and the one I wanted.

Skeet shooting - now, I really liked that. We had to shoot from trucks while going along at 20 miles an hour. The road was like a figure-eight and was one and two tenths miles long with clay pigeon houses along the side. There were 25 houses where the clay pigeons were released, and you fired 25 consecutive shots at a time. I could have done this all day!

Personal Diary During the War

January 4, 1944 - what a day! I was flying today for the first time! I got my .30 cal. machine gun; bore sighted it, had it checked by an armorer, drew my helmet and ammunition and was ready to go. I took all of my equipment over to the plane and put in my gun, then got my "Mae West" on and also my parachute and then I put on my gunners belt and my safety belt. Gosh, it sure did feel swell rolling down that runway, then climbing into the air and seeing everything getting so small. Being in an open cockpit made it feel so much more realistic. Everything was just about what I expected as far as the feeling goes, but, of course, it gave me a great thrill when I left the ground. Boy, the air is the place for me. It didn't take us long to get out over the Gulf to start firing at our tow target. The two planes were flown by civilian women pilots flying in B-26s. I saw one bulkhead with five .50 cal. holes in it. Believe me, they can have that job - I wouldn't want it.

January 6 was my first run in an AT-6. As we left the runway my ammunition fell out of the second can because the spring holding it was weak. I really had a funny feeling when I looked down and saw the ammo sliding out and going through a rather large opening in the bottom of the plane. I stepped on the ammo belt, reached down and pulled it on to my lap. My gun wouldn't lock so I had to hold my gun with one hand all the time because if I didn't, the slip stream would swing the gun back and forth and it would have hit me. I threw my leg over the side of the plane to keep the gun from sliding. With all of this going on I could hardly sight my gun, but did get all of my rounds into the sleeve target.

836TH SQUADRON

January 16 - Graduation Day! Our group had an average rating of 76.8, which was the highest in a year.

Made Corporal today! Arrived in Salt Lake City, February 6, but delayed en route on a train to my home for the first time since I joined the Army.

I was assigned to Davis-Monthan Field, Tucson, Arizona as flight engineer, arriving February 28. Here, I met my crew and found out we had three flight engineers - Jeffers, Hudson and myself. Jeffers had been there for 30 days, so he became the crew's flight engineer.

At Davis-Monthan, we went on gunnery practice missions, camera bombing, etc., flying over Arizona, New Mexico, Texas and California. I had to take pills that the Canadian Air Force had just developed for air sickness, only used them for low altitude runs. I also stopped the milk shakes and the cold barbecue I usually ate before take-off. Stopping that and taking the pills, everything was OK. I didn't want to be grounded; that would have killed me.

My co-pilot's brother, a civilian, was on the post April 30. They decided to take a chance on dressing him up like a GI and taking him along with us - he had never been up before. He took William's place in the crew. We took off and when we were only 3,000 feet over Tucson, our No. 3 prop started running away and Jeffers couldn't stop it, so he had to feather it. When he did, we started losing 500 feet a minute. Harriman, our pilot, banked our plane around and did some neat flying to get through the 20 planes that surrounded us. We headed for the field at 200 miles an hour, and Harriman told them to clear the field for an emergency landing. We were down to 200 feet when we finally reached the runway, if we had been a few more seconds away, we would have crashed. For a while, none of us thought we would make it, but when we put the flaps down it gave just enough lift to carry us to the runway. I'm sure this was an experience Rowe's brother will never forget.

May 1944 - I'm now a Sergeant. We are being sent to Lincoln, Nebraska. My pilot, Harriman, was put in the hospital with the mumps. And our radio operator, Swain's, father had just died, so he had seven days off. They almost got us another first pilot, but our co-pilot, Rowe, went to our Colonel and had him call someone in the 2nd Air Force, and they said it would be alright for us to wait for Harriman in Lincoln. The group we were to go with was sent to the Pacific. Now, we are going to the European theater. When Swain came back from California, he brought a Fox Terrier with him. We got to meet the girls then - wished we had thought of this earlier. He took the dog overseas with us.

June 2 - we left Lincoln for Bangor, Maine. On the way, we buzzed the waist gunner's home in Monroe, Michigan. Bad weather kept us in Bangor until June 5, then we took off for Goose Bay, Labrador. Weather kept us there until June 8, when we flew to a base at Reykjavik, Iceland. What an experience - the sun was up 23 hours a day at this time of year. June 12, we landed in Valley, Wales, delivering the new B-24. We were then sent to Kill Kill, Ireland, for new tactics training. While we were there someone stole Swain's dog - she was really a great dog. At

Gentlemen From Hell

Kill Kill, I found four Irish four-leaf clovers, gave two away and kept two, which I carried on all my missions. I guess it helped this Irish boy have good luck.

July 4, 1944, arrived at our permanent base at Lavenham, England - the 836th Squadron of the 487th Bomb Group, 3rd Division.

On the 15th, we flew a major to another field. On the way there we flew under a bridge! The pilot asked if it was O.K. with everyone and we all said yes. I was in the tail-last man through!

"Frenchi," our bombardier, leaves us. He was the victim of the change over from B-24s to B-17s. The reason for this was to use a nose gunner as a togglier. All the togglier had to do was open the bomb doors, reach over and throw a switch when the lead plane dropped its bombs. They did have some backup planes with bombardiers in case the lead plane was shot down.

My fifth mission was to St. Sylvain France on August 8. I flew as tail gunner. The flak was very intense. Our group lost one crew and I saw quite a few planes go down from other groups. We went in at only 11,000 feet. We had to feather number three engine. Jeffers had a piece of flak come in through the Plexiglas part of his turret. One piece went past William in the chin, turret position, and it hit McCarty, but didn't go through his flak suit. Two pieces came within a foot just behind me in the tail. There were other hits throughout the plane. I was really scared to death and felt quite a bit older after this. We landed with number three engine feathered and no flaps.

On August 10, we were made a lead crew. My co-pilot will now fly in the tail position if some air leader flies in his place.

I went to Winchester, England, on August 22 to visit Roger and Betty Edmonds, two of the students who had been sent to Winchester, Virginia, during my high school years.

On a test hop, my pilot fooled around with a P-47, an AT-6 and a Hurricane which laid its wing on ours and banged it twice and then peeled off. They were pretending to attack us. We saw a British Sterling bomber do a loop, and Harriman tried to roll our plane, but couldn't quite get roll over. A lot of stunts were pulled that day.

This was a good day, September 1 - I made Staff Sergeant and received my Air Medal.

September 30 - I flew my ninth mission to Belfield Germany as tail gunner. We flew low crew again. Just after we passed over the target, I saw a plane in the group behind us get a direct hit from a rocket and blow up. Saw three chutes emerge from the flames, but they were on fire and soon burned up, dropping the men. Contrails got really bad after this, and two ships in another squadron ran together and went down. All of the boys on one of the crews were on their last mission - I knew them well. This was also Meredith's last mission for us as our ball-turret gunner, since we were made a Pathfinder lead crew. On October 17, I was told I would also leave the crew, another victim of the Pathfinder. My 10th mission was my last with Harriman and my original crew.

836th Squadron

On my 13th mission November 2, with Bob Densmore as pilot, our target was Merseburg, Germany, an oil refinery. We flew number 11 in the low squadron - my position was togglier/nose gunner. We were flying at 27,000 feet. A plane in the group ahead of us blew up. Our P.F.F. ship was shot down. Number four engine was knocked out on the bomb run to the targets. There were over 400 guns at the target and we were in flak for 15 minutes. We also had number two engine knocked out - this caused us to drop to 13,000 feet before we could lighten the ship. Four FWs hit our squadron, but they did no damage. We had two P-51s escort us from the target to the French coast. We were down to 2,000 feet when we crossed the coast to England. Densmore did some terrific flying that day. Back at the base, Harriman, my former pilot called the "big shots" to try to find out what had happened to me since we had not come back with the group. With only two engines, it took us a lot longer to get back from Germany.

On December 11, I flew my 16th mission to Giessen Germany as tail gunner. Our target was railroad yards. We flew in the fourth position. It was a P.F.F. run with little flak, but some rockets. After the run, the planes came back over Paris to show the people our strength in the air. At 11:45 a.m., my oxygen mask froze. I took it off for a few seconds to get it to work, but passed out and fell against my guns in front of me, freezing the left side of my face. When I didn't answer an oxygen check, the waist gunner came back on a walk around bottle and fixed my mask none too soon - at this altitude, you die fast from the lack of oxygen. I stayed back in the tail until we were out of enemy territory. The rest of the trip home, I stayed in the radio room. My face hurt most when we dropped down from high altitude. An ambulance came out to the plane for me and took me to the field hospital; from there, I went to a hospital at Long Melford - still in my flying clothes. The next day, we drove two hours to another hospital in Norwich.

Three days after freezing my face, December 14, the doctors couldn't believe how fast I had recovered. At first my bottom lip hung almost to the bottom of my chin. My face really looked so bad, I thought I might not want to go home, but luckily there were some scars for a while, but they went away over time. Captains from my field came to see me to get my version of what happened. They said that I would go up on practice mission, and if O.K., I could finish my missions. I was doing better; I was one case in a million to recover so fast. When I first went to the hospital, they said it would take four to six months to recover.

December 24 - the target was an air field at Babenhausen, Germany. It was my 17th mission and I was flying as a togglier/nose gunner. We flew at 22,000 feet number three position in the low squadron. At Huy, Belgium, 50 planes, mostly ME 109s, hit us, the lead squadron and the high squadron at the same time. They came in two waves. I have since read that they were concentrating on the low squadron and that they were using timed 20mm shells that exploded in white puffs in front of the plane. The battle lasted 20 minutes and went into Germany. At the very beginning, I saw four ships in my squadron on fire at the same time. A little later, I saw two blow up. The low squadron, which I was in, started out with 12 ships and ended up with only three - of the three, our plane and one other had to turn around and go back to the base due to damage. The remaining plane, with Meredith from my original crew, joined up with the other squadron.

Our number four engine was feathered and one and two were hit and acting up. I had two holes right over my head and couldn't see how they missed me. We had no fighter escort; the fighters were late leaving because of fog. We hadn't had time to put on our flak suits. The nose filled with smoke once, and we prepared to leave, but it cleared, so we stayed.

I saw four planes work on Harriman, my first pilot, who at the time of the attack was dropping back with an engine failure. He had General Castle with him as Air Leader - they were leading the entire 8th Air Force that day. Harriman's crew got two of the enemy planes, but they were finally shot down and the ship broke up into four parts. Harriman, General Castle, Rowe and Swain were killed. Swain fell from the plane without a chute. They could only identify him by his ring. Only four feet were found that belonged to Harriman and General Castle. Before the mission, Rowe, who was displaced to the tail with the General on board, came to me and asked how to get out of the tail if they were hit. He got out of the plane, but was full of holes when they found him. When Rowe's brother attended a memorial dedication in Fraiture, Belgium, June 27, 1999, an eye witness related the details which he observed from a school yard when he was 17 years old. He said Rowe was wounded and moving in his parachute when a German pilot circled and shot him. He was dead when he hit the ground.

We headed back for an emergency field in France, but finally decided to take a chance and fly to our base. The group lost nine from the low squadron and two from the high. In our squadron, Duffy was shot completely out of the ship in the ball-turret, and Shorty jumped without a chute. Curtis' chute caught fire and went down. Blackie went to a hospital in Belgium. Sam was hit in his head by a 20 millimeter, but recovered. Both Blackie and Sam were thought to be lost but turned up a month later.

When we returned, 43 crews landed on our field when they couldn't land at their bases because of fog.

The mission was the largest air armada ever - over 2,000 heavy bombers and 1,000 fighters which finally caught up with us.

Christmas Day. It snowed last night, but it doesn't seem like Christmas - a lot of my friends were killed yesterday.

My 21st mission on December 31 was to Hamburg, Germany. I flew as togglier/nose gunner. We missed our group over the splashier and tried to catch them at the coast, but couldn't find them. While forming over England, in the clouds and fog, we missed a head on crash with another B-17 by only a few feet. It came out of the fog right at us, going just under us. Densmore said he never saw the plane, but it's etched in my memory! We joined a chaff group of six planes. We were the only plane with bombs; I don't know what we hit. Flak was heavy and I saw three B-17's shot down by fighters ahead of us, and one P-51 also went down.

This notice was sent to our base:

"For their glorious record in the month of December the men of the 487th Bombardier Group were commended, with great enthusiasm by General Arnold, Lt. Gen. Spaatz, Gen. Eisenhower and Major Gen. Partridge, Commanding General of the 3rd Air Division."

On January 1, 1945, I flew my 22nd mission as togglier/nose gunner to Ehman, Germany. I got hit at 12:01 p.m. as I was dropping our bombs. I saw the burst, a piece of flak came through the nose of the plane and went between my arm and chest, and the Plexiglas hit me above my right eye and a piece also cut me on my head. We feathered one engine over Hamburg, Germany, after it was hit by flak. Fighters were all over but didn't hit us. This was my last mission with Densmore as pilot. He was a good pilot - he always got us home.

I flew in the tail with a new crew with Martin as my pilot for my 23rd mission on January 6 to Worms, Germany. Meredith and McCarty from my original crew were with us. There was heavy flak and rockets. One rocket just missed our stabilizer, and our oxygen system was shot out over the target. We came back by ourselves at low altitude, and by the time we got to the field, we were at rooftop level - at times, we were lower than the tops of trees around our field. It was so foggy, we couldn't find the runway. We just missed the tower once, the tail of a parked B-17, plus a truck - I do mean just missed! We had to finally land at another field where it was also foggy, and we almost turned over there. As we landed, the tip of one wing was bent up and, in trying to stop, a tire was torn up on the wheel as we ran out of runway. We had used up half the runway before we touched down.

Jeffers and Hudson have joined the crew, this makes five of us from the original Harriman crew flying together again. This is my 24th mission, January 8 to Frankfurt, Germany, flying as tail gunner. There was heavy flak - three crews were forced to land in France after being shot up. There is a picture of this plane on its belly in a cornfield in "The Mighty Eighth War Diary." One of these planes was from our hut; they were a new crew and had only four prior missions. The group ahead of us was hit by fighters.

Awarded a cluster for my Air Medal - this is my third one.

I flew to Dessau, Germany, as togglier/nose gunner on January 16, 27th mission. On returning, we were low on gas and thought we were going to have to land in France, but decided to try for England. Again, we couldn't find our field because of fog, so went to Woodbridge, an English Emergency field. They were burning petrol at the side of the huge runway. Number two and three engines quit on the runway, and the other two engines quit while taxing. Seven crews had to land in Woodbridge.

On January 29, I flew my 30th and last mission. We flew to Kassel, Germany, and I was in the togglier/nose gunner position, I believe that Steck was the pilot for this mission. Before the target, the navigator passed out, but I happened to turn around and found him in time. While over the target, each bomb on one side of the bomb racks bounced off the bottom bomb - they were supposed to go off on impact. After the target, I almost passed out while helping the navigator fix his flak suit, my hose pulled loose and he had his back to me - luckily he also turned around in time to give me oxygen. On the way back, I kicked the last bomb out into the North Sea. The Germans fired a rocket at us from Holland right after I did this, and they almost hit us!

I received the 8th Air Force "Lucky Bastard Certificate" for completing my 30 missions. I was not required to fly the 35 missions because I had been a lead crew.

Going Home!

I boarded the USS West Point on February 21 for my return to the United States. For this crossing, the West Point was mostly a hospital ship. The air crews had to pull KP, and the men from Iceland pulled guard duty. There were extra rough seas - I got sick, and the regular chief did, too. The ship rocked from side to side, everything slid back and forth. Waves came over the front of the ship so badly that they twisted the steel ladders, and a sailor was killed when his gun was torn from the front and pinned him against the bulkhead.

On one occasion, 25 submarines within 24-hour cruising radius were recorded on the navigator's chart.

After rest and reassignment, I was assigned to Chanute Field at Rantoul, Illinois, where I received specialized training on Pratt and Whitney engines. When the war ended, I was stationed at Fort Myers, Florida, waiting to be assigned to a B-29 crew to go to the Pacific. I was discharged at Ft. Meade, Maryland, on September 27, 1945.

BOB DENSMORE

Densmore, 2002.

My name is Robert "Bob" Densmore, and I was a First Lieutenant. I joined the service in October of 1942, in Los Angeles. I entered the 8th Air Force when I went overseas in August of 1944. I was in the 836th squadron. I started as a co-pilot and then became a first pilot. I flew 35 missions. I was just short of 21 when I joined up.

We were very fortunate as far as people being wounded and that sort of thing. There was only one crew member that was ever wounded. Two things happened to him, and the actual wound from flak was rather minor. It was a scalp wound. We had one case where he was flying in the tail gunner's position, and we perform oxygen checks to make sure everybody's on oxygen, because occasionally somebody would take an oxygen mask off because it froze up, or it was uncomfortable, or something like that. And at altitude, if they don't get it back on, they could pass out. So, that's why we had an oxygen check every 10 minutes or so. Everybody checks in, but he didn't. So, I sent the waist gunner back to check on him - he had a walk around oxygen bottle that he used - and he found him passed out with his oxygen mask off. He had fallen against his gun, and the gun was the temperature of the outside, which was -50 or something like that, and it froze the side of his face. His oxygen mask had frozen up, and that's why he had taken it off; he had tried to clear it. So, the waist gunner was able to get the mask cleared and back on him, and he revived, but his face was frozen. On our way back, he came up to the radio room and, as we lost altitude, his face really started to hurt. The radio operator gave him a shot of morphine. Then, when we got back and landed, we had the ambulance come out and pick him up and they took him to the hospital. He was moved around to various hospitals, and they told him that he would probably be, I think like six weeks or something to fully recover, but actually he recovered in just a few days. He had been visited in the hospital by some of the squadron commanders and they told him, "Well, when you get back, we'll let you fly a practice mission; if you get along OK, then you can start flying missions again." Well, he came back, and the first mission he flew, which was without taking any practice missions, was our December 24 mission. So anyway, he got a good mission to start back to work on. But that's the only problem we ever had with people.

When we went over, we had a crew that stayed together for about eight missions. Then, they took the first pilot off for lead crew, and pretty soon they took the navigator and then, they took the bombardier off to make part of a lead crew. All the officers except for myself were changed. But the balance of the crew stayed pretty much the same. We did have this one fellow that was hurt join us later on, and he flew 12 missions with us. He had been bumped off another crew because they became a PFF crew, and that involved radar equipment, and the equipment forced him out of his position, so they had to put him somewhere else. So, he joined our crew.

I have not kept up with most of the pilots, except in one case. The problem was that they started dying. I did keep up with my crew and still do - those that are left. But both pilots that I kept up with have died. Well, and my first pilot that I started with died early, '55 I think. So, it's kind of hard that way.

I've only been to about seven reunions. The first one I went to was the one in Atlanta in 1987. I tried to pick the ones close to home to go to. My wife's health kind of prevented us from going sometimes when I wanted to.

I got into engineering after the war. I was an engineer. I designed process equipment for refineries, chemical plants and power plants. I did that all the time. I worked in Los Angeles to start with and then in the California Bay Area, which is where I did most of my living.

We were married on December 1, 1940, before I went into the service. My first child was born in 1943 while I was in the service, back in North Dakota. My wife named him Junior; she named him after me. So that was our first son and now we have a daughter and another son and six grandchildren.

I know the Germans did try to confuse the target with smoke coverage. But mainly, it was the weather, and if you bombed by PFF or radar, the accuracy was not there as it should be. I think that had a lot to do with missing targets. As far as myself was concerned, I think it was kind of funny that when we started our first mission we flew just in the northern part of France, and we couldn't drop our bombs because we had a malfunction in the bomb racks. The second mission we flew was again to the northern part of France, to Caen, and it was in support of ground troops. In other words, we were to bomb the German lines, which would help the allies to advance. We couldn't drop our bombs again because we had problems with the bomb rack. I learned about the results of this mission. I felt kind of good that we didn't drop our bombs because a lot of them fell on allied troops - Canadians mainly, but some of them did fall on German lines. But on the other hand, enough fell on the Germans that the allies were able to advance, so it balanced out, maybe. We flew five missions and only dropped our bombs once because of problems, mainly with weather, the bomb racks, or having a mission recall. It seemed like we spun our wheels quite a bit, and we didn't do much to help win the war.

Of course, any crew is a pretty close knit group. When you face what we did together you have a real bond, and that continued after the war for me. I've kept in touch with everybody that I could. I've had several missions that were not pleasant, but in the end result, nothing happened to us, so that's pretty good. We struggled through it.

The November 2nd mission I remember quite well. It was to Merseburg, which was probably one of the worst targets as far as flak was concerned. I've read that in that area, they've had from 500-700 anti-aircraft guns. This was a refinery complex in that area, and it was a target that they loved to go after, but nobody wanted to go. On the bomb run, I had one engine shot out. I was able to complete the bomb run, and as we turned off the bomb run after we had dropped our bombs and turned off, I lost another engine. So, I couldn't keep up with the group. I did with three engines, but I couldn't with two. Merseburg is not too far from Berlin, so we were well into German territory. We came back on two engines from that. Hopefully, everything would continue to work. As long as it did, we were OK. But then, there was the potential to get intercepted by fighters or something, as we were stragglers all by ourselves. But anyway, we got back.

Of course the other memorable mission was the one on December 24 when our squadron, the 836th - well, you probably know about that mission. That was the time the 487th led the entire 8th Air Force on the biggest bombing mission ever, I'll put it that way. Brig. General Castle was the air leader. Ordinarily, Generals don't lead missions, but since this was an important one and it was the first time they'd been able to fly in about five days because of weather, and they were putting up the maximum effort, he wanted to lead, which he did. The 836th squadron flew in what's called the low squadron. Actually, we had four squadrons in our group. Normally, we just flew three. This time, they made up a fourth squadron, so we had, I think, something like 48 planes up in the air. I flew on the wing of the lead plane of our squadron. I was flying in the number three position. We flew right over the Battle of the Bulge. I haven't talked to anybody that knew why we did that. Maybe somebody knows why we did that, but the only reason I could think of was that we probably did it to reinforce the morale of the troops below. The flak was extremely heavy because the Germans had a huge concentration of guns there that they could use very handily. They shot the hell out of us as we flew over. Right after we got over that, then the German fighters hit us. Personally, flying the plane, I didn't see much of the fighters because they were all behind us. What they did was they lined up behind us in two tiers and just fired into our low squadron. One of my people said there were 50 of them. I don't know if that's true or not. I don't know exactly how many there were. I only saw one, and he flew up right in front of our plane up in the squadron. Normally, they don't do that; they don't have to do that. They can stand off like most of them did and just fire into our squadron because they had 20mm guns and they could stand out of the range of our guns.

So I was flying, like I said, on the lead plane in the number three position, and we started to turn - this was Lloyd Reed's plane, and Major Lloyd Nash was the air leader for our squadron - they started to turn to the right, and I started to follow them. Then, I saw smoke trailing from one of their engines, and then I saw the fellow flying in the tail gunner's position bail out. So, I figured there was no point in following them anymore. I left them, and there was no squadron left. At that time, I had one engine damaged due to flak when we flew over the Battle of the Bulge. The fighters damaged my number one engine, and I lost power. I couldn't increase or decrease the power from the throttle setting, and it was just like half an engine out. It was running well, but what I figured was the super charger had been shot, damaged some way or other. If it wasn't working, then you didn't have a lot of power from that engine at altitude. Since I couldn't control the RPM or throttle, I figured that the throttle cables had been severed. So anyway, it just kept running along, but it wasn't doing much good. Then, I lost the other damaged engine and had to abort. We had an alternate emergency field in France that we could land at if we had trouble. I got a heading from our navigator for that, and I started toward that, and at the same time, losing altitude so I wouldn't have to work the other engines too hard. The lower we got, the better this one engine, the number one engine, ran, because of the lower altitude. So, it seemed like we had three engines, so we decided to go home. And we did.

The next day, I found out what the problem was a 20mm shell had gone through the super charger. In the process, it severed the throttle cable. But then, I also learned what happened to everyone else - Castle being shot down and all the other planes that were lost. That was the worst mission that we ever had and the only time I experienced fighters. The Germans weren't able to put up fighters like they had in the early days because of lack of fuel and oil and so forth. Those trips to places like Merseburg paid off in that it kept them on the ground, pretty much. Those were my two worst missions that I had. On others, I think I lost another engine on some mission, but I don't remember which mission it was.

JOHN C. BROOM

LEFT: *Broom (right), pictured with his cousin William Broom on Oct. 28, 1944.* RIGHT: *Broom applied his skill and knowledge to a career in the oil industry.*

I enlisted February 25, 1942 in the U.S. Army Air Corps. Following graduation from Bombardier school, I was assigned to the 836th Squadron of the newly organized 487th Bomb Group, Alamogordo, New Mexico, on November 24, 1943. I would serve as Bombardier on a B-24 Bomber. The other nine members of my flight crew were: Lt. Edgar Lee Fuller, Pilot; Lt. Wilburn E. Furr, Co-Pilot; Lt. Neil E. Brown, Navigator; S/Sgt. Hewitt J. Dickinson, Jr., Engineer; S/Sgt. Arthur Massey, Radio Operator; Sgt. Frederick E. Hernley, Gunner; Sgt. Hudie E. Graves, Gunner; S/Sgt. Willard A. Green, Gunner; and T/Sgt. Charles E. Tigh, Gunner.

Our inexperienced 487th Bomb Group engaged in pre-combat bombing exercises for about four months, including making dry runs on dams, bridges, etc. We also dropped a few real combat bombs on simulator targets such as ship outlines in white on the black asphalt beds near White Sands, New Mexico. We arrived at our brand new air base in Lavenham, England on April 13, 1944, when the 487th Bomb Group was assigned to the 8th Air Force. My age was 22.

I flew 12 combat missions as Lead or Deputy-lead Bombardier initially, then flew 21 additional missions as Bombardier/Navigator for a total of 33 missions flown. At the end of my 12th mission, I was hospitalized for two weeks with strep throat infection, and during that period, the other nine members of my flight crew were reassigned - six to a lead crew and three to a wing crew. The latter three were killed shortly afterwards when their B-17 bomber collided with another of our B-17s during a bombing-run September 30, 1944 over Belfield, Germany. They were Lt. Wilburn E. Furr, Co-Pilot, S/Sgt. Willard A. Green,

Gunner; and Sgt. Hudie E. Graves, Gunner. After returning to duty, I was trained in the use of the English "Gee" triangular radio navigation system to supplement my previous training in dead-reckoning navigation. I then flew my remaining 21 missions as a relief Bombardier/Navigator whenever a bomber crew needed a temporary replacement of their Bombardier or Navigator or both.

On October 7, 1944, I was flying as a replacement Bombardier-Navigator on a B-17. Our target that day was a factory in Lutzkendorf, Germany. As with most of our bombing missions into Germany, this one was flown at an altitude of about 33,000 feet to minimize flak damage from the very effective .88 mm anti-aircraft guns, so we all had to wear oxygen masks. On our bombing run this day, my plane was hit by four close bursts of flak - Bam! Bam! Bam! The bomber was riddled, knocking out most of the ship's systems for the landing wheels and the brakes. About the only thing still working was the plane's four engines, so from that point on, everything was manual, by the seat of your pants. The shrapnel also wounded our tail gunner and the gunner in the nose section with me. I began giving a morphine shot to the nose gunner whose leg had been hit, and while doing so, I passed out, unaware that my oxygen hose had been severed by the flak because it was still hanging from above by a thread. I regained consciousness to find that, though badly wounded, he had managed to connect an emergency oxygen bottle to my mask. We nursed the ship back to our English base in Lavenham, mechanically cranked down the landing wheels and, after touchdown with no brakes, ground-looped the plane to stop at the end of the runway.

When the Battle of the Bulge began, a 20,000-foot thick blanket of winter fog had settled over Western Europe and no one could fly. Every morning, day after day, we would get everything ready and then go out to our planes and wait. I remembered a previous flight in pea soup like this one, which I served as bombardier-navigator. We were returning from a 35,000' mission and when letting down over England, we encountered dense fog at 15,000 feet that went all the way to the ground. Using Gee radio navigation, I spotted our position on the map, then drew a course to our 487th base and gave our pilot our new heading. I then plotted our position points on my map and talked the pilot to a location 1,500 feet directly above the landing runway of our Lavenham field. The pilot then made a banking turn with me reading blips off the Gee monitor and spotting new location points every few seconds, then giving him heading corrections as the plane dropped. At an altitude of about 200 feet, we suddenly saw, shining through the dense fog, the very bright lights marking the foot of our landing runway and knew that we were home free.

On December 24, 1944, after eight days of heavy fog, the skies cleared. The American and British Air Forces dispatched every bomber and fighter plane they had. This aerial Armada was made up of 2,000 American 8th Air Force B-17 and B-24 heavy bombers; 500 Royal Air Force Halifax and Lancaster Heavy Bombers; plus 1,000 American and British fighters and fighter-bombers. The 2,500 heavy bombers targeted German supply depots, communication centers and airfields on the German occupied area east of the snowed in Ardennes battleground, where thousands of American troops had just been killed or captured in the Battle of the Bulge fighting. Five hundred of the fighter planes and fighter bombers covered the Ardennes battle area. The other fighters, mostly American P-51 Mustangs, were assigned to provide escort protection for the heavy bombers.

On this Christmas Eve morning, our 487th Bomb Group was selected to lead the entire 2,500-ship bomber force with wing commander Brigadier General Frederick W. Castle in command. All four of the 487th squadrons flew, including the 836th, 837th, 838th and 839th. I was the Bombardier on one of the B-17's in the 836th Squadron. The other eight members of my crew were: Lt. Ira L. Ball, First Pilot; Lt. Gordon R. Tomeo, Co-Pilot; Harold P. Sperber, Navigator; Lt. Cuno V. Becker, (substitute) Tail Gunner; T/Sgt. Robert H. Lull, Radio Operator; T/Sgt. Warren H. Parks, Engineer; S/Sgt/ Duffy J. Gaudin, Belly Turret Gunner; and S/Sgt. John J. Cornery, Waist Gunner.

Our projected flight path was from Clacton, England, across the English Channel to Ostende, Belgium, then across Belgium to Liege, then east to our target, a Luftwaffe airfield at Babenhausen, Germany. As we crossed the Channel, I saw RAF bombers for the first time even though I had already flown 32 daylight combat missions over England and Western Europe. I knew that the RAF only bombed at night in solitary ship sorties, never in close-order squadrons like our 8th Air Force. So here it is, broad daylight, and the Halifax and Lancaster boxcar-shaped bombers are randomly scattered all over the sky, widely separated from each other. It was a strange sight.

At noon, we were over Liege, Belgium, at 21,000 feet altitude, and our P-51 escort had not yet arrived. It was shaping up to be a milk run-no flak, no enemy planes, just smooth clear weather. Suddenly, diving at our squadron out of the sun, streaked several German Messerschmitt ME-109 fighter planes firing away with their 20-millimeter cannons. Each ME-109 was equipped with four of the 20mm cannons, and each cannon could fire 600 rounds per minute. They made that one pass, severely damaging my plane and also the command ship in the 838th squadron, then flew away, followed by all of our newly arriving P-51 fighter escorts. Our escort was no sooner out of sight than the main Luftwaffe force of about 50 more ME-109's appeared. The Luftwaffe group singled out our 836th squadron and approached from the rear in a stacked echelon formation so they could all fire together in a volley. At that point, our substitute tail gunner Lt. Cuno V. Becker yelled into the intercom, "They are coming at us Company Front - there are so many of them - what should I do?" (Now, Lt. Becker was our Squadron Armament Officer who, like General Castle, had volunteered for this mission, replacing our regular tail gunner). Our First Pilot, Lt. Ira L. Ball, had his headset switched to Flight Control VHF Radio. So, our co-pilot, Lt. Gordon R. Tomeo, yelled back, "Pick out the one you think is aiming at you and shoot him down." Our .50 caliber machine guns had an effective range of about 600 yards, while the Luftwaffe 20mm cannon had the range of about 400 yards, so we did have a brief time slot for shooting advantage. The Germans closed to within 400 yards, then began a fusillade with their 200 or so cannons, each gun firing 10 rounds per second. It was about noon on a bright sunny day, but the sky around us suddenly lit up with thousands of small bright red flashes. Our B-17's managed to shoot down 13 Messerschmitt fighter planes; however, four of our bombers were shot down outright while five more were so severely damaged they were abandoned after making forced landings nearby in Belgium. My ship and General Castle's command ship were among those destroyed. The General was killed.

In my plane, during the German fighter attack, I was operating the hydraulically powered nose turret with twin .50 caliber machine guns and could feel the ship shudder as it was being demolished by the fusillade of exploding 20mm shells. Quickly, the tail section of our plane fell off, and all four engines and the intercom went dead, everything suddenly quiet. Our navigator, Lt. Harold P. Sperber, and I quickly tore off our flight helmets and oxygen masks, snapped on our parachute chest packs and pulled open the nose escape hatch. He jumped first and, after a brief pause, I jumped out behind him. But just as I bailed out, the plane exploded in a ball of flame. I had planned to take a brief freefall after jumping to get well clear of the remnants of the plane, but when I tried to grasp the parachute's red rip chord handle with my right hand, I found my right arm was paralyzed. In reflex action, I quickly reached for the handle with my left hand, and accidentally, my left thumb hooked the red handle and out popped the little pilot chute, dragging behind it my parachute. Burning slabs of my planes wings were fluttering down around me. My hair and eyebrows were singed. The air was pungent with the odor left by the thousands of exploding 20mm shells. Everything was quiet. I looked up and in the distance saw one of our stricken bombers in flame and climbing at a steep angle. Then it suddenly nosed over and headed down in a diving spin, leaving a trail of smoke. I watched it until it hit the ground with a ball of flame. It was General Castle's ship.

My next surprise came when two ME-109 fighter planes appeared and headed straight towards me as if on a strafing pass. Fortunately, they turned away just before they reached me, waving and smiling at me as they went.

I had bailed out at 21,000 feet, and, in approximately 15 minutes, I had dropped to about 2,000 feet. I could see below a small village, a dirt road, a large pasture, and adjacent to the pasture, a large wooded area with leafless trees. There was a slight breeze, and it was blowing me towards the trees. Not wanting to land in the bare trees, with my good left arm I pulled the parachute shroud line on the pasture side of the chute. This maneuver caused the parachute to slip at an angle toward the pasture, and shortly, I was just above it and could see the ground coming up fast. I quickly released the shroud line and the parachute blossomed out fully just before I hit the ground. I had landed in a Belgium hamlet about 20 miles east of Liege and near the northern border of Luxembourg. In short order I encountered the worst and the best of villagers.

836TH SQUADRON

First, someone came running toward me with a pitchfork - I raised my left arm and yelled, "Jue A-me-ri-can! Jue A-me-ri-can!" He quickly threw down his pitchfork and ran to me, to give aid, I thought. He helped me remove the parachute harness and take my first aid kit from my flight suit leg pocket. But, he then ran away with the kit, dragging my parachute behind him. Soon, a few other villagers came and I pointed to my bloody right arm and asked, "Dok-tor? Dok-tor?" They nodded their heads and said, "Dok-tor, Oui-Oui!" and pointed to a two story red brick home a short distance up the dirt road. They led me to the doctor's house, and he came out at once. He was a Belgian gentleman who spoke perfect English. He led me upstairs to a nice bedroom, helped me out of my flight suit, and then dressed my wounded right arm and a few scratches. He helped me into a pair of silk pajamas and into bed after which he gave me a glass of brandy. A little later, his three teenage daughters brought me a snack. I had just begun to take a nap when an American 1st Army armored column arrived in the village.

Now, the American soldiers had been told that I was a shot down German pilot hiding out in the Doctor's house. I was upstairs in bed when there was a loud commotion outside. A PFC infantryman rushed upstairs and prodded me with his semi-automatic Garand Army rifle, ordering me downstairs at once. He would not believe I was an American Air Force officer, even after I pointed out the I.D. tags around my neck and my uniform. Finally, I ordered him to get his superior officer and he yelled down the stairs, "Lieutenant, this German claims he's an American and wants to talk with you!" An Army 1st Lieutenant, same rank as myself, comes upstairs and I said to him, "Lieutenant, will you please tell this dumb SOB that I'm an American and to take that damn gun out of my belly!" The lieutenant glances at the dog tags around my neck and my uniform nearby, then says quietly, "Soldier, put your rifle down. Can't you tell by the way he talks he's one of us?"

A military ambulance took me to Liege. Military Police were posted at every road crossing along the way to the hospital to apprehend any German infiltrators disguised in captured American uniforms. The M.P. password system was giving the right answer to questions about characters in the U.S. funny papers, such as: "Who is Pop-Eye's girlfriend?" and "What is Jiggs' favorite food?" Only Americans would know the correct answers, in this case "Olive Oil" and 'corned beef and cabbage." When I arrived at the Liege army tent hospital, I was given a tetanus injection and debriefed by Army Intelligence, then admitted to one of the tents.

Christmas morning was bright and quiet for a while. Then, here come two German fighter-bomber jet aircraft, the first any of us had ever seen. They flew around and around us, strafing and bombing an army munitions site, the railroad depot and the airfield. The jet's flight speed was over 500 mph, and our anti-aircraft shells were exploding about one fourth mile behind them. The two jets flew away unharmed. They had not targeted the hospital.

Gentlemen From Hell

For Christmas dinner, we had turkey and dressing and pumpkin pie. I enjoyed that dinner as only a Happy Warrior could since this last mission had completed my European Theatre requirement of 33 missions. I knew I would never again have to fly through that horrible, deadly German 88mm anti-aircraft flak and that I would soon be going home.

In the hospital tent, I swapped combat stories with the wounded soldiers; also swapped my sheepskin lined flight boots for some of their liberated German trophies. The infantrymen said they really appreciated the ground support our 8th Air Force had given them in Normandy, France back in August 1944. They said that after our pattern bombing of the German troop concentrations, most of the soldiers who were not killed or wounded were too dazed to fight, but just sat down and waited to be captured. That Christmas night, another walking patient and I went into the downtown section of Liege. I spent all of my escape kit foreign money on a large bag full of wine and brandy then went right back to our hospital tent and passed it out to the wounded. The night duty nurse never looked up from her desk.

The next day, an Army DC-3 transport plane flew me back across the Channel to a hospital in Cambridge, England. While in the hospital, I was awarded the Purple Heart Medal for wounds received in combat on December 24, 1944. I had previously been awarded the Distinguished Flying Cross and the Air Medal. After several weeks in the hospital, I returned to my 487th Bomb Group in Lavenham England. I later learned that the bodies of the seven other members of my flight crew were ultimately found in the vicinity of our bomber's wreckage in Belgium. All seven bodies were (re) buried in the Henri-Chapelle Cemetery, Belgium.

Having completed the mandatory 33 combat missions, I returned to the United States with a 30 day furlough, which was followed by an assignment to Bombardier Instructor School. Shortly afterwards, the war was over. I was discharged November 30, 1945 and voluntarily accepted a 1st Lt. Commission in the Air Force Reserve.

In January 1946, I entered the University of Tulsa, Oklahoma, studying Petroleum Engineering. I married my wife, Elizabeth Sellars Broom, on August 10, 1949 in Slidell, Louisiana. Our first child, Elizabeth Hollingsworth Broom (Holly), Ph.D., was born on December 1, 1950 in Tulsa. I graduated from T.U. in May 1951 with a BS Degree in Petroleum Engineering and immediately began work in the oil industry as a petroleum engineer. During the next nine years while living in Slidell, Venice and Lafayette, Louisiana and in Houston, Texas, Elizabeth and I would have four more children - Charlotte Broom Price; John William Broom, II; Lisa Broom Warren, R.N; and Jeanne Michelle Broom. We are now retired and living at our home in Slidell and fully enjoying our five children and eight grandchildren.

JUNIOR GOSSELL

Gossell flew 21 missions in his 39 months of service.

Dec. 7, 1941, I was a student in my final year at St. Cloud State Teacher's College. My draft number came up, and I was deferred until I graduated in June '42. The two previous summers, I was enrolled in the Civilian Pilot Training program offered by the college and the local flying school. I earned my private pilots license the first summer and took advanced training the second summer.

As I approached graduation and the end of my deferment, I applied for pilot training with both the Navy and Army Air Corp. I didn't pass the Navy physical due to the lack of a molar.

The Army Air Corps was concerned about a scar I had from a lung operation, which disqualified me. I was so desperate to avoid the infantry I even applied for the glider pilot training program. Only to be told, "Son, the draft won't even take you."

July of 1942, I boarded a bus along with about 50 other draftees to Ft. Snelling for pre-induction tests. Before the physical we were asked if we had a condition which might disqualify us. I volunteered the lung operation information and joined the long line for physicals. It seemed but a very short time after that I found myself taking the oath of allegiance to the United States of America. Followed by, "congratulations, you are now in the Army of the United States of America."

Several days later and after and unbelievable 14 to 16 hours serving KP in the mess hall, I found myself on a train bound for Camp Joseph T. Robinson in Little Rock, AR. I was assigned into Branch Immaterial, infantry basic training. This was really an eye-opener, including real Army discipline. We respected acting PFCs as though they were generals. Early in training, we were assigned a close and constant companion - a World War I Enfield rifle which was to be kept spotlessly clean and cared for. Training included long hikes in summer Arkansas heat, learning to shoot a rifle and toting a full field pack plus the rifle on bivouacs. Many of us vowed when we finally got out of the Army we were going to buy the war surplus Enfield rifles, stack them Army style and just enjoy watching them rust away.

While I was in training, I attempted to use my pilot training to get into the Air Corp. After about two months of this, I was assigned to join the 40th division of engineers at Ft. Lewis, WA. Upon our arrival we found they weren't there, but had embarked from CA. We were placed in a casual detachment. After two months of this I was assigned to a Port Battalion at Camp Knight in Oakland, CA, to learn how to load and unload ships. This provided the opportunity for me to apply for the aviation cadet program. This time, I passed the tests and shortly thereafter was sent to Santa Anna, CA, for the preflight training.

Santa Anna was not as Army tough as infantry training, but was extremely "chicken." It seemed they were just daring us to step out of line and very interested in "washing out" those that didn't fit. I was privileged to have qualified for all three programs. I chose the pilot program. I was on my way to fulfilling my dream of becoming a military pilot.

March 1, 1943, I was sent to King County, CA, for primary flight training. We trained in a Ryan PT 19. Here, about 50 percent of the group washed out, some by their own choice after their first flight.

After about three months of this, on to basic flight training in a BT 13 at Chico, CA. Here, we were introduced to a more powerful plane, night flying and cross-country flying. I was the first in my class to solo.

Another three months of this and we were ready for advanced flight training. We had to make two choices - either single or twin-engine training. I chose twin-engine and was sent to Yuma, AZ, for advanced flight training. Yuma is hotter than hell in August, and our only consolation was we could see Patton's tank troops training on the desert as we flew over them. We conceded we were better than they were.

I was in the class 43J. I graduated Nov. 1, 1943. I achieved my quest for Army Air Force Pilot's wings. Here, we were again asked for the type of plane we would like to be assigned to. I chose twin-engine, hoping for A-20 or B-26 training. My instructor seemed to be encouraging me into four-engine planes. I should have taken my clue from that as all who chose twin-engine ended up as co-pilots in four engine bombers. We were sent to Salt Lake City for crew assignment. Talk about a group of ticked off "hot" pilots.

I was assigned to a crew and sent to Ardmore, OK, for crew training. I was a very unhappy co-pilot. I asked for a transfer to twin-engine. I found out the hard way - never try to tell a B-17 pilot who has completed his combat tour you don't like flying a B-17. Instead of a transfer, I was grounded. I was able to convince a board I was merely asking for a transfer and wanted to fly, period. I was assigned to another crew.

After several months of training, we were sent to Lincoln, NE, for overseas assignment. We were assigned to a brand new B-17G to fly across the pond. We departed Lincoln at night, during a very heavy snowstorm about Dec. 30, 1944, headed for Manchester, NH. Along the way we lost an engine and couldn't feather it. Fort Wayne, IN was the nearest airport, but they were closed. When they heard of our problem, they gave us permission to land. The runways were heavily ice coated.

Ten days later, we arrived in New Hampshire, the POE. Then on to Goose Bay, Labrador. Goose Bay is not the Miami of the north in January. We were told we parked on several feet of packed snow. On to Bluie West #1, Greenland. Here, we had to land uphill. It was get down the first try or else. There was a glacier near the end of the runway.

Next, on to Iceland, a spot high on my list of "The Pits." On to Valley, Wales. The next morning, we dropped off our plane at a large airport just east of Liverpool. It was crammed full with brand new planes of all kinds. On to the replacement crew assignment station. We spent several days here. I drew an assignment to spend a day censoring mail. They gave me a razor blade, told me what wasn't allowed and then dumped bags of uncensored mail on the table for us to check for censored items.

We eventually were assigned to the 836th squadron of the 487th Bomb Group located at Lavenham. We spent several weeks getting combat ready. This included a lot of practice formation flying. The 487th practiced and flew very tight formation.

We were finally ready to get started. They sent our pilot, with an experienced crew as their co-pilot, for his first mission. The next day, we went on our first mission. Much to our displeasure, we were a chaff ship. At the IP (initial point), we were in a three-ship formation which broke away from the big formation to fly about a mile off to the left, tossing out chaff while the bombing group dropped their bombs. Being in tight formation for protection against fighters. We rejoined our group as they made a left turn off the target.

Several days later, we could see the advantages of chaff. We were on a bomb run when three other planes were dropping chaff off to the left. We were pleasantly surprised to see the German flak was shooting hell out of the chaff. That was a comforting feeling.

We flew five straight missions in five days. The pilot and I had such sore rear ends we weren't interested in any more sitting. We received our first pass to London after those five missions.

Three missions stand out a bit more than any of my 20 missions; (1) It was just after bombs away when the radio operator checked the bomb bay and noticed we had a bomb hung up. Without giving it a second thought, he rushed onto the bomb bay with a screwdriver to try and loosen the bomb. After much frantic prying, it finally dropped. It was then that he realized he was out there without any oxygen and as he looked down, discovered he had nothing but a very narrow catwalk between him and 25,000 feet of air. He was shouting to have the bomb bay doors closed as he wasn't about to travel back on the narrow catwalk to his radio room with the doors still open. The waist gunner managed to get a walk-around oxygen bottle to him. As soon as the bomb bay doors closed, it was reported he made a wild dive to get back into his radio room.

The next mission, we again had just dropped the bombs. At this point, the flight engineer would open the door to the bomb bay to check to see if all bombs had dropped. The door would often slam shut as he closed it. I was piloting at the time. I heard him slam the door shut. For the third time, I thought I heard him slam the door shut. I really couldn't figure out what was happening. About this time, I also recalled, each time I heard the door slam shut, the plane seemed to lift up a bit. A couple of more "door slams" and the lifting of the plane, I realized the door slamming was actually flak bursting right under us. Afterwards, I found out the flak was tracking on us, and with each burst it was getting closer. Some evasive actions took us out of danger. We received 50 flak holes in the plane.

On the last of my three standout missions, we were just off the bomb run to a target in Berlin. We were down to around 16,000 feet just cruising along, flak free. Intelligence had the flak well plotted, so it was not unusual to be free of flak for the remainder of the mission. All of the sudden, the lead ship just blew up right in front of us. We were flying in the number two position. For some reason or other, our part of the formation just seemed to scatter. We found ourselves out there all alone. We were well aware of our vulnerability, so we started looking for the rest of our group. We spotted it and moved to get back into the protection of the group. Since there was an opening in their formation we decide to join them until we got back to England. Shortly after we joined them, we noticed many guns in their formation were pointed at us. Our pilot quickly checked with the radio operator for the codes of the day. As soon as he communicated it to the group, they relaxed, and we were no longer a potential kill for their gunners. All groups were warned about B-17s that had been captured by the Germans and made into gun ships. They would join a formation as we did, then when they had the chance would shoot down as many bombers as they could, then dive out of there. It was a relief to know we were no longer a "kill" for that group's gunners.

I completed 20 missions when the war ended. Including three to Hamburg, three to Berlin, and two to the Bordeaux area. I returned to the States in August 1945. We were one of the last bomb groups to leave the UK.

Summary: I spent 39 months in service. I flew 20 missions (actually 21), earned an air medal with two oak leaf clusters. Two trans-Atlantic flights, received extensive flak holes on a number of missions. In spite of flak damage, not one of the crew sustained any injuries. We aborted once and had an aileron that become unattached on one end. Of our nine crew members, four are still alive.

JIM BRADFORD

My name is James H. (Jim) Bradford, (0-1167325) Rank, First Lieutenant. I entered the service in the field artillery following Pearl Harbor; later transferred to Army Air Corps in navigation training. I was assigned to a B-17 crew training at Ardmore, Oklahoma, with Ned Richards' crew 101. My good friend Bob Densmore was our co-pilot - one of the best!

We arrived as a replacement crew with the 487th Bomb Group in June of 1944. We were assigned to the 836th squadron. Lloyd Reed's crew 102 was to be trained to fly as a lead crew. I was transferred to his crew as a lead co-navigator with my good friend Roger Hatfield. Flying as a deputy lead behind General Castle on the Battle of the Bulge raid, December 24, 1944, we were shot down. General Castle, flying with Lt. Bob Harriman, went down just ahead of us; only three of his crew survived, including bombardier Paul Biri. Our crew bailed out safely except command pilot Lloyd Nash.

On the ground, I met up with our bombardier, Fred Dumler and a few others. We walked out of Germany and Luxembourg, caught up with an Army Jeep headed for Liege, and eventually made it to Brussels and then back to base at Lavenham, England.

On return to the states in the spring of '45, I was to be assigned as a navigation instructor. When the European war ended, I took reserve status in the now U.S. Air Force.

My wife (now of 58 years!) and I were married in April 1945. I studied advertising and graphic arts in New York City, moved back to Indiana (hometown: Indianapolis), taught school and started a successful graphic arts business (now retired). We have three children, six grandchildren and three great-grandchildren.

I can give you an amusing moment. We were leading a 487th group mission to Ludwigshafen, Germany. During the bomb run, a piece of flak triggered the inflation valve on our over-water dinghy. It quickly inflated and nearly filled our navigation area. My good friend and fine co-navigator, Roger Hatfield, and I climbed into the rubber raft and sang, "Row, Row, Row your Boat" while we "rowed" over our target as bombardier, Fred Dumler dropped the bomb load right on target! Our story reached Claude Tepper, our public relations officer at Lavenham. He wrote it up, and it made UP wire services in the states.

Our two crews, 101 and 102, have maintained close relationships throughout the years. We're enjoying this great Omaha '02 convention in company with dear friend Bob and Jeanne Densmore and Fred and "Smitty" Dumler.

Paul L. Biri

Biri (standing, far right), pictured with his crew, retired at the rank of Colonel after 22 years in the Air Force and spent the next 20 years teaching high school and college.

I am a retired Air Force Colonel. I was in the 8th Air Force in England during World War II. I flew as a bombardier - a lead bombardier on a B-17. One of the questions that people frequently ask me, "How did you become a bombardier?" Well, you know, in World War II, they just assigned you wherever they needed you, even though you did not prefer that position. But anyway, I was sent to bombardier training in Midland, Texas. After that, I was assigned as a bombardier instructor in San Angelo, Texas. Then, I was assigned to a crew, a B-17 bomber crew, in Rapid City, South Dakota. There, we prepared to learn to fly as a bomber crew. We flew over to England in July 1944 and joined the 487th Bomb Group. Shortly after, I was assigned to a crew as a lead bombardier with a pilot named Robert Harriman. We flew 15 missions together. Our first mission was Brest, France. Of course, on your first mission, we were very nervous and scared. As time went by, we got more relaxed and everything went fine until 24 December 1944. On that day, the 8th Air Force decided to put up the largest bombing mission in the history of the world. 2,037 bombers, and my crew was selected to lead this. Our target was Babenhausen, Germany. Everything went fine until we started to make the bomb run. At that time we were attacked by three German fighters. The radar navigator, Lt. Bruno Procopio, was wounded, and there was some damage to the left wing of the B-17 bomber.

After the second pass by the fighters, more damage was done to the plane. The first pilot, Robert Harriman, gave the order to "bail out." The plane was on fire and out of control. I bailed out at approximately 21,000 feet above ground and dropped approximately 18,000 feet before I opened my parachute. I landed about eight miles southeast of Liege, Belgium. After a few minutes, I started walking and met some Belgian people who gave me something to eat, then helped me to get to a hospital in Brussels, Belgium that night. The next day, Christmas Day, I told a doctor I was all right and I would like to leave and get back to England the best way I could. On this mission, five of the 10 crew members were killed. Now, I am the only living survivor. Brigadier General Frederick Castle was the Command Pilot. He just got promoted to a one-star General three weeks before that mission. He was awarded the Congressional Medal of Honor. I flew one more mission on March 16, 1945. Seven weeks later, the war in Europe was over, and we returned to the good old USA.

So, that was my experience in World War II. I only completed 16 missions, but it was very interesting. I stayed in the Air Force for 22 years. After retiring, I went back to college for four more years for my master's degree and doctorate degree in Education Administration. I taught high school and college for 20 years after retiring from the Air Force.

My name is Paul Biri, and I live in New Orleans, LA.

JIM ERSKINE

LEFT: *Jim Erskine.* RIGHT: *Left to right: Jim Erskine and his wife, Joe Ann, with Henry Hughey and wife, Jean, at the World War II Memorial in Washington, D.C.*

James T. Erskine, Jim Erskine. Rank: Staff Sergeant, U.S. Army Air Force. I went into service in March of 1943. I joined the Army Air Force Reserve at the age of 17. I went on active duty the 12th of June, 1943, four days before I graduated from high school. I received my diploma, but my mother had to get it for me. After training I went to the 8th Air Force. I went overseas on the Queen Elizabeth, December of 1944, arriving in England Christmas Eve, 1944, the date of the infamous, or notorious, Christmas Eve raid. I was put in the 836th squadron of the 487th Bomb Group because on the December 24th raid they had 60 percent causalities. I was 19 years of age. I was the tail gunner on the Robert Browning crew. After our co-pilot collided with another plane while taxiing on the ground, they decided they needed a crew in the pool, and this was a good one to put there. So, I flew 16 missions with 14 different crews. No one on any aircraft I was flying in was ever killed or wounded. Our plane was never shot down. We made a landing on the continent of Europe at a fighter base to refuel one time because we were flying a plane that was a gas hog. We were flying "tail end Charlie," the last plane in a formation, which uses more gas. We never ditched in the channel. I consider myself a successful aviator. I have an equal number of take-offs and landings. I was discharged from the Army December 15, 1945 on the point system. If you accumulated so many points, you were eligible for discharge, and I did not want to re-enlist, so I was discharged and sent home.

After the war, I went to work in the shop office of a factory. I had the opportunity to take the fire department recruiting exam. I placed very well on it and joined the fire department. I was married September 19, 1946 to Joe Ann. We have been married 56 years. We have six children and 20 grandchildren. Our children are Cynthia, Diane, Michael, Jane, Scott and Timothy.

My most memorable moment is when I got married. But my most memorable moment overseas, in combat, was when the ball-turret gunner called me. I was flying in the tail gun position and he asked me what was at six o'clock very low. Now, the only way I could see six o'clock very low was to lean way forward in my position to look down over the tail, between the guns. I looked down, saw a P-51 was belching smoke from its stacks and told him I thought I saw a P-51 in trouble, but that was it. He thought it might possibly be a German plane. When I sat back in my normal position, there was a hole about the size of a half dollar on each side of the fuselage, and the piece of flak that went through there would have gone through my neck if I had not been looking down. So that evening, we poured the ball-turret gunner into bed and I bought all of his drinks.

When they broke our crew up, I never knew who I was flying with. I never knew who was behind me when I was in the plane. But of the original Browning crew- Bob Browning is dead. He was killed in an automobile accident. After about 50 years, I did meet up with the co-pilot. He lived in California and was passing through Toledo and decided to stop. Also, after about 50 years I visited the ball-turret gunner. He lives within 150 miles of my home. We both knew it. He knew where I lived and I knew where he lived, but we just never got around to meeting and now we see each other frequently. Joe Ann and I meet Jack and Judy Kohl half way between Ravenna, Ohio and Toledo, Ohio at a restaurant. We go there and spend a couple of hours just chitchatting. And we meet each other at the 487th reunion. We have met them at the Eighth Air Force reunion and at a couple of Ohio Chapter meetings. He's the only one I have kept up with.

I joined the Eight Air Force Historical Society in 1981. I didn't start going to the 487th reunions right away, but when I did at the beginning it was hit and miss. I'd go to one and miss a couple and go to another one, then Joe Ann and I started going to all of them. We enjoyed the people and the camaraderie. We have a good time with the 487th – well, we have a good time with any of the 8th Air Force groups that we belong to.

I have no missions that were especially eventful for me. I can't tell you which mission it was that I was on when I had the narrow escape. I know my first and eighth missions were to Berlin, but those are the only ones of which I have a record.

JACK KOHL

My name is Jack F. Kohl. I was born in Northeast Ohio, a little town call Ravenna. I grew up there, went to the service from there. I obtained the rank of staff sergeant in a three-year period. I went into the service in October of 1943. I entered the 8th Air Force after training and arriving in England. No exact date known as to the entrance. We arrived in England late December of 1944. I was assigned to the 487th Bomb Group, 836th squadron. I was 20 years old at the time. I was an air crew gunner having flown in the ball-turret of a B-17. I flew 17 missions. We were shot down on the 17th of March flying a B-17. That seemed to be my lucky or unlucky number. Fortunately, none of our crew was killed or injured. On our last mission, we went down and were hit over Germany, south of Berlin and knew we couldn't make it back, so we headed toward Russia. We ended up going down on a small field in Poland. It really wasn't a crash landing, but it wasn't a great landing either because it wasn't a field that was designed for B-17s - period.

As I say, we were flying in a B-17 on the 17th of March in our 17th mission. Our target area was south of Berlin. During the bomb run, we took a lot of flak and lost number two and number four engines. It was decided, I'm sure by the pilot and co-pilot, that we would have a difficult time making it back across Germany, France and eventually England. Therefore the decision was made by the officers to head for Russia. We didn't quite make that goal since we landed in Poland on a small airstrip. We were immediately surrounded by Russian soldiers at that time. They didn't know whether we were really Americans or possibly Germans in captured B-17s. We were put up with a Polish family for approximately two weeks. In fact, they evacuated them from two rooms of their house, and our whole crew survived for a two-week period in this two-room situation. We then went from there to an area close to Moscow where they were picking up any American crews that were shot down and tried to make it to Russia - or did make it to Russia. It was approximately 35 days to get back to England. We went from Russia through Iran, from there on to Cairo, Egypt, where we spent approximately a week. While in Cairo, we took the opportunity of developing a severe cold in 100-degree temperature so we could spend a few extra days looking at the Pyramids and the Sphinxes. Then, we found out that we were missing in action and decided we better head on back to England. Our colds immediately got better, and we got put back on flying status and continued our journey back to England with stops in Naples, Italy; Athens, Greece; Paris, France; and eventually to Lavenham, England.

As the war was just about over by that time, we did not fly any further combat missions. Eventually, we did fly back to the United States and eventually went from Massachusetts, where we landed, to Barksdale Field, Louisiana for B-29 training. But by the time we got there and got ready for training, the war was over. And that was the end of my service experience. Since the service time, thanks to the GI Bill, I went to school at Kent State University, graduating in 1949. I was married in late 1948, and I am the parent of six. I went into business in the insurance and real estate field and worked at it for 48 years. Having retired three years ago, and the said business is now run by my son, Jack F. Kohl. That brings you up to date.

Not until about 10 years ago did I get involved in the 487th reunions. I run a one-man gang as far as my insurance and real estate business, and with a family it was just impossible to get away. It was only in the last 10 years that I felt we could take time to do things like this, and that's when I got involved.

We have nine grandchildren, three granddaughters and six grandsons, all of whom we are very proud. Our youngest son has four children under five years old. He's been busy and will be busy. Our oldest son has two boys that we are equally proud of. Number one, Jacob got a scholarship to Yale to play football. Jacob is 6-foot-6 and 300 pounds and is going to be a tremendous tackle for Yale. His younger brother graduated from high school this year. He did play football, but his thing is basketball since he 6-foot-11. They grow big in our area. Then we have the rest of them, some in college, some also parents of little children. So we have, as I say, nine grandchildren. We're busy, happy Grandparents.

DONALD FRANTZ PARTAIN

LEFT: *Partain, pictured in April 1944.* RIGHT: *Partain, pictured here in April 2001, said he "always felt that going out on a combat mission each time without hesitation that we could stop the killing and bring peace back to the world."*

My adventure with flying started at around the time I was four years old, when Charles Augustus Lindbergh, The Lone Eagle or Lucky Lindy, as he was called, took off on May 10, 1927 from Ryan Aircraft, Dutch Flats, San Diego, California (later became Lindbergh Field), in his Ryan N-X-211 single-engine Spirit of St. Louis, to New York, and his Atlantic Flight of 3,610 miles, total time of 33 hours, 30 minutes, 29 seconds. My brothers and I were there to witness the take-off.

On February 10, 1943, I was accepted into the United States Army Air Force at Fort MacArthur, California, sworn in, shipped out to basic training at Keesler Field, Biloxi, Mississippi; from basic training, shipped out to Armament School, Lowery, Field, Denver Colorado, to Panama City, Florida, Tyndall Field Flexible Gunnery Class of #43-37. Promoted to Buck Sergeant on graduation.

Travel from gunnery school to Salt Lake City, Utah, started assembling air crews, pilots, first and co-pilots, navigators, engineer, radio operator and armament gunner and set up air crews.

Moved to Brunning, Nebraska, to start our overseas phase training, on to Clovis, New Mexico, and eventually to Alamogordo, New Mexico, where we became the Gentlemen from Hell. At Alamogordo, we went through a series to Commanding Officers for our final phase training. Lt. Col., Bernie Lay, Jr. assumed command on February 28, 1944.

The first of the flyaway aircraft - B-24 Consolidated Liberators model "H" - arrived on February 2, 1944 and continued to arrive the entire month; 71 and 72

836TH SQUADRON

arrived at Alamogordo through the month of February. Our air crew was assigned B-24 model "H" number 2522636 at that time. At Alamogordo, we completed building our air crew to 10 and assigned our crew number, listed as follows: Combat Aircrew # 87-6-4; Pilot 1st Lt. Buford E. Collings; Co-Pilot F/O Marvin Kraft; Bombardier 1st Lt. William C. Mount; Engineer Gunner T/Sgt. Richard A. Doty; Radio Operator Gunner T/Sgt William J. Zaletski; Armament Top Turret Gunner S/Sgt. Donald F. Partain; Nose Turret Gunner Frank E. Horan; Tail Turret Gunner S/Sgt. Arka M. Shanks; Ball Turret Gunner S/Sgt William Herberger.

March 23, 1944, all air crews and B-24s moved to Harrington, Kansas, to have final modifications made for overseas combat, armor plates attached bulletproof glass to replace regular glass wherever needed. From Harrington, Kansas, to West Palm Beach, Florida, Morrison Field, we flew through a very violent storm. We almost had to abandon our B-24 on April 1, 1944 from West Palm Beach to Waller Field, Trinidad. In route from Florida to Trinidad, we had a malfunction in our transfer fuel pump and lost much of our remaining gas load and before our Engineer Richard Doty got it working again. We were about five feet from the water before we got full power back; all engines quit almost as soon as we hit the runway in Trinidad.

Next stop, Belem, Brazil - completely uneventful - to Fotaliza, Brazil - no problems. Next stop across the Atlantic to Dakar, Africa - we arrived early morning and landed on metal runways, lots of banging and clanging as our B-24 set down.

The airfield at Marrakech in French Morocco was our last stop before heading to Ireland, Nutt Corner and Station #137 Lavenham, Suffolk, England. From Nutt Corner, we had a Pathfinder B-17 direct us to our air station at Lavenham. Our aircrew left the United States on April 1, 1944 and arrived at station #137 on April 17, 1944. Our aircrew and the aircrew on the B-24 C, piloted by Barney Nolan, were the last two crews to land at Station #137, Lavenham, England from our overseas trip.

Combat tour started on May 11, 1944 - our 1st mission. On this mission, three of the 487th BG(H) aircraft were shot down, and we lost Lt. Col. Bernie Lay, Jr. Col. Lay eventually evaded back to England. There have been many articles on how Col. Lay and his crew bailed out - the true story is as follows from his book about the Group called "I've Had It." Chapter four, Published by Harper and Brothers, New York and London.

Our crew, flying in the low squadron to the right of the lead squadron had a perfect view Col. Lay's B-24 had been hit by heavy flak-Lay's B-24 had been damaged badly, right inboard engine was shut down because of battle damage, left inboard engine running at half power, the right aileron had been shot away and the left was sticking up, making control very difficult, damaged tail section was setting up such violent vibration it made the B 24's teeth chatter, Lt. Col. Lay's B-24 made a right turn away from the group, engines smoking and crew members bailing out. Lt. Col. Bernie Lay Jr. stayed at the controls until all the air crew members had bailed out, a loss of 2,000 feet from the original 12,000 feet-Lay's B-24 nose started to climb and then racked over to its right wing Lt. Col. Lay was at the control up until time the B-24 dropped over on its right wing tip, Col. Lay moved into the bomb-bay, grabbed the Emergency bomb bay handle - the bomb bay had been damaged and opened only a few inches, Lay's B-24 went into a steep spiraling dive, the Col. moved to the back of the bomb-bay to exit there if possible -moved forward to crawl through the opening underneath the floor of the cockpit, while crawling towards the nose wheel door, that had been jettisoned, all the time the B-24 was spinning and in a steep dive, his parachute harness had been caught, finally releasing his hung up parachute strap and dropping out the nose wheel door, as he cleared the aircraft he pulled up the ripcord. The 487th BG(H) had its first casualty that day - Lt. McCleary, a Navigator on one of the three B-24s that was shot down May 11, 1944.

1st Lt. Buford E. Collings air crew completed 31 missions on August 24, 1944. The average number of missions was 15 completed for the men flying with the 8th Air Force - we flew on D-Day. It gave me a very patriotic and historic feeling to be there on the day that the United States Army Air Force did their part in the invasion against Nazi Germany to start peace in the world and to help win World War II.

I did not keep a diary of my missions, but I can remember returning to our air station with holes in the B-24-engines smoking and burning - flying back to England under the escort of four P-51 Mustangs with a couple of engines gone. Part of the Plexiglas dome on my top turret shot/knocked away, but God willing we always made it back and completed our combat tour without losing or having any of our air crew members wounded.

I have been asked what was the most dangerous combat mission that I was on. My answer was they were all dangerous - taking off with a full bomb and gas load had its danger. Going through overreacted ceiling of 500 feet or less and topping out at 15,000 feet was dangerous. We were pulling through heavy overcast, and as we topped out at 15,000 feet, there was a P-38 Lightning that looked like I could touch it with my twin .50 caliber top turret machine guns. We were lucky. There had been aircraft crashing into each other while pulling for altitude.

One of the missions I remember was on May 23, 1944 - our 16th combat mission. We were going to bomb a German airfield at Bourges, France, our B-24 flying on the right of Lt. Joe Van Dyke's B-24 and Barney Nolan's B-24 on Van Dyke's left wing. Lt. Joseph's B-24 took a direct German 88 anti aircraft in his wing, and Lt. Van Dyke's B-24 burst into flames. Sitting in the top turret, all that I could see was large ball of flame, wing tips on the outside of the ball of flame, flames shooting out the waist window. The B-24 finally just melted apart. The tail section turret broke off and started spinning toward earth, the tail gunner still at his post and leaning over his controls. If I remember correctly, the position that Lt. Joseph Van Dyke flew that day I believe was assigned to our air

836th Squadron

crew - and because of a strange act of fate, we did not lead the element that day, and Lt. Van Dyke's air crew took the shot, and by an act of fate, we lived and returned to the USA after we completed our combat tour.

On our last mission (Mission 31) over Kiel, Germany, we took an anti-aircraft shot in our right wing, not too many inches away from the main spar in the wing. If the shell had hit the wing spar, the wing would have folded and we would have spun in. Someone was looking over us on this mission and all of our missions.

I forget the missions or where we were going to bomb, but after we made the bomb run, released our bomb load, Doty, waist gunner, called that the number four bomb-bay, with a 500-pound cluster incendiary hanging half-released, pressure fuse that was set to release the metal canister at 10,000 feet; and if I remember correctly, there were also four 250-pound anti-personnel bombs that were half-released also. The bombardier, 1st Lt. William C. Mount, and I, with the help from T/Sgt Richard A. Doty, were in the open bomb bay, working these hung-up bombs out of our B-24 without blowing the B-24 up. We could not leave the bombs in the bomb bay and land with these loose bombs bouncing around, and the pressure fuse on the canister of the 500-pound cluster bomb would have gone off at 10,000 feet and probably caught the aircraft on fire anyway, so they had to go gently.

A lot of other things happened, but after 60 years, I am surprised that I can remember the things that I have. Seeing Lt. Joe Van Dyke's B-24 go down in flames, and being as close as it was to our B-24. I still remember the flames, and his B-24 Liberator breaking at the waist section and falling uncontrollably to earth is something that I won't ever forget.

Our navigator, F/O Marvin Kraft T-123941, was born in Germany of a Jewish family, had escaped Germany before Hitler's gangster/brown shirts made their final crack down on the German Jewish population. If we had been shot down, I am certain that F/O Marvin Kraft would have gotten a much rougher treatment as a Prisoner of War (POW), being Jewish and a former German citizen. Marvin Kraft was an excellent Navigator and a very brave man to fly against Germany with this type pressure hanging over his head (Marvin, passed on this past year). It was men like Marvin Kraft and with their dedication and bravery that is an inspiration to all, and certainly helped win the Second World War.

There was one really great feeling that every time we hit the target area and the bombs released, because of dropping the heavy weight of the bomb the B-24 would jump/raise about 10 feet or more - and you, at the time, knew it was time to head for home and return to our air station.

Decorations: European Theater Operation medal, three Battle Stars for three major air battles, D-Day-Air Medal, three Oak Leaf Clusters, Distinguished Flying Cross and other minor decorations.

Flying with the 487th BG(H) and the 8th AF, that made me realize that there were extremely brave men doing an extremely hazardous job in an extremely dangerous time of our lives. I always felt that going out on a combat mission each time without hesitation that we could stop the killing and bring peace back to the world.

STANLEY E. ROLFES

LEFT: *Rofles went overseas three times during his tenure in the service.* RIGHT: *After the war, Rofles worked at and eventually owned a printing company.*

Stanley E. Rolfes, Captain. I enlisted in October, 1940. I was with the original group Eighth Air Force. We trained in Alamogordo, New Mexico and started out in January of '44. We all flew over in the early spring (I think it was March) to England as a group. We were not replacement crews. We were the original, brand new group flying over there. We went by the southern route. From Alamogordo we went to Florida; well, we stopped before that (I think it was somewhere in Nebraska) to get outfitted for where we were going. Because when we were training, we didn't know where we were going. Incidentally, we were in B-24s at that time. So, we went from Florida to Trinidad, to Belem, Brazil, to Dakar, Africa, to Scotland, and then to Lavenham. It took, I guess, a couple of weeks, because we were waiting on the weather to clear in different places. It was in the early spring. I don't remember the exact date, probably April, I imagine.

After that, I don't remember exactly, it was about eight or 10 missions I guess, they pulled me out of my crew. They were making up a lead crew and they pulled me out of the crew that I was with. And Jim Williams, the bombardier, they pulled him out of another crew, and they put us with Hugh Robertson, his crew. They made lead crew out of us. We did some training together that way before we started flying lead missions, of course. We did a lot of flying around over there, you know, in England, getting used to each other and all that sort of thing. The first couple of missions, we flew squadron lead, and eventually, of course, we started flying group lead. Around this same time, they pulled the B-24s out of combat. We were losing a lot of planes during that period. I forget what division we were in, I think it was third. There were three divisions in the 8th Air Force. Two of them, I think it was the first and second, were all equipped with B-17s, and the other one was equipped with B-24s. I guess they couldn't make them fast enough, that's the reason. But the B-24s, some people loved them, some didn't. I didn't like them at all. I don't think I would be here today if we had stayed in them because they couldn't get quite as high an altitude. We would do our bomb runs generally 23,000-24,000 feet, and they had to struggle to get up there. With the B-17s, we'd go over on the bomb runs about 28,000-29,000 feet, about 5,000 feet difference. Now they could still get their flak up high, but they lost a lot of accuracy with it. I remember with the B-24, God, when we'd get back from a mission the ground crew was swarming all over the plane and picking pieces of flak fragments out of the plane. I remember one on the nose cone of a flak, the 88mm I think the German's were using. You see, when they explode they break up into fragments of steal and spread out, as you can see on that one photograph what's happening. You don't get a direct hit by the whole shell, you get hit by jagged pieces that are perforated like, that break up like that. Well the nose cone piece, which is about maybe three inches wide and maybe two inches thick, was laying on the catwalk of Bomb A. However it came in, probably it came in after our bombs had dropped. I don't think it hit a bomb, fortunately. It was way up right there in the catwalk, it was a walkway in the bomb bay with the bomb racks on each side of it. That's about as rough as it comes, I guess.

Here are a few close calls that I still remember. Probably the closest call I ever had was, as a lead crew, we used to occasionally have to do practice bombing. We fly at what was called the "warsh" and the bombardier would be dropping sand bombs on a barge. So, we were coming back from one of these practice missions one day and dropping through the overcast, which sometimes can be 10,000 to 6,000 feet. Everybody's relaxed, we're heading back to the base, and all of a sudden I happened to look up, and I didn't know what it was, but something was coming right at us. As I started to yell to Robby the pilot, he saw it before I did, and it was the Lancaster - that's a British heavy bomber. And we were coming right at each other through the clouds on a collision course, I think. Well, the Lanc went up, we went down. And I can remember looking up and seeing the bottom of that thing. It was that close. I often thought, what if they both decided to go up or go down? There's no yellow lines up there in the air telling you what to do. That scared me more than some missions I was on.

Another mission, when we were way out towards the Polish border, about as deep as I ever went. We were still in B-24s at that time. On the way back, we were flying over the Bering Sea, which is pretty deep. Now, that's between Sweden and Germany. They told us at briefing, if you're hit and you have to try to make a crash landing, don't take off for Sweden, because if you do, one of their fighter planes will stay with you and shoot you down. They're not going to let you try to get to Sweden. But, if you turn to the left and head for Germany, they'll ignore you because they're going to get you one way or another. They weren't interested in that. They were interested in shooting the ones that were still flying. Anyway, that particular mission, I wrote down the coordinates: where we got hit, what time. When they broke off, I looked at my watch (I guess they were running out of fuel and broke off the engagement), and it was exactly 20 minutes. Boy, I'm telling you, that was a long 20 minutes. I was pretty darn lucky because in the B-24 there are little windows on each side. I used to ride backwards - by that I mean there was a little desk that I worked at, and I had these two windows I could look out, to look down on the ground. I was standing at that time and all of a sudden I heard a "ding dong," just like that. In the one window there was a hole about maybe two inches big in the little glass. The windows were only about 10 by 15 inches - they were kind of small. On the other side, where it went out, it took the whole window out. You know, it just blew it right out as it went through. It was so close, I reached my glove up to see if there was any blood on my nose. I didn't see anything, so I said, well, I'm okay.

So, we got back for debriefing, one of the pilots says, "Hey Stan, what's wrong? There's a little piece of skin hanging over on your nose." The epidermis, you know, the outer skin, it had just sort of skinned it, but it didn't bleed. It just rose it up maybe about three-eighths of an inch piece sticking up. He says, "Hey, you ought to put in for a Purple Heart." I says you got to be kidding, there's no blood up there. But, that was probably the closest I ever came to buying the farm.

One memory that maybe didn't bother some of the fellows, but it sure did me because I had to work my butt off on that mission. I forget whether we were flying division lead or 8th Air Force lead. You see, when you fly a lead, the co-pilot doesn't fly in the co-pilot seat. This is something I always felt that these guys, it was tough to be a co-pilot, particularly on a lead crew. You flew it whenever, you did "practice missions" and all this stuff. But, when you were flying on a mission, you generally had, we would have either a lieutenant colonel or a colonel or one time a brigadier general flying in the co-pilot's seat because he's in charge or command of the whole formation, whether you're flying group or wing or whatever. He makes all the final decisions about whether you're going in over that target, or different things that come up. So, the co-pilot is basically the rearview mirror of flying. He had to handle the tail turn. But, from that position he could keep the air commander advised on whether any of the planes were falling out of formation, and keep him abreast of what's going on behind us, because all we can see is what's in front of us.

Anyway, this particular mission we had a Brigadier General flying with us. Boy I'm telling you, I worked my butt off. I knew where I was every minute because I never knew when he was going to ask me.

All I can say is that I did go to Hanover three times. The reason I remember is because the name Rolfes, which is German, and my grandfather and grandmother on my father's side came from Hanover, Germany back around, I guess 1870s or somewhere in there. But the Rolfes in Cincinnati, and this is a sort of German town, you know. I think everyone I ever spoke to, even though I'm not related to, I ask them how far back they can trace their heritage. And invariably they can trace back to Hanover, Germany. There must be a lot of Rolfes there. I remember I'd be sitting there, when you're on the bomb run, which lasts generally about eight to ten minutes there's nothing for me to do. The bombardier is flying the plane. I'm sitting there and I'm thinking, I wonder how many Rolfes we're going to kill down there today? I wasn't related to them, but I'm sure there were some down there.

The way it worked on the bomber, I would get to what they call the IP, that's the initial point. Invariably they would put the IP into the wind so we would be going real slow. So if our indicated airspeed is 150 mph, sometimes we'd be into maybe 70 or 80 mph head winds, up in that altitude, sometimes more than that. So we're only going across the ground at about the speed of an automobile. We're really sitting ducks. But the point of it is, it gives the bombardier more time to spot the target and synchronize on it. Once I give the pilot the heading on the IP, the initial point, then I had to give the bombardier a lot of information like the temperature, the airspeed, the wind direction and speed. He put all this stuff in the Norden Bomb Site. Actually, the Norden Bomb Site, well today you'd call it a crude computer, a mechanical computer really, very crude compared to today's stuff. But at that time they were supposed to be a big, magic thing.

It is all sort of based on actuaries. It was pretty tough in the first part of the war. Well, towards the fall and late summer of '44 the losses weren't quite as bad. I think part of it was due to the fact that we had B-17s now, and not just our group, a third of the entire 8th Air Force. See, there were two-thirds B-17s, one-third B-24s. Now they got all B-17s and the casualty rate was going down a little bit. So they moved it up from 25 missions to 28 missions. Shortly after that they bumped it up to 35. After 35 you could go home. Well, they didn't promise you forever because they didn't know how long either one of these wars was going to last, but you could go home and they'd reassign you to something, maybe ground work or instructing, that sort of thing. Since we were flying lead crew, and we had 28 missions in, they gave us the option of going on to 35 and then go home, or go home right now for one month leave, but agree, the three of us as a team, to come back and do another tour. Well we all talked it over and agreed that this was, probably early in November I imagine, by the time we get home, we spend a month at home, we have to get back, it'll take at least two months, maybe the war will be winding down. It might be over. The trouble is, we got back real early in January and they had us flying again within a matter of a week because the Battle of the Bulge was going on. It was a bad time. That was in January and February of '45.

So I did 28 missions on the first tour and then, of course, as things went on, the war was starting to wind down, I did sixteen on the second tour, a total of 44.

836TH SQUADRON

We were running out of targets at that point. Not only that, I always thought that those last couple of missions-it was obvious that the Germans were going to have to give up pretty darn soon. It was obvious it was going to end soon. In fact, on a couple of occasions, we would be briefed for mission, we'd get airborne, get assembled, and they would call us back, scrub the mission, because they got word that Patton was 25 miles from where we were going. Things like this. So we were running out of targets. But I always thought on those last couple of missions, excuse the language, it would sure be hell to be shot down after all of this, and you know the war is about over, and your going to get to go home. This has happened to many fellows in the jungles of the Philippines. They were still fighting when the war was over. They didn't know it and some fellows got killed, but anyway, I got a Lucky Bastard Certificate.

But then the other thought I had, this would apply to any air crew member, is the contrast in psychology with dealing with combat when you're flying in an airplane as opposed to being on the ground. When you're on the ground, you're in mucking and mud and slop and rain and cold, wet feet, and all this kind of stuff. And I've talked to fellows and I asked them questions, what you do about this, what you do about that. And I'm telling you, it's pretty miserable life. When you're out in the field like this for a couple weeks at a time, I guess you just get to the point where it is so miserable, you really don't care. It's just miserable and maybe the only way out of this whole thing-well, like one fellow told me, it didn't bother him if he was killed, but he would have liked to be wounded. "Jesus, if I could just get wounded. At least they'll pull me out of here and I'll go to the field hospital or something like that." It's a miserable life. And in ours it is more concentrated, but it's so short.

I don't remember how often, but we'd get a pass to London. I don't know every other month, or whatever, I can't recall anymore, but you could be at a Tea Dance in the Savoy, dancing, and the next day you're going to be home, or home here at your base. When you get back you look at the bulletin board and there's your crew's name. You're flying that morning, you're going to wake up four o'clock in the morning and you're going on a mission. In other words, you can appreciate how sweet life can be. You got to turn it on and off when you're on the ground. I can see where it was really miserable; we always had a dry bed to sleep on when we got back, that's the big thing. I think it took a little-I don't know what you would call it-but a different kind of psychology, philosophy to think about the dangers you were facing. Sometimes they were very concentrated, maybe for five or six minutes on a bomb run, and that's the only action you saw on the whole flight. But when that black stuff is popping all around you, you know, it's a little scary, in particular when you see other planes tumbling down in the sky.

I didn't get to come home right away because I was a navigator. See, all the medium bombers were stationed in France. There werre B-25's and B-26's. These were two engine planes. Generally they only carried a pilot, I think. They may have had a gunner, I don't know. They have a crew of two or three. I don't remember. I had never seen one until this, but as they were deactivating these groups over there they had to fly them home. They wanted to fly home by the northern route because they didn't have a very long range-that's from Scotland to Iceland to Greenland to Goose Bay in Canada and down to New England. We had to do it in little hops. So they took a whole bunch of navigators and we were held…well actually I was in Iceland. We were in Iceland waiting for the weather to break in Greenland so we could fly there when VJ Day was announced on the radio. That was in late August I think. After the war ended, in late April I guess, I was just killing time you might say in a place up in Scotland where they kept a whole bunch of us just waiting for planes to come through. They would get up to Scotland and we would navigate them home. In other words I had to work my way home.

So I went overseas three times. I went out three times and back three times. I went by ship three times and flew three times. So actually I was in almost five years. September of '45 was a big month for me because I flew this hotshot plane which was a lot faster than a B-17, you know. I think it did about 240 mph, which I though was amazing in those days. So anyway, I flew home. I lined up a job, the job that I wanted and I got married, all in September.

I went to work with a printing company. I had worked for a printing company in a plant before I went into the service. Another fellow and I were eventually able to buy it out and were partners. I did okay with it. We had about 75 to 80 employees; it would vary from time to time. I had three children, two boys and a girl. Linda is my daughter. She's the first, then Dale and Mark. My wife picked one-syllable names so they couldn't get nicknames. Now I live in a retirement center.

DUANE KAISER

LEFT: *Kaiser, pictured after his 33rd mission in early April, 1945.* RIGHT: *Kaiser served from 1980-84 in the Washington State House of Representatives.*

My first combat mission was January 3rd, 1945 over Germany. Our second bombing mission was January 6, and on January 7 we bombed Paderborn. There was flak as usual, about the same as we encountered on our first missions, except we took a closer burst, causing us to lose an engine, so the prop was feathered.

When we got back to England, there was heavy fog and visibility was impaired; however, we could see the ground and some landmarks, but when the wheels touched down, we were not at Lavenham, but at Sudbury six or eight miles away. It was late, we were cold and hungry and our plane needed work by our superior ground crew. Our pilot, Lt. Harold J. McCarthy Jr., called the tower and asked for and was given permission to take off. We sat in the radio room with our backs against the bulkhead, and the take-off was as uneventful as we had done many times in training in Florida. When we got to our hardstand at Lavenham, a General in a Jeep was sitting there waiting to talk to our pilot, whom we always addressed as the "commander." The General informed the "commander" that it was against Eighth Air Force rules to take off with three engines, and starting with the next mission, he would be a co-pilot.

January 8th 1945

We were awakened at about 2:00 a.m. for another day in the sky over Germany. As this was our fourth mission and the third in three days we were already used to the routine - first breakfast, then briefing, pick up guns and parachutes, put on our electrically heated suits, and get on the truck to the plane. When we got to the plane it was dark and cold as usual, maybe even a little colder than usual, if that could be possible. After installing my guns and putting the ammunition belts in place, the engines began to start. Then, I would stay in the tail with loaded guns during take off, because we had to guard against German fighters up there in the dark, waiting for an easy victim. At the time we took off on January 8, I didn't realize that the "commander" was flying co-pilot, and a stranger in the dark was in the left-hand seat. Our target that day was Frankfurt, and it was terribly cold; in fact, the navigator said it was 72 degrees below zero. I know I turned my heat up to 20, the maximum on the dial, and just as we started the bomb run, I felt something real hot in the middle of my back, and then it went away, and so did all of the heat in my suit. That is when I found out what cold was, because from my shoes to my goggles, I had no heat.

During the bomb run, the flak got heavy and close enough to smell gunpowder from it. As we turned off the target, I heard talk up front that we had taken a hit, two engines were out and they couldn't feather them. Next, I heard someone say, "All the bombs are hung up and we are losing altitude." I remember looking out the side window of the tail and seeing the rest of the group way out in front heading back to England. What a lonely feeling, but also, no time to panic.

By this time we were down in the clouds, all alone, and it was my job to try and get those bombs out. So, I called the "commander" to ask permission to leave my guns and try to toggle out those bombs with a screwdriver. Next, I put on my parachute, got a small oxygen bottle and clamped it to my parachute harness, and headed to the radio room. When I got there, the radio operator handed me a rather long-handled screwdriver. I don't know where he kept that screwdriver, but he was quick to act. Armed with the screwdriver I inched my way out on the catwalk, over the open bomb bay doors with nothing below me but Germany.

I was lucky because as I reached across the open bomb bay, the screwdriver went in the notch I was praying it would find, so I twisted real hard, and a 500-lb. bomb was on its way to Germany. I had to keep working, because there weren't too many minutes in those small oxygen bottles. So, I then turned the screwdriver to the bottom bomb next to the catwalk, found the notch and twisted again and another 500-lb. bomb disappeared into the clouds below. I rested for a moment by leaning on the bombs behind me and holding on to that green rope as if my life depended on it, and it almost did. Just as I straightened up to continue my job, Tony, the engineer again tried his emergency switch, and all the bombs were released, including the ones I had just been leaning on. Maybe by releasing that 1,000 lbs. by hand made it possible for the electric switch to do its job. Who knows? I went back to the tail feeling pretty good, because now we could probably get deep enough in France to maybe find a landing strip or at least bail out in friendly territory. By this time, we were getting quite a bit lower, but were still in the heavy overcast. Then, I heard the pilots and navigator discussing if there could be mountains in the area. The "commander" came on the interphone and said he would give whoever saw the ground first a $20 bill. I still wonder why he used green money instead of five one pound notes. Just as I called in to say I saw the ground, he said, "I've already seen it."

We broke out of the overcast at about 2,000-feet altitude and looked for a landing strip for many miles. It was snowing and blizzard conditions prevailed outside, and it was lonely in the tail. I tried to call the waist gunner - no answer. Then, I called the ball-turret gunner - no answer. So, I crawled out of the tail to find everyone in the waist, some with parachutes on, because the engineer had earlier announced we were getting very low on gas. I took it on myself to call the commander and ask what he wanted the crew to do. He said, "Will they bail out?" I said, "Give me the order and they will." He then said, "Bail them out, Worrybird." I then pulled that red handle, gave the waist door a kick and said the commander has ordered us to bail out. As they went out headfirst, I announced their names to the commander to let him know, and when the last one had jumped I said, "They are all out now." The commander said, "Oh no, Worrybird, I'll give you 10 seconds to get out of this plane or I'll have you court-martialed." I knew he wouldn't do that, but I did ask how high we were, and his answer was about 1,600 feet. I said, "Give me 10 seconds and I am out of here." My chute opened immediately as I pulled the ripcord. As he turned the plane to find a place to belly-land, he gave me the OK signal with thumb and forefinger connected, and I waved back the same.

When I looked down, I saw I was going to land in the middle of a river, so I started unbuckling my parachute harness, but a strong wind in the blizzard carried me across the river to a very hard landing. This all happened so fast I had no chance to dump my chute, and the wind dragged me on my back up to a fence where the chute tangled and stopped. So, I was home free with just a badly sprained ankle, I thought.

Two Frenchmen with large clubs captured me and walked me down the river to a boat. They shoved me ahead of them, and that was when I first realized something was not quite right. When they rowed the boat up to shore, a GI with a tommy gun greeted me. I said, "Is that damn thing loaded?" He said, "Let me see your dog tags." I ran my hand around my neck and found none. The gunner told another GI to search me. He came on the boat, ran his hand around my neck and found no dog tags either. (The problem was it was so cold when I got dressed, I had put on two long-sleeved underwear tops, so the dog tags were between them and well-hidden.) The gunner kept his weapon leveled and asked, "What is your name?" I said, "I don't think this is going to help a hell of a lot, because my name is Kaiser." The gun stayed level, but he got a little grin on his face. Then, he asked some questions about the Eastern part of the U.S. that I didn't get quite right (I was from Seattle) because the gun stayed level. He then asked, "How many dogs does Dagwood have?" I was so relieved that I said, "one, and her name is Daisy. Oh no, wait a minute, she has had a litter of little pups." The gun came down, we shook hands and I got off the boat. He said, "Would you like to have an American beer?" By now, my answer "yes" came quickly. He said, "We have it hidden in that old barn over there." Just as we started for the barn, a Jeep drove up. He said that it was the Major - we can't let him catch us with that beer.

They turned me over to the Major. I stepped up to the Jeep and saluted him. He said that the salute was not necessary. "Where are you from?" I told him the Seattle area. He said, "Your accent sounds all right, get in." He said, "You must have had a pretty rough day - we better go down to my Chateau and get you fortified." I told him I wanted to get back to the plane to see if the pilots were OK. He said they made a good belly landing and they were fine, so we stopped at the Chateau and relaxed over a couple of stiff drinks.

Again, I told him I should get back to the plane, so he took me to where it lay in the snow. As I got out of the Jeep, there were about 50 French people milling around the plane. I knew that the guns were loaded, so I headed for the open waist door to go in and unload those guns. Just as I started to enter the plane, an officer I had never seen before stopped me. He asked me, "where do you fit in the picture?" I said, "I'm the tail gunner on this plane, Sir." Then he asked, "Are you the one who toggled out the bombs?" I said, "Yes sir." Then he asked, "Are you the Worry bird who bailed out the crew?" I said "Yes, Sir." He said "Sir, Hell, you call me Jack."

That was when I first met Jack Mulhollon, the man who started out that morning as the pilot, but when we got in trouble, he traded places with the "commander" so he could be in charge of his own crew. Jack evidently sensed the closeness of the crew and the respect we had for each other. In fact, they traded seats in the air, so with the "commander" in the left seat, he was no longer the co-pilot but the man in charge of the crew. The pilots made the belly landing in a space only half long enough to do so. They were running out of room and turned the plane 180 degrees with the vertical stabilizer, and the plane stopped sliding in the snow just a few feet from where it first touched down.

We didn't fly combat again until January 28, so I had many long nights to twist and turn in bed, wondering how we could possibly finish 30 or more missions out, considering what had happened to us on our first four days of combat.

836TH SQUADRON

NEIL F. MATZ

Matz (front, third from left), pictured here with the original crew of the "Miss Behavin'," had to bail out during one mission and said, "I was one of the lucky guys. I never became a prisoner because I was picked up so fast and brought back to London."

I was a gunner on a B-17G, the "Miss Behavin'," a member of the 836th Bomb Squadron, 487th Bomb Group, 8th Air Force. My crew was based in Lavenham, Suffolk England. The 836th was one of four bomb squadrons in the 487th- the 836th, 837th, 838th and 839th. I enlisted as a senior in high school. It must have been in March of 1943, because I graduated high school in '43 and I was still in school when I enlisted. You had to enlist to go into the Air Force. I enlisted to go into the Aviation Cadets; I was going to be a flier. I wanted to be a flier but not necessarily the pilot. I was in the Air Force 28 or 29 months.

I started pilot training at the University of Cincinnati, and it wasn't too long after that when we washed out. We were told that it was the wrong time for pilot training. They had enough pilots. They needed gunners. So, they started training us as gunners. I was put on a B-17, the Flying Fortress, as a waist gunner for the first 17 missions, and a tail gunner for the last 16 missions.

My first mission was in October of '44 to Munster, Germany. The 8th Air Force was the strategic air force, which meant we would fly three, four, five hundred miles inside Germany to bomb factories, bomb railroads, bomb oil depots. The 9th Air Force was a tactical air force; they worked in conjunction with the ground forces. I flew a total of 33 missions and was discharged as a Staff Sergeant in October of '45.

The most memorable mission I flew was on Christmas Eve, December 24th, 1944. I can honestly tell you it was probably the only mission that I ever really wanted to fly. England and the whole 8th Air Force were completely fogged in, socked down, with no missions flown in six, seven or eight days. We were grounded from the battle lines back to England. From the front lines back into Germany, though, it was clear. There were a lot of reports that the soldiers that we had on the ground there were really having a bad time. The German air force was really playing hell with them. This is why I wanted to fly this mission.

While we normally were granted leave with 48-hour passes, that week our pilot came to us and told us that we would be allowed only a 24-hour pass. They expected the weather to clear and the mission to be flown, so that's why we were offered only a 24-hour pass. Our pilot talked to us and we all agreed that we should take the pass, go for what we could get which was the 24-hour pass.

In all probability, this is why we lost the lead position we had held in our formation. By my 17th mission, this mission, we were already flying element lead. But because we had taken the pass, they weren't sure that all of us were there on the base or could get back to the base, so they gave our position to somebody else. Anyway, we did get back finally, and they put us in the number 13 spot, in the low squadron. That is hanging by yourself, no wingman. We were all four elements of three airplanes, and then one loner.

A lot of times, they didn't fly that 13th spot. They would fly 12 to a squadron. But this mission was a "super maximum" effort; really, I heard it called that many times. It was, of course, during the Battle of the Bulge, and it was the biggest mission ever flown in total number of airplanes. Where you normally would have flown three squadrons out of four, a "normal maximum," leaving one squad on the ground, on that day four out of four squadrons flew. So, they put us in number 13 and we took off. The 487th led the 8th Air Force that day. I remember it was said that when the first group reached target that day, the last group was still leaving England.

Drawing of Formation

On this mission, we were headed to Babenhausen, Germany, to an airfield. The whole target for that mission was airfields. They had figured that we would destroy as many airfields that we could and concentrate on the German airplanes at the airports that were missed on previous missions or that they didn't hit. Then the next day, they would hit the German airplanes that were left on the ground. It started out like any other mission - by the time you take off and go through the clouds and get into the formation, it takes some time.

I was left waist gunner. The right waist gunner was one of the men that was taken off when they made the 10-man crew into a nine-man crew. That's when the radio operator would come back and man that gun. Later on, they took the navigator off and made it an eight-man crew, then the bombardier would fire the chin gun. He knew enough about navigation, and we never really had to use our own navigator because we always flew in a group. The only time you had to find your way back alone was if you were shot up a little bit and you had to drop out of formation. But then you knew you could break radio silence and get guidance back.

There's a little story here about my ball-turret operator, Dave MacHauer. When you're in the ball-turret, you're really out of the plane, hanging in a ball below the belly of the plane. So when we started our missions, Dave put in for a backpack parachute so he would not have to come back into the airplane to bail out if we ever had to. Believe it or not, on this mission, Dave got his parachute.

We missed our fighter escort. Since we got there before the fighters did, the first or second pass the Germans made at us they shot us down. I knew we were hit because the shells exploded right through the middle of our airplane. It put a hole in the craft and started it on fire - the whole right side of the airplane started to burn. We were hit by fighters - the Fokker 190 and the Messerschmitt 109. They had a 20mm cannon in the nose of the airplane in addition to the .50 caliber machine guns. This is what I think hit us, because you could hear maybe three or four boom, boom, booms right through the center of our airplane.

The airplane started to go down. I didn't see anyone else on board. When I looked, Kleinman, the radio operator, was already flat on the floor. With the explosion in the craft, I thought he was dead. Our interphone was shot out. I couldn't talk to anyone. My left boot got hit with a piece of shrapnel. The whole boot was busted apart. But it was closed on top yet, and still holding. Where the foot was, that was solid, but across the front, it was blown apart. I didn't know what the hell to do, so I bailed out.

I guess I made a mistake then that probably saved my life. I put my parachute on, went back to the escape hatch, pulled the handle, the door flew off. I got down almost in a kneeling position, put my hand on the ripcord, and rolled out. As soon as I cleared the plane, I pulled the ripcord. Something we were told many times was not to pull the ripcord until you could make out a lot of things on the ground - a cow or a horse or a farmer- but like I said, the mistake I made was that I pulled the ripcord right after I cleared the plane. But that was the mistake that saved my life. We had just crossed the enemy line, but because we had a head wind going into Germany, the wind blew me back far enough that I was picked up by the men of the 125th antiaircraft artillery before the Germans could get me.

When Turnquist, the pilot, went to bail out, you're supposed to do it head first like I did. Turnquist went out feet first, though, I don't know why. Our chute was a chest pack. When he went out feet first, he was blown up against the escape hatch and he couldn't move, he couldn't get in or out. He hung with his parachute on the escape hatch. I don't know how long he was hanging there, but the bombardier Ceder came and grabbed him by his straps on the parachute. The escape hatch was only so big, and Ceder had to clear the pilot before anyone else could bail out. Ceder pulled Turnquist back in, dropped him, and then bailed out after him. Turnquist pulled his ripcord, because the chute did stream out. But it never blossomed; it never opened. He just free fell.

Gentlemen From Hell

The co-pilot, Chatterton, was mortally wounded and stayed with the airplane to keep it out of a centrifugal force spin. It was burning on his side of the plane and he knew he was not going to make it anyway. Don't forget our interphone was shot out. Kleinman was on the floor. MacHauer came back into the airplane from the ball-turret and opened up his hatch. When he got in there, I don't remember now if he told me he had talked to Kleinman, or if he had already seen Kleinman lying on the floor. I was already gone. I had pulled the door off and I bailed out.

MacHauer went back down, he needed help apparently. In the meantime, the pilot and Ceder bailed. So MacHauer decided to bail. MacHauer said later he thought he was hit, but he was burned going through the same fire that had gotten Chatterton. His gun in his shoulder holster saved his life because a portion of a shell hit his gun. Without the gun, it could have pierced his heart.

My recollection is that we were down to an eight-man crew at this time. Chatterton went down with the plane. Kleinman, the radio operator, bailed out and lived, but I never saw him after that. Four lived and four died. Ceder, MacHauer, Kleinman and I-the bombardier, ball-turret operator, radio operator and waist gunner - lived. Stanton, Gregory, Chatterton and Turnquist-the top turret operator, tail gunner, co-pilot and pilot - died. The top turret operator and co-pilot were never accounted for. They accounted for six of our men. Two were still missing in action. Chatterton and Stanton couldn't be individually identified and received a group burial after the war.

Of those of us that survived, Ceder was by far the most affected by the hit afterward. First, before he bailed out, he had seen Chatterton, the co-pilot, with his face burned so badly that Ceder said later that some of the flesh around Chatterton's eyes was just hanging. Our oxygen masks covered our mouths and noses; our helmets covered our heads and ears. Our eyes, though, were exposed, and Ceder could see the co-pilots' burning flesh just hanging there. Then, when Ceder finally bailed and safely landed, he came upon Turnquist's body - the man he helped out of the plane. Because his chute never opened, Turnquist's body was just like Jell-O. It was the 24th of December, and though there was very little snow on the ground, the ground was frozen solid. He took the pilot's watch, his wallet, his handkerchief, three or four personal things from his body and brought them back with him. It was hard for Ceder to make it home. He had a brother on the front line. I don't know if he tried finding him or what, but finally, he came back. We may have been back four, five or six days before he got back.

The Commander of the raid that day was Brigadier General Frederick W. Castle. He flew lead that day, and like us, was shot down. General Castle was killed in action - his remains were found in the wreckage of his craft.

I landed by myself. No one else. I took the parachute off after I hit the ground. The first thing you're supposed to do is try to hide the chute. We wore guns, .45 caliber guns. I only wore a gun so that I would not have to surrender to a civilian. The civilians would kill the guys on the ground if they had a chance. If you surrendered to a service man, they were to take you prisoner. They wouldn't kill you. This is after you're on the ground, you're shot down. If you're on enemy territory, though, with civilians around, the civilians would just kill you. The farmers would come with pitchforks, for God's sake. You were bombing their land, you were killing them. You heard all kinds of stories of what happened. Like Dick Ceder, for example, he bailed out of the airplane and the enemy came after him with their airplane, shooting at him as he was hanging on that parachute. That was illegal. They weren't allowed to kill a paratrooper - a guy that was bailing out of an airplane to land on the ground to fight. We were bailing out of an airplane to save our life. We were not bailing out to fight - just to save our lives. Ceder, fortunately, was met by one of our fighter escorts who circled him in the air until he landed.

My altitude when I bailed was less than 24,000, I think around 22,000, but I don't remember it exactly. When I got on the ground, a guy came over. Now I'm ready to surrender because he was military. By that time, I had already left the chute on the ground. There was some snow around, very little, and I tried to cover it as much as you could, but you cover it if you can and then get the hell out of there because everybody on the ground, Germans included, could see you coming down. So, when I got down these two guys came over and they had their guns on them. I'm ready to surrender because I saw they were military men and I didn't know whether they were Americans or Germans. They saw us bail out; they knew approximately where we hit the ground. They made sure that I was not a German parachutist, because our uniforms were pretty much the same - they were a green color. They said, "Are you American?" I said, "Yes, are you American?" They said, "Yes." One said let's get the hell out of here because at this point in time the Germans were all over the place - they had broken through the line. This was outside Liege, Belgium. I don't remember how many miles.

I asked them, "How did you know where I was or what had happened?" The two guys that picked me up told me that they had watched us. They saw this dogfight going on, had watched us being shot down, and saw some of the guys and their parachutes that had opened when they bailed out. So, they pretty much knew where I was, in fact the guy told me that there were five guys with this gun emplacement. The captain sent two guys for me, and two went after another guy. The man that picked me up made a big joke because he had red hair and they called him "Red" Baird. There was a young guy with him; Red must have been 10 years, maybe 12 years older. They were members of the 125th antiaircraft artillery. I got his full name and address in Corning, in central Ohio. I remember writing him a letter when I got home. I thanked him for picking me up and for saving my life and told him that I owe him a good drink; in fact, I owe him a drunk if he wants to get drunk because I owed him that much.

The men of the 125th put me in a truck and brought me back to a fortress outside Liege, Fort d'Embourg. Before World War I, Liege had seven mountains, seven fortresses around it and Fort d'Embourg was one of them. The one thing that I remember when we got to the fortress, I didn't know what it was, I just remember a hole or a tunnel in the side of a mountain. This Fort d'Embourg was used way, way back even before the First World War. I could tell you that if you know the fortress in Canada - Fort Henry - it was the same thing. It was an army base there. They had mess halls and rooms where they slept, and kitchens and everything else that goes with a base. An entire army camp in a mountain.

I stayed at Fort d'Embourg maybe two or three days and then got in with the Belgian underground, I guess. From there, they put me on a truck, an open truck, and brought me to Brussels. There were a lot of Americans on the ground because of the raid. At Brussels I stayed, I think one night. They were trying to get me a ride back to England. We were in a bunk, like a gym, a big open room. The next day, they got three or four of us, they brought us up to one of the air bases outside Brussels, or in Belgium someplace, and they hitchhiked a ride back to London for us on a B-24, would you believe. We had always heard so many stories about B-24s, about them blowing up, and that was the only time I ever flew on one. The B-17 was a hell of a lot better airplane - to us, the B-24 was like a flying coffin for God's sake. But it was the Battle of the Bulge, and everyone kept telling us that we had to get out of there because there were German troops all over the place.

I was one of the lucky guys. I never became a prisoner because I was picked up so fast and brought back to London. In London, they brought us into a kind of debriefing. They wanted to know what was going on and what happened, was I a prisoner and where was I a prisoner. I said I was not a prisoner. I was shot down the 24th of December. I don't remember at this point in time how many days had gone by from the day that we were shot down to the day that we got back to London. I just told them that I was not a prisoner, I did not get wounded, I was shot down. I said I don't even know if I'm the only guy alive. At the time MacHauer's news hit his paper, he was the lone survivor. The rest of us were missing in action. They didn't know. Then I got back, and then Ceder came back. Then Kleinman got back, I don't know when he got back.

When I got back to the base, Dave MacHauer was already back. I was the second guy back. Ceder wasn't back yet. When I entered the huts, our squadron had gotten hit the hardest, and they had already brought in new crews - replacement crews. My bunk was empty yet, so I took my own bunk back. But they had taken our clothes and brought them back to the Quartermaster. Then, maybe a week after that, Ceder got back. We were sitting there, a bunch of guys talking; I'm not sure, I think there were two crews in each hut.

Ceder walked in. Everybody got dead quiet. He had been missing in action. At the huts, no one really knew him, but the minute he walked in, they knew who he was without him opening his mouth. He came up, put his arms around me, and we started crying. We were kids. I was 19 years old.

At that point, we were spare gunners because the pilot and co-pilot were dead. They sent us to Henley-on-Thames, the Queen's summer home, a flak shack they called it. They sent us out there for seven days. They had hot water, you know, R&R, anything we wanted to eat.

When we went back to the base for a return to duty, David and I were put on another crew, with a pilot and co-pilot flying their second tour of missions.

Up to that mission, we had flown all 17 flights with that same crew. MacHauer and I eventually flew all 33 of our missions together. But we became spare gunners after we were shot down on that 17th mission. Spare gunners were only to fly 25 missions, because they only flew when they needed a guy, you know when a guy was sick, and they had to replace him. So your time was longer, because instead of flying two or three missions a week, maybe you would only fly two or three a month. By that point, they had reduced the number of missions required for a discharge from 35 to 25 for spare gunners before returning to America.

Like I said, at that point in the war, we were supposed to finish our tour after 25 missions. But because they had made up a new crew, we weren't considered spare gunners any longer. So then we went on to 26 and 27, then they said at 30 missions we would be finished. Then we found out we had to fly another one, that was 31, then we had to fly another one, that was 32. They were killing us inches at a time, because then they made us go up again at 33. I could see what they were doing. The war was starting to wind down. They actually flew missions until April or May of '45, by that time we were already home.

By this time, the war in Europe was winding down. Folks who flew their tour of missions and didn't want a second tour of flying were reassigned. I volunteered to do extra duty after my missions because they were sending us back home, giving us a vacation and then retraining us on B-29s and shipping us out to the Pacific. I didn't want to fly anymore. So I stayed over in Lavenham, two or three months, as CQ in charge of quarters, and worked in the office. They didn't give you a choice about retraining on B-29s. They just did it. So after mission number 33, I decided to volunteer for ground duty because there was no way in hell that I was going to be sent to the Pacific and this is what was happening. They were taking the men from the 8th Air Force or from the European theater of war, giving them a furlough home, and then sending them to the Pacific.

I was furloughed in April of 1945 and returned to America on the Ile-de-France. We celebrated V-E Day while I was home. The Ile-de-France, like England's Queen Mary, was France's biggest ship. It took us, I think, only seven days from the time that we boarded until we got into New York.

I was the only guy that didn't get the Purple Heart. Four guys got it posthumously. Some of the guys asked me why didn't I put in for one, I said, "No, I wouldn't cheapen the medal by trying to get a purple heart for a blood blister." I have my air medals; I have the air medal with six oak leaf clusters - one silver and one bronze - there were five bronze for every silver. I also have the European Theater of Operations, or ETO, medal with three battle stars. And I have the Good Conduct and American Defense medals, and one more whose name escapes me. I'm also a member of the Caterpillar Club - a pretty elite group of men that used a parachute to save their lives. And the Lucky Bastard Club because I completed 33 missions over enemy territory.

After landing in New York, we went on leave first, and then we were assigned to the Army/Air Force hospital out in Santa Ana, California. We were still in the Army at that point. They were going to make us aircraft mechanics, but then we were discharged.

My mother and father never got any notice that I was shot down. If you were, your name would be put on a list, and then after 10 days, they would send a notice that you were missing in action. I got back before the 10 days were up, and they never received a notice.

I met my wife, Eleanor, in French class when I came back as a postgraduate student. We were married four years after my discharge. We had three children who have given us seven grandchildren. It was many years before I spoke openly and at length to my family about my wartime experiences. To this day, my sisters say I was very nervous, on edge, when I first came back from England. Now, as I look back on the events of 50 years ago and recount my days of service, I can't help becoming choked-up at the memories. Particularly this last year, with all the attention paid to the 50th anniversary of the end of World War II, I have begun to record my thoughts and memories, for my sake and my family's permanent recollection. Since Eleanor and I attended our first 487th Bomb Group Reunion in 1970 in Lavenham, England, we have made an effort to attend almost every reunion held. Each year, there are fewer of us left to reminisce. At least now, my family knows what happened during the war.

KARL KANDLER

Kandler (front, far right), pictured here with his crew at training in Avon Park, FL, prior to being sent overseas, passed away in October 1994.

This is the story of Technical Sergeant Karl P. Kandler a radio operator/aerial gunner and member of Lt. Willard J. Curtiss' crew that served in the 8th Air Force, 3rd Division, 487th Bomb Group, 836th Squadron from July 17, 1944 to December 16, 1944. This story is told by his second son, Karl Jr. My father passed away October of 1994. Like most veterans of World War II, my father did not talk much about the war and his story was put together from original documents found and correspondence with surviving crew members located after his passing.

My father was born July 24, 1924 and grew up in a rural area north of Detroit, Michigan, in a small town named Allenton. He was a first generation American as both of his parents emigrated from Europe in the early 1900s. The house that his parents raised their family of three daughters and four sons was typical of the time and area with no indoor plumbing or central heat, but eventually having electricity. My father was the youngest of the children.

His service to his country was as follows:

July 24, 1942: Probably joined the United States Army Air Corp on his 18th birthday after his graduation from Almont High School that June.
March 26, 1943: Reported to the Detroit Recruiting and Induction District, Detroit, Michigan for induction into the Army of the United States.
April 2, 1943: Reported to the Port Huron, Michigan, Selective Service Board for active duty.

April 2, 1943: Transferred to Fort Custer, Michigan for basic training. Rank: Recruit

November 27, 1943: Graduated from the "Radio Operators – Mechanics Course" A.A.F.T.S. Scott Field, Illinois. Rank: Private First Class

December 13, 1943 to January 24, 1944: Attended aerial gunner school at Yuma Army Air Field, Arizona. Graduated in the top 10 out of 320 of his class. Rank: Corporal

April 1944: Trained at Army Air Field, Dalhart, Texas. Rank: Corporal

May 9 to June 6, 1944: Trained at A.P.A.A.F. Avon Park, Florida. Trained with B-17G crew commanded by Lt. Willard J. Curtiss that he was sent to England with. Rank: Corporal

June 1944: Assigned to Third Air Force Staging Wing, Hunter Field, Georgia. Rank: Corporal

June 20, 1944 to June 30, 1944: Flew from the United States (Hunter Field, Savannah, Georgia) to the United Kingdom with stops at Fort Dix, New Jersey; Grenier Field, New Hampshire; Dow Field, Maine; Goose Bay, Labrador; Meeks Field, Iceland; Prestwick, Scotland, and the final destination of Glasgow, Scotland. Rank: Sergeant

June 30, 1944 to July 17, 1944: 8th Air Force training in England. Rank: Sergeant

July 17, 1944 to December 16, 1944: Assigned to the 8th Air Force, 3rd Division, 487th Bomb Group, 836th Squadron. Flew 28 combat missions over Europe. Flew in B-17G aircraft (tail number 42-102497) named "Flack Hack" under the command of Lt. Willard J. Curtiss. The rest of the crew was the one that he trained with at A.P.A.A.F., Avon Park, Florida. During this time, he was given a seven-day rest from combat at Moulsford, Berkshire, England. Rank: Technical Sergeant

December 27, 1944: Ordered to return to "The Zone Of The Interior" (The United States). Rank: Technical Sergeant

December 31, 1944: Arrived at Fort Totten, Long Island, New York from England. Rank: Technical Sergeant

February 1945: Reported to the A.A.F. Redistribution Station No. 4, Santa Ana, California for reassignment. Rank: Technical Sergeant

March 12, 1945 to April 21, 1945: Attended and graduated from the "Instructors Course, Central School for Flexible Gunnery" at Laredo Army Air Field, Laredo, Texas. Rank: Technical Sergeant

May 1945 to October 12, 1945: Assigned to the 2nd Air Force, 16th Wing, 231st Army Air Force, Base Unit as an aerial gunnery instructor on B-29s. Stationed at Alamogordo Army Air Field, Alamogordo, New Mexico. Rank: Technical Sergeant

October 12, 1945 to October 20, 1945: Discharged from the Army of the United States. Rank: Technical Sergeant

836TH SQUADRON

When he got orders to go overseas in June 1944, he started and kept a small diary/mission log.
The following is that diary/mission log.

My Tour in the E.T.O.
B-17-G 1944
(As written by Karl P. Kandler in his shirt pocket Notepad Diary)

June 20-44: Took off from Hunter Field Savannah, Georgia enroute to Dow Field Bangor, Maine. Bad weather had to land at Fort Dix, New Jersey.

June 21-44: Still weathered in – had to guard our ship all night.

June 22-44: Bad weather yet. Got a pass for the night. Went to Philadelphia and looked the place over. "Swell time."

June 23-44: Left Fort Dix, flew over New York City and set down at Grenier Field, New Hampshire.

June 25-44: Left Grenier and landed at Dow Field, Maine. Very nice place.

June 27-44: Took off from Dow and landed at Goose Bay, Labrador, spent the night there.

June 28-44: Left Goose Bay flew eight hours to Meeks Field, Iceland very barren and was light out all night.

June 29-44: Took off from Iceland and flew about 4 hours until we sighted the U.K. Landed at Prestwick, Scotland.

June 30-44: Left Prestwick went to Glasgow where we took a train to Stone a distribution center in England for the A.A.F.

July 5-44: Left Stone for a 10 day refresher course, Nav. Bomb. Pilot. Co-Pilot and I went to Bovingdon. The Gunners went to the Wash.

July 7-44: Had a 24 hour pass and went to Watford – had a good time and got a little dope on how the English live & act.

July 17-44: Left Bovingdon on our way to permanent base. Had a three hour layover at Cambridge so went sight seeing. Saw Kings College and the beautiful chapel also all the other colleges. Arrived at "Long Melford" went out to our base-station 137 at "Lavenham" 487th group, we're put into the 836th Bomb Squadron, A.P.O.559. Our crew was again all together!

August 6-44: Made all 9 man crews so we lost Al our waist gunner & assistant R.O. He left for a B-26 base where he will get 1st R.O. Had our first 2 day pass and took off for "London" where we had a wild time with the "Piccadilly Commandos" Wow! Our pilot is in the hospital so we aren't flying missions yet.

August 15-44: Pulled out of my sack at 4 A.M. for briefing – this is it at last. Flying with "Hanner" whose R.O. is flying lead today. A successful mission into Holland to an airfield on the border of Germany called

"Twente Airfield" near the city of Hengeloo. The flak was very light but the squadron on our right got it bad – saw 3 17's go down in flames, I was scared and really threw out chaf. Am now a VETERAN! Carried load of 250 pound demolition bombs.

August 27-44: Up at 4:30 A.M. went to chow & then to briefing. Curtis is out of the hospital and this is the first mission for the whole crew together. Target-a ME 109 engine plant on the out skirts of "Berlin." Flew all the way to Northern Germany and then was recalled because there were too many clouds over target. Brought our load of incendiaries back. Saw a little flak. Got credit for mission. –milk run–

September 1-44: Called at 3 A.M. went to chow and had a plan "A" briefing. Going to "Mainz" Germany which is on the Rhine a little ways south of "Frankfurt." Hitting an ordinance plant. We got to the target but the cloud cover was 10/10 and the P.F.F. didn't take us in so we came back with our load of 1000 & 500 pounders. No flak but got credit for the mission. Some saw flak.

September 8-44: Up at 3:30 A.M. to brief at 4:30–target is "Mainz" Germany that we didn't hit last time. Had plenty of P-51's and dropped our load of 500 lb. demos. Flew at 29,000 ft. & was 47° below zero. Damn cold! Our tail gunner didn't go, we took a boy on his last mission! Had a lot of flak but it wasn't very accurate. Our Bombardier was hit in the leg. "Purple heart" Good mission! Ordinance depot was our target.

September 10-44: Briefed 4:30 A.M. target was "Nuremberg, Germany." A large tank assembly plant. Dropped 20-100 lbs. fragmentation bombs from 27,600 ft. The air was quite cool 47° below. We had 3 flak holes in our left wing it was damn accurate. Had fighter support. Rough mission.

September 11-44: Briefed at 4:30 A.M. and our target was a synthetic oil plant on the outskirts of "Leipzig, Germany." We had a load of 500 lbs. demos. Had a good escort. They saved us from fighters. Got a big hole in our right wing from flak. Lucky we didn't lose an engine. Those "Nazis" (used swastika symbol here) are a rough bunch. "Bohlen" was the target.

September-13-44: Up at 2 A.M.-briefed at 3 A.M. Target was "Stuttgart, Germany." A engine plant for airplanes. When we got there the target was under a smoke screen so we went to the last resort at "Darmstadt, Germany," a rail yard. We dropped our load of 500 lbs. from 26,000 ft. We had light flak and a few rockets – "Darmstadt it is just about due south of Frankfurt." Was quite an easy mission compared to the past few.

September 19-44: Just got back from "London" last night but had to get up and go to "Limburg, Germany" to bomb a large bridge. We dropped 20-200 lbs. bombs from 25,000 feet. Good fighter support, had quite a bit of flak but no damage was done to our SQDN. It was about 35 below and our heated suits felt good!

836th Squadron

September 25-44: Briefed at 4:30 A.M. and the target was "Ludwigshafen, Germany." The weather was very bad but we bombed P.F.F. Had a load of 500 lbs. GP. The flak was moderate and the fighter support was good. It was a good mission! 26,000 ft. Very cold. Hit the rail yards.

September 26-44: Briefed at 8:30 A.M. target was "Bremen, Germany." We carried a full load of incendiaries and bombed from 27,500 ft. 42 degrees below zero. Our engineer is in the hospital with a cold! Had a lot of flak and saw a B-17 blow up when hit by a fighter. 410's hit one group but our escort took care of them. Really blew the target up. Target was an aero engine plant.

September 27-44: Briefed at 2 A.M. and our target was "Ludwigshafen, Germany" again. This time we got the big chemical plant. Carried 20-250 lb. GPs. Heavy flak but not very accurate. Bombed from 26,000 ft. and had good fighter escort! Ball gunner's oxygen supply failed and he nearly died before we got him on another supply line. Gave us a scare. No flak damage. Our engineer still in hospital. Rough mission.

September 28-44: Briefed at 4 A.M. Our target was "Merseburg, Germany" in the Leipzig area. We bombed from 26,000 ft. and carried a load of propaganda leaflets. The flak was the worst I have ever seen. You could land on it. We lost 2 ships out of 13 and all the rest where full of holes. Saw 2 men bailout and saw one 17 with an engine on fire. We had 5 to 10 holes and they had to put a new wing tip on our plane. Saw a jet-propelled fighter but it didn't attack 4 P-51s took after it. Had very good fighter support. It was the roughest mission so far. Oil refinery was our target.

September 30-44: Briefed at 5A.M. Target was "Bielefeld, Germany" a large rail yard behind the front line. Carried 12-500 lb. G.P. and bombed from 23,500 ft. Flak was very light and it would have been a good mission but we went through some clouds and 2 ships in our formation hit in mid-air and spun down. Saw 2 chutes. One crew was "Jackson's" his engineer flew 2 missions with us. Our engineer is now with us again. Good fighter support and no enemy fighters. Sad day. Going to London to get tight tomorrow.

October 6-44: Briefed at 4:15 A.M. Target was "Berlin" a large tank factory on the out skirts! We carried 12-500 lb. incendiaries and bombed from 25,000 ft. The flak was accurate and quite heavy. Had 3 large holes in our wings. It was a good mission and it was clear. Berlin looked big from where we were. Good fighter support and didn't see any enemy fighters. All our ships came back.

October 7-44: Up at 3 am to brief; our target was "Lutzkendorf, Germany" a large synthetic oil plant – Take off – 7A.M. Landed – 3P.M. Carried 12-500 lbs incendiaries and bombed from 24,800 ft. To low for our health! The flak was very heavy but we just had one small hole. Fighter support was good & they shot down 3 jet jobs. The Squadron in front of us was wiped out by "Nazis" (used swastika symbol here) fighters. One engine #4 went out over Holland and we came the rest of the way on 3. Good mission.

October 9-44: Briefed at 8 A.M. Our target was the marshaling rail yards at "Mainz, Germany." We carried a load of propaganda leaflets. Bombed from 26,000 ft. Couldn't see the target so bombed P.F.F. Flak was very inaccurate and the fighter support was good. Mission lasted 6 hours 15 min.

October 14-44: Up at 3 A.M. for briefing our target was the Ford Motor Co. at "Cologne Germany." Bombed from 27,000 ft. temp - 42 degrees. Bombed P.F.F. had a load of 12-500 lbs. G.P. & incendiaries. Flak was not very accurate or intense. Good fighter support. No damage to ourselves although one tail gunner got hit in the hand by flak. May lose finger. 7 hours 15 min.

October 15-44: Up at 1:30 A.M. to brief. Target was one of the large rail centers in "Cologne Germany." Bombed from 27,000 ft. very cold. Had 6-500 lb. incendiaries and 14-250 lb. G.P. bombs. Flak was very heavy and accurate. Lost two of our ships. Saw 2 ships blow up. Had good fighter support & hit the target. Flak was so close could hear it explode. Had 12 to 15 holes in our ship. No one hurt. 3 men in our group were wounded. "Happy Valley" is a bad place to go.

October 18-44: Up at 3 A.M. briefing 4 A.M. Our target was the tank and heavy equipment factory at "Kassel, Germany." Bombed from 26,000 ft. Had 6-500 lb. GPs and 6-500 lb. Incen. Flak was very light and inaccurate. No damage or ships lost. Had good fighter support. Bombed P.F.F. but had very bad weather on the way back. Were up for about seven hours. Broke in a new pilot today, his first mission.

October 19-44: Briefed at 4 A.M. Target was the aero engine plant at "Mammhiem, Germany. Carried 6-500 lb. GPs and 6-500 lb. incendiaries. We bombed from 28,000 ft. Temp was - 45°. We went up to 31,000 ft. and were out of reach of the flak guns. No damage was done to us and no ships lost. Fighter support was very good. Flak was very heavy below us. Bombed P.F.F.

October 22-44: Briefed at 7:30 A.M. Our target was the rail yard at "Munster, Germany." We carried 12-500 lbs. GPs. Dropped them from 26,500 ft. Flak was very heavy but not very accurate. No flak damage was done. Fighter support was good and the mission only lasted 6 hours. Was an easy mission P.F.F.

October 28-44: Briefed at 5 A.M. Our target was the large rail yards at "Hamm, Germany." Carried 12-250 lb. GPs and 4-500 lb. incen. Bombed from 26,000 ft. Flak was very light and no damage was done to us. Fighter support was good. Mission lasted 7 hrs. Bombed P.F.F.

836th Squadron

November 4-44: Briefed at 5:30 A.M. Our target was the Cokeing and Benzol plant at "Neuenkirchen, Germany" which is a little north of Sarrbrucken. We carried 12-500 lbs. G.P. and dropped them from 27,000 ft. - 42°. There was no flak at the target and we had good fighter support. Bombed P.F.F. No damage or planes lost. Good mission.

November 5-44: Briefed at 4:30 A.M. Our target was "Ludwigshafen, Germany" a large chemical plant. We were supposed to drop 2 miles in front of the troops but the clouds were 10/10 so we went to "Ludwigshafen." We carried a load of leaflets and the other ships carried 4-1,000 lb. We bombed visual and really hit the target. Flak was very intense and one of our ships was shot down – Swarzon's crew. We had 8 holes in our ship, but no one was hurt. 3 men on other crews were wounded. Saw 2 ships go down from group behind, 1 blew up. Had good fighter support Was a very rough mission.

November 16-44: Up at 4 A.M. to brief. Our target was troop installations near "Duren, Germany. We bombed in front of our troops – we carried 30-260 lb. frag. Bomb and dropped them from 23,000 ft. Flak was light and no damage was done to any of our ships Had fair support – really blasted the target and should have done some good for our boys – good mission.

December 2-44: Briefed at 5 A.M. Our target was the rail yards "Coblenz, Germany." We carried 12-500 lb. GPs. We got just about to the I.P. when we turned back because of the weather. We didn't drop our bombs. Received credit for the mission which made us VERY happy.

December 4-44: Briefed at 5:15 A.M. Our target was the rail yard at "Mainz, Germany" in the Frankfurt area. We carried 12-500 lb. GPs and dropped them from 25,000 ft. Temp. - 35° - Good fighter support and we bombed visually. The flak was heavy but not accurate so it wasn't to bad. Good mission lasted eight hours.

December 6-44: Briefed at 4 A.M. Our target was the oil refinery at "Merseburg, Germany." We carried 20-250 lb. GPs. Bombed from 25,500 the temp - 47°. Good fighter support but the flak was very heavy. Most of the ships had holes – we had 3 in our ship. Bombed P.F.F. Was a very rough trip which lasted 8 hrs.

Crew Member List That Shipped Over
- Lt. Edward M. Ghezzi, 1314 Bellaire Pl. Brookline (26), Pittsburgh, Pennsylvania
- Lt. James K. Merritt, Federal, Wyoming
- Lt. Willard J. Curtiss, Reubens, Idaho
- Thomas W. Collins, 3 East Fairview Ave, Dover, New Jersey
- Frank J. Callaghan, 39259443, 3010 Vine Street, Denver, Colorado

Gentlemen From Hell

Roscoe J. Stephens, 35773163, Route 2 Hoods Creek, Ashland, Kentucky
William J. Hiser, 38405745, Route 2, Wanette, Oklahoma
Alferd J. Byrnes, 32851079 14, Van Zandt Street, Schenectady 4, New York
Robert D. Watson, 37485725, 2501 East Street, Omaha, Nebraska

The aircraft that the crew of Lt. Curtiss flew their missions in was a B-17 G with the army serial number of 42-102497 and named "Flak Hack."

As what happens in times of conflict, the destiny of individuals are not in the hands of any person but that of an Almighty Entity. I say this because four of the enlisted crew (including my father) were removed from combat flying and replaced by the direct actions of their Pilot Lt. Curtiss after the December 6, 1944 mission. When the newly formed crew flew on December 24, 1944 in the lead squadron commanded by General Castle in the largest air raid of history supporting the "Battle of the Bulge," enemy fighters shot down their aircraft. According to a copy of the "Missing Aircraft Record" (number 12177), General Castle's plane was attacked first by enemy fighters and lost, then Lt. Curtiss' plane came under attack and was shot down with the loss of three crew members. Those crew members were pilot Lt. Curtiss, the engineer/top turret gunner T/Sgt. Callaghan (both from the crew my father served with) and the radio operator/gunner S/Sgt. Saporito. If my father had flown this mission, my family would not have been.

My parents married on June 10, 1945. After being honorably discharged from the United States Army Air Force, my father started his own business as owner and operator of a retail grocery store. Through the years, their family grew to four sons and one daughter. My father was quite successful and was able to have three of their children attend and graduate from college. I had the honor of being the first descendant of my Grandparents to attend and graduate from college.

In closing, this short history on my father and the crew that he flew into combat with during World War II, let me say that while putting it together over the last couple of years, I have come to realize the tremendous amount of sacrifices, courage and honor that all who lived during that time exhibited. It is no wonder that you have been named "The Greatest Generation." For without each and every one of you, the world would not be as it is today. My thanks to all of you for what you accomplished.

JIM WANDLESS

LEFT: *Wandless was part of the "Hades Lady" crew.* RIGHT: *Wandless, pictured in December, 2002.*

I think you've jogged my memory, so I think I'll start right out with some recollections of the missions that I remember and the different things that happened. I thought I'd start out with a mission we were out on when I saw a P-51 Escort take a direct hit from anti-aircraft fire. We were coming to the target area and flak was coming up, pretty much all over the sky. I saw a P-51 Escort climb up about 1,000 feet above us. The only reason he would be there would be to give us escort in case we ran into any enemy fighters. It always feels good to see those guys hanging around. As I was watching the flak burst, for some reason I just kept glancing back and forth to see what that P-51 was doing up there. Out of the corner of my eye, I just sort of looked back, and what was once a P-51 was now just a big white puff of smoke in the sky and sort of like sparklers falling out from that white cloud. It looked very much like if you took some burning sawdust and just threw it out across the sky. It just kind of floated down with all those sparklers and then you realize, that what used to be a P-51 was just smoke and sparklers. And that was the end of that.

To continue the missions remembered, I call this one the B-17 spy plane mission. We were coming back home. Our tail gunner informed us that we had a stray B-17 arriving back right off our tail. It had tail markings of a bomb group that he was not familiar with. I took a look back there myself, and I didn't recognize it. I can still see that pilot and co-pilot sitting up there in the cockpit and, sort of occasionally, smiling and talking back and forth to each other. We were down low enough at that time that we didn't require any oxygen masks, so you could see their faces real good. Our pilot picked up the conversation and said to keep an eye on them. There had been several incidents of the German Air Force sending up rebuilt or captured B-17s and joining in on the formations of 8th Air Force. I don't remember if it was our pilot, or the squadron leader, or who it was, but they tried to make radio contact with the plane that was riding off our tail there. There was no reply. Evidently, if this were to happen going into a target area, it would have been taken more seriously because if it was a German spy plane they could contact ground units and let them know exactly what our speed was, altitude and all that sort of thing. But as we looked back at the plane, we became more and more convinced that it was a German crew. Being that we couldn't make radio contact, there was really nothing you could do. If you tried ... well, you just couldn't take the risk of trying to shoot the plane down because there was always the possibility that it was an American crew aboard. So, we just let them hang on our tail. After about 10 minutes, sure enough, they sort of winged over and went off about a mile away off our left wing. Staying there for about another 10 minutes, just sort of tagging along. Then, they just did a U-turn and went back to wherever they came from. So, I suppose that really was a German-manned spy plane. I thought to myself at the time that they'd have to really be very brave or awfully brazen to pull off a detail like that.

We had heard sometime previous to this about the 8th Air Force headquarters passing down word that they were going to try to do something about these spy planes drifting into formation and all that sort of thing. So, they passed the word down; from the way I understand it, this all happened before we had joined the group. But they passed down the word to put some kind of secret marking on each aircraft in the 8th Air Force. Anyone who showed up in any formation without the marking on it, the word was, you just shoot it down. Sure enough, shortly thereafter, the way I heard the story, a B-17 drifted into a formation and he did not have the markings that would give him the password. The word was given to open fire, and they say that the plane had so many holes in it that it looked like a sieve as it went down. The way I understand it, there were no more spy planes for quite a period after that.

This is a very brief recollection of a mission we had. It was probably very late in the war. We were flying pretty much solo at only about 2,000 feet and going up a winding river, and we came out to a German town. As you looked down, there wasn't a soul in sight - no vehicles, nothing. Nothing was moving at all. But I can still remember there was a huge gas storage tank. Maybe being the eager gunner I was, I called the pilot and said, "You think I ought to open up on that gas tank over there." He said, "No. I think these people have already suffered enough." I think it must have been an area that was fairly safe from anti-aircraft fire or anything that the Luftwaffe would put up because our pilot was a very daring person, but I don't think he had any suicidal tendencies about him. But it was quite an experience to fly that low over Nazi Germany. We returned to base after that, but I thought it was very interesting to see first-hand that low to the ground an eye witness account of what was going on down there in Germany.

This would be an eyewitness account of what a B-17 flying fortress could do and the punishment this aircraft could really take. We were out on a mission to bomb a German fighter base, I suppose it was a fighter base, that's about all they had left. It was just dirt runways, and at briefing we were told there would be no anti-aircraft opposition. We came in very low - I don't suppose we were over 8,000 feet. We lined up for the target, and as we get on the bomb run, a little bit of flak started showing up off the right wing. Shortly thereafter, we released our bombs and the flak was the type that they call tracking flak. They adjusted it to the speed of the aircraft and it just follows you right along. I called up the pilot and I told him that we have anti-aircraft bursts right off our right wing. I suppose the whole formation at that time saw it also because we made an immediate left turn, a good 45-degree turn to the left. As we turned, I could look back and get the best panoramic view I ever saw of a formation of B-17s going through a flak barrage. The bomb group that followed us was the 486th from Sudbury, our sister bomb group. They were about six miles down the road from us. As we turned, I could see the whole thing. They came into the bomb area and the German 88s were just cramming huge black bursts right into the formation. You just stand there in amazement as you watch the whole group just fly right through all that. As far as I know, they lost no aircraft, but they did give out something like 95 Purple Hearts up at Sudbury that day. But I'll always remember that panoramic view I saw. Like I said, it's just amazing that a group of airplanes would go through something like that and still make it back home.

I thought I would give a little change of pace at this time and tell of an incident we had on a three-day pass to London. We were in this pub with quite a few service people and local residents. I remember standing at the bar, and there was a real buxom, beautiful blond-haired barmaid standing behind the bar. She was pouring a draft of beer, and it was about half-full when in came a V2 Rocket. They usually, the ones that I always heard, had two explosions. You hear the first one, the "woomp," and that blows the warhead off, and then when the warhead hits the ground, you hear the big "BOOM!" So the barmaid, being in the midst of pouring this draft of beer, she just finished pouring it and stood it on the bar and then said out loud, "Oh dear, there goes another pour soul." That was quite something because it so typified the stiff, upper-lipped British type Londoner at that time.

I can recall a mission, I don't remember which one it was. When we got back to Lavenham Base, the weather was so bad that they sent us over to the coast to a specially-built landing field that had these huge gas pots they'd light. It would burn the fog off right over the runway and give you enough visibility to make a landing. When we got over to this emergency field, as we approached the area, and as they guided us down from the tower, we suddenly found ourselves coming out of the fog and you could see the runway right below. It just looked like a huge valley going right through the fog. Of course, down at the other end of the runway, you'd run right into the fog again if you continued down and tried to circle around or whatever. That was the only occasion we ever had to use that particular field, but it's something that really sticks in your mind. I only saw it one time. It's something that you just don't ever forget.

In remembering the days of Lavenham, one of the most unforgettable characters at Lavenham, or anyplace else, was our tail gunner Bill Kneeley. He was from Brooklyn, New York and had an absolutely fantastic sense of humor, like most people from Brooklyn at that time. They just give you the lighter side of life - something to laugh about every day. I can remember we were on a bomb run and Bill Kneeley came on the intercom, and he was a very talented person. He could sketch and draw. He was a real artist. He could imitate all the celebrities of that day. We were coming into the target area and he comes in over the intercom doing a perfect imitation of Bing Crosby. It was so good that you'd swear it was Bing Crosby himself. So, the pilot comes in and he says, "Look, can you hold that down until we get out of the target area?" So immediately he says, "Okay, I guess that's customary." But it was just one of those things that he would do at the drop of a hat, just spontaneous, when you weren't expecting it. I just had a couple of other things I remembered about him. This is the same guy I wrote that poem about on the 24th of December '44, during the Battle of the Bulge. He said many times that he was going to carry a brick along and tie a message on there and drop it over the target area from the tail position, saying, "You have just been bombed through the courtesy of the 487th Bomb Group." I don't know if he actually ever did, but he sure threatened to do it many times. I don't know if you're familiar with Brooklyn type humor at that age, but they were probably some of the funniest people around during World War II. There's a little poem that he used to recite. He used to get the Brooklyn Eagle, I think it was, which he said was the best newspaper in the world. They had a poem in there about spring. It goes something like:

Ah, 'tis spring, 'tis spring
And all the boids is on the wing.
My, my, how obsoid,
I thought the wing was on the boid.

One other thing I can remember about him was he used to imitate, like I said, people in the movies and show business. One of his favorites was Peter Lorre. We used to have conversations with Peter Lorre, and one day he said to me, "How are you?" I don't know whether you're familiar with Peter Lorre, but he was in quite a few movies. It went something like, "How are you? My name is Peter Lorre." And I said, "Yeah, I've seen you in several pictures and all that." And then he brought this other guy in and he says, "This is my brother." I said, "I didn't know you had a brother." He says, "Oh yes. This is my brother." I said, "What's his name?" And he says, "His name is Motor Lorre."

This would be a recollection of a conversation I can remember that our radio operator George Brennen had picked up. P-51's, they were out chasing down an ME-262. That was a famous jet that was flying at that time of the war. I guess it was a good 70-80 miles faster than anything we had. Their method was if they had a group of them started chasing an ME-262, they'd radio ahead and the idea was that any P-51s up ahead of them would pick up the message and they would start coming from the opposite direction. If they could box in that ME-262 coming from front and back, the probability would be that he would go into a turn. That's when they would get him, because a P-51 can turn inside the turn of an ME-262. But like I say, it's just one of those little things that I do remember. It was really quite interesting to hear the whole conversation and the procedure of how to knock down an ME-262.

Life at Lavenham included some good liberty runs. They go a lot of places: Sudbury, Bury St. Edmunds, and on and on out further. But I remember one afternoon, we were off duty and they had the liberty run. I don't remember exactly where it was going, but we all climbed up on the truck. We were driving up the highway and another truck come up along side of us and passed us. We got a real good look at it, and it was the truck going to the junkyard. Right on top of the pile was the remains of bomb bay doors of a B-17. It must have had a burst right underneath the aircraft because I don't think there was a half inch of metal shown between the hundreds of holes that were in those bomb bay doors. It was just another witness to the fact of the B-17 and just how well built that aircraft was. I don't know what the history was of that aircraft, or whether it ever flew again or not, but I would be inclined to doubt it, but at the same time I wouldn't be at all surprised if it did take repairs and fly again. The B-17 was sure a rugged, rugged aircraft.

This is my recollection of our mission to Nuremberg. This was February 20, 1945. I'll just proceed with when we arrived. Near the target, there were bomb groups ahead of us. Someone had been behind schedule, and everybody was circling the city. This was not good news because the weather was clear that day and the Germany flak crews could see us. That meant if they could see you they could also hit you. I think we were up there around 27,000 feet, give or take a few feet, and we were circling the city in a wide perimeter. You couldn't see very much because it was so far away. Finally, it was our turn, and we picked up the IP and set course for the target. We immediately picked up heavy tracking flak all around the formation. I was standing looking out the right waist window, and right there at my eye level was a continuous burst of tracking flak about every three or four seconds. I had to turn my head every once in a while because it just kind of mesmerized you if you just stared at this continuous bursting flak. Of course, you realize that with every burst of flak there was hot steel flying all over the sky. We hadn't reached the bomb release point when I felt something similar to something like a sledgehammer hitting me in the stomach, just about two inches below my bellybutton. Seconds later, I felt something hit me in my right thigh. I can still hear myself saying "Ough!" or something like that. I looked down on my stomach and I could see there was a hole in my flak vest. The shrapnel piece was lodged into the steel plate that had taken impact in my flak jacket. This no doubt saved my life because the flight surgeon told me later that a stomach wound that far from home would mean certain death from loss of blood. There's no way you can put a tourniquet on that type of wound. The only alternative would have been to bail out and possibly hope to be treated in a German hospital if one could be found.

My leg wound was not serious, just left my leg numb for the time being. When we returned to Lavenham Base, the flight engineer fired a red flare signaling we had wounded aboard. The ambulance came roaring up to our aircraft right after we turned off the runway. The first man arrived and said to me, "Where's the wounded man?" I said, "That's me." He said, "Well, I don't see anything wrong with you." I think he thought it was a false alarm. So I said, "Well, I do have a piece of shrapnel in my leg." They brought a stretcher with them, but when they saw I wasn't in serious condition he just said, "Okay, follow me." So I hopped out of our B-17 and walked to the ambulance, limping ever so slightly. The flight surgeon looked at my leg and took some x-rays. He said I'd have to go to the hospital because the shrapnel was in too deep for him to get out. I still have a piece of fine German steel in my leg because the surgeon at the hospital said it wouldn't be worth going in that deep to remove the piece of shrapnel. I saw the x-ray and it was about two inches from the bone. The surgeon said he might do more damage than good if he tried to remove it. I supposed he was right. The only bad point of the wound was that I had to stay in the hospital for about three weeks because they didn't want any infection set in from any piece of my uniform which might have gone in with the piece of shrapnel. It really was quite embarrassing to be in the ward that I was assigned because it was full of infantry and paratroopers with really severe wounds of various types. After they saw the hole in my leg they just kept asking me, "Well, what are doing in the hospital?" I could only say I wish I knew how to get out of there. It was also very amusing to find out that my doctor was a Japanese American with a very heavy Japanese accent. Every morning, day after day, I would say to the Japanese doctor, "Doctor, can I go home today? I don't see any reason for me to be here." He would always give me the same reply, "You cannot go home today, maybe tommolow."

Our B-17 picked up about 200 holes that day, and our crew chief had all the holes patched and put a dab of red paint on there so we'd know how many hits the Hades Lady had taken. After that, as we arrived at the plane each time we went out, she just looked like she had a real bad case of the measles.

This is just a brief recollection of a mission we were out on returning to the base. We were still over Germany and it was a very clear day and you could see 50 or 60 miles. I think it was the tail gunner or the ball-turret gunner who spotted a plume of smoke way off to our right wing. We figured it was probably an underground factory, because at that stage of the war Germany was moving a lot of its factories underground. In a lot of cases, they wouldn't even fire them up until after dark because they didn't want the location known because there would probably be a quick bombing raid on that area. Our navigator, he took a fix and made a plot exactly where this plume of smoke was coming up. When we returned to base, this information was turned over to whoever would be responsible for going out and taking care of that factory.

Life on the base and in the barracks was mostly drinking beer, playing snooker (a British game), black jack, poker, chess. As far as U.S. shows, we just missed the Glen Miller Band by two or three weeks. Shortly thereafter, he was lost while flying over the English Channel when he was headed over for France. We also took a lot of opportunities to go out on the Liberty Runs to all the neighboring towns. Us fly boys could sure drink a lot of beer. It did take your mind off a lot of things.

Lifestyles and customs were a little bit different as we soon found out shortly after we got to Lavenham. We went on a Liberty Run, hopped on the truck and went up to, I don't know if it was Sudbury or Bury St. Edmunds, and went in and had our first round of local beer. After about three or four beers, our tail gunner said he was going to have to take a trip to the restroom. He came back and he said, "Now you're not going to believe this. But when you go to the restroom around these parts, it's co-ed. Whether it's male or female, you just got to wait your turn." He said he went out to the restroom and there was a lady out there, and she says, "Don't go away. I'll be through in a minute, deary." The Liberty Runs were always lots of fun. The secret of a successful one was not to miss the Liberty Truck going back to the base. If you did, the only way back would be to hail a taxicab. It was very convenient, but also very expensive. I can still taste those delicious chips neatly wrapped in newspaper. If you had time you just ran back in and get another beer.

A story came down from headquarters about a Luftwaffe fighter pilot who was a POW. They brought him over for interrogation, and he was still very confident that they were going to win the war and all that sort of thing. He insisted that we couldn't possibly keep losing aircraft the way we were, that pretty soon we were going to run out of aircraft. They decided to take him up to the depot where they stored all the incoming replacement B-17s. They took him up there in a jeep and let him take a peak through the fence at all those B-17s parked in there. He just took one look and shook his head and said, "Okay, I give up."

The Luftwaffe was still apparently active in the winter and spring of '44-'45, but nowhere near as active as they had been. They just kept taking too many losses, but I can remember a mission we were on. There were quite a number of enemy aircraft in the area, mostly some brave souls flying independent of one another and coming in from different directions. They never could get close enough for us to take a shot at them because the fighter escort would pounce on them when they were still quite a ways out. It was quite a sight to watch from that height and just watch a wing or a tail assembly of any 109 or whatever else was coming in, and just watch that thing tumble over and over and over and over and over as it headed for the ground. We couldn't help but admire the gutty performance of these pilots of the German Air Force. I believe this was the same mission that we saw our first German Rocket ship, the ME-163 Comet. They were way up above us around 50,000 feet. You could see the contrail, and we figured it had to be the Comet Rocket Ship because there was nothing else around at that time that could fly at that high of a speed and that high of an altitude.

I'd like to make a continuation of the mission I already sent you before about our abort from Berlin. After we landed at Dijon, France at a B-26 base, the final diagnosis of our aircraft was that it had four burned out engines. I don't understand all the technical parts of it, but it had something to do with the innercoolers and the internal part of the wing, there's a mechanism in there, something about a tailgate. It was locked in the close position, and this had something to do with the function of the engines, and that's why we had lost power and had to drop out of formation and fly back over Germany by ourselves. But after we got to the Dijon B-26 base, they came and picked us up in the truck. We were riding around the perimeter, and as we passed the end of the runway, there was a B-26 Marauder sitting there at the end of the runway. The entire nose section was gone, right back to the wing. Also, the engines were just stripped right off it. We just took a look at it and turned and wondered what in the world happened. A person on the base said that everybody knows that the B-26s are a real hard plane to land. This particular aircraft, a few minutes before that was coming in for a landing and it nosed over. The tail went up and the nose just went right down the runway with the engines. The friction made everything just sort of vaporize and absolutely disappear. Of course the first thing you say is what happened to the pilot and the co-pilot. He says, "Well, just take a look down the runway. They're out there somewhere. You can't see them, but they're there somewhere." Evidently we had arrived just after it happened because they were just putting a ladder up to the door that goes from the cockpit into the bomb bay area, and as they put up the ladder, the door opened and out stepped the flight engineer. They did pull the truck over so we could take a good look at all this. You just sat there amazed, trying to figure out what had actually happened. It was a little hard to believe and really sink in. You had to think about it a little while to figure out what actually had happened. The truck started up a little short distance down, and all of a sudden we heard this horrible high-pitched whining and we said, "Now, what in the world is that?" The guy said, "Well, that's a regular occurrence around here. These B-26s have a bad habit of throwing a propeller." He said, "We've found some of them a quarter a mile away, maybe even almost a half a mile away." So we were only too happy to board our DC-3, which was going to fly us up to Paris.

After arriving in Paris, we became acquainted with a drink called Calvados. It's made out of apples, I believe. We were three days in Paris because the weather was so bad they couldn't get us a flight back to Lavenham. So, we did have three days in Paris and consumed quite a bit of, among other things, Calvados. I remember our tail gunner. He was really susceptible to this drink, and he probably consumed more than anybody else did. I can remember he tried to write a letter to his wife, and his hand was shaking so bad that he had to wait a day or two because of the after effects of this Calvados drink.

Some other interesting things that we found in Paris were, well of course when we got to Paris it was mostly infantry personnel on leave. Here we were, the fly-boys, we didn't even have our regular shoes with us. We had our heated boots, they looked like, sort of like black felt, and they hooked into your electric suit to keep your feet warm. The infantry, as we walked down the streets of Paris, they called our shoes "fruit boots." They used to get after us with sayings like, "There's no wings on a fox hole." So our only reply was, "There's no fox hole in a B-17." Another sight was the Parisian taxis. At that time there was no gas whatsoever for civilian use. It was a strange sight to see what used to be a motorized taxi hooked up to a horse. You just grabbed a hold of the steering wheel and said, "Gitty-up!" I can also remember our tail gunner come through again with the laugh of the day. He had taken high school French and he was really proud that he could handle himself in a conversation with most Frenchmen. We were going down the street and got lost. So, he walked up to a Frenchman and started speaking in French. I believe the Frenchman was having a little trouble understanding what he was saying, so he started speaking English. Our tail gunner was so proud of his French, he just kept asking questions in French, and the Frenchman replied in English. That went around for about three or four rounds and we were all laughing so hard, including the Frenchman, that it just made our day.

Getting back to Lavenham, one of the worst things I can remember about flying missions was on the long trips when you had to get up very early in the morning. You'd get everybody airborne and it would still be four or five o'clock in the morning and it's absolutely pitch dark. When all those aircraft up there are trying to assemble (the process that they used at that time) each group and the squadron would fire these flares in different colors. So, if your squadron color was two yellows and a green, that's the one you'd be looking for in the sky. In every direction you could possibly look, it would be all these different flares all over the night sky. It was just one of the most spectacular fireworks display you could ever imagine. I suppose that even a Technicolor camera wouldn't be able to capture the depths in the color of the sights that you would see at those times.

I can also remember very late in the war that I saw a sight that I suppose very few people saw. It was the RAF. At that stage of the war, they were also flying daylight as well as night missions. I don't remember where the target was for that day, but I'll never forget the sight as I saw the RAF was flying in mass formation. We were in a perfect position for a full view of them coming from our left at nine o'clock position. They were flying not too much beneath us. They were very close, actually, when they finally switched under us. The radio operator had picked up their signal and said, "Here they come." I looked out the left waist window and as far as I could see there was nothing but four-engine RAF bombers. I understand that there were 1,000 out that day, and it's a sight that I'll never forget because it's a piece of world history I'll never be able to see again. I can still see the co-pilot seated in the nearest bomber as they passed underneath us. He was looking down at a map or a chart very business like. We were all flying low enough so that we weren't wearing oxygen masks, and he didn't even have his hat on and his hair was sort of a sandy blond color. It just made such an impression to see such an air show of 1,000 bombers just as far as you could see. It's just another one of those things that even if you had a moving picture camera I don't know whether it would have done the picture justice. It was just so three dimensional and just out of sight, completely overwhelming, really.

I am now recalling a morning when we were sitting out on the hard stand right next to our airplane, "Hades Lady." I believe it was the navigator, Captain Oaks, who spotted something. He was just kind of leaning back on his elbows in the grass and it was a perfectly clear day. The sun was just starting to come up, and he saw these V-2 rockets that were pretty much directly over head. You couldn't hear anything, but if you just happened to look that way with the early sunrise, they were reflecting off these V-2 rockets. Once you spotted them, you could get the faint indication of the flame from the rocket engine. You could just watch it go right across the sky on its way down to London. That morning, I think we spotted three or four of them. Then, I guess the sun was getting up too high and there were no more reflections up there in the sky. That was one of the few times, I guess it was the only time that we ever spotted them. I guess if you were out there on a similar morning, you would probably be able to see it. We just happened to spot them that morning, and it was just one of those times when you just happened to look in the right direction at the right time. That was the first time I ever actually saw them going in. We had heard them crash down there in London town on passes, but that was the first time that we ever really spotted one in flight.

I think that one of the strangest things that I can ever remember was going out on our very first mission and looking over at the B-17 directly across from us and watching the bomb bay doors come open. See, those bombs drop out of there. It seemed like we dropped our bombs before they started firing back with those German 88s. I had seen this sort of thing in newsreels and moving pictures, but somehow it's just not the same at all. It's got something to do with reality, I guess. When you see a picture and then you see it happening right before your eyes, it's a lot different somehow. When they started firing back with those German 88s, my first reaction was, "What are you shooting at me for? I didn't do anything to you." It's just something that when it happens for the first time …the only thing similar I can think of is someone who is playing on a football team. Getting out there on the playing field for the first time, it's not as dangerous, but it's really similar. When you're on the sidelines and then you're in the game. Boy, here is reality facing you right straight in the face, and it's just a whole lot different that way.

This is another incident that I credit our radio operator George Brennen with. He picked up on the radio and piped it in to our intercom, P-51s bombing the Siegfried Line. It was one of those days we were flying quite low; there were scattered clouds. But after we picked them up on the intercom, we looked around and, sure enough, we looked down and we could actually see them. You could hear them giving each other instructions on who was going to go next and what they were going to try to hit. We could see those big dragon teeth that the Siegfried Line was famous for. Once those P-51s put their nose down, they just go down and dropped those 500-pounders, I guess they were, or maybe something a little smaller possibly. It was really fascinating to hear them converse on the radio and watch them perform.

On the subject of flying overseas, I thought it would be kind of interesting to go back and tell you about the landing field at Greenland. The, I guess it was a code called Bluey West #4. The only way you could get in there would be in daylight hours with good visibility. As you came up through the entrance, which was a canyon, it had a river flowing down through the canyon. In that area, as you come off the Atlantic Ocean - or I guess the Arctic Ocean - you'd see this big cliff that would just drop straight off. I guess, probably, it sure looked like at least 150-200 feet. As you came up to the entrance to the canyon there was a freighter that either hit a rock or been torpedoed and just the bow was sticking out of the water. As you fly down the canyon, once again, you'd feel a lot better if you had a real good pilot sitting up there because when you look out the side windows of those B-24s, the wing tips looked like they weren't too much more than a couple hundred feet from the canyon wall. As you fly down the canyon it kind of winds down with the river. You make a right hand turn, and that's the airfield. It was a flat area there, and the instructions were that once you make your approach you have to land. If you tried to go and take her around one more time, you're going to run right into another part of the canyon wall, which goes up and over 200-300 feet. I can remember after we landed, there we were looking up at the wall, and you see these black splotches up on the wall. The way it was explained to us was that that was the remains of previous fly-ins who did try to go around. They just went up and hit the canyon wall. Right at the base of the canyon wall was a cemetery for wreckage airplanes, and they either crashed, or they were just junk there, but there were quite a few laying in all degrees of destruction, I guess you'd call it.

Getting back to the beach at Blackstone, Wales ... When the 487th flew back home, taking all our aircraft with us, we went back to Blackstone, Wales. As I recall, we carried quite a few people. We were really crowded in there. I think, probably - it must have been pretty close to 20 people on each plane, at least on the plane I was flying on. While we were waiting to go ahead and fly back over to

Iceland, Greenland and Labrador, a bunch of us went down on the beach there. There was a B-17 right on the beach that had overshot the runway. I don't know whether it was an emergency landing or not, but it was a belly landing and it was just sitting right there on the beach, lying on the belly. I suppose they probably retrieved that airplane somehow over the years. But anyhow, we were down there on the beach and somebody said, "Boy, it would be a good day for swimming." It was late spring and the temperature was just about right. Somebody said, "Yeah, but we don't have any bathing suits." So somebody says, "Who needs a bathing suit?" And then boys will be boys. The first thing you know, the beach looked like one of those nudist colonies. We were romping and splashing in the surf and not a stitch of clothes on any of us. We had a wonderful time.

Getting back to life in the barracks ... One of the crews that we had in our barracks there had the misfortune of going to Merseburg two days in a row. I think they didn't fly for two days, and I believe they went back to Merseburg again, and that was three days at Merseburg, which was one of the worst targets at that time of the war. It was synthetic oil. Last count that I heard, they were supposed to have 1,500 antiaircraft guns spread out around the city there. They would just throw up a barrage in the sky; they say it was so thick you could walk on it. The sky just turned black because ...well, 1,500 guns would put a lot of black puffs up there in the sky. But I remember we weren't flying that day, but we talked to the crew when they got back. One of the things that I remember was about the flight engineer. He was in the upper turret. One of those pieces of shrapnel came in there right through the plexiglas and hit him right on the elastic band on his goggles and snapped it off. I guess it probably missed his head by a quarter of an inch, something like that. The ball-turret gunner had a piece come up through the ball-turret, and he brought it back with him. It wasn't too much smaller than the size of an English walnut. Those guys were just about flak happy after their third trip out that way.

I thought I'd tell you about our trip up to Scotland. We went up there on what they call flak leave. After you fly so many missions, they give you a break. They send you out in the country, someplace where they think you can sort of get away from it all. We were up there not too far from Glasgow. I remember there was a little loch up there. I can't remember the name of it, but I remember we were staying at the, I believe it was the Bailie Nicol Jarvie Hotel. It was a very nice spot, but once again we spent a lot of our time going into town. I was just recalling another thing that happened on our flak leave. We went to Glasgow and got aboard one of these, we call them double-decker trolleys, I think they call them trams over there. We got aboard and I put my money in the till, and then Bill Kneeley, he came up in back of me, and he was fumbling around for some change and he come up a hay penny short. It was really quite funny because you always hear about these Scotsman and how frugal they are with their money. While he was trying to find his other hay penny so he'd be able to pay for the ride, a little Scotsman was right behind him and he says, "Do not worry,

836TH SQUADRON

lad. I've got it," in his Scottish Burr. And he put a hay penny down in that till there and we got a big laugh out of that. Then, we headed back and found a seat and sat down.

After we sat down, I guess the thing that followed was one of those things that happened during the war years, sort of like the case of ships passing in the night. That sort of thing. We were sitting there, and the seat up in front of us was a little Scotch lass, and she had beautiful blond hair and these big blue eyes. She was sort of like the Doris Day type. The real wholesome type that you'd be thinking about taking home to meet your mother or something like that. I was 19 years old and still looking for Miss Right. There was something very fascinating about her, so I found a way to strike up a conversation. She wasn't too interested. I just kept the conversation going and finally asked her if I could take her out to a movie or possibly out to dinner or something like that. She said no. Her mother wouldn't allow it. She was living at home, and she heard about these wild Americans, and she just wasn't allowed to get involved with something like that. I said it would just be a movie, and I'll take you out to dinner and just take you home. She said she couldn't do that. So finally we got around to the point where I said, "Well, how about if you take me home for dinner and I'll do the dishes for you?" She got a big laugh out of that. She said, "Okay, I'll give you one chance." She wouldn't give me her address or her phone number, but she did say that she'd meet me at this bank at the corner of - I can't remember what it was. I copied it down at the time. We were supposed to meet there at four o'clock that afternoon. This was right up around noontime, so I suppose she was out on her lunch hour or something like that. I was really looking forward to that date because there was just really something special about her.

We went back to the hotel. When we got there, we were informed that we got word that we were going to have to get back to the base immediately. I said, "Well, I have a date at four o'clock." They said, "No, you don't." The only thing I could think of was here I am - I have a date with a girl. I don't even know her name or her address or phone number, but I know where I could meet her at four o'clock, but I won't even be in town at four o'clock. You start thinking about things like, maybe I ought to go AWOL for a couple of hours. I guess your duty or common sense calls first. Anyhow, I returned to base and often wondered what that girl thought of me. I guess if she waited anytime at all, she was really burning because I stood her up. I was probably more disappointed than she would be. But, that's one of those things that you just never know. I think the little time I knew her, I was thinking of really going steady. She was really something special, but that's the way it is in time of war. You just keep right on moving on.

A mission that our crew flew to Bordeaux, France, carrying Napalm bombs. It was one of the last amphibian landings in Europe in World War II. As we approached the target we could see some big battle-wagons off shore lobbing those big broad sides toward the beaches. I could see the flash of the big guns and then the black smoke being belched out of those long barrels. The Napalm bomb was a nasty weapon, as you no doubt already know. The casing for the ones we carried were made of pressed paper and had a bad habit of leaking. When they hit, they splatter jelly gas, which stuck to anything and whatever, it burned furiously as soon as the air hit it. I was very glad that I would not be at ground zero when they hit, but I was equally glad when they said, "bombs away." We didn't have to sweat out any mishaps that might have occurred in antiaircraft fire. A hole in one of those paper mache bombs we were carrying would have turned our fortress into a flying Ronson lighter.

I know I'm jumping back from one thing to another, but here it goes anyhow. I'd like to tell you about our landing at Valley, Wales after our Transatlantic crossing on our way overseas. We brought in a brand new B-24 and we left it there at the base at Valley, Wales. From there, we went into town, and the very first folks we met were two little Welsh kids about 10 or 12 years old. They walked right up to us and said, "Any coins or gum, chum?" Well, how could anybody resist? So, we shared with them and sent them on their merry way. My family is Welsh on my grandmother's side. Her maiden name was Lewis. I just love to hear that Welsh accent and enjoyed any conversation I could strike up with any Welshman that was available.

Bolt Studs: I don't remember his name or rank, but I do remember his pep talks. He was never failing to remind us - don't forget your bolt studs. It's impossible to charge a 50-calliber machine gun without one. He usually did his pitch before the black curtain at briefing that was pulled back and displayed the target for the day. Usually, it went something like this, "Well guys, we are going out to kill some krauts today." This meant a city target, and his attempt at some lighter humor to ease the tension somehow always worked.

Our pilot stated that he would barrel roll our B-17 over the home base at the end of our tour. We knew it was a known impossibility, but we also knew that if anyone could do it, it would be Lieutenant Battschinger. At this time, we believed he was capable of doing the impossible. We all gave a sigh of relief when he gave a low pass to finish our tour and our last flight as a combat crew.

I remember a radio show that we listened to in the mornings in our hut in Lavenham. It was called the Duffel Bag Show. The theme song was Tommy Dorsey's version of "Opus One," one of my favorite big band numbers. It was always pleasant to start the day hearing this and all the big band selections that would follow. One morning, they had a special announcement. It brought stone silence to the room. The announcer said that our commander in chief, FDR, had died at Warm Springs, Georgia. Nobody said a word. We went about our business, leaving everyone to his own personal thoughts. Mine were, "Well, it might take a little longer, but we're still going to win the war."

We had a crew member in our hut who was of German descent. After he told us that he had a grandmother still living in Frankfurt, we couldn't help but have some good-natured fun. We reminded him every time we went to Frankfurt that if he put in a good word with his grandmother, if she was manning one of those antiaircraft German 88s, maybe she could aim a little off just to spare her grandson's outfit. We used to kid him that his grandmother probably operated a pedal type 88. Every time she stomped on it, she'd get that "Kapoom, kapoom, kapoom." He always laughed right along with the rest of us.

One evening, I was sitting at the Non-Commissioned Officers Club when a woman showed up with an assistant carrying a slide machine. He started setting it up, including a screen, while the woman announced her purpose for being there. She said that they had a half-hour show demonstrating the dashing Cossacks of Russia and some scenery of mother Russia. The public relations set up by who knows who - just a little propaganda show. I think at that time of the war, most of us felt the same way General George Patton did. That was even though the theme of government policy was that Russia was our ally, we still had our doubts and did not trust the Russians any further than we could throw them. To a man, we all vacated the room. With no audience, the Russians packed up and left.

I thought I would add a little bit of humor by recalling a story when I was going to gunnery school. The story goes something like this. The particular gunnery school used open-cockpit two-seater Ryan planes - the pilot in the front and the gunner in the back. This pilot took a gunner up for the first time to shoot at a target sleeve pulled by a tow plane. He explained to the gunner all the rules and procedures and emphasized the fact that he should be sure that the bag was attached to his gun to save all the brass cartridges so they could be reloaded and used again. After all soldier, there was a war going on, you know. Everything was going fine. They were airborne and the tow plane was coming into range. The gunner hand-charged his gun, lined up his sights, pulled the trigger and started blasting away. The pilot heard the cartridges hitting the skin of the plane and then knew that the gunner had not attached the bag. So, he immediately called on the intercom as loud as he could to be sure the gunner would hear him. He shouted, "Save your brass! Save your brass!" At which time, the gunner abandoned his gun and bailed out.

I have a memory here that I've labeled the "Heavenly Choir." We were on our way home from a mission, everything quiet and calm. I heard an a cappella choir singing what sounded like a beautiful hymn that I had never heard before. It sounded like a very large choir, at least 100 voices all in perfect harmony. As much as I like to hear the Mormon Tabernacle Choir, this one sounded even better. In fact, I'd have to say there was no comparison. I thought to myself, where was this coming from? Is it actually coming in over the intercom or am I just imagining things? Your ears can play tricks on you flying in the state of the art equipment of that day with the sound of the engines vibrating through the airframe and the noises of whistling air going by. I decided to switch my head set in my helmet to intercom to UHF or VHF. I don't remember which, but the choir never missed a note and it was still coming through. So, I switched back and forth from VHF to UHF back to intercom. Nothing changed. It was still coming through. So just to be sure, I unfastened the chin strap on my leather flight helmet and took my helmet off. There was no more sound of the choir. I was almost afraid to put my helmet back on for fear I had lost contact with the choir. But, when I put my helmet back on, I could hear them again. There was no explanation for what was occurring. I just decided to listen and enjoy. My only regret at this time was that I had no knowledge or talent for writing down the music of the sounds that I was hearing. It was like nothing I had ever heard before or since. I think it lasted for about 10 minutes, and then the choir was silent, much to my regret. I never brought the subject up because I knew from my experience in the service that anyone dwelling on such a subject would be in for some intensive interview with a head shrink. You might end up on the funny farm with a section eight status for your troubles. I never told anyone about the heavenly choir until I was safely back home in civilian clothes, and then only told folks back home and let them give me an understanding nod. I know there are a lot of things going on in this world that we don't understand or have any knowledge of. I have no idea who or what or where the sounds of the heavenly choir came from, but I know it wasn't from me. If I was capable of imagining those kinds of sound, I would have produced some of the most astounding music that was ever heard.

836TH SQUADRON

JOE GAFFNEY

LEFT: *Gaffney's crew decided on "Elliot's Idiots" - in reference to their pilot, Robert Elliot - as their name, but it was never painted on their plane because "we had completed half the required 25 missions with no paint. Superstition had taken over, and we trusted to good luck."* RIGHT: *Gaffney, right, with friend and fellow serviceman Chet Berg.*

Our-nine man B-17 Crew, after completing combat training at Ardmore, Oklahoma, flew from Kearney, Nebraska to Nutts Corners, Ireland, stopping at Gander Bay, Newfoundland. One waist gunner, Harold Patrick, had been transferred to ground work because of air sickness. Here are the rest including their final rank:

Pilot: First Lt. Robert Elliot; Co-Pilot: Lt. Ruperto Casillas; Navigator: Lt. John Jackson;
Bombardier: First Lt. Don Broadbent; Engineer and upper turret: Tech/Sgt Larry Schooner; Radio Operator: Tech/Sgt: Joe Gaffney; Waist Gunner: S/Sgt: Hugh Brooks;
Ball Gunner: S/Sgt: Gori Gervassi; Tail Gunner: S/Sgt. Don Murray.

After a stop-over at Stone, England, we went on to Lavenham and joined 836 Squadron in the 487th Bomb Group of B-17 Flying Fortresses, which were replacing the B-24s at the base. That was July 1944.

The first mail from home and wife Jane brought both good and bad news. The bad vee mail letter told me that my brother Jim had been killed while fighting new St. Louis France in company G Ninth Infantry. The good news was Jane's confirmation of her pregnancy and the expected birth in January 1945.

"Elliot's Idiots" crew flew our first mission August 9, 1944, and the last December 6, 1944. Sometime between the first and last mission, we decided on

"Elliot's Idiots" for our ship's name, but that was never painted on our craft - why not? Because we had completed half the required 25 missions with no paint. Superstition had taken over, and we trusted to good luck.

We were directed not to keep a diary (I kept mine in a metal Prince Albert Tobacco can). Here is what I wrote in my diary after a mission in October.

"Twenty-first mission, October 14, 1944: Target Cologne, primary Ford Motor Company, and secondary, marshalling rail yards. Beans (Don Murray) was hit by flak over the target, no point to write details as it is marked in my mind."

Here is what I remember: we started the day a little pissed off after being advised that the number of missions required had been changed to 30 and then to 35. We were going after trip 21. Usually, this was heard from Don Broadbent, our bombardier: "Bombs away!" After looking I would say, "Bomb bays clear."

Our routine changed a little that day. Don: "Bombs away" - Joe: (That's me) "Bomb bays clear." Then from the waist gunner Hugh Brooks, "Beans has been hit."

When Murray came through the door from the waist to my radio room, he was a sad sack. His oxygen mask dangled loose against his chest and was not connected to any O2 supply. (We were flying at 27,500 feet - too high to be without oxygen). His right arm hung close to his body. I could see blood spurting from a hole in his torn glove.

First I hitched our emergency oxygen supply to Beans' mask, then knowing that the first aid kits included a pair of scissors, I opened the one hanging on my main radio. Guess what? No scissors. I needed some way to cut through the many layers of flight clothing Murray had on so that I could apply a tourniquet to his arm so the oozing blood would stop.

While I searched for scissors in six or more aid kits thrown by our engineer Larry Schoonover from his end of the bomb bays to me, I watched Beans pointing at one of his flying suit pockets. When my eyes caught up with his finger, I followed to the right pocket. Inside was a shiny boy scout Jack Knife. In seconds, I cut through several layers of clothing, exposing our tail gunner's arm on which I wrapped a tourniquet, tightening it enough to stop the loss of blood from his hand. In fact, his finger had been nearly severed. A small amount of flesh held it together.

Shortly, another crew member appeared in his flying clothes with flak vest, crash helmet, "Mae West" flotation jacket and fur boots. Unable to identify one crew member from another, I thought he was Broadbent. No matter what we all looked alike. It was Schoonover who helped tape up Murray's injury.

Upon "Elliot's Idiot's" landing, Beans Murray was rushed to the base hospital where his finger was removed.

Whenever Beans met any of us at future reunions, he held up his hand and shouted, "I have four!"

One of his fingers was left at the hospital in Lavenham, England. And Beans carried that Boy Scout Jack Knife for the rest of his life.

JIM HYLAND

"Three things sustained me during the POW ordeal: the power of prayer and a strong knowledge that God answers prayer, writing letters back home and a positive belief that our Allied forces would conquer the German war machine."

While I have been asked to tell you what life was like as a POW, permit me to provide some background. I was trained as a navigator at Ellington Field, TX and graduated in April 1944. My next assignment was to Dyersburg, TN to train on B-17s with a crew headed by Pilot Lt. Lloyd Kersten. In July of that year, we were sent to Kearney, NE to pick up a brand new B-17 and fly it to England. Upon arrival in England, we were assigned to the 487 B.G., 836 SQ. I celebrated my 21st birthday in a big and unusual way ... we went on our first combat mission on that day, Aug. 8, to support ground troops in northern France. This was no picnic as it involved a low-level (10,000-ft.) attack on bridges near St. Sylvain, France. Flak was extremely heavy, and the 8th Air Force sustained heavy losses.

Twenty-nine missions later (our 30th), it was Nov. 30th ... a cold clear day over Europe. Our mission was the oil refinery at Merseburg - a deep penetration of Germany and close to Leipzig. Roger Freeman records in his book, *The Mighty Eighth*, that "this last mission of November was the most formidable yet, with ... 29 heavies lost. Most of the losses were sustained by the 3rd Div. (including the 487th BG) due to an unfortunate sequence of events. The bomber column was led by the 1st Div., briefed to attack the Zeitz synthetic plant, while Merseburg was to be bombed by the 3rd Div. The divisions were to separate for their prospective runs at Osnabruck. However, the 1st Div. overshot the turn point, and the 3rd Div. followed. By the time the error was appreciated, the 3rd Div. wings were 15 miles south of their correct course. This brought them into the range of 90 guns defending Zeitz and on the wrong approach to Merseburg ... for periods of up to 18 minutes, each group was subjected to a concentration of anti-aircraft guns without parallel. Some 80 percent of the Division's 539 Fortresses were damaged in this last visit to the most dreaded of targets."

Immediately after we dropped our bombs, we were hit by flak in the right inboard engine, and possibly two additional flak bursts after. The interior of the aircraft behind the pilot was in flames, and the craft rolled over into a flat spin. The bombardier and I exited through the forward escape hatch. I remember only getting my head out of the hatch, then passed out from lack of oxygen ... we were about 25,000 feet. Somewhere around 5,000 feet, I revived enough to realize that I had to pull the ripcord to open my chute. I drifted over the southern edge of the Merseburg refinery as other bombers were preparing to release their bombs. I landed just a few hundred yards from the target. My landing site was on the embankment of a small stream and next to an orchard. In coming down through trees, para-jumpers are taught to cross legs to prevent serious injury and hang up in a tree. Thus I was just able to clear the nearby trees, but in landing on the steep embankment, my feet crumpled under me and I suffered a severe fracture of the right knee.

I was just a few yards from a farmhouse, and within minutes, the farm family was out to get me. Discovering my injured condition, they brought a ladder, placed me on it and took me into an animal shelter adjacent to the house. While I knew a little German from high school days, I couldn't make out the entire conversation, but gathered that the SS trooper who arrived later would just as soon annihilate me. He was, however, convinced by the family that I should be sent to a hospital for care.

The next morning, I was picked up by a military truck along with my bombardier and several other fliers, and taken to a POW hospital in Leipzig. There, my broken leg was reset after X-rays were taken and a plaster cast was applied. Later, that cast would be a source of entertainment for me as I had a number of visitors who could only be eliminated by a daily dousing with an insecticide powder to delouse the cast.

In mid-December, the German guards at the hospital gleefully gave us the disturbing news that the war would soon be over because German forces had been very successful at the Battle of the Bulge. Christmas Eve, however, produced a rather somber change to their attitude. What I did not find out until later was that our very own 487th Bomb Group had led the entire 8th Air Force on its first raid since the start of the Battle of the Bulge. For over two weeks the 8th Air Force was down because of bad weather. On Dec. 24, the weather cleared and General Frederick Castle come down from 8th HQ to take command of this raid in support of ground troops around Cologne. This was the largest mission of the war by the 8th, and General Castle's aircraft was shot down and he died in the crash. He is remembered as the only general in his country's history to die in a direct act to try and save the lives of his subordinates.

Our hospital guards were older men, probably not fit for fighting, and were a bit more lenient than the young Germans. On Christmas Day, they brought a small Christmas tree into our ward, set it up and presented us with a homemade cake to celebrate the holiday.

There was a Christmas gift that day which I didn't learn about until returning home. The pilot's wife gave birth to a baby girl that Christmas Day. The pilot's wife, Helen Kersten, passed away just last month, and with that passing, I have a new contact - their granddaughter has now contacted me seeking more information about her grandfather.

On Dec. 28, 1944, I was marched a mile or so in bitter cold on crutches to a waiting cattle car along with other fliers. This would be our home for the next four days ... a straw-lined boxcar. The train pulled out and headed for Frankfurt and the interrogation center there. We arrived on Dec. 31, but not before being left locked in the boxcar by our guards in the marshalling yards a Frankfurt when the 8th AF came over on another bombing mission. Fortunately, the marshalling yard was not their target that day! In late January, I was moved to another Lazaret, or hospital, at Meiningen, Germany, where I would remain until Gen. Patton's tank force freed us in April.

The German-supplied food was frequently leftover turnip and potato peelings boiled up into some kind of thin soup. To this day, I can't stand turnips! While the food was life sustaining, it didn't stop me from losing about 25 pounds during my internment. Red Cross packages were supposed to come each week, but we were lucky to get one a month. That was one of the highlights of the week, as it would contain a chocolate bar, cigarettes, Spam and dried fruit. Cigarettes were traded with the Germans for whatever. The prunes or raisins frequently ended up in a mixture of water and sugar to ferment until we thought it sufficiently potent to drink!

I spent much of my time writing letters home (which never got there until well after liberation), learning some French from a French primer and several French officers in the camp and playing bridge or poker for money we didn't have! We got exercise whenever the guards would allow us out into the compound yard.

One of our great delights was to confuse "Bed-check Charlie," the guard who came each night to be sure all were accounted for. As he would begin his count, we would begin moving about the room for one reason or another. He would count, then count again and again; "ein, zwei, drei, vier, funf ..." The makeup of prisoners in our Meiningen camp was quite diverse. There were a number of U.S. fliers plus French, English, South African, Indian and Sikh.

Early in April, the weather turned warm, and about April 2, we could hear gunfire in the distance, and truck traffic at night became very heavy. We knew something was up, but weren't sure just what was happening. The British in camp had been able to get BBC news regularly, and they advised us that Allied forces were on the move in Germany. On April 5 at 8:30 a.m., there was a bombing and strafing attack by our planes, including bombing of the bridge just 100 yards or so from our compound. At that point, someone placed an American flag on the ground in the compound to alert the Air Force of our presence. Light gunfire could be heard throughout the day. At 5:30 p.m., Patton's tanks came roaring into town, and a few minutes later, one tank crew stopped in front of the compound and advised us that we had been freed, but told us to stay within the compound for the night with American guards. The German guards left hours earlier.

The celebration that night was indeed a happy one! The hospital was a converted boys school with an auditorium/gym. That evening, we held a stage show in the auditorium with various prisoners putting on skits, songs, etc. My greatest recollection of that evening was of a British soldier with a beautiful tenor voice singing "Danny Boy."

Gentlemen From Hell

I was moved by ambulance to a field hospital near Frankfurt, then flown to England on April 12. It was there that we learned of the death of President Roosevelt a few days later. Some 47,000 men of the 8th Air Force lost their lives or were reported missing in action, which included the nine men of our aircraft. Two of us survived by jumping, and seven died when the plane went down.

Upon my return to the States, I made it a point to visit the parents of each of the men of my crew who were killed and the pilot's wife. Three things sustained me during the ordeal: the power of prayer and a strong knowledge that God answers prayer, writing letters back home and a positive belief that our Allied forces would conquer the German war machine.

To many people, the American flag seems something to be burned or desecrated. To me, it is a powerful symbol of freedom and honor. The U.S. is indeed the greatest country on earth. May God protect this great land and its people.

837TH SQUADRON INTRODUCTION

This squadron will lead off with the three men who were Prisoners of War. They are Jim Brooks, who has written his own book, *A Glimpse of Hell: The World War II Years*; George Phillips, who tells the story of all 10 members of his crew bailing out of their plane and subsequently being captured by Germans and made POWs. The last of this group, Leonard Davis, tells of only having one two-minute shower and no change of clothes in the eight months he was in prison camp. His story, up until his very last paragraph, will bring you to your knees.

George Battschinger tells his own account of being a waist-gunner, coming under heavy attack and having his oxygen hose cut in two at 30,000 feet. Next will be Clark Yocum's chapter, where he recalls the day the base intercom came on with a Red Alert - "Attention all personnel." They all thought a bomb was going to hit their control tower. In John Besson's chapter, he says, "The zenith of my career was the command of a B-52 Strategic Bombardment Wing!" Quite a few of these men continued their military service after their time with the 487th was complete.

Walter Zmud tells of how he decided to stay in the Air Force. He was assigned to Counter Intelligence School in January 1947, and he became an intelligence officer assigned to Headquarters, Wiesbaden, Germany. Follow his career until July 1959-1963, where he was assigned Air Chief of Staff Intelligence responsibilities/management of USAFS Clandestine Collection Operations Worldwide.

The next account is Julian Headley, who flew 35 combat missions over Germany. Then there's Tom Valentine, whose last paragraph states, "If you are wondering what it was like to live through those times, imagine getting up at 2:00 a.m., knowing you must cross an icy pond which is cracked under your feet and some of your buddies are falling through the ice with no one to help them. Your life seems to stop until you finish your tour and are reborn." That's just an analogy to the sheer horror of war.

The next three veterans were all members of the same crew. Pete Peterson's account is a great pilot's story. He tells the logistics of a day in the life of a pilot in combat. Alan Wheasler tells the co-pilot's story, and David Dahlberg's is the story of a flight engineer and gunner. As Dahlberg states at the end of his chapter, "The Germans never turned back the Eighth Air Force, and the Eighth Air Force never failed to complete a mission once it started."

JIM BROOKS

LEFT: Brooks served as the radio operator on the crew of the "Blonde Bomber." RIGHT: Brooks, 1989, at the dedication of the 487th Bomb Group in Dayton, Ohio.

I am Jim Brooks, and this is the story of my experiences while serving in the Army Air Force. I was a tech/Sgt. in the 487th bomb group, 837th squadron at Lavenham Field in England from July 1944 till November 25, at which time my crew and I were shot down over Merseburg, Germany, and became POWs of the Germans. I was originally inducted into the service in February 1943 at Leavenworth, Kansas and assigned to the Army Air Force. My basic was at Greensboro, North Carolina. Man, was I homesick. I was ready to leave that place at the end of the six weeks I spent there.

After basic, I shipped out for Scott Field, Ill, a radio school. I was now a P.F.C. Whoopee! It was here that I first begun to enjoy my life as a soldier. The school held classes around the clock in eight-hour shifts. Every 30 days, we changed shifts. If we kept our grades up, we were given a 72 hour pass every four weeks. I liked that! I never missed a pass, because I could make it to Springfield, MO, to see my sweetheart, Claudia. We were engaged to be married, but decided to wait until after the war. It was at Scott Field where I took my first airplane ride in a little L-5, the type of plane used for practice.

Upon completion of radio school, I was promoted to corporal and shipped out to Yuma, AZ, to gunnery school. Yuma was an eight-week course in aerial gunnery. We were instructed on how to maintain and shoot .50 caliber machine guns and learned how to stay alive at high altitudes and recognize enemy aircraft.

Gunnery school was a breeze for me. I'd been handling guns since I was nine years old. Back on the farm where I was raised, I did lots of quail hunting, so I knew how to lead a moving target. It was at Yuma that I took my first flight in a B-17 bomber. What a thrill that was! Of all my training, though, I think high altitude worried me the most. There was so much to learn about it and such a short time to do it in.

By the first of March, 1944, I'd finished school and was given a 15-day delay-in-route, with orders to report to Lincoln, NE, where I would be assigned to a combat crew. I was promoted to Buck Sgt., issued my wings, and put on flying pay. Now, I was rich! I arrived in Lincoln in the middle of March and met the crew I would be with for the rest of the war: Pilot, Craig Shields; Co-Pilot, Bob Meier; Navigator, Dennis Carey; Bombardier, Jim Peyton; Engineer, Max Alcar; Radio Operator, Jim Brooks; Waist Gunner, Johnny Marthaler; Waist Gunner, Billy Snider; Belly Gunner, Virgil Drake; Tail Gunner, Clifford Pflieger.

These were the men I would be training with, the men I would be going off to war with. They were a good bunch of guys. I liked them all. We had some good times and some bad times, of course. We shipped out of Lincoln in just 24 hours for Ardmore, OK. It was late March 1944.

Ardmore, OK, a place I will never forget. One of the most important events of my life happened here - Claudia and I were married on June 17. We had two weeks together before I left for war. Ardmore was an overseas-training unit for combat crews. After 90 days training, 42 new crews shipped out of Ardmore for Kearney, NE. There we picked up 42 new B-17s and headed for war. We touched down in Bangor, ME, and flew from there to Gander, Newfoundland, onto Nuts Corner, Ireland and finally to England. My crew was assigned to the 487th bomb group, 837th squadron, Lavenham.

Our first mission was the Belle-Forte Gap in France, important because it was a key pass for the railroad lines. I remember that well. We flew two more missions in France; the rest were deep into Germany. Our targets were oil refineries, marshalling yards, airfields, submarine pens and factories. The Germans were tough fighters, and we had our share of close calls, but we soon learned that the fighter planes and the anti-aircraft weren't the only enemy out there. Weather and high altitude were just as deadly, plus mechanical trouble. We had to deal with them all.

After 22 missions, we got two weeks off for what they called "flak leave." We were ready for a rest. We returned and flew six more missions. Then, on November 21-23, the 487th celebrated their 100th mission. November 24th was Thanksgiving Day. On November 25th, we were scheduled to fly our old "Blonde Bomber" on our 29th mission. Just three more missions and I would finish my tour. We were all getting anxious. When we went into briefing that morning and they raised the curtain on the map to show us our target, my heart sank. We were headed back to Merseburg and the oil refinery. It was a rough target, we knew, because we had been there twice before.

On this mission, we hit heavy flak before we ever got near the bomb run. We lost one engine on the start of the bomb run and two more after we got our bombs away. The old Blonde Bomber's wings were covered with oil. We were losing 2,000 feet a minute. We threw out all the weight we could, trying to keep our altitude. Then, one of the engine's props ran away - we couldn't feather it and it began to smoke. We were afraid it would catch fire and blow us up, so we bailed out - my first and only parachute jump. I dove out, just like I used to do in the old swimming hole back home.

We had been taught to count to 10 before pulling the ripcord, but I tried to pull it just as quick as I cleared the plane. But for some reason, I couldn't move my hand. I seemed to be standing still in midair. I began to pray. It must have been 20 seconds before I could move. Then when I could move, I jerked so hard my hand went clear around my back. My chute opened and it really shook me. I said out loud, "Thank you, God." As I drifted down, it was so quiet, and I began to count the other chutes. When I saw the last one, I said, "Thank you, God," again.

Then all of a sudden, I saw the ground coming up fast. I came down in some small trees. I grabbed the top of one of the trees and swung gently down to the ground without even losing my footing. It was snowing. I pulled my chute down, crawled into a brush pile, covered up with my chute and spent the night there. I spent the next three days on the run. I was shot at and chased by a dog and two old men, but I escaped to walk 80 kilometers before being captured by an SS Trooper. He turned me over to the Gestapo. They searched me and questioned me, put me in the city jail, and fed me my first food in four days.

The next morning, I was awakened by a big old German soldier yelling at me. He had a tommy gun hung over his shoulder. He kicked and shoved and yelled at me and pushed me out to a waiting panel truck that held two other German soldiers. I thought they were going to shoot me on the spot. After two days of traveling and being kicked around, I arrived at a staging area for all airmen. There, I met the rest of my crew, all except the navigator, who had broken his leg when he hit the ground. It was here they separated the commissioned officers from the noncoms. The next stop was a base overseen by the International Red Cross. They took all our flight clothes and issued us regular army ODs.

Then, we boarded a train - next stop, Stalag Luft 4 up near the Baltic Sea. I was now behind the barbed wire with 8,000 other airmen. This place was so overcrowded that we had 22 men in a room for 16. The weather was cold and damp and food was scarce. The diet was dehydrated cabbage and kohlrabi soup. There was no obesity here. By February, the Russians were headed our way, so the Germans prepared to evacuate us. On February 6, 1945, we marched out of Luft 4.

This was the start of 85 of the darkest days of my life. I prayed a lot in those 85 days, and I saw lot of my prayers answered. There have been a lot of stories written by different men about the march where each of us has his own story and his own memories of that nightmare time. And each of us, because of who we were and what we've become, will choose different aspects of the march to write about. Probably all of the stories are true, but even if you put them all together you couldn't have an inkling of what it was like to live through it. Even today, more than 50 years after the war, it's hard for me to find the words for some of the things I saw and did. I won't even attempt to describe them because they still make me sick and it makes me cry to think about them. It was called the "Black March."

After 85 days and 600 miles, the march ended at Falling Bostel, Germany. It has been said 1,500 men died on the march. After being liberated by the British 7th army, I was flown to the 91st General Hospital at Oxford, England. After spending about three weeks in the hospital being examined and after receiving partial pay, I went back to Lavenham and the 487th to see if I could find any of my old friends, but they had quit flying combat and there was no one there I knew. So, I returned to the 91st and boarded a hospital ship by the name of Jeredith M. Huddleston.

Eighteen days later, we arrived at Charleston, S.C. As I stood on the deck of the Huddleston, I remembered the day I had seen the shores of my country slip behind. In my mind, I retraced my journey and I realized that God had given me a glimpse of hell. He had showed me a place where there was no light and only darkness. There were no smiles, no laughter, no music, and no sweet smells. There were just foul odors, and once proud men were groaning and wallowing in their own filth and dying. I know now what the wailing and gnashing of teeth means. You know, you don't have to spend much time in hell for it to seem like eternity.

"But I'm back now, and I'm about to experience the opposite of hell, and I think now I know what it's gonna be like whenever I step into the gates of heaven," I told myself. It had been a little over a year since I left my country. There is no way I can explain the good feeling I had down inside when I walked down that gangplank and stepped back on American soil. Well, I knew what it would be like to step into heaven.

I spent two days in the Stark General Hospital in Charleston while they examined me again. Then, I was sent to O'Reilly General in Springfield, MO, where I was examined yet again, and then given a 90-day convalescent leave to report back to Jefferson Barrack, St. Louis. After being examined again, I was given a 60-day convalescent leave, with orders to report to Santa Ana, CA, for discharge December 6th, 1945. It would be many years before I would be ready to tell my story. In 1987, in order to answer the questions of my children and grandchildren, I sat down with a tape recorder and told the complete story, which has been published as the book, *A Glimpse of Hell: The World War II Years.* Many stories, funny and sad, as well as much information that I could not include in this short chapter, may be found in that book.

GEORGE PHILLIPS

Phillips spent nearly a month as a POW in Germany. He is pictured with a number of other POWs on or about May 4, 1945, the day the group was liberated by the 9th US Army after a truce was reached.

I was inducted into the Aviation Cadet program of the Army Air Corps on July 27, 1943 in St. Louis, MO. After having six weeks of basic training at Jefferson Barracks, MO, I was sent to Butler University in Indianapolis, IN for the required college classes needed. In January '44, I was sent to the classification center in San Antonio, TX.

I washed out of the Cadet Program there and was sent to Aircraft Armament School in Lowery Field, CO. Within a few days, we were sent to Buckley Field, CO for the required classes to learn about Aircraft Armament systems, which included various types of bombs, explosives and fuses.

From there, I was sent to Gunnery School at Laredo, Texas for some weeks of training in learning the .50 caliber machine gun parts and how they all work together; also, how to disassemble and re-assemble it blindfolded (I enjoyed that). We also had instruction in how to shoot the .50 Cal., as well as some instruction in shooting the Colt 45 Automatic pistol and the Thompson submachine gun. We enjoyed some skeet shooting both on the range and from the back of a moving truck. We did our duty as clay target operators, also.

After Gunnery School, we were given a two-week furlough to show off our two stripes, after which we went to Lincoln, Nebraska for crew assignment, when the combat crews were made up.

From there, the crew was sent to Biggs Field, TX for Phase training, flying as a crew in Aerial Gunnery practice, formation flying and learning our jobs as a crew. I was assigned as a waist gunner. The crew was broken up,

837TH SQUADRON

and I was assigned to a different crew. The pilot of this new crew was Lt. Robert L. Goodenough. This was a good crew, and I was happy to be a part of it.

We finished Phase training as a crew and were sent back to Lincoln, NE for processing for going overseas for combat duty. We were sent to a processing center at Center Kilmer, NJ near New York City. After a few days of processing, we boarded the Isle de France for the journey overseas.

We left port Nov. 29, 1944. After several days on the ocean, we arrived in Greenock, Scotland Dec. 7, 1944. After a few more days of processing, we boarded a train bound for a town named Stone for assignment to a group. We were sent to the 487th Bomb Group, 837th Squadron, Station 137, located near Lavenham.

The plane we were assigned to was a B-17G; the number was 297970, a good plane with several miles on it. We had an excellent ground crew. The crew chief's name was M/Sgt. Albert Mazzole, or Muzzy. After a few days of getting acquainted with our new surroundings, we started flying orientation flights to get accustomed to our duty and the area.

I was assigned as the togglier (dropping the bombs) on our crew. I liked flying that position. We started flying our combat missions on January 7th, 1945; the first mission was to Paderborn, Germany.

After we took off and were at maybe 5,000 feet the crew would leave their take-off positions in the radio room and go to their stations in the plane. The first time I went through bomb bay to pull the pins out of the fuses and saw the bombs hanging in their shackles was a real wakeup call. This was the start of the real thing we had been waiting for. The target was railroad marshalling yards and the bombs were 1,000 pounds each. The first mission went OK.

The second mission was the next day January 8, and the target was the railroad marshalling yards in Frankfurt, Germany. This mission turned out to be quite interesting. On the return flight, we were having an engine problem and using more fuel than normal. We were unable to keep up with the group and lagged behind. Darkness was fast approaching, and being low on fuel, the pilot decided to land at a base in France. It was a former German Air Base that the Americans had captured some months before.

Apparently, our base failed to receive the message that we would be landing in France due to the problems we were having. Anyway, we didn't return to Lavenham until January 10, and since the base didn't know where we were, they had gathered up all of our belongings, thinking we had been shot down. What a confusing mess. But it was finally straightened out, and we were able to get to bed. Everybody on the base enjoyed excellent food, fresh eggs, plenty of good milk and other healthy food we needed. I think I could have made a meal on the dark brown gravy the mess sergeant served. It was super.

Our third mission was to Mainz, Germany on January 13, 1945, with the target being more railroad marshalling yards. These yards were being hammered very heavily due to the Germans moving troops and equipment to the front lines. The bomb load was five 1,000 pounders.

Gentlemen From Hell

On the 14th of January we went to Osnabruck. This may have been the secondary target, as the list of missions in the 487th history book indicates the target was Magdeburg, Germany. The target was more marshalling yards.

Our fifth mission took us to Augsburg, Germany on January 15, 1945, and again we bombed the railroads.

On January 18, we went to Kaiserslautern, Germany and tore up their railroad yards. On our seventh mission we bombed the marshalling yards in Wesel, Germany. The eighth mission was to Berlin, Germany, which we called "Big B," to drop our bombs in the center of the city. On February 8, we flew to Chemnitz, Germany, which was a long mission to bomb the railroads. This was our ninth mission. We enjoyed several three-day passes to London, where we took sightseeing trips when we were not flying and needed a break in the action.

Our 10th mission was to Weimar, Germany on the 9th of February to bomb armament works and vehicle factories. On February 15, our 11th mission went to Cottbus, Germany to bomb the locomotive shops. These missions were all targeted on the German transportation system to destroy or disrupt the flow of vital materials to the front lines.

Our 12th mission took us to Frankfurt Germany again. This was a rough target due to the unusual number of anti-aircraft guns there, but we bombed the railroad yards this day. The 12th or 13th mission was Neumarkt to target the marshalling yards. Our 14th mission was on February 24. The target was the Bremen, Germany shipyards and some ships in the harbor.

On February 25, 1945, we flew our 15th mission to bomb the oil storage depot at Nurnberg, Germany. This was low-altitude bombing at the target, less than 10,000 ft. I couldn't see any target and wondered why the bombs were being dropped on what seemed like a wooded area. But when the bombs began hitting the ground, huge balls of flame erupted, and I was amazed that it was a camouflaged oil storage dump.

The 16th mission was on February 28, and the target was the locomotive shops at Kassel, Germany. All of the targets and some flak with some heavier than others and we did suffer some damage on most missions, either an engine out or structural damage or both. There were not many milk runs.

On March 1, we bombed the marshalling yards at Ulm, Germany, the house of German General Rommel. Brunswick, Germany was the target on March 3, which was our 18th mission, halfway home on the missions. At Brunswick, we bombed some Armament shops. Our 19th mission on March 8 sent us to Frankfurt again to bomb aircraft parts manufacturing factories. The 20th mission was to Dortmund, Germany to bomb the railroad yards on March 10. Our 21st mission on March 11 was to Hamburg, Germany to bomb the submarine pens. The 22nd mission went to Hanover, Germany, and we bombed a tank factory.

On March 17, the target was an oil refinery at Ruhland, Germany. This was our 23rd mission. The target for March 19 was the railroad yards at Bielefeld, Germany. Now for some R&R.

On March 20, 1945, we went to Aberfoyle, Scotland for several days of flak leave, which was standard practice. We flew to Preswick, Scotland and went on to our destination. It was beautiful country, which had not seen any war damage. We enjoyed good food and some sightseeing to Loch Lomond, also visited Edinburgh, Scotland and did some sightseeing. We did a lot of relaxing, but the time ended before we wanted it to. Then, back to combat.

On March 30, the target for the day was Hamburg, Germany. We lost an engine before we got to the target and had to turn back at the Holland coast. The bombs were jettisoned into the English Channel. Not good to spend all of the time, money and effort to put bombs on the plane and then have to drop them in the Channel, but orders are orders.

The next mission was to Brandenburg, Germany on March 31 to drop the bombs in the center of the city. On April 2, the target was an airfield in Vandel, Denmark, but the mission was called off and we returned to base. Our 28th mission on April 3 was to Kiel, Germany to bomb ship building installations and ships in the harbor.

The next day - April 4, 1945 - we returned to the same target to bomb again. On April 7, the target was a German fighter airfield at Parchin, Germany. The target for April 8 was some railroad marshalling yards at Hof, Germany. The 32nd mission on April 9 was to Nuremberg, Germany to bomb an oil storage facility.

On maybe four occasions, we returned from the mission with an engine out and several flak holes in the plane. On two occasions, we had to land at a base in France due to problems, low fuel and equipment failure. On April 10, 1945, my crew was flying as one of the deputy lead crews.

I was flying my 33rd mission with a different crew when the plane was attacked by a German ME-262 Jet fighter before we even got to the target. The plane was hit with rockets and the No. 2 engine started burning. This continued for some minutes, and the crew started bailing out. We had a Mickey Operator (Radar Jammer) on the plane that day.

All 10 members of the crew bailed out safely and were all captured by the Germans and made POWs. I landed rather hard in a field that had been cultivated with crops of some kind. A welcoming party was waiting for me consisting of a civilian of some rank with a couple German military people and a civilian car. When we left the field, the driver took a paved road a short distance away and turned left.

There were many German tanks on the side of the road hiding under some trees. We proceeded past those and on to some sort of a military camp and stopped in front of an administration building. I was escorted inside to be searched and questioned briefly. I also heard the familiar statement, "For you, the war is over." As I was sitting in a chair, the Navigator was brought in and went through the same procedure. We were taken to the brig at a German Air Base, and there the rest of the crew was gathered. We were locked in cells, and as I remember, had a choice of a bench for sitting or the floor for sleeping. We bedded down for the night as best we could. One German man and a police dog served as guards. As I remember, we were there for maybe three days. We had some freedom from the cell, as the guard was a decent fellow. I can vividly remember an American P-47 strafing the field and setting some parked planes on fire, as we could see and smell the smoke. The guard left us during the attack to man an anti-aircraft gun, but when he got back he said he didn't try to hit the plane. I think he knew the game was up for Germany anyway.

Later, we were loaded on a truck with a wood or charcoal powered engine that traveled about 10 mph. We went into the town of Magdeburg that had a lot of damage. On the way, we picked up the top turret gunner who was being marched at a brisk pace by a young German trooper. We ended up at a German hospital complex and were taken to a large room on the top floor. Several other POWs were there from infantry, artillery and armored divisions.

The next morning, the Allies started shelling the area with artillery. As the shells would come in, the more knowledgeable of the POWs would seek what cover was available on the marble floors, but the Air Force POWs would stand by the windows watching the action. We soon learned better. When the first shell landed, there were some wounded German hospital patients walking around outside. When the shelling started, they threw their canes and crutches up in the air and started running as hard as they could for cover. No laughing matter for them, but we thought it was funny.

That night, we were told to get ready to travel and left sometime during the late night hours. Small arms fire could be heard very distinctly. We walked for some hours until we were well out of the city and were permitted to rest for some time. Since I left my shoes in the airplane before bailing out, all I had to wear was a pair of flight boots that were far from comfortable. We continued walking for several days until we got to Camp XI-A located in the vicinity of Altengrabow, Germany, which is about 30 km east of Magdeburg. The facilities were WWI calvary stables, and everything was loaded with lice.

I don't remember many of the details from the time I spent in POW Camp XIA, but I was not abused in any way. About the only thing I do remember is there was not much food available. Potato soup seemed to be the usual thing, and there was the heavy German black bread that would really stick to the ribs.

On May 3, 1945, arrangements were mutually made between the American Officers camp, the German Commander of the camp and the American 9th Army which had a bridgehead on the West Side of the Elbe River. A mile-wide corridor was established between the camp and the American lines, and the next day (May 4, 1945), the camp was evacuated of all Allied POWs. This was before the war was officially over in Europe.

We were taken to a captured German Air Base and deloused, and we enjoyed hot showers and received clean clothes. What a good feeling. We were also given some good food for a change, and several, including myself, got upset stomachs, but that was over in a day or so.

After that, we were loaded on C-47s for a flight to Nancy, France, and then on to Camp Lucky Strike. While there, General Eisenhower made a speech and promised the Ex-POWs they would soon be on their way home. I think it was about June 1, 1945, when we loaded on a troop ship at La Harve, France, bound for the good ol' USA, arriving about June 12, 1945. After a quick processing, it was on to Jefferson Barracks, MO for me and a furlough from June 14, 1945 until September 22. Then, on to San Antonio for discharge, which was October 27, 1945. A civilian again, it was an interesting experience.

LEONARD DAVIS

"With only the German rations, you were really on a starvation basis. The thing that strikes me about that, in the state of starving, the depths to which human relations sink, because there was no longer a civil word amongst the prisoners. It was all fighting each other and obsession with food."

My name is Leonard Davis. I went into the service in June 1943. I entered the 8th Air Force, I guess, when we arrived in England in July 1944. I was in the 837th squadron of the 487th bomb group. I'm now 77 years old and approaching 78. I was air crew. My job was navigator. I was on my 12th mission when I was shot down. One of my crew was killed. The pilot died rather by accident, a parachuting accident. One of two causes was either his chute didn't open completely or else the fact that he came down in immensely high pine trees with branches on them only at the top and it caused him to split his chute. If he wasn't fortunate to have something to hold onto, he fell the rest of the way through and died from that fall. We're not sure which. None of the other crew were wounded or injured in any way, but they all parachuted.

I was discharged finally in about November, if I remember, of 1945. After the war I continued engineering school and became a mechanical engineer and worked at that for the rest of my life - the rest of my working life. I got married on September 18, 1950. We had two children, a boy and a girl.

So far, things I particularly remember about my experience in the service are that the pilot was a little dubious about my abilities as a navigator because I was criticized by the crew training establishment for not keeping a complete log. I didn't see the sense in writing down all the little towns that we crossed over in Oklahoma. I watched, I knew where we were all the time, but writing all that stuff down I didn't feel was useful for anyone. So, I got criticized for that, and I think that worried the pilot because he was determined that everyone on that crew do the best job possible. He wanted to get us back in the worst way. So, one day he said to me, "Davis, do you really think you can get us across the ocean?" Because that was a prospect that we had to fly a plane by ourselves across the ocean. I kind of tongue and cheek said, "I don't know, I never tried that." I don't think I helped his confidence any. But anyway, that's the way it was.

One of our crew, the bombardier, was kind of a nervous guy. One day, he said to me, "Davis, if we ever have to bail out, you get out of the road because I'm going to be in a hurry." I said, "George, if we ever have to bail out, you go first." I didn't like the prospect of bailing out. I wasn't really sure that I could

837TH SQUADRON

do anything like that. So when the time came, there was George. His eyes were as big as saucers saying, "Get going!" I said, "Go ahead, George," which he did.

A memorable moment to me, if I try to think of the most memorable thing, was coming down by parachute, because here we were in Germany, and I look down at the ground and I thought, there's no one down there to offer any help, you know. I'm solely alone here. There's not a friend anywhere down there, and that was a pretty sobering moment to think of that. After I landed, though, I was joined by the co-pilot, who had gone out after me but delayed opening his chute and watched me come down. We were both down in a very dense forest - big forest, too. Maybe four miles long. But he could come down and was able to meet me, and we continued on together. After a while, we heard a terrible noise in the forest, like a bear running full speed through the underbrush. We crouched down and looked carefully, and low and behold, here came the bombardier fast as he could run, right through the forest, brush and all. So we calmed him down and the three of us went ahead together, and we were continuing in the direction the plane had flown because that was the direction of the shortest distance to Belgium, to get out of Germany. Consequently, following the path of the plane we came upon the pilot's body, which I told you about before.

I think there's one other thing that seems worth saying to me. I think most people are aware that the bombing killed a lot of civilians in Germany, and they should remember that the Germans had killed a lot of civilians in Britain. But on top of that, I don't think everyone understands that the 8th Air Force was not wholly responsible for a lot of that. As far as I'm concerned, I was never assigned a target, and I don't think any other 8th Air Force member was ever assigned a target that was not of specific military value. That is, it would be an oil refinery, a switchyard in the railroad, a factory producing munitions or tanks or something like that, an airfield, a military airfield. We were never ordered to bomb a city, a residential area or anything like that. But, you have got to remember, too, that we couldn't always manage to hit the thing that we were aiming at, because the Germans were doing the best they could to keep us from hitting. They were bracketing us with flak and attacking us with fighters and covering their targets with smoke screens and everything possible to try and make sure that we didn't hit what we were aiming at. Often, the target would be in the midst of a city somewhere. The railroad marshaling yards were invariably in cities. Sometimes, you'd miss a little bit and you'd get some of the civilian homes in the vicinity. But that's not what we were aiming at, and it wasn't our intention. Most of the civilian damage I'm sure was done by British bombing, which didn't aim specifically at military targets. Their mode was to area bomb and flatten the cities, just as the Germans had done to them. They bombed at night, where you couldn't see very well specific military targets, whereas we bombed in the daytime, particularly in order to see those targets and hit them directly if we could.

Gentlemen From Hell

I learned of one of the very early reunions that was in 1972 in Saint Louis. I had two crew members in Saint Louis at that time, the co-pilot and the bombardier. In Indianapolis, where I lived, the tail gunner also lived. The tail gunner and I got together, and we drove down to Saint Louis and met with the co-pilot and the bombardier, and we all went downtown to the hotel where the reunion was being held. We walked in and looked around and, of course, we didn't know a soul, but we didn't know that was typical. We felt like we ought to know someone, and we didn't. We just decided to leave and go back to the ball gunner's home and hold our own reunion, which we did. So I didn't attend another reunion for 20 years, whereupon I'd been over to Europe and visited Lavenham, our old airfield, with my son. That fall, after getting home, I saw advertised that the group was going back to Lavenham next year. I thought, well you know, it would be nice to go with some of the guys in the group. So, I signed up and went that next year by myself. I was assigned a roommate and got to know him well and continued with that - Clark Yocum from Ohio, living on the Ohio River in Ohio. Since then, I've attended all the reunions except one. I went that following year to the Buffalo Reunion, in '93 I guess it was, and it continued.

I told you before about the pilot's concern for my navigating across the ocean. Actually, we had to fly from Gander, Newfoundland to the city of Belfast in Northern Ireland, which is a distance of about 2,000 miles. Well, we got out over the ocean - the crew was a little concerned about me, too, because I'm only 19 years old and navigating the North Atlantic for the first time with nothing to guide you but the stars. Well, there were 56 airplanes going, but each one was on its own - one taking off after the other and not following each other, but each going independently. Though consequently, every once in a while, a crew member would see the lights of another airplane, he'd call up and he'd say, "Davis, there's one over there, and it's headed off that direction." You know he was concerned - am I going the right way? Later, they'd call and say, "There's another one, and he's going off that way." And I say, "Well, I don't know what's the matter." But I tell you, one of the most memorable moments of my life was when we came right down the center of Donegal where we were supposed to be and landed right on schedule near Belfast in Northern Ireland, in an airport called Nuts Corner of all things. And I'll tell you, when we got on the ground, I was a hero - probably for the only time in my life, and at least never again equaled in exhilaration. That was a very memorable moment.

I hadn't told you either about the results of my landing by parachute in Germany. Virtually everyone who came down in Germany was captured. Very few ever got out of Germany, as some did out of France or other friendly countries. I was captured - and the remainder of the crew. The co-pilot and the bombardier, the officers of the crew, were all in prison in Stalag Luft I, which is on the Baltic Coast, straight north of Berlin. People usually ask, "How was it in Stalag Luft I?" I guess if I were to tell you the worst things about it, I would say there was starvation, lousy sanitation and some loss of life, taken those one by one. Following Thanksgiving in '44, the amount of Red Cross parcels that were issued were diminished and diminished and diminished, until about March of '45, there were none whatsoever. With only the German rations, you were really on a starvation basis. The thing that strikes me about that, in the state of starving, the depths to which human relations sink, because there was no longer a civil word amongst the prisoners. It was all fighting each other and obsession with food. You forgot about girls for a change, and the only topic was food, to the extent that you were copying down in your notebook recipes that others might recite, and your favorite meals. You wrote out what your favorite meal was when you went to your grandparents and asked other prisoners, "what was your favorite meal?" You were obsessed with food.

The sanitation in the eight months I was in that prison camp: I had one two minute shower, and I had zero changes of clothes. I only had the clothes on my back, and being wintertime, even if you could shower or sponge off, there was no other clothes to change in to. So, you put the same dirty clothes back on. But being that cold with nothing to wear, you weren't going to wash your clothes, either. So, I wore that same set of clothes the whole time - eight months, if you can think of that. There was no running water in the barracks, so some people had their washrooms in two corners of the compound. The compound measured about 300 feet on the side, so you might have to walk as far as 300 feet just to get there to brush your teeth or wash your hands. After dark, you couldn't do that. You couldn't leave the barracks after dark, so you couldn't go to the latrine and the washroom. Sanitation was a horrible problem, and we were really fortunate there weren't some epidemics there, but there were not.

We were located between the advancing armies, so our camp didn't have to march out as some others did. Our crewmen imprisoned over in what's now Poland had to march out, and for 83 days march to and fro in Germany. The Germans didn't want to surrender them because they were a bargaining chip. Consequently, they just marched them around. They didn't have a prison camp. Finally, we were liberated by the Russians. We had to wait a couple of weeks until our evacuation could be negotiated. Finally, our Air Force was able to arrange to fly into the local airport and fly us back to France in B-17s - the same planes we had flown. So that was a joyous, joyous experience to see those 8th Air Force B-17s arriving and to get onto that airplane and lift off out of that horrible mess of German imprisonment.

Another of the worst experiences in Stalag Luft I was some of the prisoners being shot dead by the German guards. The occasion was that it was against the rules to go outside of the barracks if there was an air raid on. Sometimes, prisoners would be occupied in some fashion. They wouldn't hear that there was an air raid and they'd inadvertently step outside. They'd soon realize that the raid was on because there wouldn't be anyone out there. However, before they could get back inside the barracks, several were shot dead by the German guards.

George Battschinger

Left: Battschinger, pictured here in September 1945, spent 12 years in the Air Force Reserves after returning from overseas. Battschinger retired at the rank of Captain with the Air Force Reserves. Right: Battschinger now lives in Sanford, North Carolina.

I was an 11th grade student when we learned on Sunday, December 7, 1941 at 1:00 p.m. EST of the bombing of Pearl Harbor. I always dreamed of joining the Army Air Corps in anticipation of becoming a P-38 Pilot.

Back in the '40s, everyone was patriotic. I don't remember any anti-war demonstrations - most of the young men wanted to get into the war to help their country. There was pride! I was one of those men. I couldn't enlist because I was underage and my parents refused to sign the necessary papers for my enlistment.

At the age of 19, I tried to enlist in the Army Air Corps; however, I was not classified for the draft. I went to the Draft Board and requested to be classified 1-A, and my request was honored.

In September of 1942, I was processed in the Federal Building in Newark, NJ. I later passed the physical and written test at the 113th Infantry Armory. Of course, all I could think about was becoming a P-38 Pilot, however that was not the Air Corps plan.

On November 27, 1942, I was sworn in as a "buck private." On February 2, 1943, about 800 enlisted men, of which I was one, departed for Atlantic City, NJ for 30 days of basic training and getting prepared for uniforms. On our 31st day, 495 men of the original group were sent to the University of Vermont for a 90-day refresher course. After a week or two, our entire group (495 men) developed German measles and were hospitalized for a week at Fort Ethan Allen in Winooski, VT.

837TH SQUADRON

From Vermont, we were on the move again, and this time to a Nashville, Tennessee Classifications Center, where it was necessary to pass a 6/4 physical. After five weeks, I received orders to report to Maxwell Field in Montgomery, Alabama for Cadet Training. At last, I was on my way to becoming a pilot! (Perhaps a P-38 pilot?) After nine weeks of physical training, learning code, and still learning to satisfy the requirements of the Army Air Corps, I was hospitalized for a five-day period for the removal of a cyst on my chest.

My next venture was Dorr Field, Arcadia, Florida for primary flight school. I was instructed in the PT-17 Stearman (220 HP Bi-plane). This was a very special "stop-over" point for me because it allowed me to enjoy Christmas Day, 1943 with my brother, Bob, USMC, prior to his leaving for the battle on Iwo Jima, where he was awarded the Purple Heart. Nine weeks later, I was sent to Bush Field, Augusta, Georgia for basic flight school. At this point of my flying career I was instructed to fly the BT-13 and BT-15 (425 HP), a low-wing, primarily all-metal aircraft.

Nine weeks later, I was sent to Moody Field, Valdosta, Georgia. It was here I learned to fly the AT-10 twin-engine, low-wing plane. This aircraft was constructed primarily of wood and fabric.

My graduation was May 23, 1944 (class of 44-E) in Valdosta. It was with great pride that I accepted my wings on becoming a Flight Officer. It was at this point of my career that I received my first leave - a delay-en route, which for me was a "delay-en route" trip home to New Jersey to visit with family and friends.

My next station was Plant Park, a stadium in Tampa, Florida. I remained there for a week, and then on to Buckingham Army Air Base in Fort Meyers, Florida, where I trained to fly the B-17F four-engine bomber. That was when I realized my thoughts of P-38 flying were over - that four engine aircraft revealed my future with the Army Air Corp. Our duties were to fly "gunners" who were to shoot at targets being towed by B-26 two-engine bombers.

On June 6th, 1944 while eating breakfast, I learned of the invasion of France (D-Day). I prayed all the way back to my quarters. Five weeks later, I was sent to Avon Park, Florida, where we formed a combat crew. Our crew consisted of Leno Pezzato, Pilot; George V. Battschinger, Co-Pilot; Robert Martin, Bombardier; Stanley Lankiewicz, Navigator; Herb Walton, Engineer; Robert Wood, Ball Gunner; Blair Campbell, Waist Gunner; George Graham, Radioman; Robert Pittis, Tail Gunner.

We received instruction in formation flying, high-altitude bombing (20,000 feet) and night flying (500 mile round robin runs). Bailing out of a B-17 was not an easy task, but our instructors really educated us as to the proper procedures. They also schooled us in "ditching" just in case it ever became necessary. Fortunately for me, as well as the entire crew, these were two obstacles we did not have to exercise.

After our B-17 training was completed, the crew was sent to Hunter Field, Savannah, GA, a staging area, before going overseas; and from there, we traveled by train to Camp Kilmer in New Jersey for winter clothing, briefing, etc. We crossed the Hudson River in total darkness on a ferryboat to board the 45,000-ton Il De France. We sailed the southern route to avoid German U-boats and nine days later we arrived in the Firth of Clyde, Scotland. We then traveled by train to Stone, England, a staging area. We then moved on to Lavenham, England, where we became members of the 487th Bomb Group (station 137). We were assigned to the 837th Bomb Squadron and "Miss Bea Havin'" - a B-17G four-engine bomber.

My first mission was on December 6, 1944 to Merseburg, Germany. There was never a thought that crossed my mind as to whether it was right or wrong. I was sworn in to do my job, and my job was to fly my crew to Germany and give them hell! It was an oil refinery in an area defended by over 800 heavy guns in a 40 square mile area. The sky was filled with flak, thousands of bursts all around us. As I reminisce about this, I don't understand how we were missed so often. We had many holes in the aircraft, but no real damage. Our losses were 25 aircraft.

After my sixth mission, I flew two missions with newly formed crews as an instructor check pilot, to enlighten them of my experiences and to help them cope. The new crews were well trained. They listened to what I had to offer and worked really well.

Every three weeks we were entitled to receive a 56-hour pass to go into London. This gave us the opportunity to do sight-seeing - i.e., Big Ben, London Bridge, Westminster Abbey, etc. It was around this period of time that I was called up to Division Headquarters. I had to stand in front of the high command officers and answer questions that were "tossed" at me regarding the handling of the B-17 Aircraft in many different situations. For me, it was a very "nerve-racking" experience. I did pass the verbal test, and a short time later, was promoted to 2nd Lieutenant. When it was suggested that I continue on with another newly formed crew, I requested of Captain Smith to permit me to return to my regular crew. I explained to the Captain that if I was supposed to die, I preferred to be with my full crew. I was then sent back to my regular crew and flew 27 more missions with them.

During a mission to Magdeburg, Germany, January 14, 1945, we took a hit just after "bombs away." The plane rose about five feet in the air, and I knew immediately we had trouble. I called for an oxygen check. The crew answered, but our waist gunner did not. I asked the radioman to check on the waist gunner, and as suspected, he was down. His head was looking out through a hole the size of a basketball in the floor. He obviously was trying to get air - his oxygen hose had been cut in half. Since we were in formation, our navigator asked permission to go back to the waist gunner. After permission was granted, the navigator went on portable oxygen and went to the waist gunner. I told the crew to be sure the waist gunner was receiving oxygen because we were at about 30,000 feet. Lank, the navigator, fitted a portable mask on Blair, the waist gunner, and then he tried to stop bleeding. Blair had been hit in the hip by the fuse end of an 88mm shell. Lank and Graham used every first aid kit aboard to stop the bleeding. We had over 60 holes in the plane. I asked for permission to abort to go home. We left the formation with fighter escort. We made a straight-in approach to our home field, and although firing red flares (a distress signal), we were flying in with another B-17 shooting landings. The tower called him off, and with just minutes to spare, he powered up and allowed us to land. Blair was removed from the plane and taken to the hospital nearby. We saw him the next day, and he was in a plaster cast and ready for transport. A week or so later, he was back home in California.

On January 16, 1945, our mission was to Dessau, Germany, which we were told was a long one. We had the ground crew top off the fuel tanks. The weather was to be "socked" in at our time of return. If we were on time, we would be OK; if not, we were to go to an alternate field some 100 miles away. The weather was so bad that we could not locate any field in the area. Suddenly, we saw a B-17 ahead of us circling for a landing field. We could not see the ground yet, but followed anyway. Unknown to us, we were following our squadron leader, and we landed on a British base for the night. The next morning, the Brits put 100 gallons of fuel in each main tank, which was a blessing. When we returned to our base, calculations showed that we landed at the Brits with almost dry tanks. The mission was nine hours long.

On a mission on February 15, 1945 to Nuremberg, Germany, a cylinder head on number three engine burned away. We lost power in that engine; we feathered it and came home on three engines. On just about every mission, we came home with many holes in our aircraft.

We had missions to Hanover, Mainz, Coblenz, Aschaffenburg and Mannheim, and twice to Hamburg, Berlin, Nuremberg and Bremen.

After our 29th mission, we were sent to an English country house in the English countryside. We spent seven days there resting, having a good time with lots of good food. The American Red Cross was responsible for these activities. We partook of many sports activities: horses, bicycles, tennis, etc., and to boot, we were given a bottle of whiskey for medical reasons.

All in all, we had quite an experience for young men, however, I do think it helped to make us better citizens. There was an inspiration that made us love our country, respect our flag and Constitution.

When we completed our 35th mission our "Miss Bea Havin'" had 79 missions to her credit. We were sorry to leave her. A few years later, she was found in the desert of Arizona just waiting for more action. I remained on the 487th air base for an extra week after our 35th mission to receive a promotion to 1st Lt. My trip home was on the same ship that took me over, the Il De France. During a leave of 21 days (the only leave I had in my three years), my fiancée and I were married. My wife and I were sent by train from Atlantic City, New Jersey to Lake Lure, North Carolina for 30 days of R and R which took a full day of traveling to get there. The scenery was beautiful along the route. The hotels at Lake Lure and all the entertaining were in the hands of the Red Cross. Dinnertime was always special - we were entertained by the GI orchestra, which was very entertaining. The music was beautiful. The Navy supplied a boat to take us up the lake to the Officers and Enlisted Men's Clubs for dancing. We went swimming, fishing and hiking and enjoyed an extended honeymoon. We returned to Atlantic City, New Jersey by train for a week or so, at which time I received orders to report to Lockbourne Army Air Base in Columbus, Ohio. At this time, I was a rated first pilot. We flew 500-mile round trips to keep in shape. Since the war was almost over in August 1945, we were then sent to Langley Field, Hampton, Virginia. On or about the 18th of August, I was sent to Fort Dix, New Jersey for discharge, at which time I enlisted in the Air Force Reserves. Twelve years later, I was again discharged from the service, attaining the rank of Captain.

While in England, I was awarded the Air Medal and Five Oak Leaf Clusters. I also have a Sharp Shooter Award, a Good Conduct Medal, the European, African, Middle Eastern Campaign Medal, the World War II Medal and the Distinguished Service Medal from the State of New Jersey.

CLARK YOCUM

Yocum retired from his radio and television repair business in December 1992. The radar shop that he worked out of in the war is still standing, and he was in it his last two visits to Lavenham.

The following is a short story of my life during WWII on Sept. 4, 1942. I was drafted into the army of the United States. I was 21 at that time. I was given two weeks at home to get things in order. On Sept. 18, 1942, I went back to Fort Hayes, Columbus, OH. I was then issued clothing and equipment.

On Sept. 25, 1942, I was sent to Jefferson Barracks, St. Louis, MO for basic training. Out of our group, I was the only one to go to the Army Air Corps. Tests were given on Sept. 30. I had been told by an Army friend of mine, "If you want to go into a certain job, don't make too good of a grade on that exam."

I took an exam for photography, and my grade was 100. I deliberately put down the wrong answers on the radio exam. I was selected for radio school on Oct. 20, 1942. I left for Truax Field, Madison, WI for 12 weeks of radio school.

Christmas at Madison was very nice. I had a Christmas dinner at a family home on Christmas day and another the day after Christmas. There were not enough soldiers to go around. I completed school and on Jan. 21, 1943 went to radar school at Boca Raton, FL. On March 1, 1943, my birthday, I received three presents - box of home made cookies from home, a diploma from radar school and a set of corporal stripes. This was for having completed two technical schools.

The army eventually didn't know what to do with us. There were not enough radar units for the men to work on. This was classified material. We were not allowed to talk about it to anyone. On March 6, I got a 15-day furlough and went home.

On May 30, 1943, I was sent to Plant Park, Tampa, FL. From there, I went to Will Rogers Field, Oklahoma City, OK. The first thing I heard was,

"What are you doing here? We don't have any radar." This outfit had A-20s and B-25s.

I remained with this outfit about five months. I worked as a radio mechanic. I did learn a lot about how the flight line works. They had one man there that had previous radio experience. His name was Isay. He had worked on the jobs no one else could fix.

This outfit went over to England after I shipped out. It became part of the 9th Air Force. I saw Isay in Cambridge one day. He asked me to transfer back to the old outfit. "You will only have to stay inside and repair radios. You will be a master sergeant in three months." Something in my head told me to turn it down, and a few weeks later they shipped him to France. I don't know what happened to them.

Now, to get back to the previous story, on Nov. 1, 1943, I was sent to Hammond, LA. This was a sub-base of Harding Field at Baton Rouge, LA. We had P-47s. It was at this base that I met a young lady (Mattie Mixon) who later became my wife. All good things must come to an end. During January of 1944, I joined the 487th Bomb Group, 837th Squadron. I was in the base hospital for three weeks. I had picked up trench mouth on the way to join the 487th. I had to gargle every two hours with hydrogen peroxide.

One day, an officer from the 837th came to the hospital and talked to the doctor. I left the hospital the next day. I drew my new equipment and shipped out with the ground crew.

On the way east to Camp Kilmer, NJ, we passed through my hometown of Bellaire, OH. We went across the Ohio River into WV. Just then, the officer in charge of our coach said, "You boys have been on this train for several days with no exercise. We are going to stop in Wheeling, WV and march you through the town."

I had a sister who worked in Wheeling. As soon as the train stopped, I jumped off the train. I saw a man standing in a doorway. I ran up to him and said, "Call the Warwick China Co., ask for Esther Yocum, then tell her, her brother is up here." He didn't answer me, just took off. When we got back to the station after marching around town, she was there. I did get to talk to her for a few minutes.

We went over to England on the Duchess of Bedford. I won't go into details, but I did not like the crossing.

We arrived in Scotland April 3, 1944. We were met by The Red Cross. The coffee and donuts were well liked by all. We all got "two k" rations while boarding the train that would take us to our base. We ate the dinner ration and saved the breakfast ration for the next morning.

Upon opening the breakfast ration the next morning, I was about to discard the pack of toilet tissue contained in the box. Something told me to keep it. I was later glad I did.

We departed from the train in the little town of Long Melford. Trucks were waiting to take us to the base. The base was brand new and we were the first to arrive.

We were given quonset huts to live in. The radar men shared the same hut as the radiomen as this was a new base. We had no supplies at all. The RAF cooked dinner that first night. The dinner was good compared to what we had on the ship. One of the dishes was corn. This was baked in a large container. I didn't take any.

That night, Axis Salley welcomed the 487ths to England. Early the next morning, a base doctor came in the hut along with two helpers. Each helper had a gallon jug in each hand. "Anyone who ate the corn last night, if you don't have the runs, you will have them. The corn was bad. Take some of this medicine." I was glad I didn't eat the corn, with most of the ground crew down with the back door trots and had no toilet tissue on the base. The Stars and Stripes was used for other than its intended purpose. Also, all of the grassy area was covered by the boys who didn't make it to the latrine.

Lt. Warner (later a captain) was our radar officer. We had a nice outfit. Everyone pitched in and helped with the work. We worked one week on day shift, then had a day off. You then worked a week on the night shift. On the night shift, you check out the "Gee Box" or later "Loran" set in each plane. This meant you got up in the navigator's department and make sure the set was working proper. If it wasn't, you took it back to the shop. We had two spare units. If you needed more than two units, you stayed while one was fixed to put it back in. Otherwise, the bad sets were left for the day shift to repair. When the work was done, all but one went back to the huts. One person had to stay all night.

While with the 487th, I went to school to learn how to service the British "Gee Box." This was used by the navigator as an aid to navigation. This was a good piece of equipment, but its range was limited. Our engineers took it and increased its range by quite a bit. Ours was called "Loran," for long-range navigation. I also went to school for this.

One of the other jobs we had was to see that all the planes had plenty of "chaff." This was similar to Christmas tree icicles. It was dispensed by the radio operator via a chaff chute. It was used to jam the German guns that fired using Radar, thus the flak didn't hit the plane.

One of the days I remember was June 6, 1944. I was working the day shift. I reported to the radar shop at 8:00. The night shift was still there. Also, Capt. Warner was in his office. "This was unusual," the boys said; "something is up. We worked all night. We had to shoot off all the IFF sets. We almost called you out to help."

At 8:20, Capt. Warner came out of his office and gave us a report. "Right now, our troops are landing on the shores of France. Our planes will come back one at a time. They will get more gas and bombs, you men will load chaff, two kinds on each plane." The night crew went off duty at this time.

We had a Jeep, but that was not enough to cover the job. I was sent to the motor pool to get another vehicle. All I could get was an old command car. We loaded this with boxes of chaff (both kinds). I drove it around the perimeter strip. I had two men with me. They rode on the running boards; I went in one direction and the crew with the Jeep went in the other direction.

Gentlemen From Hell

When the plane landed, I pulled up, the two men each grabbed a box and put it in the back of the plane. Then, on to the next one. This went on all day. I did not get any lunch that day. I did get a battle star for "D" Day.

We all remember Aug, 15, 1944. About 5:00, the base intercom came on - attention all personnel - "Red Alert." Buzz bomb, east side of the field. Just then, the motor in the bomb quit. This means the bomb is going down. We all rushed out in our underwear and in our bare feet. From where I stood, it looked like the bomb was going to hit the control tower. The man who gave the alarm was in the tower. He got out in a hurry, no wonder he stuttered. It missed the tower and the hanger. It landed in a field about a third of a mile from the base.

Life went on as usual. Everyone on the base did his job the best he could. On May 2, 1945, I had a seven-day furlough. I went to Scotland. I was in Edinburgh. I just had my picture taken. I walked out of the studio. A lady was running up the street yelling, "The war is over. Churchill will speak at 2 o'clock." I heard Churchill's speech, got my bag and got on the late train for London. Thus, I was in London for VE Day. I took my daughter back to London for VE Day + 50 years. We both enjoyed it.

I have been back to Lavenham three times with the 487th. The treatment has been wonderful. The people of the area have gone all out to help us.

One thing I might mention at this time. The first Sunday at the base was sunny. Six of us walked into town. We could see the church tower from the base and could hear the bells toll. We just walked towards the church till we found a road going to town. We did go to the church service. The route we took was later called the Burma Road. The back way into town - a lot of boys used this route.

The aircrew came back to the states in July of 1945. The rumor was that we could train for B-29s and go to the Pacific. Any member of the ground crew that came over with the 487th could fly back. The rest would close down the base and come back later by boat. I had to get back to marry the girl I met while serving in Hammond, LA. She came up to Ohio. We were married Aug 1, 1945, and are still married today. We have one daughter, Beth. The three of us attend reunions. While on our honeymoon, the war ended in the Pacific.

After my 30-day R and R was over, I reported to Indianapolis, IN. They sent me to Drew Field, Tampa, FL. During Sept. of 1945, I got my honorable discharge from the army of the United States. This is a brief story of my time in the service during WWII. After the war, I went back to my old job of fixing and servicing radios. Later on, we added television. When my boss passed on, I purchased the business. I ran it till Dec. 31, 1992. I then retired. Smokey Silva of the 487th got my number in early 1992. I went to the reunion in Savannah that year. I also went back to England that year. I have not missed a reunion since. However, I have not met any of the ones I worked with, nor have I met any of the ones who were in our quonset hut. The radar shop that I worked out of is still standing. I was in it the last two visits to Lavenham.

837TH SQUADRON

JOHN BEESON

LEFT: *Beeson also served in the Air Force during military action in Korea and Vietnam, with the zenith of his career being the command of a B-52 Strategic Bombardment Wing.* RIGHT: *Beeson, second from right, pictured with members of his crew.*

This chronology was compiled in October, 2002 by John D. Beeson (tail gunner) as I remember it.

The word "available" in Jack Leon's name came from the character Available Jones in the comic strip Lil' Abner. Available Jones was available, for a price, to do anything. Although we didn't think that Jack volunteered us for specific missions, it seemed like we were always on the "availability list" to fly; thus the name.

Our crew was formed in the late summer of 1944 at Walla Walla Army Airfield in Washington State. It was a B-24 training base. Crew members were: Pilot, Jack Leon; Co-Pilot, Robert Polen; Navigator, Leo Dolin; Bombardier, Robert Shaw; Engineer, Leonard Marino; Radio Operator, John Sunberg; Waist Gunner, Lucien Osieki; Waist Gunner, Ralph Moore; Ball Gunner, Reese Hopkin; Tail Gunner, John Beeson.

Upon graduation, we were sent to Hamilton Field, CA (a port of embarkation). Since we were already on the West Coast, we assumed that we would be sent to the Pacific Theater. Not so! As I learned many years later during a Personal assignment at SAC Headquarters, you send the troops where the replacements are needed (in war time usually because of losses). Instead, we were loaded on a troop train for a six-day ride to Camp Kilmer, NJ, an East Coast port of embarkation. The car that the enlisted members of our crew rode on was a WWI troop car. In other words, a plain freight box car (sliding doors on each side) with bunks built into the interior. What an interesting and exciting trip for an Indiana farm boy just turning 19 years of age on 1 Nov., 1944. We had the sliding doors open most of the days on the trip. A hobo could not duplicate that trip today. After a few days at Camp Kilmer, we were sent to the Port of New Jersey, where we boarded the British ocean liner Acquatania, sister ship to the ill fated Lusitania. We crossed the Atlantic Ocean unescorted at near the top speed of the ship, making frequent irregular course changes to avoid submarines. Needless to say, the accommodations and food did not rival the fare of a modern cruise ship. Upon docking in Scotland, we transferred to Camp Stone, the assignment depot where every 8th AF replacement crew member (who did not fly his own aircraft over) passed through. There, we were introduced to the "three biscuit" mattress which was standard bedding at all air bases in England. Still, better than the tents and canvas cots of the 9th AF in France.

In a couple of days, we were loaded onto a train, destination unknown (at least to the enlisted men) for transport to our assigned unit. We arrived at our destination in the middle of the night, and we were informed that we had been assigned to the 446th BG near Rattlesden, and that it was a B-17 base. After about three more days, we were suddenly transferred a few miles away to the 487th BG at Lavenham. Again, the old personnel logic that the replacement troops go where the recent losses have been the greatest.

We spent December retraining into the B-17, where both our pilot and navigator flew a couple of missions with experienced crews for indoctrination. 8th AF crews flew with only one waist gunner. Lucien Osieki was removed from the crew and completed his 35-mission tour as a spare. We missed the max-effort mission on Christmas day of 1944, but got to help load the bombs for it. Just after that, we started flying our missions.

When the 8th AF started flying missions over Germany, the losses were catastrophic. Later, as training and tactics improved along with modest fighter support for part of the way, the tour length was established at 25 missions. The statistical probabilities were that most crews would not complete the tour. They would be shot down, killed, taken prisoner or, in a few cases, evade and return to England. Some would die aboard in combat or in crash landings resulting from combat damage. The odds were not good. Later in the war, when we developed long-range fighter escort and the Luftwaffe's effectiveness was subdued, the tour length was increased to 35, but the odds of completing the tour remained about the same.

On one of our missions, four German ME-262 jet fighters attacked and in two passes shot down our entire low squadron. Fortunately, we were in the high squadron or this story would be different, if written at all. Because of the performance differential, the P-51 escort fighters were ineffective against the jets. I didn't recognize the significance of this event until years later when I read in the Air Force magazine that this was the only time during the war that German jets shot down the entire squadron.

We were shot down on our 23rd mission. On 18 March, 1945, our target was Berlin, Germany, which we bombed. At that moment of bombs "away," our B-

17 was struck by anti-aircraft fire. Two engines became inoperative. The propeller on one of these engines would not feather, thus creating additional drag. Smoke and fire were visible in the oil cooler outlets behind one engine on the right wing. Obviously, we would not make it back to England in this condition. The co-pilot, Bob Polen, had been hit in the leg by flak. Bailing out over Germany would be extremely unfriendly as a result of increased bombing. The decision was quickly made to continue eastward in an attempt to reach the Oder River, which was the position of the Russian front lines.

We did make it to the Oder River, but not without losing altitude from 25,000 feet down to 12,000 feet. After crossing the Oder River, the Aircraft Commander gave the command to "bail out." As we were bailing out, Russian Yak 9 fighters came up and started attacking our aircraft. Two of our crew members, Marino and Sunberg, were killed by being strafed (shot at) by the Russian fighter aircraft while descending in their parachutes. I and two other crew members were strafed but not hit. One of the surviving crew members observed Sunberg lying on the ground, but the Russian captors would not allow him to approach the body. To this day, there has been no information concerning the plight or disposition of these two men.

An interesting aspect of the bail-out had to do with the survival gear. We were instructed to take along a pair of Army boots to wear after landing. Our in-flight foot wear was electrically heated inserts inside fleece lined flying boots. Not ideal for walking any distance on the ground. I, the young Indiana farm boy, was the only one on the crew that followed this instruction. When bailing out of the tail gunner's hatch, the parachute harness on my right shoulder caught on the door frame. My right hand was guarding the parachute rip cord handle, and the boots were in my left hand. Since prohibiting the opening of the parachute until clear of the aircraft was more important than the boots, I had to drop them. Some Russian or Pole probably got an almost new pair of boots. The other crew members, none of whom carried their boots, have teased me about this event, but I still fail to see the humor in it.

The Oder River is the border between Germany and Poland. To the best of my recollection, after bailing out, we landed two to three kilometers from Landsberg (Rorzow) (Wielkopolski). I think it was south and slightly west of where I landed. Our aircraft, B-17G tail identification number 44-8276, preceded on eastward. As it was already badly damaged descending rapidly, the attack by Russian fighters probably hastened the descent. None of the surviving crew members observed the crash of the aircraft.

I landed in a reforested area with the new trees just slightly taller than the height of my parachute. This resulted in a landing with about the force of stepping down from a chair. I assumed that the fighters might try to strafe me on the ground. I instantly got out of the parachute harness and ran through the forest until I came to a dirt road. I went back about 40 feet from the road, laid down under a tree, pulled pine needles over my body to break the outline. In the meantime, the fighters made two strafing passes at my parachute. After a few minutes, I heard voices and made the decision to walk out onto the road with my hands up. It was a Russian infantry squad, with guns drawn. Upon identification, using the "blood chit" (we carried it for that purpose), I had to shake hands with each one of them before we could leave the spot. I'm sure I was the first "Americanski" they had ever met. From that point on, I was treated royally; as well as could be expected that near the front line. I recall hearing some cannon fire to the west.

I was taken to what appeared to be a temporary Russian Army headquarters in the town of Landsberg. There, I was reunited with Reese Hopkin (ball gunner). Hopkin had seen Sunberg lying on the ground, and since no other crew members were brought in to that location, we assumed we might be the only two who had survived. Communication with the Russians was difficult since they could speak no English and we could not speak Russian.

The following morning, we were assigned to ride on a Russian tanker truck convoy which was returning east from delivering fuel to the tanks at the front line. A P-51 fighter pilot who had been shot down joined our group. The drivers could speak no English but knew they were driving Studebaker 6x6 lend lease trucks which were Americanski. During this trip of about three days, we passed a German concentration (death) camp. It certainly made an impression on me, although it obviously was no longer in business. The food fare for that trip was Russian black bread and some captured German corned beef (about 90 percent fat). We were picked up at an airfield near Lodz, Poland in an Army Air Force C-47 and flown further southeast to a former shuttle bomb base at Poltava, Russia.

Upon arriving at Poltava, we learned that all of our crew members had survived except Marino and Sunberg. They had arrived there before Hopkin and I. We stayed about three weeks in Poltava due to an operational incident between the U.S. Air Force and the Russian Base commander. During that time, he would not allow any U.S. aircraft to come in or depart. When we were finally cleared to leave, we traveled aboard Air Transport Command aircraft. The routing back was to Tehran, Iran (overnight); Cairo, Egypt (two nights, and went to the pyramids); Athens, Greece (pax and fuel stop); Naples, Italy (overnight); Marseilles, France (pax and fuel stop); Paris, France (pax and fuel stop); and on to London (overnight), returning by train to Lavenham.

Upon return to Lavenham, the group had stood down for the end of the war. We had been scheduled for our "flak leave" (rest and recuperation) at a hotel in Southport, England the day after we were shot down. Since we had been through an experience that would definitely qualify us for it, we requested that we be allowed to go now. It was approved. While traveling to Southport we spent VE (Victory in Europe) night in London. What an experience to see the celebration of the people after such a long war. Only persons traveling on orders were allowed off base during this period, so we were among the few Americans in London that night.

In July, we flew (with three replacement crew members) the B-17 G 46315, named "Fearless Fosdick," back to the United States. It had crash-landed in Europe, been repaired, flew a little out of trim, but made the trip safely and reliably. Overnight stops were made in Iceland (it never got dark); Goose Bay, Labrador (the most mosquitoes we had ever seen); Grenier Field, NH (diverted for weather) and finally on to Bradley Field, CT. To my knowledge, none of us ever flew in the B-17 again.

What has happened to the crew?

Marino and Sunberg died in combat. Leon, Polen and Dolin died of natural causes. Shaw was recalled for the Korean War and died in a C-47 crash in the United States. Beeson, Hopkin and Moore are still kicking.

Jack Leon had a career as an executive with GE finance in New York City.

Bob Polen returned to Southwestern PA and worked in the family business, which was the ownership and operation of coal mines.

Leon Dolin was a tax lawyer in New York City, but finished his career as a partner in a meat processing plant (a more lucrative business).

Ralph Moore returned home and, with his brother Paul, operated an auto dealership and repair business that his father had started.

Reese Hopkin returned to Harmony PA. He operated a 101-acre farm (mostly on the side of one hill). He was also a supervisor in a welding shop in a steel mill. His address has not changed.

I (John Beeson) returned home and finished college. Upon graduation, I received an ROTC commission, re-entered the Air Force and became a pilot. Flew a combat tour (also 23 missions) in the Korean War as a B-29 co-pilot. My tour during the Vietnam War was Chief of Maintenance of the 8th Tac Fighter Wing (F-4s). There were many interesting and satisfying assignments, but the zenith of my career was the command of a B-52 Strategic Bombardment Wing. Betty and I are now retired in Cocoa Beach, Fl. We live adjacent to Patrick AFB, just one mile north of the Officer's Club, from which it is all right-hands on the way home.

WALTER ZMUD

LEFT: *Zmud, pictured with other officers at a training course at Mather Air Force Base.* RIGHT: *Zmud, pictured with his wife.*

I enlisted in the Air Cadet program while I was in college, and in September 1942, I was sent to Kelly Army Air Field, San Antonio, Texas for my indoctrination, medical and psychiatric testing. The tests were to determine my health status for continued training as an air cadet. I took the eye aptitude test for my pilot training and was sent to Muskogee, Oklahoma for pilot training. But due to my reckless flying practices, I was transferred out of the pilot training program. However, because of my high scholastic and aptitude tests, I was allowed to remain in the program. I was given the choice of going to navigation training or bombardier training. I chose the bombardier training program and was sent to Ellington Air Field in the spring of 1943. After I completed my training at Ellington, I was sent to Laredo Army Air Field to take a gunnery course, and then went to Midland Army Air Field for my advanced training. I was commissioned a 2nd Lieutenant in October 1945. After graduation, I went to Salt Lake City, Utah to pick up my combat crew. The crew were as follows:

2nd Lt. Fred L. Smith, pilot; 2nd Lt. Sam M. Williams, co-pilot; 2nd Lt. Mullins, navigator; 2nd Lt. Walter V. Zmud, bombardier; Sgts. Robert W. Beckman, engineer; Gunners Lester Paul C. Bon, Veston Satterfield and Fred H. Armstrong. Our radio operator was Pvt. John W. Sweet.

A short history of my military service follows:
Oct 1943-Dec 1943: We were sent to heavy bomber training in Davis Monthan Army Air Field, Tucson, AZ.

837th Squadron

Dec 1943-Jan 1944: Alamogordo, N.M. Continuation of B-24 training and preparation for departure to the 487th Bomb Group in England.

Jan 1944-March 1944: left Alamogordo, N.M. for Florida to Trinidad, Venezuela to Belem, Brazil to Dekar; Senecal, Africa to Ireland, and then to Lavenham, England. Our B-24 Bomber was called "The Black Widow." Our squadron was the 837th Bombardment Squadron (H) Station #127 of the rd. Bomb Division, Eight Air Force.

March 1944-Oct 1944: I flew 25 combat missions, including day before D-Day, during D-Day and after D-Day. Our losses were heavy as well as those in other 8th Air Force Bomb Groups. I took Navigation courses after D-Day to allow our navigator to become lead navigator. My reassignment orders following my completion of 35 combat missions on 24 Oct. 1944 read:

> Position: Navigator-Bombardier; Combat Hrs: 225:55; Missions: 35
> Awards: Five Air Medals, four Battle Stars and The Distinguished Flying Cross

After Mullins was transferred to Lead Navigator, I became a busy crewmember for each following mission flown. We were very lucky, even though we returned from our missions over Berlin, Heidelberg, Castle, Hamburg and other cities in Germany with over 50-200 holes in our fuselage. We only had one casualty, a shattered elbow/arm to Sgt. Sweet (gunner). On our return from the target area, after giving the flight path return to our base in England, I crawled out of the nose pit to the rear and doctored the wounds, bandage with sulfa and administered a shot for his severe pain. I stayed with him until the pilot, Fred Smith, called me to give him a short route so as to get to our airfield sooner. We shot the usual flares on arrival over the airfield, indicating someone was wounded on board. The doctor, nurses and ambulance met us as soon as we landed. This is a short commentary on a normal combat mission, and now that I think back, it appears a miracle that I lasted 35 missions. The majority of the original combat crews, who manned the initial 487th Bomb Group at Lavenham, only flew 25 missions. However, we had severe losses and needed experienced veteran combat crews to break in the replacements, which were now arriving after D-Day because of 8th Air Force losses during the invasion. I was allowed to return to the states in Oct. 1944.

Oct 44-Dec 44: Home leave and AF Rest and Recuperation Center - Atlantic City, NJ.

Dec 1944-April 45: Bombardier instructor in Midland Army Air Field, Midland, TX.

April 1945-June 1945: Bombardier Instructor at Carl's Bad Army Air Field, Carlsbad, NM.

June 1945-Jan 1947: Assisted the closing of various air fields at the end of WWII, such as San Angelo Army Air Field, Army Air Field, Midland,

TX; Carlsbad Army Air Field, Carlsbad NM; Big Springs Army Air Field, Big Springs, TX. and others.

It was about this time that I decided to stay in the Air Force. Many of my friends got out and returned to their jobs back home or went back to school. I decided to make the Air Force my career.

Jan 1947-May 1947: I was assigned to Counter Intelligence School, Holabirtd Signal Depot, Baltimore, MD.

May 47-Juue 1948: Attended Russian Language School, Presedio of Monterey, Monterey, CA. I attended the first Russian course given at the Presedio.

Sep 1948-Nov 1949: (Intelligence Officer) Assigned to Hdqrs. USAFE, A-2 Wiesbaden, Germany. While assigned there, I was sent to Hq. USFA in Vienna, Austria as a Russian Interpreter to interrogate two crew members that had defected from the Soviet Union in a U-2 Twin Engine bomber.

Nov 1949-Jan 1951: Returned to the states - Mather Air Force Base, Sacramento, CA, to upgrade my navigation skills. Upon completion of my studies, I was retained at the base as a Navigation Instructor and supervisor in the Radar Target: Intelligence Section.

Jan 1951-May 1954: I received orders to report to Central Intelligence Agency (CIA) in Langley, VA. I remained on active duty as an USAF officer during this assignment, but wore civilian clothing at all times. I was assigned to the Ukrainian Desk Operations within the USSR Division. When the Chief of the Division was transferred to another job, I became the Ukrainian Interim Chief. Our operations were strictly clandestine covert operations in support of the UPA (Ukrainian Nationalist Army), still actively in armed engagement with the Soviet forces in Western Ukraine. We trained UPA members, armed them and dropped them in the Western Ukraine Carpathian Mountains.

May 1954-Oct 1955: Recalled back to active duty by US. Air Force. I was to report to Mather Air Force Base as a Navigator instructor. It was a short one-year assignment when a cable arrived from the Pentagon directing me to report to Rhein - Main Air Force Base in Germany.

Nov 1955-June 1957: Assigned to the 7000th Support Wing, Frankfurt, Germany, and my tasks were as an Operations Officer for all 7000th Support Wing clandestine activities targeting the East German, Mid-East and North Africa areas. The targets were Soviet and Satellite Air Forces and Missile Forces operating in these areas.

June 1957-July 1959: Assigned as Team Commander of USAF Clandestine Special Team in Bremerhaven, Germany. The clandestine collection effort was against Soviet and East German Air Forces located in those

837TH SQUADRON

areas. Specified interest was new weaponry and aircraft and strengths of forces.

July 1959- May 1963: Assigned to the Air Chief of Staff Intelligence (ACSI) in Washington, DC. My responsibilities were the management of USAFS clandestine collection operations worldwide. I was an intelligence officer assigned to headquarters, Wiesbaden, Germany.

April 1963: I retired from military service. Accepted a position as a civilian with the Air Force Department as an intelligence specialist (the same job as I had in uniform), but now as a civilian. This position was in a special intelligence group at Ft. Belvoir, VA. In 1980, I retired from the Federal Government.

I got married while I was a cadet at Ellington Air Field, April 1943. We have four children - Robert W. Zmud, Ph.D., Oklahoma University, Oklahoma; John Peter Zmud, Special Ed. Director, Huntington, Mass; Johanna P. Zmud Arce, Ph.D., President, NuStats Marketing Research Co. Austin, TX; and Ann Marie (Mia) Zmud Dougherty, Director, Environmental Protection Department, Austin, TX.

There were many memorable moments in my military, civilian and retired career. I take great pride in the accomplishments of my children. I returned to Lavenham, England in 1992, a memorial event.

The most memorable event in the war was when I worked in CIA as a civilian. I gained much experience in covert/clandestine operations which 95 percent or less Air Force officers would ever receive during their entire career. The other memorable event was when I received my orders to return to the States after completing 35 missions without any mishaps.

JULIAN HEADLEY

LEFT: *Headley flew 35 combat missions over Germany during his six months overseas.*
RIGHT: *Headley, pictured with his wife Sibyl on their 60th wedding anniversary Sept. 6, 2002.*

Julian Headley was born in Empire, Alabama. His family moved to Baytown, Texas when he was 16. After he finished school, he was employed by Humble Oil and Refining Company Market Department as Transport Truck Dispatcher.

On September 6, 1942, Headley married Sibyl Alford. His draft notice arrived while they were honeymooning. When they returned, a friend from his office personally delivered the notice to their home. He was also presented with his vacation paycheck, which amounted to 13 cents. He still has the check.

Headley was sworn into the U.S. Army Air Corps as an aviation cadet on September 25, 1942. He was placed in the reserves until March 25, 1943, when he was ordered to active duty. His first destination was Santa Ana, California, where he was classified as a pilot and assigned to a 12-week course in pre-flight training. His wife came to join him after he had settled in. From there, he moved on to Thunderbird Field in Phoenix, Arizona for 11 weeks of primary training. The next move was to Pecos, Texas for Basic Flying Training, and then on to Fort Sumner, New Mexico for Advanced Flying Training. Upon completion he received his Pilot Wings and was commissioned as a 2nd Lt. in the Army Air Corps on February 8, 1944. At this point, he had logged 280 hours of flying time.

Upon graduation, Headley was granted a 10-day leave, which he spent with his family and friends.

The next assignment was to Roswell, New Mexico for three months. Here, he received his B-17 Pilot Transition Training and became a B-17 pilot. From

837TH SQUADRON

Roswell, he was sent to McDill Field, Tampa, Florida. His wife did not accompany him to Florida. She went home to Baytown to await the birth of their daughter.

At McDill Field, a combat crew of 10 members was formed and received their Combat Crew Training. On their practice runs, they dropped bombs consisting of 95 pounds of sand and five pounds of explosives. This was how they measured their accuracy while using a minimum amount of explosives.

After completing their combat training, they were ready for overseas duty. The crew went to Savannah, Georgia for staging and picked up a brand new B-17 bomber to fly overseas (staging was the term used when the crew members received their briefing before going overseas). They left Savannah and flew to Manchester, New Hampshire. After spending the night there, they were ready to depart for their overseas destination, which was unknown. Headley was given a sealed envelope marked "secret" and was told not to open it before leaving the continental United States. Upon leaving the U.S. from Presque Isle, Maine, the envelope was opened, and they found they had been assigned to the 8th Air Force in England. This was on September 10, 1944. Their first stop was Goosebay, Labrador. On September 14, they left Goosebay and flew to Reykjavik, Iceland; left Iceland on the 18th for Valley Wales, arriving at Lavenham, England on September 24, 1944. They were assigned to the 487th Bomber Group, 837th squadron.

New crews leaving the States flew new bombers to their overseas destinations. However, from there the crews were assigned to different Bomber Groups, and they had to fly whatever planes were available. Headley and his crew had the good fortune to get a new plane for their first mission.

With the 487th Group, Headley flew 35 combat missions over Germany. All of the crew members were briefed before each mission. These sessions stressed flying at a high altitude and staying in formation at all times. Their primary targets were railroads to stem the flow of supplies to the German troops, and also synthetic oil plants. Secondary targets were assigned for each mission, and if both the primary and the secondary targets could not be bombed for any reason, then the bombs were dropped on a target of opportunity. When clouds obscured the primary target, they dropped their bombs by radar.

Headley's plane was hit by anti-aircraft fire on some missions, but there was never any serious damage to the plane, nor were any of the crew members injured. They always returned home safely.

The mission on December 24, 1944 was led by General Castle, Commander of the 4th Bombardment Wing. He insisted on flying as the lead bomber with the 487th that day, leading 2,000 bombers and 1,000 fighter planes. Their targets were the Luftwaffe fields and communications centers to interrupt information and air support for the German offensive in the Ardennes.

At 23,000 feet over Belgium, Castle's plane was hit. Two more hits set his engine on fire and damaged the controls. Then, the right wing tank exploded and the plane spun out of control, killing Castle and the pilot. A total of nine planes were lost that day. Headley was flying in the third group behind Castle. Usually, the lead plane of each squadron was the only one equipped with radar, with one other back up in the group.

After completing the required number of missions in February of 1945, Headley returned home on board the Troop Transport, U.S.S. *General Gordon*. On board were 1,000 army ground troops that were being sent home due to injuries, and 200 men from the Army Air Corps. They departed from South Hampton, England and landed at the New York City Harbor.

A visit home was the first thing on the agenda. Headley had his first meeting with his new three-month old daughter in March 1945. She was born on December 4, 1944.

He then served another year with the Air Transport Command. During the first six months, he was stationed at Memphis, Tennessee serving as a ferry pilot. It was his duty to transport planes to wherever they were needed.

In the fall of 1945, he was reassigned to Fairfield, California. Here, he served as a Foreign Transport pilot, flying to Manila, Panama and France transporting troops, mail, cargo and U.S.O. personnel.

Headley was relived of active duty in March 1946, but remained in the reserves. In 1969, he was transferred to the retired section of the reserves and earned retirement as a Lt. Colonel.

Awards and decorations received are: The Air Medal with five Oak Leaf Clusters, European-African-Middle Eastern Campaign Medal with 3 Bronze Service Stars for the Rhineland, Ardennes and Central Europe Battle Campaigns, American Campaign Medal and World War II Victory Medal.

After being released from active duty, Headley returned to his old job with Humble Oil and Refining Company in Baytown. In 1948, he was transferred to Schulenburg, and he and his wife are still making their home there.

837TH SQUADRON

TOM VALENTINE

LEFT: *Valentine, pictured Oct. 1944 after he completed his required missions.* RIGHT: *Valentine describes what it was like to live through World War II: "Your life seems to stop until you finish your tour and are reborn."*

My name is Tom Valentine. I was a co-pilot in the 837th Squadron, and I was with the group at its inception in Alamogordo, New Mexico. I graduated from the class of 43-J at Albany, GA. in October 1943, and was sent along with many of my classmates, directly to the group, making up the crews in Salt Lake City for the 487th bomb group. The rush was on for combat crews for the 486th and the 487th. We had no formal training for the job of co-pilot (on the job training as it were). The 486th and the 487th groups were the last to join the 8th Air Force, 3rd division.

We trained in New Mexico from January 1944 until April 1944, and from there we were sent to England. We were all inexperienced, although out pilot, Dick Munson, was an excellent pilot, having flown many hours on submarine patrols.

The B-24 was a very difficult plane to fly, being unstable and underpowered. It took much physical effort to fly. It cruised at 160 mph and stalled (fell) at 150 mph with a bomb load.

The B-24 was poorly designed. There were six gasoline heaters on the flight deck which had to be turned off during combat, which meant no heat over Europe. The average temperature was minus 30 degrees, and the wind comes in the front, around the nose-turret and out the back. The gas gauges were glass and had to be drained before crossing the channel.

The maximum altitude we were able to fly was 19,000 feet. The plane first rushed along, and you felt as if the engines were the only thing holding the plane in the air. Formation flying was extremely difficult. When you saw the B-17, which flew at 30,000 feet, and even though they only flew at 150 mph, (10 miles slower than B-24), they would be passing us because of the difference in altitude and increases in the ground speed.

The B-17 crews had a saying that they would rather have the B-24 group with them than the fighter protection. The German Pilots would always pick on the B-24s because of poor formation and stragglers.

We became a lead crew in May '44 (lead plane in a squadron) with an extra navigator and new bombardier. We led our group on D-Day. We were to bomb a railroad junction in Normandy. We flew at 12,000 feet and were to fly over the invasion beaches at 6:30 a.m., the time of the landings. We were excited that we would have a grandstand view and be a part of the invasions. Imagine our disappointment when we hit the channel and it was totally undercast and we couldn't see a thing. This was the worst letdown in our lives.

A week later, we were leading a mission into France. On the bombing run, our No. 1 engine blew the pistons through the top of the engine and gray smoke poured back. We were already having trouble with the No. 2 engine. We had to dump the bombs (we were losing 300 feet a minute) so we dumped the guns, ammunition and flak suits to lighten the plane. We called the fighter planes (four P-47s came and escorted us to the channel, which is about 100 miles at Normandy). We were losing altitude steadily, but our navigator put us right on a Canadian Fighter Base (Red Hill). They welcomed us with open arms and a steak dinner.

My best friend, Paul Chavez, had somewhat the same trouble and had to bail out over occupied Belgium. He evaded capture for three months, until the American Troops came through.

We changed over to B-17s in July '44, and it was like going from a beer truck to a Cadillac. We went from the bottom in bombing accuracy to second in the 8th Air Force. The 17s were extremely reliable, easy to fly and would go to 35,000 feet empty. Most of our missions were flown at 30,000 feet.

Our targets became more difficult when we changed over, as the 8th Air Force said. The more dangerous targets would go to the 17s. The B-24s losses were higher. The 2nd Division (all B-24's) were taken off flying missions in August '44 and were assigned to flying supplies to the Army in Europe - gasoline, maps etc.

I finished my tour of 30 missions and returned to the states. I married my wife Pat in November of '44. I was assigned to Fort Myers, Florida until June of '45.

We went to Buckingham Field in Florida. The field was a gunnery school. Terrific job, flying gunnery students four hours a day. The rest of the time was just enjoying Florida. I was very fortunate to have been in the war and returned home with no wounds, mentally and physically the same.

The strangest feeling when I finished my tour, I felt guilty that I wasn't going with the group when they flew overhead on their way to Germany, although I wasn't about to volunteer for another tour.

If you are wondering what it was like to live through those times, imagine getting up at 2:00 a.m., knowing you must cross an icy pond which is cracked under your feet and some of your buddies are falling through the ice with no one to help them. Your life seems to stop until you finish your tour and are reborn.

HOWARD (PETE) M. PETERSON

I was enrolled in the University of Texas in Austin, Texas. At the time I was getting in they had a full complement of people in the pilot training, so I went into the reserves for about five months before I was called in. I was called in and sent to Shepherd Air Force Base for basic training. From there, I went to Peabody College in Nashville, Tennessee, which at the time was known as a college training detachment. They had about 600 cadets there, and we took college courses while we were waiting for classification. We were then sent to Nashville classification center, and I was classified for pilot training. From there, I was sent to Montgomery, Alabama for preflight.

How and why they chose which cadets did what job is sort of a mystery. In some cases at the classification center, people were washed out, some people were made navigators, some people were made pilots. They did give you some coordination tests, which I don't know whether that was one of the determining factors or not. They never really did reveal why you were classified as a pilot, others as navigators, others bombardiers.

We were sent to Bennettsville, South Carolina, and that's where we took our primary training. From there, you went on through basic, and whether you were going to be a fighter pilot or a bomber pilot was determined by, I think, the need. If there was a need for fighter pilots and you fit into the physical qualifications, you would then go to an advanced school for single engine. In my case, I was sent to George Field, Illinois to twin engine. Then, I knew I'd be in some type of bomber.

We were sent to Smyrna Air Force Base in Smyrna, Tennessee. There, we went into B-24s. That type of training consisted of four trainees getting into an aircraft and flying two hours apiece, so the whole shift was an eight-hour flight. During the course of that eight hours, each of the four individuals would shoot landings and do all sorts of maneuvers, but the others would sit in the back of the airplane and study. It was kind of monotonous, six hours being in the back of an airplane with somebody who is in the transition stage shooting landings and doing steep turns and various maneuvers required to get proficient in the B-24. We would study meteorology, navigation, the particular aircraft, emergency procedure and anything to do with what you'd need. Plus, you coordinated with other aircraft and did formation flying, which was a big, big item when you got overseas because you were in formation sometimes as much as eight hours in a stretch.

Sometimes, the instructor would pull the throttle on one engine before you even got off the runway. In one case, a good friend of mine was killed because one engine was pulled before they left the runway. Just after they got off the ground, another engine on the same side quit, and they crashed into the village and killed the whole crew. As a matter of fact, one of them was supposed to be the best man in my wedding.

I was sent to Westover Field, Massachusetts, and there I met the crew. The crew was from all over the country with various backgrounds. From Westover Field, where we assembled, we went to Savannah, Georgia to Chattam Field where we trained for combat. This consisted of an awful lot of formation flying, cross-country flights, night flying, and all the things you might need in combat. We did some low-level, over-water gunnery practice, but we never did get an actual simulated fighter attack in this training.

At that time we were still a B-24 crew. It wasn't until we landed at the base with the 487th Bomb Group at Lavenham, England that we found out that we were going to be flying B-17s. We went over to England on a ship that had brought German prisoners to the United States. At that time, the losses weren't as large, so all crews were not flying aircraft across. The ship hadn't been as cleaned up as it should have been. The crew was subjected to all sorts of filth and everything else. Most of them were sick for nearly the whole time going overseas. We shipped out of Brooklyn and landed on the west coast of England. When we left the U.S., we had no idea where we would go in England. After we landed at Liverpool, we took a train clear across England under combat conditions in that everything was blacked out.

The whole crew was delighted that we were converting to B-17s. It was a much more forgiving aircraft as far as the problems you have with inclement weather in England. We did have one surprise in that when our co-pilot arrived at Lavenham with the crew, he found that his brother was stationed there. We had to take transition training in B-17s where we learned to convert to B-17s. We had to do quite a bit of formation flying, linked trainer training, all sorts of training to accustom us to the B-17.

The 487th Bomb Group arrived in October of 1943. They had gone through some pretty serious and heavy losses during the time they'd been there. We replaced a crew whose pilot was named Thompson and "Happy" for short. He trained us in the aircraft that we were to get, which was called the "Piccadilly Lilly." We flew the "Piccadilly Lilly" for 13 missions and when we were on leave in London, another crew took it and we didn't see it again. We have heard since that the crew possibly made it back to England after they had been shot up, but the plane was so badly damaged that it was used for parts for other aircraft. It had landed at another base away from ours. We were assigned a brand new aircraft. The radioman on our aircraft was also an artist. We dubbed the airplane the "Queen of Hearts," and he painted the appropriate girl on a big heart. It wasn't as good an aircraft as the other one because it had too much sophisticated equipment, like a formation stick.

The Germans had made their final thrust for the Battle of the Bulge and England had been blanketed by fog for a solid week. We had been sitting there unable to get off the ground because you could not see more than a few feet. When the fog finally lifted on December 24th, it so happened that our group was chosen to lead the Eighth Air Force on the largest raid that the Air Force ever had flown. The Air Force was led by a General. When the group was chosen to lead the Air Force, General Castle was assigned to the lead aircraft. Every aircraft where it was possible to get off the ground was used that day. Since our group was the leader of the Air Force, the Germans, who had saved up all of their gasoline and ammunition and so forth for one last stand, attacked our group, and General Castle was shot down and killed. Our group lost 12 out of 36 aircraft. Some of them probably became prisoners of war, but we never really knew of their fate. I'm sure there has been research done on that and somebody has those statistics. But the fact that we were flying our first mission, the pilot of the crew always flew with an experienced pilot, so I was co-pilot to a Captain Smith from Kansas. Captain Smith had been on too many missions, and during the course of the mission he was on the radio in contact with all the other aircraft that were going down and so forth. So he got quite disturbed and was unable to continue to fly the aircraft. I was given controls and he thought I was quite cool, but it was just due to the fact that I was on intercom and didn't realize the gravity of the situation. I was given a Distinguished Flying Cross, which I admittedly don't feel like I deserve.

We were one of the crews that did make it. It is a rather impersonal war in that unless your crew is wounded-and we were very fortunate that nobody was wounded - you don't see the problems that occur. So we didn't experience that directly. The crew was pretty well shook up. But I will say that our crew felt that they were blessed. They have always said that. They felt that somebody was looking out after them. They were always optimistic, and this wasn't the case with a lot of crews. I was always very proud of them, and I'm still proud of them today because all of them have come back from the war. They all have made a great success of their lives.

They would wake us up around four o'clock in the morning to go to briefing. At that time, the curtain is drawn and you are shown the target. Well, of course, if it's a rough target, the Kaopectate is brought out, and it does affect those, particularly those who have been to a rough target. You are briefed and told the course you are going to take. The course is not a direct course because during the previous missions flak areas have been plotted so that the course you take is usually on a zigzag route that avoids the heavy flak areas. The course lengthens the missions so that sometimes the biggest problem you have is fuel. When you leave the briefing room, you check the aircraft over. Everybody gets on board and waits for the signal from the tower to taxi out or, if there is radio contact, you would be given an audio signal. When you taxi out, you're in line with all the other airplanes and as you come up you take off at about 30-second intervals. After you take off, you have to assemble into formation. That is done by a radio beacon that you circle. The leader starts circling the beacon and his wing men form on him. Then, the second echelon of three forms under him. The leader of the second echelon is where we flew. Then, there is a third echelon with a wing man on each of the wings of the leader that forms underneath them. After all these are formed into the squadron, then it is formed into the group. Three or four squadrons in the group, and the squadrons are stacked in a sort of ladder arrangement. The wing is formed by several groups to the target. What it amounts to is that everybody had to come over an initial point at an exact time so that you're not over there with 36 airplanes at the same time. Well, as you leave for the enemy territory you're in groups, wings and air-forces. If you're all going to the same target, you would all fly along the same quarters in intervals of just a few minutes apart. When you get near the target area you come to what they call the initial point. That is the point at which the bomb groups turn to the target in squadrons. In other words, they peel off in squadrons and they bomb as squadrons. Over this initial point as the squadrons peel off toward the target, there can be no deviation from the course. There can be no evasive action from flak or anything else because the bombardier is in control in the lead aircraft. When the bombardier in the lead aircraft drops his bombs, everybody else drops at the same time, so that a pattern of bombs come down on the target from each of the squadrons.

After the bombs are dropped, it is necessary for the group to reform as a group. The reason for having the group formation stacked like it is for fire power. The more guns you can train in this pattern, the better off you'll be under a fighter attack. As a matter of fact, in most cases, the enemy would not attack a group that was in excellent formation.

Towards the end of the war, they did have electric flying suits. Those were good because they gave you more freedom. As you approached enemy territory, you put on what they called "flak apron." It was a big heavy thing that covered the whole front. Of course, your back was protected by the steel seat. Then, you wore a helmet that looked sort of like a German WWI helmet. The glamorous things you see in the movies of pilots with a fresh hat and all, this really, as you go into combat, is not very practical. We would also wear an oxygen mask. You sort of looked like a turtle sitting in a seat. I wore an electric flying suit with electric boots and just a lighter flying suit over that. It wasn't that practical if you have to bail out, and particularly if you had to experience extremely cold weather when you hit the ground. Fortunately, we didn't have to bail out and I didn't have to put up with that problem. If you wore the lighter equipment, it did give you more flexibility to move about. There was always a problem of using a relief tube in the back of the aircraft. You had to put on an oxygen tank that you could carry and go through the bomb bay to the back of the airplane. There is another thing that people think, that you're free to talk to each other during the course of the mission, and that just isn't the case. You can talk through the intercom, but you are restricted from doing much by the fact that the pilot and the co-pilot are setting their flying close formation and they're so busy that they really don't have time for these glamorous things like you see in the movies.

I'd say the average bombing altitude was between 24 and 25,000 feet. Sometimes, when you were forming into your squadrons and your groups over England, you would form vapor trails. I'm sure most people have seen pictures of vapor trails from combat aircraft. Sometimes, you would be forming and you'd form so many vapor trails that the visibility would get so bad that you'd have to keep moving up to keep reforming. We would climb all the way across the English Channel and try to be at our bombing altitude by the time we got over enemy territory. The bombing altitude was usually about 25,000 feet, but in one case we were going to bomb Hamburg and we were encountering considerable flak. The group commander chose to climb, and we got to 29,000 feet. The navigator reported ground speed of about 300 mph, and we always bombed at 150 mph indicated airspeed. This was our first encounter with the jet stream. When we left the target and turned back, we had to lose altitude to get back because we were making no progress as we came off the target and into the jet stream, which we had benefited from on the way in.

We flew the full 35 missions, which was the amount you were supposed to fly at that time. After 35, we were there about a week, and we were being shipped out of South Hampton, England, when the European war came to a close. They let us go to London for VE night.

We went to Berlin twice. Of course, by the time we went to Berlin, it was quite torn up. Fortunately, on one of the Berlin missions (it was a visual mission), we did get glimpses of the destruction. Probably our longest mission was to Dresden. That was toward the end of the war. We did go to Kiel in an attempt to get one of the German ships. I don't recall which one it was. We went to Nuremberg a couple times and Cologne. We headed for Norway once, but we had to turn back because we lost an engine. We went to several of the Ruhr Valley's smaller towns. Our last mission, we did go to a railroad yard near Czechoslovakia. On that mission, they had moved in rail cars with guns on them. This hadn't been anticipated so we went in at 12,000 feet. We caught a lot of flak in which the leader of our squadron was hit and both the right engines were on fire. The crew bailed out. This was quite a traumatic experience for our crew because we could see the people come by our aircraft very close. Some of them failed to get their parachutes snapped to the parachute harness properly, and so we knew they didn't make it.

We had some fighter attacks, but our group flew such good formation, and it was demanded of us, that other groups were losing aircraft where we weren't. We did get attacked by the German jet that was new to the European Theater, but it didn't do any damage. Lloyd, our ball-turret operator, thinks that he shot it down. We do not have a confirmation. I think that Lloyd was quite proud of the fact that he at least thought that he had gotten the German jet.

There was always a debriefing routine. Of course, the navigator had plotted where flak was encountered. This was important for future missions. They wanted to know any unusual circumstances that you encountered on the mission. I think they were also evaluating your emotions and so forth.

In the time period that we were in the European Theater, the losses had been cut considerably. We realized the losses when they would pick up the crew member's belongings from your quonset hut. It was kind of a matter that when you came in and landed, if another crew had been shot up you didn't see the goriness of that because that would be removed off to the side, so we usually escaped that. Whether that was done purposefully or not, I do not know.

We didn't have a bombardier in our aircraft. Because we bombed in a pattern by squadrons, bombardiers weren't necessary in all the aircraft. The lead and his wingman on the right both had bombardiers. The wingman took over in case the lead was shot down. The navigators and co-pilot and pilot were all trained in the use of the bomb site so that we could take over in case of an emergency. Early crews had 10 men, but ours was a nine-man crew.

One of the biggest problems that we had during our combat was the English weather. You hardly ever had good flying weather in England. When you were coming back with airplanes in a group formation, all low on fuel and you encountered a real serious weather condition, it was a matter of airplanes trying to get into this little English air field. You came over the radio signal that was your signal for the base and you peeled off of formation so that airplanes were peeling off at very close intervals homing on the beacon and you would often encounter heavy prop wash. You might be completely on instruments, and you didn't really know where some of the other aircraft might be. We didn't have an instrument landing procedure and probably wouldn't have had enough fuel to go through that procedure anyway. Mortars were shot off at the end of the runway. If you saw one of the mortars in the clouds you would dump all your power and do your best to get into the runway. One of the biggest problems was trying to get into this base along with all of the other airplanes. If the base got socked in completely to where there was no chance for you to get in, they did have a base in which they had 10,000 feet of asphalt runway. On each end of that runway, they had 5,000 more feet. They had a ditch around the whole runway complex that they could pour gasoline in and light a fire in order to get airplanes in under the worst conditions. We never did, but some of the crews did have to go to that base and then it was a matter of getting back to your home base. It was also a common occurrence in this area where bases were so close together that planes would actually land at the wrong base. Of course, this was rather embarrassing, but if you could get into a base sometimes, it was your only choice.

ALAN H. WHEASLER

Wheasler's crew completed its 35th and final mission and was waiting its trip home when the war ended in Germany.

My name is Alan Wheasler, Indianapolis, Indiana. As a young man, I made model airplanes and was very interested in flying. After the war broke out, I was drafted into the Army and was sent to the infantry. During basic training, I learned that they wanted air crewmen. I applied for consideration for aviation duty. After a lot of mental and physical tests, I was accepted. After my basic training in the infantry, I was sent to a college for five months of study and then further tests. We had a lot of mental tests, physical and psychological tests. At this time, you were placed in training for bombardier, navigator or pilot. I was accepted into pilot training and sent to primary flight training in a biplane, which is an open-cockpit plane. I saw it for the first time, and it was very thrilling to pilot an airplane by myself. One of the students was flying, and the instructor had him make a loop. He hadn't fastened his seat belt, and when he was upside down, he fell out. The instructor landed the plane, and the student was picked up uninjured. He was placed immediately back in the airplane and forced to perform another loop successfully. This is done to make sure the experience hadn't made the student afraid of flying.

We then went on to basic flight training for more acrobatics. I had wanted to fly in fighters; however, I was given twin-engine training, and I believe then I was destined to be in bombers. I don't know how they pick men for bombers, but since I was tall, this might have been the reason. Also, bombers were in big demand at that time. More bomber pilots were needed, as it took two pilots in a bomber and only one in a fighter. I went on to advanced flight where we received more instrument flying, night flying and formation training. After about

837TH SQUADRON

a year of flight training, I graduated. I was then sent to a base where I was assigned to Howard Peterson's crew as a co-pilot. At this time, members were assigned as navigators, radio operator, engineer, nose gunner, waist gunner, tail gunner, and ball-turret gunner. Altogether, we had a crew of nine men. We were sent to Savannah, Georgia for more training in B-24s.

We trained in formation flying for practice missions. We'd go out over the ocean and the crews could practice firing their guns. We also dropped practice bombs. We also made 1,000-mile over-water flight so that the navigator could practice navigation by the sun and the stars. All this was done to practice functioning as a team. After about three months, we were prepared for embarkation. We received more shots and were briefed for overseas duty.

We left on a convoy ship for England, which took 10 days to two weeks. The ship was crowded, and some men were seasick. In times of bad weather, the men were below deck, and at times it was rough. As we got closer to England, there were more submarine alerts. We landed at Liverpool and were then placed on trains to a small base where we were assigned to bomb groups as replacements for other crews. At that time, you had to fly 35 missions over enemy territory and then sent back to the states. We received more shots and were advised as to which bomb group we were assigned. Then, I was surprised to learn that I would be going to the 487th Bomb Group, where my younger brother was assigned as a gunner. We arrived late in the evening and learned that this was a B-17 group, and we had been trained in B-24s. I inquired at headquarters about my brother and, apparently, headquarters had notified him that I was at the base. Since everything was blacked out, I knew I couldn't find him that night. About an hour later, my brother arrived at headquarters and we had a very joyful reunion. He was just finishing his tour of duty, so he decided to take an assignment as a gunnery instructor to remain in England with me.

Since we had been trained in B-24s, we had to transition to B-17s. It was not difficult; however, it did take about two weeks of lectures and flying to learn the difference in the systems of the two aircraft. We practiced more flying in formation and working as a team. About the middle of December, we were ready for combat. At that time, bad weather had arrived over Germany and France and we were unable to fly. The Germans proceeded to attack in what was known as the Battle of the Bulge. Since we couldn't give our troops any air support, it created quite a battle.

On the 24th day in December, the weather cleared. It was a very big day for the Eighth Air Force. Every airplane that could fly was put in the air, creating over 1,000 bombers in the air. Our group, with General Castle, was assigned to lead the entire Eighth Air Force. This was the first mission for our crew, but I was not with them. The first mission is to be flown with an experienced pilot, and our pilot was to be flying as co-pilot, so I remained on the ground.

Normally, the German aircraft didn't attack until we were over enemy territory, but the Germans expected this and attacked before we received our fighter escort. They attacked the group, and 13 planes were shot down from the group. Some bailed out or landed in friendly territory. However, General Castle's plane was shot down. He and the other members of his crew were killed.

The next few weeks were very hectic. We flew 13 combat missions and many unknown practice missions before we received our first leave into London. London was quite an experience. This was our first real contact with the English people. The English people were friendly, and I believe we were well received. We went to Westminster Abbey, saw Buckingham Palace and other sites. We ate at different restaurants and local pubs. The English food was different, but very good. London was bombed heavily, and it suffered a lot. However, their spirits were high. They seemed to have very little fear. Sometimes on leave, we would hear and feel the V-bombs exploding.

When you were assigned a mission, you would be awakened about two in the morning. We would eat breakfast, then briefing. We'd be shown the target, altitude, time for takeoff and the position you would be flying in the formation. We then would go to the airplane and prepare the plane for the mission. We would takeoff about 6 a.m., climb to a certain altitude over England with the rest of the squadrons, and then assemble into groups. Usually, there would be 13 planes in a squadron and three squadrons for the group. Sometimes, there would be four squadrons. Then, the whole group would assemble into a wing and depart for Germany. The groups would be about 10 miles apart. By this time, we had been in the air about two or three hours. We would all start climbing so that we would be at the appropriate altitude for bombing by the time we arrived in enemy territory, which is usually 29-30,000 feet. Once we reached our initial point we could not deviate from our course. The bomb run was maybe 10-20 miles long. The plane had to be level and straight or you could possibly miss the target. Usually, this is when the anti-aircraft fire would start. The sky would be black from exploding ant-aircraft shells. After the bomb drop, we would usually dive about 1,000 feet and turn for home. Again, there was anti-aircraft fire and possibly enemy fighters on the way in and out. After we would get back in friendly territory, we could relax a little bit; however, we would still be in formation.

The duties of the co-pilot were similar to a pilot. I had to monitor instruments to see if they performed properly. Also, when not flying I had to look out for enemy fighters and maintain contact with the crew by intercom. We would check on the crew about every 15-20 minutes for any problems. The pilot maintained contact with the group or squadron leader. The radio operator maintained contact with the home base. The pilot and myself would exchange flying formation every 15 minutes because formation flying is very demanding. You have to focus your vision on the plane you are following. Depending on your position in the formation, you may have planes above you, below you, and on each wing. Once back over the base we would land in sequence and go in for debriefing. We would be questioned on what we observed from enemy fighters, airplanes that were shot down, and any other pertinent information that we had seen. A typical mission was about 10 hours of flying.

After a dinner you could relax, write letters, we received our mail, and checked to see if we were assigned for a mission the next day. If so, we had to get some sleep. If not, we could go to the officers club for some relaxation. Sometimes we could walk into the town of Lavenham and go to the local pub.

On one of our missions, we were having trouble with our hydraulic pump that supplied our brakes. As we were taxing out on to the runway for takeoff, our brakes failed. To avoid other aircraft, we went off the runway and into the mud. The airplane was stuck in the mud, and because of the heavy weight, it took two half-tracks to pull us out. Needless to say, we were delayed and didn't fly that day. My brother always checked all the planes coming back, and he didn't observe my plane returning. He was quite distressed until he found out we didn't go. He then became angered with me because I hadn't told him.

On the crews 35th mission - my 34th - we were bombing a railroad yard in a small town in Germany. There wasn't to be much anti-aircraft fire and we would be bombing at 10,000 feet for more accuracy. At that time, we were flying section lead, where we would be just below the leader. There were planes on each wing and three other planes just below us. We received very heavy anti-aircraft fire all the way in and out. The fire was so heavy you could feel the concussion below us, and the smoke from the explosions was entering the cockpit from the open bomb bay. Just as we dropped our bombs, the leader was hit in the bomb bay and caught fire. We moved to the right and observed some of the crew bail out from the rear of the plane. I observed one man jump out and just missed our wing tip. Another opened his chute and just barely floated over our plane. No one seemed to be emerging from the front of the plane and the plane exploded.

Since I didn't go on the first mission, I had to go on one more with another crew. Some of my crew wanted to volunteer to fly with me on my last mission, but I didn't want them to endanger their lives. The crew I did fly with didn't have much experience, and I must say that I didn't see much discipline in that crew or any teamwork.

Our quarters were small. They were little quonset huts, and there was very little heat. It doesn't get real cold in England, but with the moisture present, it feels very cold. There was very little hot water for showers. The meals were adequate. We had a lot of powdered eggs. One good thing was that when we flew missions, we were served fresh eggs. You had powdered milk, as the English milk was not pasteurized and the army didn't want us to drink it.

I believe we were well received by the English people, although I never had too much close contact with them. One time we had to land in a rural air force base because of bad weather at our home base. We stayed overnight, had dinner and were very well received. They did everything they could to make us comfortable.

After we were there for about three months, they sent us to a rest home for a week. It was a large British estate that the army had leased. The Red Cross operated it for them. It was a mammoth building with large bedrooms, hallways and sitting rooms. They had a small lake where we could row a boat, fish, hike in the woods or in the fields. They had several farm animals and we could walk around the countryside and visit some of the small villages in the area. We were served some of the best meals we ever had in the Army. After that rest, we went back to flying missions to Germany.

Our crew seemed to live a charmed life. No one was injured, but we did receive several holes in our aircraft. One time, a piece of anti-aircraft shell came through the nose of the airplane and struck my rudder petal, saving me from any injury. We completed our 35 missions and were relocated back to the United States. While we were waiting to go home the war with Germany ceased. The night the war was over in Europe, we had a big celebration.

I was then sent to Edinburgh, Scotland and embarked on a larger ship than I went over on. It only took us five days, and it was a very pleasant trip. We arrived in New York as one of the first ships to arrive after the cessation of hostilities. They welcomed us with fireboats spraying water and very much celebration. There were large bands playing. My brother and I had a leave to go home and shortly after that, I was released from active duty and was home when the war ended in Japan.

In the last 10 years, our crew has had several reunions.

DAVID B. DAHLBERG

Dahlberg described himself as "a little heavy" during his service - 118 lbs. Our last mission, our 35th mission, was to Nurenberg, which was a railroad yard on the outskirts of the city.

This is Dave Dahlberg, flight engineer/gunner aboard the Howard Peterson crew. My rank while in the service when I left was Tech Sergeant. My job was that of a flight engineer. I monitored the mechanical things on a B-17, plus acted as a gunner on a B-17. Before being assigned to the Peterson crew, I went through gunnery school in 1942. If at that time I had gone overseas, I would have been dead by now, because losses were huge in that period of time. I later was shipped to radio school, where I graduated. Then to mechanic's school, where I graduated at Keesler Field. That is the height of my training before being assigned to the Peterson crew as a flight engineer.

During our time with the Peterson crew, we trained at Chatham Field, Georgia, to become a crew on a B-24. The same members that were assigned to the crew at that time stayed all the way through our tour in Europe and completed our trip there. During our time there, we learned to work as a group, and each person doing his assigned job and getting together as a group. The pilot is the overall command officer and takes responsibility for the whole crew and its activities. As a flight engineer, I felt that I took charge of the enlisted men and conveyed the information the pilot had that affected the enlisted men. From Chatham Field, we were shipped north to Mitchell Field, Long Island. Half the crews flew over to Europe, but our crew was in the other half who went by boat. We all went over on the USS *General Brooks*, which was a small troop ship that carried about 5,000 soldiers. Most of the soldiers were engineers and construction workers, but there were about 25 crews aboard that ship - Air Force crews.

When we arrived in Europe, we had to make a transition from B-24s to B-17s. The biggest job was for our pilot and co-pilot. It was entirely a new airplane, and they had no time in it at all before getting there. For the rest of the crew, the B-17 transition could be made fairly easily. Basically, the rest of the crew was little affected. During the time we flew our missions, we would wake up in the morning. We would have what you'd call a "red alert." There was a light, which was red, and if that was on, you had an alert for the next morning. You knew that the crews were going to fly. There was a good chance, if there was a maximum alert, that everybody would be flying. They would fly as many airplanes as they could depending on the target. We would go to breakfast and we would draw out our flight clothes, parachutes and the like. We would go from there and get our gun barrels, which we cleaned, and we would take them over and install them in our turrets. Meanwhile, we would go to briefing. During the briefing, we would learn what the target was and what we could expect from antiaircraft, how many guns were there and whether or not the Luftwaffe would attack us during the flight and what kind of fighter support we could get, depending on the target, the distance and how far we'd go, how much fuel we'd have and what we'd have to do for the day. So when we finished the briefing, we would go out to the airplane and install our guns and just generally get ready. Then, we would leave the ground and we would form over England. England's always overcast, so we would go up to about 15,000 feet and we'd be up above the clouds. Up there, the sun is always shining and so we would always see the sun. We would get up at 15,000 feet, and we would form by groups, squadrons, wings and then the whole Eighth Air Force, and we would start across the Channel to bomb our targets.

All missions were not basically the same because the more important the mission was, the more heavily armed it was on the ground, so you could expect more flak, and it would be more heavily defended and you'd expect more German fighters. The main targets of the Eighth Air Force were strategic targets, which we figured were important. What we were trying to do was break the German's ability to wage war by destroying ball bearings, oil and things of that nature. We would also bomb railroad yards, shipping, submarine pins and that sort of thing, too. But basically, it was industry that we were trying to put a stop to. There were some bombing aircraft factories and things like that, but that was not a high priority. The British wanted us to bomb aircraft factories and places where they made airplanes because they didn't want airplanes to fly back over to Britain. But the Americans wanted to put a stop to the Germans' ability to wage war by hitting heavy industry and oil targets and the like. The American army wanted the Eighth Air Force to provide support for its troops, but the Eighth Air Force was committed to a program of strategic bombing, which was to interfere with the ability of the Germans to wage war. They did do the other jobs as well, but they tried to stay right on target and complete that.

The type of flight gear we wore at the time I was there were heated suits. Originally they wore fleeced lined suits, heavy suits. They were hard to maneuver in, hard to move around in, and they were not too warm. The temperature up there was about 65 below, so it was not conducive to keeping too warm. When we were there, we used heated suits; the heated suits worked pretty effectively. You had to be plugged in, along with your oxygen and your radio equipment, but the heated suits worked. The problem was when they short circuited or there was a short across, it burned the hell out of you. But other than that, they were effective.

By the time we got to England, the Americans controlled the air. This meant that they could send P-51s with us with auxiliary gas tanks. They could follow us all the way to Berlin if they had to. They would stay with us and they could drop their tanks and get enough gas to get home. Before that, the Air Force could only escort you a short ways and then they'd have to go back to refuel. So once we controlled the air, the Germans had a very hard time to compete. Also, because of the lack of oil, the Germans were having their own problems. The head of the Luftwaffe told us in St. Paul a few years later that they would train their pilots on the ground because they didn't have enough fuel to send them up. So when the pilot first got in an airplane to fly, that was his first flight. He had trained on the ground, but they didn't have the fuel, so the first time he flew, he went right into combat without much training.

As a gunner, we would test our guns when we were up over the North Sea when we were forming, then we were ready. Once we were attacked, it was up to each gunner to make his own decision. He would fire when he wanted to. Usually, the enemy aircraft was called out over the intercom. The word would come over the intercom, "fighter at two o'clock," etc. In most cases, all the gunners would be alerted to an aircraft and whoever could see it could fire at it, depending on which way it was attacking. Generally, the Germans liked to attack straight across the front. They liked to come right at the co-pilot and pilot. That's the decision that they make, and that's the decision that they usually follow in their attack - straight at you and attack the pilot and co-pilot.

Our last mission, our 35th mission, was to Nuremberg, which was a railroad yard on the outskirts of the city. The Germans have all their railroad yards on the outskirts of the city. We were briefed that there would be no flak there. I can't remember exactly, but I think we were flying rather low (usually we flew at about 31,000 feet), but because of that I think we were down to about 18,000 feet. The Germans had moved in 88 anti-aircraft guns on railroad cars. When we were about 10 miles away, I called out to the pilot that I could see the flak up there coming already. So there was flak right there. When we approached the target the ship that was flying number one was hit, and we were flying number four locked up underneath. The crew started to bail out, and the one that struck me was a guy who was up at the door to get ready to bail out. Somebody pushed him and he went right out the door, but his chute rolled right over his head because he hadn't gotten it attached yet. On a chest chute, you just snap them in place and he hadn't gotten his snapped in place yet. He went out without his chute. I remember that very vividly because the guy rolled right over my turret.

The type of living facilities we had were quonset huts. We were given one can of coal, a small can of coal, like a four-quart can of coal, and that was supposed to take care of you for the whole day. It was never enough to even warm up the thing, but that was it. At the time we were there, the British had very little food. Our accommodations and food on the bases were fine, but when you were in town, there was very little to eat and very little that you could buy in the way of food, no matter how much money you had. It was not very good, but the facilities on the base, as far as food and so forth, were good. The usual recreation was that we would go to London and maybe take in a movie or a show and see the girls, see the night life. We would go to the Covered Gardens, where they had great big dances. The British girls would stand in the middle and they would cut in on the other girls, whoever you were dancing with. If they wanted to dance with you, they all stand out and cut in. For airmen, it was a great time. That was the type of recreation that we had. Most crew members stuck fairly close together. They would separate some, but generally we stayed pretty close together. The enlisted men stayed together, and the officers stayed together. Sometimes, officers and enlisted men would be together, but usually they remained separate.

When we were at the local base, we would go over to the Swan Hotel, which of course is still standing, and I visited there last year in England. We would go there and have drinks at night. During this time, England had a blackout. Also, all street signs would be removed so Germans couldn't find their way. We would take a shortcut across the field and run through the fields and back to the base. There was a land army camp there. A land army was girls who would do harvesting and that sort of thing during the war. If they couldn't serve in the regular service, then they used them for land army girls to harvest crops and stuff. They were close to the bases, so that was part of the entertainment that was available.

The only real contact we had with the RAF was when we saw them in England every once in a while. One time, we did land at an RAF base and they gave us a tour of their airplanes. They were doing all the night flying. They did not fly formation. They flew all different altitudes and all different speeds, and they would come across a target in all different directions. They would have target markers who would stay right in the area there and drop flares for half an hour when they were bombing a target. The rest of the guys would fly in there and drop their bombs. The thing that impressed us is that we were being rotated at 30, 35, 25 missions and the RAF, by then, since they had been in the war for so long, had like 500 and some missions. It was just a never-ending thing for them. They didn't have a set number of missions that they could be rotated. It was almost like a death sentence. You just kept going until you got it. But they had .30 caliber machine guns in their airplanes, where we had .50 caliber. They were impressed by our guns. They would say, "Look at the size of that "beaut."

837TH SQUADRON

The size of our guns was impressive to them. They were flying at night, and you would see the lights from the tracer bullets. At night, it is a diffcrent kind of a thing than it is in the daytime. There was one time when we had contact with the British. We stayed overnight there and then flew back to our base the next day.

When you completed your missions you were sort of a casual thing waiting for the army to make up its mind what to do with you. We completed our 35th mission and we went on leave. I forgot to mention that halfway through the tour, you are also sent on what they call "flak leave." By the time you're halfway done, you need a leave. You get kind of crazy, and everybody's got a hang-up on the missions and everybody's nervous, so they send you on flak leave. We went to Henley on Thames, which was the old Prince's Palace. It is now a sports club where they serve dinner. It is a very expensive place, but it is where they have the Henley Regatta right on the river. We went up there, and it was staffed by the Red Cross. They would give you civilian clothes. We would have blue clothes, a shirt and pants and sweats that we could wear. For a week, all you would do was eat and sleep and whatever recreation you wanted. You could ride bikes, or this or that. You would do that, and then you would be returned and finish your tour.

I came back on the Il de France. When we went over on the USS *General Brooks*, it took 18 days to go overseas in convoy. When we came back, we came back in three days. So it was quite a difference. I landed in New York on VE Day. Although it was a wonderful time of celebration, I didn't get to celebrate much because we were with a bunch of troops and we had to stay there. They didn't release us or anything. So we couldn't do anything. On the ship back, I went through Fort Snelling, and then we went on leave for 30 days. They gave you a 30-day leave when you came back. I went from there to a rest camp in San Anna, California, where they had double-regular rations. They had all kinds of fruits and vegetables and everything. You could eat all you wanted. The food was very, very good - excellent. In fact, that's the finest food I ever received in the Army. This was to get you built back up and ready for reassignment.

I went from there to Chanute Field, and from Chanate Field I went to Langley Field. From Langley Field, I went to Sioux Falls, where I was discharged. During the time that I was in the service, I was stationed at about 27 different bases, which meant I was moving all the time in three and a half years. One time, when I was shipped from Salt Lake City to Gager Field, I got pneumonia. I went on sick call there, and they sent me over to the hospital at Fort George Wright. I was so sick then, and they tell you to stand up, and I couldn't stand up. Finally, I got up there and they put me in the hospital. I had pneumonia, so I forget exactly how long I was there - a couple of weeks or something. When I came out, my outfit had shipped out. I didn't have anything except for the clothes I was wearing when I went into the hospital. I went over to the company headquarters and I said, "Where's my stuff? Where's the clothing and everything?" They said, "Well, your outfit's gone. They shipped out to Eprath, Washington." I says, "Well, how do I get to Eprath?" And they said, "We don't know. That's not our responsibility. Your outfit's gone, and we don't have anything to do with your outfit." I said, "Hey, I don't have any clothes, I don't have any money, I don't have nothing." Finally, they agreed to get me a train ticket out to Eprath.

They shipped me out there, and when I got there, they were living in tents. There were outdoor latrines, and they had trenches for latrines. They had tents out there in the middle of the desert in Washington. So I went over to the tent, and I said, "Where's my outfit?" They said, "Well, they've gone out to Blithe, California." I said, "Well, I don't have any clothes or anything." And the guys says, "Well, you'll have to get a mess kit to eat." He said, "You'll have to get that." I said, "Well, I don't have anything. How do I get that?" He said, "Well, you'll have to see the mess sergeant and have him give you a mess kit. Then we'll have to get a supply sergeant and get you some clothes." I said, "Yeah, but where is all my stuff?" He said it's all gone to Blithe, California. I said, "Oh, I'm going to Blithe?" They said, "No. You're going to Rapid City, South Dakota. Your outfit went to Blithe, but you're going to Rapid City, South Dakota." So, I went to Rapid City, South Dakota shortly thereafter, and it took a full year for my clothes that were sent to Blithe, California to catch up with me. So that is one of the things that was very interesting.

Our crew was very fortunate. We survived the 35 missions. In fact, we just got the report from all the crews down during WWII in the 487th Bomb Group, and they did an extensive search on where they were killed and what happened to the different flyers, including General Castle, who was shot down on our first mission. There were seven bombers from our group that went down out of 13 total planes on that mission, and General Castle received the Medal of Honor for that mission. In covering this information, we found that the original ship we flew was "Piccadilly Lilly." We flew that for 22 missions, and we quit flying that, and two days later it was shot down. We were flying the Queen of Hearts for the rest of our missions. Two days after we finished the Queen of Hearts, it was shot down. It's a matter of fate, but it's also a matter of luck that a crew can count on. Crews are very superstitious, and you'll begin to believe that you are lucky. You'll maintain that until something else happens that changes that. We try to keep in contact, particularly Pete and myself. We try to, at least once a year, send everybody a Christmas card and keep track of them. When we were a crew, our ages ranged from about 21 to 17. This wasn't an old man's war. Anybody that was 27 or 28 years old looked like a grandpa to these air crews. The Eighth Air Force suffered 50,000 casualties during WWII. We had 28,000 men in prison camps, and we made the sacrifices and we paid the price, but we did the job. The Germans never turned back the Eighth Air Force, and the Eighth Air Force never failed to complete a mission once it started. Some missions were scrubbed because of the weather or something, but once a mission was started, the Eighth Air Force never failed to complete the mission. We did suffer some horrendous losses, but we did do the job.

That's about all from here.

838th Squadron Introduction

The first three men were in the same crew flying the "Red Growler" out of their base in Lavenham, England. The first chapter is that of Julian Messerly, who was a good friend of my dad's. He was one who paid that supreme sacrifice, having drowned in the English Channel on May 30, 1944 when their B-24 ditched due to flak damage. Therefore, I have put his chapter at the beginning of this squadron. Read his personal diary entries, given to me by Laura Richman, Julian's niece.

This squadron is especially personal to me because the second chapter is that of my father, Tommy Craig, from whom I drew the love of my country, respect for all servicemen and the deep-rooted values to never forget the supreme sacrifice that many of those men made - their lives! My dad was an engineer and waist gunner who received the Purple Heart along with the EAMET Campaign Medal with eight Bronze Service Stars.

Richard Atkins, their co-pilot, I called to interview on the telephone three weeks before he passed away. He was the last living member of my dad's crew.

Pete Riegel's story was told to his family and sent to me for his chapter. His story about a World War II pilot, captain and operations officer is riveting. The next account will be my personal interview of Henry Hughey, who helped me line up all the interviews I did at the 487th Bomb Group reunion in Omaha, Nebraska, where I began my book. Henry was a ball-turret gunner on a B-17 and flew 32 missions. Read about how his plane had to make an emergency landing when they lost a third engine - later to realize their landing spot was a German mine field. The tail gunner of Hughey's crew is the next chapter - that of James Spurlock. He flew 32 missions on the B-17. He wrote, "I would be a fool to say I was never frightened. But when you were flying over the different targets and your anti-aircraft were going off all around you, you had to be afraid."

Roy Hon is the very emotional interview of a tail gunner's story. He says, "I love the reunions, and I love the men. We're a band of brothers so to speak. It's great." Read his experience with the 487th and his future years of experience with a Strategic Air Command group that was carrying the A-bomb. Hon and the man interviewed for the next chapter, Art Silva, were crew members. Silva was a waist gunner, and in his chapter, he tells several stories of how relatives of several men killed in action discovered how they died. He speaks of the flight surgeon, Dr. Lerner, and that chapter you'll read next. Dr. Lerner says, "I could never understand what kept them going. Perhaps seeing some crews making it to number 35 and the youthful sense of immortality and duty gave these men the will to complete their missions." No one could describe these feelings better than the veterans themselves.

William Bowers is the next chapter, that of a technical sergeant and radio gunner on B-17s. He says, "The December 24, 1944 mission to the Ardennes, in support of the Battle of the Bulge, when the 8th Air Force launched the mightiest Air Armada ever assembled, is one of the most vivid memories for the 487th airmen." Major Francis Eberhart's story follows, and he was a Squadron Commander. Roy Levy flew four missions with the 838th squadron, then an additional 16 missions with the 836th squadron, because his original crew was shot down while Levy was hospitalized. "The only one to get killed, in the crew that was shot down, was the young man who made everyone go to church on Sunday." This young soldier, who died, obviously made a huge impression on his fellow troops.

William Rich was a Major who didn't retire from military service until 1984. Chuck Haskett's account leaves the reader spellbound as he describes his plane under attack. The next chapter is from Mike Quering, whose feelings can only be expressed in his own words, "One of the difficult things of explaining to somebody what it's like in combat is to really get you to feel what it's like without embellishing or anything like that, but just to tell how it is. I say to you that it's hard to do if you haven't experienced it. But let me say this: you feel like you're going to jump out of your damn body and your skin. When you see the flak bursting around you and you see these fighters coming in at you, and you see the goddamn 20-millimeter shells bursting in front of you, you know you say, 'They're going to kill me, they're going to kill me.'" These were Quering's emotional words to me in his personal interview in Omaha, Nebraska concerning his involvement with the 838th Squadron.

Walter Moore is the next story in this particular squadron. He details the harrowing experience he had while shot down in enemy territory and how he made it back home safely. The last story in this squadron is that of Paul White, who tells of a chilling reunion with his flight base. When his plane didn't arrive on time, the members of the base had arranged his clothes as if he had not returned from his mission.

JULIAN MESSERLY

Messerly's crew was forced to ditch into the English Channel due to flak damage on May 30, 1944. The plane sunk with Messerly still hanging on to it, and he drowned. Information submitted by Ron Messerly, brother of Julian, and Ron's daughter, Laura Richman.

Julian graduated from High School Fort Dodge, Iowa, June 1942 and entered the Army Air Force 24 Feb. 1943. The following is his story as taken from official Army AF records, letters and conversations with the surviving crew plus his letters that were sent to family members.

24 Feb 1943: I'm going to be an aerial gunner and mechanic. As soon as I'm through with my 18 days Basic Training, I'll be going to gunnery school.

22 Mar 1943: This sure is a beautiful place, we're staying in hotels on the beach. The beach is perfect, we go swimming about three times a week. The waves are quite high and we ride them into shore. The water is chilly, but is sure is fun. I've been on guard duty two times and KP once. Washed dishes and peeled onions from 4:30 AM to 7:30 PM. I have eight days left in my basic training, before I go to gunner's school.

Apr 1943: I graduated from gunnery school 18 Apr. 43 at Tyndall Field Florida, class number 43-20. I've got my Silver Wings, a medal for expert gunnery and a promotion to Private First Class.

24 May 1943: I'm here at Sheppard Field, Texas for mechanic school. It will probably be a month before I start school and four months to go through. After that, I go to three months advanced gunnery and then the Japs better watch out.

2 June 1943: Wow, I got seven letters last night, a box of cookies from Marie, candy from Mom and a carton of cigarettes from Marvin. They sure came at the right time, because I was broke. It's nice to have lots of brothers and sisters.

29 June 1943: I've started school, and I work on the B-26 and B-25 bombers. I like the B-26 the best. It is real fast, carries a big bomb load and has lots of guns. It sure is a good ship.

11 Aug 1943: They have been keeping us awful busy. I'm in the electrical branch now studying the electrical parts of the plane and the wiring; next is carburetors, generators, magnetos, etc. I will graduate here about October 20 and hope to get a furlough around Christmas.

17 Aug 1943: I'm studying carburetors now. I still have propellers, instruments, engine operation, inspection and 10 days when we camp out and put a B-25 and B-26 together.

22 Sept 1943: I've been studying all week for a test and finally had it today. It was hard, but I managed to pass it. We are in our last branch of school, so it won't be long before I'll be leaving this field, probably by the first of November. Chuck Foote, Jim Davis and Dean Tuel, three fellows I went to High School with here, shipped down here Saturday. It was sure good to see them.

19 Oct 1943: We have been camping out in the woods, about 10 miles from camp. They have planes out there that we work on under combat conditions. They roll us out in the middle of the night and have us set up a lighting system and go to work. We have been pulling engines off and everything else. We go back out for six more days, and then we will be through school and I will be a Sergeant.

2 Nov 1943: I will be home Friday the 5th. I won't be coming through Des Moines; they have a different route mapped out for me. I hope you (Verna) and Erma can get to Fort Dodge before I go back.

1 Dec 1944: Davis Monthan Field, Tucson, Arizona. Well here I am again, only further West and South this time. I've seen a lot of the U.S. since the last time I saw you - Missouri, Kansas, Colorado, Utah, Nevada, California and Arizona. This Field is the best I have been on since I've been in the Army. Salt Lake City was sure a hellhole, it was cold and damp, we slept in tents, everyone caught colds and some ended up in the hospital.

23 Jan 1944: Alamogordo, New Mexico. Today, we had ground school in the morning and flew this afternoon from 12:30 to 6:30. There was low ceiling and the weather was rough, the roughest ride I've ever had since I've been flying. We couldn't fly over 9,000 feet because of icing conditions and low clouds. Too dangerous flying formation when you can't see anything. I was supposed to be in ground school again tonight; I didn't go and will probably catch the devil for it.

838th Squadron

28 Feb 1944: We are all through training now and will leave here soon for our POE. When I leave here, I won't be able to write for a while, so you will know what is the matter if you don't hear from me for a while. The Army will send Mom my POE address. Maybe we will be bombing Tokyo soon.

During the First, Second and Third Phase of my flying gunners training, I have had five Air to Ground Malfunction missions, operated the ball-turret four times, the top-turret 13 times, Air to Air tow missions about 20,000 ft. four times, fired 1,000 rounds ammo above 20,000 ft. and completed all my proficient checks.

1 Jan 1944: Crew members were assigned (Crew 3-D-1132). The crew were as follows: Walter W. McCarty, Richard S. Atkins, Willard J. George, Thomas W. Craig, Fred C. Sweeney, Keith E. Coles, Julian W. Messerly, Henry W. Blaha, Robert L. Williams, Raymond G. Spoerl.

The "Red Growler," a B-24h Serial number 42-52739 built by Ford Motor Co. at Willow Run, Michigan.

Thomas Craig said that the plane was named after the pilot 2nd Lt. McCarty, 23 years old, red haired, played football and growled out his orders. The crew started calling him the "Red Growler." The plane had a picture of a bulldog dressed in a football uniform carrying the bomb.

Fred Sweeney said the crew left New Mexico 16 Mar, 44 to Herrington, Kansas in preparation for overseas movement, stayed there a few days then spent the night at Macon, Georgia, then to Morrison Field, Florida. We left there 27 Mar. 1944 to Puerto Rico, Trinidad, Brazil and Dakow, Africa, Marrakech, North Africa and to Scotland and finally England on 12 Apr. 1944.

24 Apr 1944: Just a few lines to let you know I'm still OK. It is rather bad day today, cold and damp, good weather for catching a cold. I sure would like some candy and cookies if you could send some. Can't get much of that here.

30 Apr 1944: Hi, Ronnie. I suppose you will be out of school for the summer pretty soon. What do you plan to do for the summer? If you need any of the money I send home for something, use it but don't waste it. Have you heard anything from Marvin lately?

2 May 1944: The Red "Growler" is really on the ball. We are doing Okay. We have a few pictures of the crew that we are going to try and send home, but they have to be censored first. I knew all the time that Howard would be coming over soon, but he told me not to say anything. I guess Russell will probably be home on furlough by now.

24 May 1944: I just got back from pass to London today. Sure did have a good time. We went sight-seeing around London. I couldn't begin to tell you everything we saw. They have a lot of penny arcades and you could sure spend plenty of money if you've got it. I'm getting so that I

GENTLEMEN FROM HELL

like tea, and am learning how to balance a cup of tea on my knee. I've been invited out, and they usually have tea. Send me some candy in my next package.

27 May 1944: Well, here it is, Saturday night. Not the old Saturday nights like there at home. Just a gang of dead-tired guys sitting around writing letters and some in bed already and it's only about seven o'clock. Is Ronnie still working yet? I sure get a kick out of his letters. (This was the last letter that Julian's' Mom received from him.)

Combat Missions - Sgt. Messerly flew the following missions with the crew of the "Red Growler."

7 May 1944: Liege, Belgium (Marshalling yards). No planes were lost and none damaged. This was the first Mission for the 486th and 487th Bomb Group

9 May 1944: Leon Cauvron Airport, France, 487th dispatched 34 aircraft, nine received minor damage and two major damaged. This was the start of the pre-invasion bombing of enemy installations in France

11 May 1944: Troyes, France, 487th dispatched 34 aircraft, 17 received minor damage, five had major damage and three aircraft from 838th Sqdn. were shot down. The lead formation, 838th Sqdn., was led into a flak area due to navigation problems. The lead plane flown by Lt. Vratny of Fort Dodge, Iowa, was shot down. Lt. Vratny survived and currently resides in Fort Dodge. Two other aircraft from the 838th Sqdn. were also shot down. The "Red Growler," Lt. McCarty and crew landed in Southern England (Exeter) because of major damage and severe flak wound to Thomas Craig, the Engineer.

25 May 1944: Monitique Sure Sambre, Belgium. 487th dispatched 38 aircraft, six had minor and one major damage. Targets attacked were rail installations and airfields.

29 May 1944: Politz, Germany. 487th dispatched 27 aircraft, 11 received minor and three major damage. The targets were aircraft plants and oil installations. Strong enemy fighter formations opposed the bombers. The 838th Sqdn. had one shot down by enemy aircraft.

30 May 1944: Munster Germany. 487th dispatched 37 aircraft, 21 had minor and five major damage. Attacks were on aircraft industry targets. Lt. McCarty and crew were forced to ditch in English Channel due to flak damage. Aircraft ditched approximately 10 miles from Lowestoft. Sgt. Messerly, gunner, drowned before rescue arrived. Lt. George, Ssgt. Blaha and Sgt. Cole were wounded.

Missing Aircrew Report 15237 - 30 May 1944, B24H, 42-52739 Code 2C. Badly damaged by flak, had to leave formation after bombing and return alone. When flying off Lowestoft, Suffolk, the last engine went out and the pilot ditched near some small fishing boats. The B-24 sank within three minutes. The RO tossed out the rafts and the crew filled their Mae West and were picked up by the fishermen within 20 minutes. Sgt. Julian W. Messerly (37661921) could apparently not get his Mae West working and was hanging onto the tail of the aircraft. He could not be reached by the others and drowned when the B-24 sank. (Sgt. Messerly is MIA on the "Walls of the Missing" in Cambridge.)

War Duty Room, Lowestoft, 30 May 1944 - I beg to report that at 1300 hours, Tuesday, 30 May, 1944, a Liberator aircraft, No. 252739, crashed into the sea of Lowestoft. Nine members of the crew were brought ashore at Lowestoft by H.M. Drifter De Rosa. The following member of the crew was lost: Sgt. J. Messerly. The above information was obtained from the Royal Naval Base, Lowestoft, who stated they had taken the necessary action concerning the crash. Passed to War Duty Room, P.H.Q., 1630 hours 30.5.44.

26 June 1944: Lt. George, letter -We were over Germany, the exact location I cannot mention, on May 30, 1944. We had two engines shot out due to anti-aircraft fire over the target. We took a heading for home, and on the way over the Channel, another of the remaining engines quit. Going into the Channel we knew was going to be next. The pilot gave orders to stand by for a crash landing. He then ordered me and four men, including Julian, to clear the rear of the ship of its loose cargo to prevent anything from flying through the air when we hit the water. We then took positions for the crash. The ship hit with a hard knock as we were all expecting. The water began to fill in rapidly. I thought for sure there was no escape. Only by an act of God did I finally get out. I swam to the life raft and then passed out from shock. When I awoke, after two days in the hospital, they told me about Julian. "Mess," as he was called by the boys, was a happy and jolly fellow, but also a hard-fighting man.

29 July 1944: 487th Group Chaplain, letter - When it became apparent that the body would not be recovered, I arranged a memorial in the Chapel on the base. This was held Sunday, July 23rd at 7 o'clock.

16 Aug 1944: SSgt Blaha, letter - When we first got our orders that we were on the way down, "Mess" and I worked together getting rid of the guns and ammunition. I was not in a position to see him at the last. I was draped over the edge of the dinghy with my head hanging on the bottom of it. During the crash, I had my little finger all but torn off. It was sewn back on now and doing very nicely. We really miss him. He and I seem to always draw a double bunk together, he below and I on top. When we got over here, he slept right next to me. SSgt. Blaha was transferred to 15th AF in Italy and parachuted out of a damaged B-17 and became a prisoner of war.

Sept 1944-Mar 1945: TSgt Sweeney, letter - No, Julian was not the tail gunner. He flew Top Turret on the ship. Tommy Craig and Robert

Williams are still down in Italy, the last I heard. As for Henry Blaha, the last report from Craig and Williams was that he was shot down. They claim he got out of the ship alright, as parachutes were seen. That was several months ago.

31 May 1945: Letter from Keith Cole's Mother - You know, Mrs. Messerly, Keith's crew was grounded after going down in the North Sea and didn't have to fly again, only by choice is the way I understood it. He told me after three motors went out on them (I don't remember whether they were shot out), they got within about 10 miles of land and radioed for help. Two English fishing boats heard and saw them coming down. Keith told it in just short jerky sentences, and maybe I don't remember either exactly what he said, as he was in such a strain. He said he and Julian were holding on to the tail of the plane. The waves were four feet deep. Keith's life belt was only half tied. He said "Mom, I looked at Julian and am positive his belt was ok, for it was inflated. I told him we should try to work our way up to the front of the plane." Keith did, and I think partly pulled himself up on it. He said, "One of the men on top was fighting to get the rubber boat afloat. Nothing worked as it was supposed to." It was finally thrown out, and the boys that got into it pulled Keith in. "The plane broke in half and went down. Mom, I believe Julian was hurt and that was the reason he couldn't do as I did." Keith had three-four broken ribs, and fingers on the one hand were broken. Keith was in the hospital during Christmas, I think from flak wounds. His back has terrible scars on it. It's a wonder he isn't crazy from what he's gone through. He's grounded now, won't fly anymore and I am so thankful.

Aug 1999-Feb 2002: Richard Atkins, Conversations with Laura Richman (Julian's niece)

Atkins was the co-pilot; he said that they sent SOS to Air Sea Rescue and were picked up by them. When they crashed into the sea, the waves were 3-5 ft. They hit the water real hard, and the front fuselage of the plane peeled back like a banana and folded back over the bombardier compartment. The pilot was knocked out. Atkins had to push the pilot out of the escape hatch

Atkins thought they had everybody in the rafts when he looked over and saw Julian hanging on to the antenna wire at the tail of the plane. Everyone was yelling at Julian to let go of the wire and move forward. He would look at them, but never said a word.

Atkins then got back in the water and got close enough to tell Julian, "give me your hand" - again, he looked but did not say a word. The plane went down real fast with Julian still hanging onto the wire. Atkins was sucked under twice and had to back away. He said Julian's Mae West was inflated, but he was unable to move. Atkins said on this mission, Julian flew as the side gunner.

May 1980-Apr 1990: Fred C. Sweeney - Telecon with Ron Messerly (Julian's brother) - Fred was the radio operator on the plane, sent out the SOS and also got the life rafts out.

Over the Zuider Zee in Holland, their 3rd engine quit. The pilot told the crew that he thought he would be able to make it back, but gave the crew their choice to bail out or stay. The crew elected to stay. They ditched into 4-5 ft. waves. Julian was able to get out of the side window and was hanging on the tail section. Sweeney said they talked to him but he would not answer. They tried to get him to come toward the raft, but he wouldn't. They were trying to get him with the raft and came close when the plane went down with Julian still hanging on to the plane. Sweeney said the plane created a lot of suction and he thought Julian got sucked down. He didn't know if his life vest was inflated or not.

Fred said that on the 11th of May mission, they were hit by flak and flew back at tree-top level to Southern England. Came over the Islands of Jersey and Gurnsey. Air Force records show that they were forced down in Exeter, England because of major damage and severe flak wound to T.W. Craig, Engineer and Waist Gunner.

29 Apr 1990: Thomas Craig - Telecon with Ron Messerly - Craig called and thanked me for a picture I had sent him. He told about how the "Red Growler" was named after the pilot, Lt. McCarty, and that Julian was top-turret gunner on the plane. He said Julian must have been hurt really bad. When the B-24s ditched, the crew really took a beating, much more in a B-24 than a B-17. The B-24 had the high wings and usually broke in two. Craig, who suffered serious wounds on 11 May mission, was told by the crew that they came real close to saving Julian, that if the plane had stayed afloat a few seconds more, they would have gotten him.

This is the text of the Western Union Telegram that was delivered to Julian's mother after he died: It was delivered 1944 June 12 at approximately 10:45 AM.

The Secretary of War desires me to express his deep regret that your son Julian W. Messerly was killed in action on Thirty May over Germany period. Letter follows UL.IO Adjutant General.

Julian had three brothers in the service. Howard and Earl were in the Army Infantry. They were both wounded in combat and received the "Purple Heart" medal. Earl was also rewarded the "Silver Star" for Gallantry in Action. The third brother, Russell, was in the Navy and survived the war with no injuries or wounds.

THOMAS WILLIAM CRAIG

LEFT: Craig entered the service in February 1943 and was Honorably Discharged on September 7, 1945. RIGHT: C.C. Neal, author of this book and Craig's daughter, said her father encouraged others to live life the way he did: "Don't look back on yesterday, that's gone, just live for today and look forward. You can't get back yesterday and you don't know if you'll have tomorrow, so live life to the fullest and enjoy today." Craig passed away October 30, 1998.

Tommy Craig was born August 19th, 1922, in Charlotte, North Carolina, where he grew up on a farm milking cows before he went to school. In the ninth grade, he moved with his parents to Concord (20 miles away), and after high school graduation, he attended North Carolina State University for two years. Then, Pearl Harbor was bombed, and hence, the course of his life would be changed forever. He enlisted to serve his country and fight for freedom.

I am the author of this book, Cynthia Craig Neal, and the proud daughter of Tommy Craig, who passed away October 30, 1998. He left me with such a sense of pride in our country, love of the flag, and respect for those who served their country in World War II, that I saved his chapter to do last. I knew it would be the hardest emotionally to complete, because I wanted to be very sure that the values and lessons he verbalized to me were put into print and saved forever for future generations to read. His date of induction into the service was Jan 28, 1943. His date of entry into the service was February 4, 1943, and he was Honorably Discharged on September 7, 1945, making his time in the service two years, seven months and 12 days. During these years, his battles/campaigns included Air Combat Balkans, Central Europe, Normandy, PO Valley, North Apennines, Air Offensive Europe, Western Europe and Rhineland. He received the EAMET Campaign Medal with eight Bronze Service Stars, Good Conduct

Medal and the Purple Heart. He also received the Air Medal with 1 Oak Leaf Cluster with the 15th AF, Jan. 26, 1945.

Before going overseas, he graduated Engineering Mechanics Course at Keesler Field, Mississippi on August 15, 1943. He also graduated Aerial Gunnery Course, Harlingen, Texas.

On April 11, 1944, Tommy Craig arrived in Lavenham England, station 137, having been assigned to the 8th Air Force, 487th Bombardment Group (Heavy), 838th Squadron. From records researched at Maxwell Air Force Base in Birmingham, Alabama, his first mission was flown on May 7, 1944, and his last on April 21st, 1945. He was stationed in England from April-October 1944 and in Italy from October 1944 until May of 1945 in the 484th Bomb Group 15th Air Force.

He flew B-24H and B-24J to July 19, 1944, and B-17G in combat from August 1, 1944. He handwrote in one of his war books that he was in the 484th Bomb Group in Italy after having been in the 8th Air Force in England. He told me that he had gone to the 15th Air Force in Italy after his tour while stationed in England. According to the roster Flight Echelon 487th Bomb Group list sent by Pete Riegel, the original crew was Walter McCarty, pilot: Richard Atkins, co-pilot; Williard George, bombardier; Raymond Spoerl, navigator; Thomas Craig, flight-engineer; Fred Sweeney, radio-operator; Henry Blake, tail gunner; Keith Coles, nose gunner; Julian Messerly, top gunner; and Robert Williams, ball gunner. In a letter dated 5-4-87 from Fred Sweeney to Craig, he recalls their plane a B-24 that they named the Red Growler, and a picture of a bulldog holding a bomb with the number 39 on it.

One of the most memorable missions for my dad was the 487th Bomb Group mission over Chauteaudun, France on May 11, 1944. The 487th lost three aircraft to flak that day, including the command aircraft with 487 Bomb Group Commander, Lt. Col. Bernie Lay, in the right seat of the Frank Vratney crew aircraft. Col. Lay successfully evaded capture. Tommy Craig sustained serious flak wounds to his right shoulder for which he received the Purple Heart. His plane made it back to England on three engines, and he was hospitalized for several weeks.

The official report of this event follows:

Thirteen B-24, Aircraft Airborne at 1020 For Troyes, France. One aircraft aborted. Engine failure, returned this station. Twelve Aircraft met flak barrage over enemy territory before reaching target. Three aircraft shot down. One aircraft, piloted by 1st Lt. Vratney Lt. Col. Lay, Base Commander aboard, suffered major damage and crew forced to abandon ship. All crew members were reported to have successfully bailed out. One aircraft, piloted by Captain Brodsky, caught fire and was reported as exploding. No crew members were reported as successfully bailing out. One aircraft piloted by 2nd Lt. McCleary reported as sustaining direct hits and exploded. No crew members were reported as successfully bailing out. One aircraft piloted by 2nd Lt. McCarty suffered major damage, and on return trip was forced down in Southern England. T Sgt. Craig, T.W. Engineer, suffered severe flak injury in the right shoulder.

Then, on May 30, 1944, while Tommy was still in the hospital, his crew's B-24 was so badly damaged by flak that it had to leave formation after bombing and tried to return alone. However, when flying off Lowestoft, Suffolk, the last engine went out and the pilot ditched near some small fishing boats. The B-24 sank within three minutes, and the crew filled their Mae West's and were rescued by the fishermen within 20 minutes. Apparently, Julian Messerly couldn't get his Mae West to work, and he was hanging on to the tail of the plane. He drowned when the plane sank. In one of his books, Tommy Craig wrote beside Julian's name "my friend." He actually spoke quite a few times about how uncertain life really is and how you have to enjoy each day. Any time that friends or family of my dad have died and have lived their lives fully, he would remind me to "be thankful that they had lived a long, full life. My friend Julian, who died in the war, never lived out that full life, but he's the reason you have the freedom you have today." He could not talk about Julian Messerly without getting emotional, and he rarely talked about his missions other than to say, "We were doing what we had to, ready and willing to do anything to defeat Hitler!" Almost every week of his life, he'd take the opportunity to say, "Don't look back on yesterday, that's gone, just live for today and look forward. You can't get back yesterday and you don't know if you'll have tomorrow, so live life to the fullest and enjoy today."

Tommy was married for 53 years to Louise Carpenter Craig and resided in Concord, North Carolina until his death in 1998. I, Cynthia Neal, am their only child and married to Dr. Larry Neal. My dad's pride and joy were his two grandchildren - Sherry Honey Barrow, married to Klay Barrow; and Thomas Anthony Honey, called "Tommy," and he is married to Kate Miller Honey. He loved his family - took us boating, water skiing, and went to every basketball game, soccer match and tennis matches of his grandchildren that he possibly could attend. He went with us to church and taught us the value of a hard day's work. He worked for his dad at International Harvester Tractor Company after the war, but after having a heart attack at age 39, he began going up to Concord Boating a few hours a week. That became a few days a week, and he soon purchased the company and had his own boating company, called "Craig's Marine," until he retired at 74 years old.

How I wish I had asked more questions about his war years and had started going to the 487th Reunions before he passed away, but in his words, "You can't get back yesterday, so just live life to the fullest today," and that's what I'm trying to do by compiling this book, in his memory and the memory of all those who died in the war and to the remembrance of all the 487th veterans that are still alive! The next time you see a World War II Veteran proudly wearing his veteran's cap filled with emblems, take a minute to stop and thank him for his service to his country, for your freedom, and watch him beam with pride!

RICHARD ATKINS

Atkins, who flew 30 missions during World War II, passed away three weeks after his final interview providing information for his story in this book.

The start of my service as a pilot was in 1942. I was sent to Davis-Monthan Field, Tucson, Arizona. This is where I had my first transitional flying in order to get used to the B-24 and to drop bombs on target. General training was what I and the entire crew received. We all practiced our individual positions learning everything we could. Here, we ended up with out final crew. However, our first navigator had to be replaced because on our 1,000-mile practice run, when we were not supposed to go out of the United States, we found ourselves in Mexico. This resulted in the loss of the navigator. He was replaced by Spoerl.

Our group went from Davis-Monthan to Alamogordo in January 1944. Here, we were assigned to the 487th Bomb Group. The entire 487th flew to England and became part of the 8th Air Force. My rank was flight officer when we went over, and when I got out of service I was Captain.

We flew over to England via the long route over Africa. When we arrived in England, we were immediately assigned to our Airgirl. We flew from Scotland, where all groups transitioned from, and right on to a brand new base. We were there as a first-time unit. This station became 137, Lavenham, England.

I was 24 years old when I went into service. I was considered an old man. I flew 25 missions. Then, I flew five more missions as an instructor pilot.

Let me describe the way our first mission felt. I was a 24 year old co-pilot, and neither I nor the rest of the crew had ever seen flak. We didn't know what it looked like. We saw it off in the distance and if you know what a weight-lifting dumbbell is - well that is what flak looked like in the air. I said to Walt, "Do you know what that looks like?" He said, "Yeah, it looks like a dumbbell." I said, "Boy! You're sure right there - it sure is pretty." About that time, we had flak streaming through the windows and through the gunnery positions and throughout the airplane. It was coming in around us all the time.

On the first five missions, we had to ditch once and had to emergency land at the airbase three times after being badly shot up. The flight engineer, Tech Sgt. Thomas W. Craig was wounded on one of our very first missions. He was in the base hospital and not with us when we ditched in the channel. On this mission, we lost our waist gunner, Julian Messerly, who drowned after we ditched. This was in May of 1944. Those surviving the ditching were made members of the "Goldfish Club." I escaped death by use of my emergency dinghy. I have a copy of my original certificate making me a member of the Goldfish Club. Early targets were Liege, Brussels, and Lyon.

After the war, I worked for Pacific Telephone and retired as Assistant Manager in 1981. My wife and I had two sons and two grandchildren.

It was a memorable moment in my life when I graduated from school and entered the Air Force. The most memorable of my war memories were the early mission when Tommy Craig was wounded and the ditching experience when our crew member drowned.

When Talking About Your Father, Tommy Craig

He asked if I was the Richard Atkins that was the co-pilot. I told him yes, I was. Then, he and I just talked about what we each remembered. I told him I didn't remember much because the two of us only flew on about five or six missions together.

Julian Messerly. He is the only one who died of the crew that I know of, even afterwards. I went over to England with the original group. He, your father, was one of the original group, otherwise I wouldn't have his picture. I was 24 when I went in. I was the old man. I flew 25 missions. Then, I flew five more as an instructor pilot.

Julian Messerly was the only one in the crew to die. He drowned. He was a gunner. He was a waist gunner. He, your father, was wounded. I think two of them claimed to be wounded when we ditched. I don't remember who, or a claim being made. We got him, your father, out of the airplane because he rode in with us and we landed safely, you know, in the air-girl. But the time your dad got wounded, we did not land safely. We had one engine out, and Tommy was the only one who got wounded that I know of.

I got a copy of my original membership in the Goldfish Club. I was certified Flight Officer Richard Atkins, as qualified as a member of the Goldfish Club by escaping death by the use of his emergency dingy on May 30, 1944. But now that you say May of '44, I believe that your date is more correctly oriented than mine.

838TH SQUADRON

Second Phone Interview

My rank was a flight officer when I went over, and when I got out I was captain. I went into service in 1942 and I entered the 8th Air Force in Alamogordo - that's the first time. I flew over to England via the long road - that is the route through Africa. We flew the whole group (the 487th Bomb Group) from ... well, we all got assigned at Monterey, and that's where the general order came from that I have. January 1, 1944, so it was in 1944 that the general order was made.

Well, the start of my Air Force experience was in Tucson, Arizona. In order to get used to the B-24 and in order to drop bombs on target, general training is what I had and what we all had as a crew. We all practiced our various positions and did everything we could and ended up with our final crew.

We arrived in England, I'm not just sure when because we were immediately assigned to our air-girl. We flew from Scotland where all the groups transition from. We flew right into our brand new base. Nobody had been there before. But we were there as a first time unit - as far as I know. I'm not sure the date that we arrived there. I always called it; we were stationed at Bury Saint Edmunds. The targets on all of those three dates: the first one is Liege and the second one is Brussels, the third one is Lyon. That's about all I can say about that. The replacement groups were more interested; they were the B-17 group, and they seemed to be the only ones interested in maintaining and keeping a record and history of the 487th.

The most memorable moment in my whole life was when I graduated from school and then had to go into the Air Force. My most memorable moment in the war was the ditching, and the loss of one of our men, and Tommy being wounded.

Author's note: This concluded our conversation. About three weeks later Mr. Atkins' wife called to tell me that he had passed away.

PETE RIEGEL

LEFT: *Riegel spent 30 years in the Air Force and retired as a Lt. Col. in 1972.* RIGHT: *Pete Riegel's crew - Top row: Rodney T. Cooke, nose gunner; Grayson Hayes, engineer/ top gunner; Charles Rasmussen, co-pilot; James Pete, radio operator; Steve Kulik, bombardier. Bottom row: Glen Hollifield, gunner; Ed Simmons, ball gunner; Pete Riegel, pilot; Frank White, tail gunner.*

This is Pete Riegel. The day is the 27th of August, 2002. My purpose is to record a few instances in my experience during World War II. I was drafted into the service on June 3, 1941 at Jefferson Barracks, Montana and transferred to March Field, California, where they assigned me as a radio mechanic on P-40s. I was then transferred to Hamilton Field, California as radio mechanic of P-38s. Here, I had an opportunity to take a leave back to Washington, Montana, where I married Melva Hoelscher. We both returned to Hamilton Field, and I soon joined the cadet program at the encouragement of the P-38 pilots whom I met. Eventually, I passed all the tests and was sent to Nashville, Tennessee. Here, I was joined again by my wife and proceeded to Dorr Field, Florida, where I trained in Stearmen aircraft, then further to Bainbridge, Georgia, where I trained in B-13s. In Columbus, Mississippi, I flew AT-9s and AT-10s. I completed my training and graduated as a 2nd Lt. on July 28, 1943 (Class of 43G).

I was further transferred to Smyrna, Tennessee for B-24 transition; this was a three-month program. At completion, the class was transferred to Salt Lake City where I picked up part of my crew. At this time, I received two telegrams, one stating that Mel was having a rough time in the delivery of our child, Marsha, and another telegram telling me that my brother was killed in an accident in Hawaii. I was granted a 10-day leave to join my wife in Washington, Montana. Upon return to Salt Lake City, I found that my original classmates and friends had transferred out. I was placed in a completely new group of people. I picked up my co-pilot, Charles Rasmussen, who was as qualified a pilot on B-24, or any other aircraft, as I was.

We then proceeded to Alamogordo, New Mexico via Kansas where we began phase training with crew integrity in B-24s. This was a three-month program. Mel visited me in Alamogordo the month of December while our six-week old daughter, Marsha, stayed in the loving care of her grandparents. After being completely satisfied that we could fly combat according to our Commander, we proceeded to make plans to transfer to England. We left Alamogordo and flew to Herrington, Kansas, where we fell in line with all groups transferring to England. At this location, my mother and father, with Mel and daughter Marsh, joined me for a few days. This was to be the last time I would see them because we proceeded to Florida where we finally agreed to the name of our B-24. This was the original B-24 assigned to me through the purchase of war bonds from our home in Franklin County, Montana. We named it "Stardust." The song "Stardust" was played at my first dance with Mel in our hometown of Washington, Montana.

We proceeded en route, which is very vague to me now, and we flew to Natal, South America, across the Atlantic Ocean to Dakar and then into Marrakech for a two-week layover. We then proceeded up northwest of Spain, west of France and into Scotland, where we had to wait for further guidance to our home base, Lavenham, which was newly constructed. At Lavenham, we had several practice missions, and some time later we began to fly combat.

On our third mission, our target was Chateaudun, May 11, 1944. Our Commander, Lt. Col. Bernie Lay, was to lead the formation and he selected an altitude of 12,000 feet. Our target was an airfield, and we had a full-group formation. I was in the 838th squadron, and at 12,000 feet, it was quite evident that these experienced ground gunners could target engines rather than aircraft. They were very good. I was 24 years old and pilot, and as you look at the formation sheet, I was to fly position number nine, and the number six position was to be flown by Lt. McCarty. As we formed above the "Splasher," which is a radio beacon some distance from the base, I noticed that the number six slot was not occupied, so I flew up into that position. The B-24 on my right, Lt. McCleary, received a direct hit and exploded. I assumed that all were lost, but later found out that Harold Owens, a crewman, had bailed out and was a POW for the duration. He has quite a story to tell. The number one position, with Commander Bernie Lay, was hit and immediately lost altitude. We followed and saw that 10 parachutes were observed. At the same time, the number two position, with Captain Brodsky, aborted the formation and disappeared from sight. My original navigator, Lee Johnson, was flying on this aircraft. I did not have a navigator on the mission.

Trying to rejoin the formation, we find that all aircraft were heading back to England. The words "fighters in the area" caused us to descend to the deck. On the way down, we dropped our bombs in a wooded area. As we were on deck, I'd say 15 to 20 feet above the trees, we noticed people on the ground waving at us. We were heading in a direction of 300 degrees, as our bombardier indicated, and were heading for an estuary. We knew there were pill boxes or machine gun emplacements on the coast line. We did get a few shots from the pill boxes, and our gunners returned the fire, but we were too far away. As we approached the estuary, we saw that we had a B-24 on our left wing with an engine feathered. Later, we found out that this was Lt. McCarty. We could see land ahead of us, which we first thought was England, but then realized England wasn't that close. As we raised to 500 feet, we saw water on the other side and realized we were coming up on the Jersey Islands. We skirted to the right and proceeded with a new heading of 330 degrees. We kept flying and then began to realize we better make a heading of due north. Finally, we saw land a little to the right. As we approached England, two Spit Fighters were on our wing, and one immediately flew over our nose, indicating he wanted us to land. But England was a great country not getting lost. They had low-frequency radios called "Darky." Anytime a plane needed directions, a call to Darky would give him proper directions. We called Darky for Lavenham and a heading was given due east. The Fighters recognized us and left. It wasn't long before we reorganized the area. We landed and found out that Lt. McCarty had already been on the ground for 30 minutes. Someone said that they were about ready to declare us missing.

As we parked the aircraft and returned to Operations, our Commander wondered why we didn't proceed as the leader of the formation to complete our mission, but without a navigator that was impossible. This was one of the many exciting experiences as I flew a total of 46 missions in B-24s and B-17s. I returned to the states after 28 missions with a promise to return for a second tour. I desired to be with my wife who was about to have her second child as she had quite a problem with the delivery of her first child. The request was granted and I returned home. Even though I was late, all seemed to go well. I was home with my wife and two children for 45 days when I received orders to return to England for my second tour where I flew 18 more missions for a total of 46. Many times, I can relate to some of the strange and exciting days in which I flew until the end of the war. I lost my original navigator, Lee Johnston, while he flew as an added navigator on Capt. Brodsky's crew on May 11, 1944. My original bombardier, Stan Slusarczyk, who flew as a spare when Jos. Willis was lost in the North Sea on May 29, 1944.

I made the Air Force my career with 30 years. I retired as a Lt. Col. in 1972. I spent a year in Korea in 1951 flying personnel and cargo. In 1969, I spent a year in Vietnam flying reconnaissance. I have a total Air Force flying hours of 5,000 plus and combat time of 1,023 hours. Since retirement, I became involved in instructing religion in our parish for children attending the public school. Now, I am completely retired.

We have been married 60 years on August 24. We have five children and one, unfortunately, has passed on at the age of 54. He was our second child, the one in which I tried to get home in time for his birth after my 28th mission. Their names are Marsha, Mark (now deceased), Cynthia, Patricia and John. We also have 10 grandchildren and 14 great grandchildren.

Since I have met you, Mrs. Neal, I think of you and your father often. I knew your father but did not know that he had been injured on the mission on May 11, 1944. I think he was the crew chief of that B-24 that was flown by Lt. McCarty. I often think of him as I switched with Lt. McCarty's crew from number nine position to number six position - strange. Hard to tell, maybe it would have been a different situation. Just thinking about it.

Pete Riegel's Additional Information

There are many occasions that I can remember very clearly happenings of many years ago, this one 58 years ago. The date was May 11, 1944, and I was flying my B-24 called "Stardust." This was my 3rd mission of a total 46 missions, and we all were still quite unfamiliar flying combat. Our target was Chateaudun Air Base, Troyes, France. Our Commander, Bernie Lay, selected 12,000 feet as our altitude. This was the first and last time we flew missions at such a low altitude.

We were flying in the No. 6 position in the lead formation. It was the Commander's decision to have two navigators fly in the Lead and Deputy Lead aircraft, so we were flying without a navigator as "follow the leader." My former navigator was Lee Johnson, who was flying with Capt. Ed Brodsky's plane in the No. 2 Deputy Lead position. He was considered a highly-qualified navigator.

Approaching the target, still quite in the distance on a clear day, 88 mil. explosions appeared at our altitude. McCleary's B-24 had a direct hit and exploded, and it appeared that the whole crew was lost. However, on gunner, Harold Owens was blown clear, wearing his parachute, escaped and was a POW for the rest of the war.

A burst also hit both the Leader and Deputy Lead's aircraft, and they left the formation. I followed the Lead's aircraft as he gradually descended, also viewed the Deputy's aircraft as it left the formation. After counting 10 chutes out of the Lead's aircraft, our Commander, I made an effort to return to the formation, which had reversed its course, having no leader, and scattered all over the sky. We could not catch up. We felt all alone.

When we heard "fighters in the area," we dropped our bombs in a thick wooded area and hit the deck. I asked Kulik, my Bombardier, to give me a heading back home. After going through several maps, he being unprepared, gave me a heading of 300 degrees. On the deck, we observed Frenchmen waving at us. We must have made quite a sight and noise to them. Ahead was an incline as the surface wasn't too level. Starting to climb a bit, reaching to top, we observed a church steeple right ahead of us. A sharp bank to the right, and we continued at 300 degrees.

Gentlemen From Hell

We anxiously waited to approach the coastline, but we knew the Germans would have pillboxes all along the coast. We finally saw a large body of water, an estuary, leading to the coast. We followed it, but we did get a few rounds from the German guns. I advised my gunners to fire back. At this time, I noticed another B-24 on my left wing with one engine feathered. We recognized it as McCarty's aircraft. He soon left and took up a more northerly heading. Did he have a Navigator? Later, we learned that he did.

Out of range of the German gunners, I began to climb over the water and immediately noticed land. England wasn't that close. Changing our heading to 330 degrees, we realized that the Jersey Islands would have more German gun emplacements.

We continued our heading until we saw land far to our right. We then took up a heading of 360 degrees and approached the southwesterly coast of England, possibly Plymouth. We thanked the Good Lord for a clear day. Where would we have flown if we hadn't seen land?

Approaching the coast of England, two Spitfires were on our wing. One remained on my right wing and the other on my nose, indicating that he wanted me to land. Now, England had low-frequency radio stationed on many locations for emergency purposes. They called this "Darkie." I began to call "Darkie," and when they answered, I asked them for a heading to Lavenham. The Spitfires must have recognized us and took off. "Darkie" gave us a heading of 80 degrees. Within a short time, we were approaching familiar grounds and landed at our home base.

McCarty had landed 30 minutes sooner. Of course, he had a navigator on board. Our ground crew considered us one of the missing as we had lost four B-24s that day, our lead with our Commander Bernie Lay and Frank Vratny as pilot, a good friend, Capt. Bodsky with Lee Johnson, my former navigator on board. McCleary, whose plane had disintegrated off my right wing, (the only survivor was Harold Owens), and in the lower squadron, Duncan's B-24.

Each of the survivors of these four aircraft all had different experiences, and they are interesting stories in themselves.

WILLIAM HENRY HUGHEY

LEFT: *Hughey was one of many servicemen to see battle during the Battle of the Bulge on Christmas Eve, 1944. Right: Hughey, front, third from left, pictured with his crew.*

My name is William Henry Hughey. I was born in Memphis, Tennessee, October 30, 1925. I went through Bruce Elementary, Bellevue Junior High School and Central High School before I was drafted into the U.S. Army Air Force. I left home on New Year's Eve, 1943 and reported for duty on January 1, 1944 at Camp Shelby, Mississippi. At that time, I was a private. I did, however, go through Corporal, Sergeant, and Staff Sergeant. I was discharged as a Staff Sergeant, November of 1945.

My crew was assembled in Lincoln, Nebraska and became members of the Eighth Air Force when we arrived in England in October of 1944. We were sent to Stone, a replacement depot. We were told that our crew had been assigned to the 100th Bomb Group. Because of the 100th's reputation of the crews lost on missions, we were not too happy with this assignment. However, our orders were changed and our bombardier, Johnny Welko, informed us that we had been reassigned to the 487th Bomb Group. We were to be assigned to the 838th Bomb Squadron. The commander at that time was Major Francis C. Eberhart. Captain Pete Riegel was our operations officer. If my memory serves me correctly, I was 19 years old the day we landed in England.

I was a ball-turret gunner on a B-17. We flew 32 missions. Our pilot, Richmond C. Young, flew 33, and the co-pilot, Larry Boss, flew 34. The pilot was required to fly the co-pilot with a seasoned crew before he was allowed to take us, a new crew, on combat missions. The co-pilot had to fly two missions as a co-pilot with a seasoned crew before he could go. Then, we were allowed to fly together as a crew.

Gentlemen From Hell

No one on our crew ever received a scratch, although we did have some close calls. We were only shot down once, on March 2, 1945 on a mission to Dresden, Germany. We got off course going into Germany, probably eight or nine miles south of the course and out of the flak corridor, an area, in theory at least, in which the enemy could shoot at you but could not hit you. Apparently, we were off course just enough to let them fire and hit us. While we knew we had been hit, we thought we had no serious damage. When we turned to the IP, the number four engine was smoking. Our co-pilot informed us we were losing oil pressure on number four. He feathered the prop and shut the engine down. Immediately after "Bombs Away" was called, we lost another engine, and it was shut down. While the aircraft was capable of crossing Germany on two engines, I don't believe the German Air Force would have allowed it. We were ordered to fly to Warsaw, Poland. When we arrived in the Warsaw area, we found ourselves flying in a terrible blizzard. The wingtips were not even visible. We had no idea where we were, and then we lost a third engine.

Our pilot asked us what to do - if we wanted to bail out or ride it down? Because of weather conditions, we decided it was best to ride it down. The pilot and co-pilot made a beautiful emergency landing, and we all walked away without any injuries. We were picked up by members of the Russian Air Force, stationed at Warsaw, and taken to individual homes to be quartered for the night.

We returned to the aircraft the next day to get our A-3 bags. The Russians would not allow us to approach the aircraft, informing us that we had landed in a German mine field. We stood there and watched them blow up mines all around the aircraft, some being detonated right between the wing and the tail where we had been walking the day before.

We spent two weeks with the Russian Air Force in Warsaw. At the end of this period, the Air Transport Command sent at DC-3 to pick us up. Two other crews that had landed there in the meantime were picked up as well. We were flown to an American base in Russia, at Poltava. From there, we were flown on a C-46 to Tehran in Iran, which was headquarters for the Persian Gulf command. After spending several days there, we were then flown to Payne Field in Cairo, Egypt. There we had a sort of humorous situation. The sergeant demanded to see our shot records before he would allow us to board the airplane for London, and we said, "Officially, we are still on a mission." If we had shot records with us, we'd be subject to court marshal because we were not allowed to carry anything legally but our dog tags. However, I had my shot record with me, my driver's license and everything else my wallet held - I just didn't tell him that.

We then were routed across North Africa into Naples, spending three days there. Leaving there, we went to Paris and on to London. We returned to our base in Lavenham, where we flew five more missions. On April 21st, 1945, I flew my last mission. For me, the war was over. My tour in the ETO was over. As it turned out, this mission, April 21, 1945 was the last mission ever flown by

838TH SQUADRON

the 487th Bomb Group. The 8th Air Force flew its last mission of the war on April 25, 1945.

My tail gunner, Jimmy Spurlock, and I went into service January 1, 1944. When we touched down on the runway at Lavenham the evening of January 1, 1945, we had just finished our first year in the military and our 16th mission. I was discharged November of 1945. I had been 20 years old for one week at the time of my discharge. It was really a quick tour of duty - it lacked two months being two years. Others not quite so fortunate spent several years, but it was in and out for us.

I guess the worst mission for the 487th Bomb Group that was flown (and you may hear this again in other interviews) was Christmas Eve, 1944 during the Battle of the Bulge. The German infantry put forth a last gasp effort to retake land they had lost and push us back into the channel. They caught the United States ground forces in a position of being unprepared to repel such an offensive - the troops were being pushed back and encountering terrible weather. The severe weather of December 1944 kept the 8th Air Force on the ground. We were alerted for a mission Christmas Eve, 1944, and the day dawned with beautiful weather. Normally, we put three squadrons made up of anything that would get airborn. We were going to fly ground support for the American troops by hitting the German field at Babenhausen. German fighters from this field were giving ground support to German infantry. Our mission was to take the field out. The 487th Bomb Group on this day, 24th December 1945, was leading the entire 8th Air Force. The mission consisted of over 2,000 bombers and 1,000 fighter escorts - the largest mission ever put up by the 8th Air Force.

In the air, the Germans unexpectedly crossed over our lines and got behind us. We normally didn't pick up our escort until after we had crossed enemy lines five or 10 degrees, but this time the Germans came from behind us on our side. I saw them coming, thought it was our escort and said to myself, "What in the hell are they doing with their landing lights on?" Well, those were not landing lights - it was cannon fire coming from German fighters. From my position in the ball-turret, I began to see bombers fall left and right. It is the only mission I ever flew that I figured was my last one. I didn't see how any of us could survive it. We were told that about 200 German fighters jumped us.

This mission was being led by General Fred Castle. Our aircraft was right off his left wing. As my turret came around to the one o'clock position, four ME-109s (German fighters) came down through our squadron. This is the first time I had seen a German fighter that close and that big black cross on the side is the ugliest thing you will ever see in your life. These ME-109s hit General Castle's aircraft on their first pass. His number three engine was on fire. He lowered his landing gear and then retracted it. We can only assume that this was his signal to the deputy lead to take over. He moved out of formation and that was the last time we saw General Castle's aircraft. Five members of the crew bailed out of the General's aircraft. Four survived the bail out. One was so badly wounded, he died the next day. I believe Colonel Paul Biri is the sole survivor of that crew. Our squadron lost two aircraft - General Castle's lead aircraft and the crew flying Tail End Charlie. The low squadron was the one that really caught it. Out of 13 aircraft, 11 went down. It was one sad day when we got back.

When we returned from the mission, our squadron armament personnel met us on our hard stand where we parked the aircraft. They told us to go on to interrogation and then to the mess hall and said, "We'll take care of cleaning your guns." This was a job the gunners always did at the end of every mission. We thanked them profusely.

We were alerted for a mission Christmas Day. After briefing, we went to personnel equipment to pick up oxygen masks and parachutes. As I came out of the personal equipment building, it was snowing very hard. I threw my A3 bag upon the truck just as the tanoy alerted us, "Red flare from the tower," mission scrubbed. I put my equipment back in my locker and my crew and I walked back over to the mess hall and had breakfast again.

For 50 some years every Christmas Eve, I have called my crew because it was a very significant day in our lives and is to this day. When I came home, I went back to work for a company that I had worked for previous to going in the service. I got married in March 1948 to Jean Ann Luther, a young lady working at the same company. The company switchboard operator and receptionist had written to me while I was overseas. In one of her letters, she had said there was a young girl she wanted me to meet and meet her I did and married her. We have two children a boy, William Henry Hughey III, who was born at MacDill Air Force Base, Tampa, Florida where I had been recalled to serve during the Korean War, and our daughter, Julia Ann Hughey Yakobsky was born seven years later in Birmingham, Alabama. We have six grandchildren and one great-grandchild. After I was discharged, the English Air Force did not remain foremost in my mind. I was raising a family and making a living.

In 1983, there was a symposium held in Atlanta about the Air War (Air War Europe comes to Atlanta). I attended and heard Francis Gabresky and Bob Johnson speak. Adolph Galand, the German ace, was also a part of the program and I got his autograph. When I registered for the symposium, I was told that a Georgia Chapter of the Eighth Air Force Historical Society was being formed. I signed up not knowing if I would ever hear about this again, but now, 18 years later, we have what I think of as the most active chapter in the nation. I am sitting here today as we speak in Omaha, Nebraska at the 35th annual reunion of the 487th Bomb Group being interviewed by Cindy Neal - whose father was a member. We are enjoying comradeship that has gone on all these many years. It is a pleasure to be here and we thank God we are here.

JAMES SPURLOCK

My name is James E. Spurlock. I entered the service on January 1, 1944. I arrived in England sometime in September of 1944. I was in the 838th squadron of the 487th Bomb Group. I was 18 years old when I went into the service. I was tail gunner on the B-17. I flew 32 missions.

No one on our crew was ever injured, but it was shot up pretty badly twice. The last time was on March 2, 1945. We lost an engine and we went down in a fighter field eight miles south of Warsaw, Poland. We stayed there for 18 days, and the ATC (Air Transport Command) sent a plane to pick us up. They took us back to a base in Poltava, Russia. We stayed there several days, and then we left and went from there to Teheran, Iran, to Palestine, and from Palestine to Cairo, Egypt. We spent Easter Sunday in Cairo, Egypt. We left the next day, and we went to Tripoli. From Tripoli, we went to Tunis and then across the Mediterranean to Naples, Italy. From there, we went to the southern part of France, up to Paris, and then across the Channel to London and back to our base. We were gone for a total 35 days. That was definitely a very enlightening experience for a man that was just 18 years old. I think what I just told you was probably the most interesting part of my whole entire service career in the fact that until I left home, I had never been more than 70 miles away from Memphis in my life. In that 22 months that I was in the service, I was at 26 different states in the United States and 22 different foreign countries. On top of that, I was being paid to do it - not much, but paid.

We lived in the same hut (barracks). Naturally you just had to get to know each other and certainly you got more friendly or closer to some rather than others. Like Henry Hughey and myself, we lived in Memphis together and we came back to Memphis together, and we've been friends for the last 60 years. All of our crew members stayed pretty close together. Of course, some of us started to die. Today, there are only three of the nine left - Henry, Richmond Young and myself. The other crew members were John McKee, David Cherry, Anthony Ciserano, Larry Bross, Bruce Bavender, John Welko, and then the three I just mentioned.

I was overseas from September '44 until, I don't remember the exact date we left England, but it was sometime in September of '45.

We came back one day, no one on that plane was injured, and we counted after we got down on the ground, there were 293 holes in that airplane. Henry probably knows the date. I do not. Henry is certainly our group historian. I do not remember where we went on that mission, but he will. He's got a list of all of them - the date, how it went, was it good, bad or what.

I would be a fool to say that I never was frightened. Also, I realized that it was part of my job and that I was going to do the best I could, but when you were flying over the different targets and your anti-aircraft was going off all around you, you had to be afraid.

Our plane never ditched in the English Channel. We started to one time, but we knew we were about to run out of fuel. But, we went on and we made it back to the ground without having to leave the airplane.

As I said, there are just so many different things that every now and then they run across your mind. All and all, it was a very, very awakening experience. That's when it was over and we got to come back home.

I got married on April 12, 1946. There were two children, subsequently. One was born on March 8, 1947 and one born on June 14, 1949. They're both living in Memphis today, but my older daughter has moved to Kansas City, and wants to move back home. After the war, I went into the cotton business. I attained a job there. My starting pay was $20 a week, and I started on the 6th day of May of 1946, and that's the only thing that I've ever done. I worked for a man for 21 years. After that, I finally saved enough money that I could go into business for myself. From then until now, I've been in business for myself. On the 6th day of May, I will have been in the cotton business for 57 years. The name of my business is Delta Cotton Company, and for 55 years we were on what was called Cotton Row in downtown Memphis on Front Street. In July of 2001, I moved out east to what is known as the Agriculture Center. A lot of people call it the Penal Farms - 5,000 acres that the county owns. Our office is maintained there.

I went to Savannah one time. I don't remember how many years ago it was. Henry has invited me to all of them, but having owned a small business, and I was the principle in this small business, I felt that I would like to spend my time more at home then going to the conventions. I would like to have helped, but I did not.

As I say, I admire Henry Hughey. He is very enthusiastic about the 8th Air Force, 487th Bomb Group and our squadron especially, and he is probably the best historian that anyone has. I just depend on him for those memories and so forth, and he does a mighty good job of it.

ROY HON, SR.

LEFT: *Hon spent 16 months overseas during World War II.* RIGHT: *Hon, pictured kneeling at a 487th Bomb Group plaque at Arlington Cemetery.*

My name is Roy Hon and I'm from Los Angeles, California. I've lived there all my life. I went into the service six months after I got out of high school. I went to replacement depot on the 8th of April 1943. We were all testing. We were there for about five days. We were tested and everything like that. At the end of that five days, we were loaded on buses. There were eight buses full of us, left the reception center and when the bus caravan stopped for lunch in Bakersfield, California, there were only five buses left. We asked the man in charge of the caravan what happened to the other three buses, and he said, "Oh you guys are lucky. You're going to the air corps. They went to the Army." That's how I got in the Air Force. I didn't have any choice about it. But I was very happy that it worked out that way. We got into the Air Force. After I'd gone through gunnery school and armament school, we had crew training and things like that, flying together with the crew, and then I guess that's when we were assigned to a group to go to England. As a group, we were one of the last groups to go over as a complete unit. We got ready to go, and it seems that they didn't have enough room for everybody that they wanted to go with the airplanes. In case anything went wrong, they wanted to send the ground crew to fly with them so they could make repairs or anything like that if they needed them. So they took a couple men off each crew and put them on a boat. So I was on a boat for 14 days going across the Atlantic Ocean, weaving back and forth dodging German submarines and everything! I'd never been on a boat before! I didn't get really seasick, but I can't eat lamb anymore because on the boat we had oatmeal and raisins for breakfast. It was watery oatmeal and it wasn't too good. This is a typical English meal, I guess, because it was an English boat, Duchess of Bedford. So we had two meals a day, oatmeal in the morning, and then at night they had mutton or some form of lamb. It was pretty good to start with, but then it got awful tiring. So anyway, I can't eat lamb anymore!

We left New York on the 23rd of March 1944, because that was my mother's birthday, I remember it. We landed in England the 1st of April. We got to the base and we went operational on the 7th of May. I was hit on the 27th of May 1944 and was removed from the crew. In the meantime, I had flown the four missions and I saw one really bad thing happen. There was an airplane off our right wing that took a direct hit from antiaircraft fire. The airplane caught fire and I saw one of the waist gunners jump out the waste window and pull his ripcord and his parachute strung out behind him in flames. It was already on fire, and he just went down like a rock. That was about the saddest thing that I ever saw.

I flew with the 838th squadron in the 487th Bomb Group. I was a little over 19 when we started, and my position was a tail gunner. My pilot was Huff and my co-pilot was Webber. My bombardier was Rogers. The navigator was Lacy. The engineer was Gene T. Burrage, who died quite some time back. Our radioman was Ballman, Bob Ballman. One of the waist gunners was Art Silva, the other was Cosme P. Marquez. He also lives in Los Angeles. I don't see him very often, as often as I would like to, but Art Silva, the other waist gunner, is still with us. He is doing fairly well. I only got to fly four missions with the group because I was hit on the fourth mission. I went to the hospital. I was in the hospital 54 days. While I was in the hospital, they changed the group from B-24s to B-17s, and they cut the crews down to nine men, taking one man off each crew. There were 10 originally. Of course, I was the one that got taken off because I was 15 missions behind the rest of the crew when I got out of the hospital. I stayed around there from July to November as a spare gunner. I didn't get to fly any more combat. I flew enough practice missions during that time to keep my flight pay up; four hours a month, you had to fly to get your flight pay for that month.

Then they shipped me to Italy and I was in the 15th Air Force. I got down there, and it was the same thing. They had B-24s, of course, down there, and I got assigned to the 459th Bomb Group, originally as a gunner. They had so many new crews, replacement crews coming into the group, that they started a gunnery school. They put me in the gunnery school as an instructor with all my past experience - four missions. But anyway, I enjoyed trying to teach the new guys coming in about the combat, the way flak looked and what you had to watch out for and all that. It was pretty interesting. Then they said we're short of bombardiers. You could fly as a togglier. If somebody is out, we need another bombardier, and you could fly as togglier. They gave you about half-hour schooling on how to set up the intervalometer, which spaces the bomb so that they don't all drop at one time, they drop in train, you know. Then, you watch the lead ship when you're on the bomb run. You watch the lead ship and when you see his bombs fall out, you press the toggle switch. That releases your bombs, and they drop out in train after that. So, that's all there is to being a bombardier, but it was a job that I didn't mind too much. One thing about it, American Air Force is different from the German Air Force. When we bombed, we bombed military targets. When the Germans bombed, they bombed anything they could see, any people or anything, they didn't care, like the railroad stations in London and things like that. I always felt good about the American Air Force because they had such high standards of morality in that respect.

So, I flew a total of 11 missions. I was overseas for a total of 16 months. I was sent home in July of 1945 after the war was over in Europe. When I got home, they sent me to San Pedro, California for orientation on going to B-29 school and going to the Pacific, because the war was still going on in Japan. I was sitting in one of the orientation lectures one day and this Sergeant comes in and calls out my name. I said, "Yes sir." And he said, "What's a matter Hon? Don't you want to go home?" I said, "Oh yeah, I sure do." He said, "They recounted your points. You can get out now." So that's how I got out. That was after 27 months in service.

My experiences with other crew members weren't too connected after I left the 8th Air Force because I didn't know anybody. I was a spare gunner or a spare bombardier, and I didn't really know any of the crew or the crewmen personally very well. I was just put on that crew and flew with them that day. I'd come back up maybe two, three weeks before I flew again, and then I would fly with another crew. I never really got to know any of the Italian 15th Air Force men that well. But these reunions are fantastic. Getting to meet all the guys again, and even crews that I didn't know before, are just wonderful situations. I didn't know much about the reunions until the '70s, early '70s. Art Silva, living in California up about 200 miles north of me, came here to Los Angeles one day on some business he had to take care of and found my name in the phone book and gave me a call. He said, "We're having a reunion in San Diego this year. Would you like to come?" I said, "Well, I sure would." That was my first reunion in San Diego, 1976. I missed a couple and then I had a couple. I've been to almost every one of them since about '81, something like that. Chicago, I didn't get to Chicago. That was '82. I went to Denver in '83, New Orleans, Seattle, Lavenham. Seattle was interesting because we went to the factory in Seattle where the B-17s were built. That was very interesting. Buffalo, New York, I missed that one.

That's the nice thing about this bomb group. A few men die every year. You think this place was getting smaller, but then there's a few more to come. So, it keeps the population up pretty good. It's just wonderful. I love the reunions and I love the men. We're a band of brothers, so to speak. It's great.

After I got out in '45, I worked five jobs in different places. I worked with my dad mixing cement and pouring driveways and sidewalks and brick walls and that type of thing. When I was drafted the first time, I was working at Lockheed, so I got drafted out of Lockheed. I went back when I got out of the service. I went back, I guess in '48 because I got married in 1949. I met this girl in '47, and we went together for six months and broke up for six months, and we went together for another year and got married. And we're still married, 53 years now. We have two kids that are both grown, but they are both single and they're both still living at home, and I don't have any grandchildren, and it makes me so mad. But anyway, after I got married and before I had the kids, I was recalled for the Korean War. I went through a little B-29 training, not too much, because I was already a gunner and they needed gunners. So, they assigned me to a group as a tail gunner on a B-29. That was interesting to me. Then the group I got into, I don't even remember the number of the group, but it was a strategic air command group and we were carrying the A-bomb. So as far as combat was concerned, there wasn't any. We flew to Guam and spent 70 days at Guam waiting for Truman to say, "go in and drop the bomb." He didn't, so we came back and another group replaced us there.

After I got back to the states, I decided I didn't want to fly anymore. The army was trying to get officers, and they were asking anybody that wanted to be an officer to change branches of the service from the Air Force to the Army and go to an OCS (Officer Candidate School). I did that. I went into the Army and they put me down to a PFC, and I finally made it back up to Corporal. I went into 16 weeks of basic training, which was just like I'd never been in the service before, running with a rifle over my head, up and down the field and everything like that. Basic training center number eight was in Fresno, California, which wasn't too far from home. But anyway, after I got through basic training, I went to another school previous to going to OCS. I went to that fine. My work was good and all that. I passed all right, but they said, "Well, we're not going to let you go to OCS." I said, "Okay, let me back out of here and I'll go back in the Air Force." My discharge from the Air Force read for the purpose of attending OCS in the Army. I'm not going to OCS, I'm going back in the Air Force. They said, "Well, you can go to OCS if you want to." Well, all they had to do was put me in OCS for six days and wash me out and they accepted me in the infantry for the rest of my life. Well, that's not what I wanted. If I can't get a commission, I don't want to stay in the Army. So, I went back into the Air Force and I went to school for link trainer repairmen. I worked as a Link Trainer at Randolph field for two years, I guess. I rose up to lead man over the Link Trainer Department. Then, I had been in for a total of seven years during the Korean War and after. I decided I didn't want to stay in the service and make a career of it, so I got out.

I went back to school. I got a teacher credential and taught school for two years and dropped out of that. I didn't like it. Then, I joined with the company that built ground support equipment for the airlines. The first company was Nordskog Company, Inc. and they built the kitchens, the galleys for the airplanes. I worked up to where I was running the electrical crew for wiring the galleys for coffee makers and whatever equipment went into the galleys, a lot of it electric.

I would have retired except that my wife keeps me busy now. She's still working. She teaches at National. She's great at it. She loves the people and she works real hard at it. She's got a lot of friends that she's made through that. And she's still at it, that's the thing. Her last job was principal at Hollywood High School. She was there for six years. One of the nice things she did was start an alumni museum. There were an awful lot of stars that went to Hollywood High, and a lot of them came back to see the museum since she started it. They donated their things to the museum, too. So they're recognized there, too. The other thing was that with small items, she raised $6 million for the school from the neighborhood. This probably shouldn't be in here. Forget it. She wouldn't bring any of the money home, but I did get to meet some celebrities. It was fun.

ART SILVA

LEFT: *Silva entered the service three days before the December 7, 1941 attack at Pearl Harbor. He spent 35 years in the oil business after the war.* RIGHT: *Silva (far right), pictured with Pete and Mel Riegel and Patty Riegel Eads.*

My name is Arthur W. Silva. My rank was staff sergeant. I went into the service December 4, 1941, three days before Pearl Harbor. I entered the 8th Air Force February 1944. I arrived in England March of 1944. I flew with the 838th squadron while with the 487th. I was 24 years old. I was a member of the air crew. My job as an air crew member was as a waist gunner on both the B-17 and the B-24. I flew 16 missions in the B-24 and 18 missions in the Fortress. No one on my crew was killed. One was wounded by friendly fire over the Channel. My plane was never shot down. We never had a crash landing. We never ditched in the English Channel. I went overseas in March of 1944. I was discharged by the finishing of the war by the surrender of Japan. That was August of 1945. What I've done after the war was work about 35 years for an oil company. I got married twice. I wasn't married overseas. I have three children and three stepchildren.

My most memorable moment was, I would say, D-Day, June 6, 1944. Then, we had a troop support. It was the first time that bombers were used as tactical weapons. Eight hundred bombers bombed right ahead of the allied lines off of Normandy. That was about August of 1944. The third most memorable moment was the invasion of Holland, which we were bombing flak guns prior to the paratroopers coming over. The C-47s were going to be shot at by the 88s, and we bombed prior to them coming over. One was a mission to Berlin, but really nothing eventful happened. Probably the thing I remembered most about it was we lost 12 fellows out of my hut within three weeks. Six enlisted men were lost

838TH SQUADRON

May 11, 1944 and six more June 6, 1944. So, that was 12 inside of three weeks. One had three missions and one had five missions. We had 30 more to go, so it did look like it was going to be a long haul.

The start of the mission was about four in the morning, depending on how far the target was. We had breakfast at about five o'clock, and then you went to your ready room where you picked up your clothing, your parachute, and one of the things at the end of the line was a member of your religion. He was in a small hut, and mine was a priest. I remember talking to him and him telling me, "You're going to make it." So I said, "Well, the last one, Father, I made it." But you know something, I'll tell you, I went to a fortune teller in London to find out for sure if he was right. I didn't trust him, I don't know. I probably would've gotten my money back if she said something else.

Before the mission, we were briefed where the target was. The crew met out on the line and we all went to our positions. We went to what you call a splasher or a buncher - a joining area where they all joined, where all the bombers joined before they went over across the channel. You were looking at about at least 1,000 bombers going towards Germany at different places. The missions were cold. I flew from May to September and that was the warmer part of the year in Europe, but it still felt 40 degrees below zero. So, the biggest part was the cold weather.

In 1995, I went to England for the VE Celebration. They stopped at the Madingly Cemetery out near Cambridge while we were there - I saw the crash happen, I saw the guy, it didn't look that bad. There were two guys killed that day, right at the field in a B-24, and I never forgot that one. While we were at the cemetery, we stopped; this co-pilot was killed. His name was Joel Isaacson, and CBS was doing it, they were interviewing me, and I said, "You know, the folks ought to know about this." A little town in Mentor, Kansas, and I thought, I got to tell someone about this. They mentioned who his brother was, so about a year ago, I got a letter from a lady in Wichita, Kansas. She was the sister of this guy, and she was looking for my name. She heard me on that CBS program and said, "I was looking for your name." She said, "I wanted to know what happened to my brother that day. How he was killed?" She hadn't been over to England, so while she was there on the plane she talked to an ex-Air Force retiree. She told him what she was doing, she was going to England to her brother's grave there at Cambridge, and he said he could get her in touch with somebody. So I got the call from her. It was really touching for her to find a flight to this reunion. She said she saw that thing on the television and her brother had seen it. He sent her three rolls of video that he had taken. It was on national television. It was funny how that thing had worked out.

Another one was one of the crew members had lost a foot. I sent him all the stuff for this reunion. He never came. He didn't show up for it. So that was one story, and these stories are spin-offs. Here's one that I had about two years ago. A guy went over to London, crossed the channel and to the Normandy Cemetery, and, apparently, he must have been Jewish because he found one grave, one of those ones with the Star of David on the side of the cross. He got a hold of me, I guess because I'm the contact guy. He wanted to know who was in that grave. It was my navigator. He wasn't flying with us that day, and he was killed. Anyway, that was another spin-off story that one of the pilots was a guy by the name of Roberts, John Roberts. I sent this story to the guy in Holland. Roberts never talked to us. A young reporter had got him in Pennsylvania. He was the mayor of the town at one time; he was a civic-minded guy, Roberts was, but he never told the story. Him and the co-pilot got out, but there were six men, they crash-landed in France. Six men were trapped. They couldn't get them out; they were trying to get them out of the aircraft and it caught fire. They couldn't put it out. He never forgot it. So that was his story, but he never revealed it until this young reporter got it. I got the story; they sent me the story, but where my navigator was that day was another story when he was with this Roberts. Then, here we go again, I get this magazine from a Jewish Legionnaires Magazine; it's like American Legion, Jewish people. It was cited this guy who went to this cemetery and chased this story down, and a librarian in San Diego California, she did it also. And this magazine says that this man should be commended for finding this story, you know, chased this thing down and pursued it right to the very end.

This is stuff that maybe I didn't participate in, but these are stories that I have years of in my scrapbook. There was this crew coming back; they aborted. The engine caught fire. They tried to go out toward the channel, I guess to put her on automatic, and it came back, and him and the radioman didn't get out. The rest of the crew bailed out. There were about seven guys who bailed out. The radioman was killed; his chute didn't open. It hit the aircraft. And the pilot didn't get out fast enough. When they were building an apartment complex over there, they had dug up the crash of the airplane. It was so battered that they just buried it. They didn't even salvage it. This was March of 1945. The British are great for history, and they went to, "What the hell? Who was in that airplane?" And they asked, "Were there any survivors still living?" We found one gunner in Alabama, James Bane. But anyway, they wanted to know the pilot's name; Porsche, the guy that was killed with it. There were two descriptions of the crash, one by the civilian authorities in Britain and one by the military. So I went to the library and I got the addresses of two newspapers in Morristown, New Jersey, and they wrote up; it says, "British to Honor American Airman." It was written in a newspaper in New Jersey. But there was a lady who had read the article and sent it to Britain, and it came back to me. Anyway, the folks, the father found out the story. His son - Robert Porsche was his name. There happened to be Mrs. Porsche, the mother, passed away. They put his footlocker and his stuff on for the garbage men to pick up. His Momma died, and they just threw it out. But there was a lady next door by the name of Mrs. Testa. She knew she had read the story, and she took her own money and shipped it over to England to a museum. She paid for it. It was a footlocker, and his social security number and the date was stamped on the back of a photograph of when he was killed. They got a video back with this museum curator, how he found the wreck, and they brought it over to this museum. In the meantime, you know, this museum curator wrote me a letter and he says, I think I'm going to ask the building people there in this little town of Colton, Coleville, if they'll name the streets after these people. It was a pilot and radioman. So anyway, I got pictures of that, too. It was Fortress Way, this radioman's name, the pilot's name and also a plaque after the apartment complex was built. So that was all done because of what they found when they dug it up to build an apartment complex. So that's another story that would never have come about. But everyone, somebody told me this, every one of those grave sites has got a story. They've all got a story.

After a mission, it was pretty bad. So, I went to a flight surgeon. You went to a flight surgeon when you had a problem, more than my priest. But I wanted to quit. I wanted to quit. There were no heroes. There was a ward full of guys, they call them flak happy, or combat fatigue is a fancy word for it. This is when men break down and cry, "I'm not going back. I'm not going back." I found out that some of them, they took their stripes. I don't know what they did with officers, but they took their stripes away from them and put them in menial jobs. We were all volunteers, so in the infantry, you couldn't do that; but in the Air Force, they would find something like permanent KP or guard duty, or some other jobs you didn't like. But this ward, it's fit for two rows of guys, and a flight surgeon would come up one side, come up that side, and he would say, you know, "You going to go back?" He asked me. He asked me, "So what are you going to do?" He said, "You got to live with yourself for a long time afterward." I saw the flight surgeon last year in Saint Louis, but remember the words he said, "Silva, you're going to have to live with yourself a long time afterward." Here I am. I made it. The flight surgeon was Dr. Lerner. The flight surgeons had really one hell of a job. He said the hardest was to keep the pilots because they had so much responsibility. Us gunners, some of us along for the rides, I guess. Like I say, how many of these guys come out of those wars, that they went back, I didn't ever know. But we had one on our crew that was thoroughly grounded. He kept faking illness. Now, this is not a hero's story. He kept faking illness. Finally, the pilot told us. He talked to each one of us and said, "We're going to have to do away with Mac. We're going to have to get him off the crew." But there were other cases like that. But nobody ever talks about that kind of stuff. They want to be the hero business and all that, the razzle dazzle. I don't think these guys will talk about it either. Nobody wanted to.

For two years, I worked with the Dutch. It was a book for a missing air crew reports. There was one report says, "Killed by a pistol accident." When I was at the cemetery, we were sitting there with the thing around us, the camera crew, and we were at this grave site. I remember this guy's name was brought up and the guy behind me, I wish I knew who it was. "I was there," he said. "He was the bunk below me." He said, "He shot himself. He just couldn't take it." The report said it was a pistol accident; it's happening in, probably anytime where those who just can't take it any more. Men break down. When you see men break down and cry, that's it. They're hurting.

We had one crew member in my hut, that first six crew, six men that went down. They were blown up, it was McLeary's crew. Some guys did it, right above their locker, or maybe their cot. There was a little shelf and some guys would take a piece of paper and a pen and write a will to mom and pop, a wife, or something like that. Some did; I never did, but some did. One was, I got it in my scrapbook. One was wrote to these Jewish people, I saw them get hit with a B-24, just blew up. It said, "Mom and Dad, I loved you. I want you to know how much I loved you." These were wrote before, in case it should happen. He said that he was Jewish and he said that he hoped these things would right our rights and our wrongs. It was published in the Chicago Tribune. I've got the clippings. I kept it because I had seen it when it happened, the date. But there were people who did that, who wrote their wills, I guess to mom and pop, or wife, or whatever. I never did. I never even thought about writing one like that. I never thought about it.

I had a brother shot down. That was the biggest blow to me. He was flying out of Italy, a B-24. He was a prisoner of war for a year, and he never talked about it until his wife died about five, six years ago. He never talked about it with the family. But I see a lot of letters that come to me about, "Dad never wanted to talk about it." That's the old cliché. "I wonder if he'd ever want to talk about it."

The flight surgeons, the problem was laid in their lap. They're the ones that had to handle the guys that were on the fringe, or combat fatigue, or flak happy as we called them. Then, I don't know if the squadron commanders had anything to do with it, but when we lost this one crew member, a pilot decided - he told us, each crew member - he said, "I'm going to have to take Mac off the crew." It was because he was faking illness. We couldn't get him awake on purpose, it was a hangover, or whatever it was - we drank a lot, that's for sure. What do they call it, "false courage." We did that. Getting into an airplane at six, seven o'clock for a mission in the morning and you got a big hangover because you, what we'd do, we'd turn the oxygen on full rich, that was an instant cure. I wonder if they even know that today. But I got air sick, that was one reason I wasn't a cadet. I wasn't a cadet because I got airsick so much. I knew that I wasn't going to make it, but how in the hell did I ever make it through with the drink and then getting into an aircraft to go on a mission? But the oxygen sure did the job. Yeah, that was good times.

But you know, we were talking about it the other day in the briefing room about we were invincible. It was going to happen to the other guy, but it wasn't going to happen to us. They were just kids. I mean they didn't have any idea ... you did after a while [have fear]. At first, you knew everything was gung-ho.

You flew the flag and had patriotic reasons, and when you got in combat for a while you were realistic and thought, this is a bad business I'm in, how did I ever get here? Most of us were volunteers. Most of the Air Force guys, we weren't drafted as pilots or gunners. We were volunteers. That was one reason they couldn't court marshal us, really. They took the stripes away from you and stuff like that, but a lot of guys, I think the higher up, they'd say, send them to the infantry; make them do it whether they like it or not. Nobody likes to get shot at everywhere you go. But as far as morale was, we had a good crew. My crew had good morale. I think they got me through it. When you have a crew, and I think the British said this, that one thing to keep a crew together was your loyalty to your crew. You weren't going to back out from the other eight guys and say, "I quit." And they said that was a secret and they knew that these guys in the infantry had a squad the same way that the men were so loyal to each other that one guy felt like he was dishonorable to the other guys he was flying with. How could you face somebody and say, "you quit us"? They couldn't do that. The British knew that secret - yep, I guess we did, too.

After all these years, I've been thoroughly engulfed in this stuff right. My family cared enough. My son doesn't know much about it; my daughter does. I've got two beautiful daughters. Kathy, she came a couple of years ago with my granddaughter. And these guys - my youngest granddaughter, she's about 25, she stops traffic. The guys say, "Well, it runs in the family." But this thing never finishes. The worst is we're on the web now. I get my addresses there, but not my name. I get South Africa, Switzerland, I've got a whole lot of Europe. I've got the little tips of the addresses, only part of it. People want to know this and know that. But something that makes me mad, I get peeved about it, is you got 50 years that a guy has forgotten about his crew and now he wants to know what happened to his crew. Why would a guy wait so damn long to want to find out about his crew, what happened to them? Somebody said they were looking at that movie Saving Private Ryan and they got patriotic. But after 50 years, it kind of gets me peeved about it, because why did you wait so long? You're close to these guys as you think you are now, why didn't you communicate with them? Others told me they never communicated with their crew, never heard from them. My crew was very loyal. I've lost one guy about two years ago, my co-pilot. So what's left of our crew is my pilot, my radioman, and then I've lost my bombardier, the navigator's alive, the pilot died October 2002, and I got a tail gunner whose alive. There's about four of us. Roy Hon - he didn't fly with us very long - he was wounded over the channel.

My middle-aged sister, she kept all my V-mail letters and she asked me after the war, she kept every damn one of them, and she said, "Do you want me to save them?" And I said no, and I wished I had them. I got one left. I was going with a gal from Kansas. And you know something, I always thought about this, I told somebody this, but she wrote me just about everyday. It was, you know, a real thing. Somewhere, we were waiting to take off on a mission, and I thought, something's wrong, there's got to be something wrong. It was intuition. So when I got back home I got the "Dear John." That's what it was. My sisters didn't like her. She stayed with my folks and my sisters, they said, "You can do better than that." But I've been in two marriages. I've been married eight years the first marriage. I got these two daughters. And then I've been married 40 years the second time.

I've been back to England twice, and like some guys, I thought, why the hell do men want to go back to where they spent some of the most traumatic experiences of their life? Why would they want to go back? I can't answer that. I don't know if they could. One guy told me, he says, "I ain't going back, because I never left anything there, and I don't intend to go back." But you did leave something. You lost your youth there. You sure as hell grew up in a hurry. You grew up quick - made old men out of us. You could see it in the crew pictures. That was an aging process that made you mature beyond your years. Kids were 18, 19 some of them. But why would they want to go back to Lavenham, to England, to a spot where they had the most traumatic experiences of their life? And some go back. I was interviewed by a gal at a radio station. I said, "Well, it's beautiful today." I said, "Lavenham is a beautiful place. But you know something?" I said, "I couldn't get the hell out of here fast enough." I hated it. But when I come back in '70 and '95, it was beautiful. It's beautiful countryside. The British people, when you go over there, they're gratitude is real. They lay out the red carpet for you. We've been over there six times since the war. Roy Levy has taken people over there. The town of Lavenham has become a tourist place. The buildings are all like this ... You look down the street and the buildings are like this ... This is where they wrote this poem, "There Was a Crooked Man." I've got some friends there. That plaque, I'll take credit for that. I did a little cheating on it. It was 1969 and the auxiliary paid $175 for a brass plaque right there in the Village Square. You can see it right there, and they said, "Silva? Art, pick the words out if you want." I went to the Legion Park where I lived, and it was to the men who were there, it says, "Who died for American democracy." I put it in Britain, so I took the American out. I say what the hell, I didn't want to offend the British who died for American democracy - we died for everybody's democracy. That's the way it should have been. So every word I copied exactly the way it was, except I took the American out of it. But they put two more plaques right there underneath the tower. There's two of them there.

And the Alston's, I knew her, the mother. She was the one that had the push behind us guys going over the first trip in '70. She got the city council, and we stayed there at the Swan and someone stayed over at Long Melford. It was two busloads. It was more than this reunion - 150 people went. And she was the one; she told me they won't build here. She already had 40 addresses that had visited her after the war.

In fact, here's another story. There was a writer from a San Diego television station wanted to know about this Bernie Lay. I don't know if you know about

Bernie Lay and the "Twelve o'clock High," but he was a reluctant guy. He never talked about it. We had a bad mission, and he never wanted to talk about it. So anyway, the writer talked to me on the phone and I says, well, we brought everything over there to England. Everything from pencils to bombs, we brought it over, including Coca-Cola. The American had to have his way, and so he wrote this article, "The Keepers of Little America." This was the next major influence. We married their girls. And I'll tell you, I've said this to guys, we weren't always a good guest, a grateful guest. We would let the English know that we were there saving their bacon. I don't know how they put up with that. I don't know how they did. Guys would get drunk or raise hell and tell the British, "If it wasn't for us, Adolph Hitler would be marching in the streets." The British were mad, I guess. Well, he said, over here over-sexed and overpaid and all this. So, it was probably the truth.

They sent us to rest homes. We had a big one in Southport, great big. It burned down a few years ago. That's where they sent you for flak leave; what they had for, you had 10 missions or 15, they sent you to a flak home for rest and recuperation. It was a nice place with sheets and good food, and there were girls in the town. It was a recreation area. Blackpool was another place. And that's where the crews went for flak leave; they'd call it your flak leave. In London, they were something else. That was another place you'd go to do the things you weren't supposed to do. But you know, life was here today, maybe gone tomorrow. We drank a lot and your life expectancy was not … like I say, you made the most out of it, out of life. The crews themselves were pretty close together - mine was. I know maybe some weren't, but we were very close.

ISADORE LERNER

We were in the operations office of the Grand Island, Nebraska air base, trading stories about our Army experiences. I had just bid goodbye to 20 crews we had been training for the last few months, and now they were off to Europe as replacements. I had just mentioned that Uncle Sam had sent me to every area of the United States except New England and Florida. "Lieutenant Lerner, you have orders." The sergeant handed them to me and I felt as if I had won the jackpot. Florida! Orlando! I hopped a ride in a B-17 and was soon in the Sunshine State. What a contrast to the dreary, chilling climate of Grand Island.

I joined a group of 75 men that made up the original cadre of the 487th Bomb Group. Training began immediately. Lectures and flying training left little time to enjoy the warm climate. In a short time, we were packed onto a long train loaded with many more group personnel, only to end up back in Nebraska. Bruning, Nebraska, a field so unworkable that in three weeks the whole group was transferred to Alamogordo, New Mexico. It was here the group melded and became a well-trained unit ready for overseas duties.

The group began a long journey. The ground personnel to Camp Kilmer, New Jersey, to join a huge convoy crossing the Atlantic to England. The air crews were to fly their planes to England via Brazil, North Africa and to our base at Lavenham.

After our arrival at Lavenham, we immediately set to work organizing our medical department. The dispensary consisted of several offices, a laboratory, x-ray lab, group Surgeon's office and a large room for the doctor's to meet and study. This room also contained a bed for the doctor on call. Attached to the dispensary was a 20-bed hospital for lesser cases. Serious cases, such as injuries, burns, acute appendicitis were evacuated to the station hospital at Acton six miles away.

The flight surgeon's duties were generally similar to those of a general practitioner but also with an understanding of aero medicine and psychological problems needed to care for the flight crews. The base had approximately 3,000 ground and flight personnel at any one time. Most of the ailments were due to stress, backaches, abdominal pain, upper respiratory infections, minor injuries, and gastrointestinal problems.

One day, I received a sheaf of red-bordered letters, high priority! One was signed by President Roosevelt and others all the way down the chain of command to General Eisenhower, and finally, to me. I had to attach my report explaining why this GI in the ground detachment could not get his asthma medicine. His mother had written to the president about it! So, I called the man in.

We had no previous information about his asthma. He brought along a tiny vial about one dram size. The contents were a small amount of diluted adrenaline into one quart of sterile water, making a concentration matching his medication, and I gave it to him with instructions. I then made out a "suitable" report and attached it to the sheaf of letters and reluctantly sent it back through the chain of command. If I only had those letters today!

Stress was a problem with the combat crews. To go out everyday, to face the Nazi's extremely accurate anti-aircraft shells and their fighter planes, seeing their buddies going down was terrifying. They would figure the odds of surviving. Based on a percentage of the losses, they would calculate their chances. So it was not surprising when some men could no longer go on.

One man (they were all 18 to low 20s) came in and told me he couldn't go on. I told him to take the weekend off and come back Monday. He reported back and told me he was ready to fly. He had spent the weekend with an English family, and somehow he felt ready to fly again. Subsequently, he flew 35 missions with no problems and was sent home on schedule.

After the May 11, 1944 mission when we suffered our first big losses, I went over to the barracks of those who survived to talk to them about their feelings. At times like that, I wondered how I could comfort men who had just experienced such emotional trauma. To those that appeared to need it, I gave a sleeping pill. Perhaps I may have helped, but I needed to know more, so on June 15, 1944, I arranged to go on a combat mission. Fortunately, it was basically uneventful. We did get some flak at our level, but no one was hit. I saw our target blasted. With the bombs gone, we turned for home. I felt better having flown the mission.

In the beginning, the losses would prey on your mind, so we learned not to dwell on them and to blot them out. It was necessary defense. By the end of the day, we accepted the fact of losses, but always hoping those men in the planes were able to bail out. Although we developed an accommodation for the battle losses, it was never complete. When the planes returned, we still counted the numbers anxiously and wanted to know how many chutes were counted when a plane went down.

I could never understand what kept them going. Perhaps seeing some crews making it to number 35 and the youthful sense of immortality and duty gave them the will to complete their missions.

To counter stress, the Air Force had taken over many English manor houses. Crews would be sent to these magnificent homes for a week of R and R. For one week there was no war, no discussion of war. One could take walks, read, skeet shoot or just loaf around. Flight surgeons were assigned to these "flak houses." I was fortunate to be assigned twice.

On May 17, 1944, I took my first leave, and as everyone else did, I went to London. Walking down Oxford Street, I ran into a close friend and medical school classmate. After our street reunion he invited me to come with him to meet his "English family." He had met them in a bomb shelter during an air raid.

Gentlemen From Hell

During the war, many Londoners closed their homes and evacuated to the country to avoid the bombings. The government took over these homes and used them to billet officers stationed in London. My friend was billeted across the hall from his "English family." That evening, they invited us for dinner.

After an excellent home cooked dinner, sitting in the living room, enjoying conversation, the doorbell rang. In walked a beautiful young brunette. It was Sylvia, a cousin of the "English family." From that time on, I spent all my leaves in London visiting her. Her family was very close and loving and probably concerned about my intentions. So was I. I couldn't bring myself to propose marriage, take her away from her family to an uncertain future. When the war ended, I returned to Chicago to complete my unfinished residency. All through those months, I couldn't stop thinking about Sylvia. On May 18, 1946, I called Sylvia and proposed. She accepted on condition that I come to London for the wedding. That was fair enough. We were married on September 1, 1946. We met May 17, 1944, and I proposed May 18, two years later. It has been good.

838TH SQUADRON

WILLIAM BOWERS

Bowers (third from left), pictured with fellow servicemen at Sloppy Joe's Bar.

I am William Bowers, Jr. I was a Tech Sergeant and Radio Gunner on a B-17 in the 487th Squadron Stationed 24, Lavenham Field. I was born in Varnville, South Carolina on April 1, 1918. I remember growing up in Varnville, which was a very small town, during the really tough times of the Great Depression. I attended the local schools and was employed by the South Carolina Highway Department until I was drafted into the military on January 9, 1942 at the age of 24.

I was assigned to the 30th Army Division 117 Infantry Company and I stayed at Fort Jackson for about six months. While at Fort Jackson, they took us to Myrtle Beach for two weeks. We pitched tents on the beach during this period. They would get us up real early each morning, and we had to walk about 10 miles. At about four in the afternoon, they gave us leave to go into town.

We were then transferred to Fort Benning, Georgia. We were to stay there for approximately six months and then were transferred to Fort Blanding, Florida. We stayed at Fort Blanding for a short period of time and went to the Tennessee maneuvers while in Tennessee. I transferred to the Army Air Force and was sent to Greensboro, North Carolina to take a test and be assigned to a school. This was the first time I had been assigned to an area that had a lot of snow and a lot of time to stay indoors. After I finished radio school (in the winter time), I was transferred to Yuma Air Base, AZ, to go to gunnery school. When we left Scott Field, Illinois, the temperature was about 15 degrees, and when we got to Yuma, it was 90 degrees. What a change! After finishing gunnery school, I was transferred to McDill Air Base in Tampa, Florida. This is where we were assigned to

Gentlemen From Hell

a crew to take our advanced training before going overseas. The crew I was assigned to is as follows: Pilot-Robert J. Gasser; Co-Pilot-Robert Fuchs; Navigator-Harry Katz; Bombardier-Richard D. Adams; Engineer/Gunner-Jack Hawkins; Radio Gunner-Billy Bowers; Ball-Turret Gunner-Kenny Drinnon; Waist Gunner-Fred Belt; Tail Gunner-Elmer Zeidman.

We were assigned a B-17 at McDill. We flew many training flights to targets in the gulf. I believe these flights were for bomb-run and aerial gunnery practice. We flew and fired at floating targets while we were skimming the wave tops. We also flew navigation training flights. On one of these flights, we slowed to look at the forest fires. On another flight, hedgehopping with two other B-17s thrilled us! The chickens and cows sure did scatter. We lost an engine on one of the flights and felt like some kind of heroes, because we came home singing "Coming in on a Wing and a Prayer." We also did some night flying. We learned to wear "Mae West's" and practiced ditching procedures from a B-17 fuselage in pool water.

After completing air crew training at McDill around mid August, we were sent to Savannah, Georgia for overseas staging. During this transition, we were given a 48 hour trip to Havana, Cuba via B-17. While in Havana, we stayed at the Hotel Nacionale. I remember visiting Cuba's Capitol building. Some of us visited Sloppy Joe's bar where we tasted rum and coca-cola. I brought home a souvenir picture of this place. In general, I believed we all had a good time with this trip.

During our stay in Savannah, there was much speculation as to whether we would be going to the Pacific or to Europe. I remember we visited in Savannah and spent lots of leisure time playing cards as we waited to go. Our overseas flight began in Savannah. If my memory is correct, Gasser informed us for the first time, after we were airborn, that we were headed to the European Theater of Operations. We were ferrying a brand new B17G. Our first leg was to Bangor, Maine. On the flight north, we flew over Varnville at tree-top level, and we also flew over Philadelphia, where Elmer Zeidman was from, as well as New York City, the hometown of Fuchs and Katz. While in Bangor, we traded in our summer uniforms for winter wear. It was there that a supply Sergeant suggested that we had a double that had been through the day before. It was there I got a new watch and gave Kenny my old one.

Our next leg was to Goose Bay, Labrador, where we refueled and spent the night. Some of us pulled guard duty in the extreme cold of our B-17 - or was this Iceland on our next leg? We completed our overseas flight at Wales, British Isles near the end of September 1944. While in Wales, we learned that the British Isles was completely blacked out at night. We went to a movie in town and heard the British National Anthem played before the picture began.

From Wales, we were transferred to AF station 137, Lavenham England which was the home of the 487th Bomb Group. We were assigned to the 838th Squadron, commanded by Major Eberhart. We were given our very own B-17G, which we named "Tru Love." We enlisted men were assigned to a quonset hut that already had two older crews living there. We also discovered that at this stage of the war, the groups were flying with only one waist gunner. Somehow, it was determined that Bob Wisdom would not fly in combat with us. Even though Bob would not fly in combat with us, all of us always considered him to be one of the old "Tru Love" crew. Bob was assigned CQ duty for our squadron. He really took care of his buddies.

Before we flew our first mission, we flew some training flights around England and did some night take-off and landing practice. On one of these night practices, during a light rain, we cracked up at the end of the runway. Gasser told us later that he did not have air speed indicated after accelerating nearly to the end of the runway. So, he cut power and applied the brakes. We skidded off the end of the rain-slick runway and mired the landing wheels deep into the mud. The plane tilted tail-up, and smashed the nose. Then, it slammed back down and smashed the tail; I believe Elmer got a few bruises from being bounced around. I happened to be seated with my safety belt on, Fred was bounced around also. Luckily, there was no fire. We quickly evacuated the plane. Elmer crawled out because his knee was bruised. Someone had failed to remove the pilot tube cover. I believe the ground crew chief, as well as Hawkins and Gasser, were held responsible for this oversight. We had to fly our first three missions with Gasser riding in the CO pilot's seat, because, in his mind, no one could fly like Gasser. Bob Fuchs had to fly with some other crew on the first few missions.

A few days after our crack-up, another plane crashed within our hearing while checking out night landings. By now, I was beginning to develop a worrisome feeling that flying into the ETO was more dangerous than it had been back home. Our first mission to Germany was flown around September 30, 1944. The first few missions were routine and without incident, as were the majority of our missions. A few missions later, to gun emplacements at Metz, France, I saw my first B-17 shot down by flak. One wing was ablaze as it spiraled down, eventually breaking apart. I remember counting several parachutes, which were reported to Gasser and again in debriefing. After this, I was scared of black puffs even though we all knew that you did not need to worry about the one you saw.

The mission on which we flew downward through a clearing in the clouds to around 10,000 feet to bomb a railroad yard is remembered vividly because of seeing box cars flying through the air like match boxes. We had some kind of view, and there were no flak guns shooting at us.

Those missions to the oil fields at Merseburg were particularly scary because of the acres of black puffs of flak. It was on one of the Merseburg missions that I was looking directly at a B-17 when it disintegrated in mid air from a direct shell hit. The plane fell in small pieces. As I recall, there were no parachutes. How close it was to us! We knew it could have been any one of us.

On a mission to bomb an oil dump in the Black Forest, I witnessed a fantastic air battle between bombers from another group and both German and American fighter planes. It seemed as though everywhere I looked, planes were going down in smoke and flames. The air was full of parachutes.

There was one mission when a piece of flak, about a half an inch by 10 inches in size, went through an inboard engine propeller hub on our B-17. Black oil spewed forth from the hole and covered the underside of the plane. I was really scared because of the fires I had seen on the other planes in flight. We suddenly, and without warning, dropped out of formation, seemingly out of control. We could see the remainder of the formation leaving us in the distance. We were alone. However, Gasser soon had the plane under control and flying level. We were all worried about the wind-milling of the propeller until he got it feathered. Since our group had gone on and we were alone with a full load of bombs, powered by only three engines and over friendly territory, we turned back and headed for home, knowing that we would have to carry our bombs back to the English Channel before dumping them. A friendly P-38 Lighting appeared and escorted us back across Europe. We finally made it home to our base, "Coming in on a wing and a prayer."

We landed an hour later than the remainder of our group, which had completed their mission and returned to base. Fred's brother, Dave, had come over to our base that morning for a visit. He was patiently waiting by our hardstand when we arrived.

The December 24, 1944 mission to the Ardennes, in support of the Battle of the Bulge, when the Eighth Air Force launched the mightiest air armada ever assembled, is one of the most vivid memories for the 487th airmen. There were 2,034 heavy bombers carrying an army of approximately 18,000 men and 6,000 to 10,000 tons of bombs. The 487th group was leading the Eighth Air Force armada, and our squadron, the 838th was the lead squadron. Our crew, flying in "Tru Love," was in the four position. General Frederick Castle, who was task commander, was visiting the 487th for this mission.

Our fighter escort had been delayed on take off due to bad weather over their base. It seemed as though the German Luftwaffe knew all this because they launched a small flight of around 20 fighter planes, which attacked the 487th group. The Germans made a head-on pass and crippled General Castle's plane. Before they were through, they shot down 13 of the 487th's planes, which was a one-third loss. They seemed to be flying at us from all directions after the first pass. Kenny spotted one coming up from beneath us at about five o'clock and quickly identified him as an FW-190.

He then set his wingspan in his turret gun sight. As he approached, he kept him framed in his sight by letting off on his foot, actually operating by his heel control. When he was coming into range, he began to think, "Should I open fire?" That is when he pressed his guns and started firing. He shot down one FW-190 and hit another, and also Elmer hit another of the FW-190s from his tail-turret. None of the German bullets hit our plane. Our crew reported shooting down three FW-190s at the debriefing.

838th Squadron

We also learned at the debriefing that our fighter escort showed up in time to destroy all the remaining German planes the B-17 gunners had left for them. Our plane moved up to fly in the third position to the target and return. After the battle, there was a plane flying along within our line of sight, with a large gaping hole at its left waist position. It flew onto the target and returned to base, never to fly again.

A crew of our buddies who lived in our barracks was shot down. I believe it was Lt. Cromwell's crew. We found out that they were crippled on the first pass and then attacked by several Germans who finished them off. They bailed out over friendly territory and all but one eventually returned to our base and resumed flying their mission. I believe their crew received credit for three or four Germans destroyed. The crewmember that did not return suffered a broken leg.

General Castle rode this crippled plane down, staying with it so that his crew would be saved. He was killed. The Congressional Medal of Honor was awarded to him posthumously. I believe he was the last airman in the ETO to be awarded the Medal of Honor.

It seemed that we dreaded missions that took us over the North Sea. I believe this was because we had been warned that if it became necessary for us to ditch or bail out into icy waters of the North Sea, a human could not live for more than three to four minutes. We flew quite a few of these missions. There was a strange name, Zeider Zee, which we flew over on some missions. Then, there were the beautiful white cliffs of Dover, which we could see on some of our return flights.

I remember we flew several missions to Kassel and to Merseberg. We also flew on the first daylight mission to Berlin. On one mission, we were forced to land in France because of bad weather and fog back in England at our base. We and several other crews landed at a fighter base with a short runway. The next morning, we taxied down the runway and turned and took-off with airfoil and engines set as if it were a maximum load take-off. I remember we were so light without gasoline and bombs that we had the sensation of mushrooming into the air. I remember that a movie was shown that night. The screen and seats were set up in open air. The local townspeople were invited. Some of us got to practice our high school French with them.

We aerial gunners were experts in the care and use of .50 caliber machine guns. Ours were detailed and cleaned after every mission and cleaned of excess oil before every mission. We could detail, strip and reassemble while wearing gloves. On every mission, we test fired our guns while we were over water.

Somewhere around the 20th mission, we were given two-weeks rest leave to Southport, where we relaxed and took it easy. We also got regular 72-hour passes to London. I remember visiting Westminster Abbey, St Paul's Cathedral, Madame Toussaud's wax museum and Leicester Square. I saw Big Ben and Buckingham Palace. I visited the bombed ruins and heard V-2 and V-1 buzz bomb blasts. While in London, we ate in fancy restaurants and traveled many miles on the subway. London and all of England was completely blacked out at night.

Bob Fuchs was promoted to first pilot and given his own crew after about 20 missions. Of course, he will always be part of our crew. I do not even remember who flew as our co-pilot after Bob left. I remember that on one of our missions, we heard that Bob's plane was shot up really bad. They lost three engines and had to throw everything including the radio equipment off the plane in order to conserve fuel and limp home on one engine. I remember how much we admired Bob for bringing his crew home safely. You see, he was "one of us." That was really "coming home on a wing and a prayer."

Life in our Quonset hut was fairly comfortable except for the cold, dreary climate. Our only heat was a tiny stove, which could be fueled by most any solid fuel. We were given a coke (charcoal) ration each week. Since the ration did not last long, we supplemented it with scrap wood. Elmer and Fred and some others were excellent wood scavengers. Kenny established himself as the official wood-chopper, using a sharp hatchet. He being from the hills of Tennessee knew about such things.

An Englishman came regularly and took our laundry to his house where it was done up real nice for us. I wish I could remember his name. I remember he was polite and friendly. We paid him a fixed amount for each item.

We went to the local towns of Lavenham, Sudbury and Bury Saint Edmunds fairly often. The pubs seemed to be the center of English social life. The local citizens seemed to enjoy the company. We learned to play darts for milds and bitters. Occasionally, we were invited to their homes for tea and biscuits. We donated chocolates to our hosts. We also learned about the English fast-food items of fish and chips.

We sent all of our letters by v-mail. All of us received food packages from home. I believe mail call with the letters and packages from home were the most enjoyable moments of our existence.

Our last mission, number 34, was flown February 28, 1944. One of the longest missions was 11 hours and 56 minutes. Our shortest mission was eight-plus hours. We had flown approximately 400 hours in combat.

All 10 of Tru Love's crew made it through the war safely and returned home. The four officers had each advanced from second to first lieutenants. The enlisted had advanced to staff and tech sergeants.

No one really knows what happened to the aluminum, the steel, rubber and plexiglas that made the B-17 named "Tru Love." But many of the planes made it through the war only to be chopped into scrap aluminum back home in America. But no matter what happened to the plane itself, not a man alive who flew in her will ever forget his Odyssey in Tru Love. After we finished our 34th mission, we became members of the Lucky Bastards Club on February 28, 1945. All of our crew was shipped back to the U.S.A with the exception of me. I stayed with the 838th squadron until after VE day, and was in London on May 8, 1945. I

838TH SQUADRON

flew back from England a member of the crew with Alvin Moser Jr. We deported England on July 6, 1945 and arrived in the U.S.A on July 13, 1945. I was then transferred to camp Gordon, Georgia and given a 30-day delay in route to Tampa Florida, where we were to train in B-29 to go to the Far East. While I was home the Japanese surrendered, so when I returned to camp Gordon, I was discharged on August 22, 1945 and returned to my home in Varnville, S.C.

FRANCIS EBERHART

Eberhart was a Squadron Commander, and flew 33 combat missions during World War II. He served over 23 years in the Air Force.

I joined the Eighth Air Force when the 102nd Observation Squadron was assimilated into the Eighth Air Force. The date of my entry into the service was March 15th, 1940. I was wondering what was going to happen to me in my service career. I remember the day I became a squadron commander. I was called in by one of the Captains and was told I was being made a squadron commander. At the time, I didn't think I was good for this job. I really didn't appreciate the magnitude of my duties. I was told, "Take care of things. You have to see things are getting done. That's your job." With the squadron one night while we were being briefed and I had to explain why I was going to be squadron commander, I did with these words: "You know why I'm here. Let's go." That was my introduction to pilots and the people in the 838th squadron. I just floundered around till they told me what my responsibilities were. If they wanted a mud hole filled up, then I had to get after the men and see that it was filled up.

I was about 22 years old when I arrived in England in November 1943. I flew 33 missions - 13 in the B-24 and the rest in B-17s. The reason we changed airplanes was because the B-24 had a tendency to wander. The nose was not stable. But the B-17 came on solid. A bombardier could plan his bomb load with the position on the target and it would be there at "bombs away." It was much more stable. The B-17 could fly higher than the B-24, but it was slower by 10 miles per hour. Missions were flown at 150 miles per hour. I had good pilots that could really fly - exactly to the letter, which made it really easy for the other guys at the tail end. It made it easier for them to stay with it especially during a maneuver such as a turn. If we flew all over the sky - God help us!

There was a mission where we flew through the clouds - that was my most memorable by far. I was leader this day and assigned to some target in Germany. Everything went according to Hoyle during the early part of the mission, but we got over the water clouds which made us fly all over. We were dispersing, climbing, going lower. I chose to go lower, and we eventually got down to 1,500 feet which, is impossible to fly over enemy territory. I had no alternative except to climb, trying to get on top of the clouds which were very, very thick. We were flying up at 150 miles per hour, and the only airplanes we could see were wing tips of two airplanes on the side. Gradually, we came up. An entire unit came up without being able to see each other. When we reached the top of the clouds, every plane was there in just about the right position, only because they flew with instruments and at 150 miles an hour - so, dangerous, but no crashes. We were not supposed to fly on instruments. The clouds dispersed, and it opened up when we got over this enemy territory, but then it closed in again and we were once more on instruments. We could not see; the only aircraft were the sideman's wing tips, and we were on instruments, knowing there was a wing ahead of us doing the same thing because he could not see either. I thank the good Lord above we didn't get killed or run into one another. Those were the best pilots, and I wish many times since that I had called them in and given them the Distinguished Flying Cross - they sure deserved it that day. I don't know whether we hit the target or not, but the bombardier released the bombs. This is one mission I remember as being really different.

I began to feel I had developed a bit of steam with my job, and felt I was doing a good job. Air leaders didn't fly the airplanes, but they were responsible for them to fly correctly and on time at a certain place. Earlier, some air leaders flew up to get away from the gunners down below and some of them would change courses to avoid flak - not us. We flew directly as the instruction dictated. Therefore, my evaluation came out pretty good, and I soon became what they called a good air leader, of which I was real proud. My missions went according to the orders. I kept copies of all the flight plans for our wing throughout the whole war. I later lost the trunk that they were packed in when I returned home. I regret not having the records of these missions. I had a lot of planes shot down, especially in B-24s. When the gas tank in a B-24 was hit, it always exploded. The B-17 was a little different.

Usually, everything went according to plan and there was no great mess about it. One thing you had to do was the IP at a certain time at a certain altitude. That is when the bombardier took over and set his sites on the target.

There was a time when guns were exploding around us and that's when I got so scared I was numb. If you think you've ever been scared before, you haven't come close. There were several missions that were very scary, but the good Lord was sure looking out for me.

There was a part of my life when I was trying to find out who I was, where I was going and why, so this is a beautiful story, if you look at it from the standpoint that all my life I knew I wanted to fly! It was the only thing I really wanted to do! In college, I didn't care about my courses - I wanted to fly! There was no way of doing it because of the cost involved.

After I returned from England, I went to law school. Then I went back into the Air Force and finished out my 23 years, six months and three days. I was a member of JAG for six years until I elected to give this up and fly. We received an allowance for flying.

I got out of the service to build airplanes. Four of us rented the airport at Baldwyn, Mississippi. We had an engineer who had a patent on an airplane used in the 102nd observation squad.

ROY M. LEVY

It is August 9 of the year 2002. We're here in Omaha, Nebraska for the 37th Reunion of the 487th Bomb Group. My name is Roy M. Levy. I held the rank of Staff Sergeant. I went into the service, maybe April or May of 1943. After our crew was trained and we arrived in England, we were sent to Stone, England, where there was a depo base - that's to transfer people to different groups - and that's when we went into the 8th Air Force. I arrived in England at the beginning of '44. I was with two squadrons. I was with the 487th Bomb Group. I flew with the 838th squadron for four missions and then I flew with the 836th squadron for an additional 16 missions. The reason for that, on the fourth mission my oxygen came off and the pilot called for an oxygen shift. I didn't respond; the radio operator, Angelo, came back and he said he heard about people's skin turning blue. I was blue. And I replaced the oxygen mask, and on the second oxygen shift I was off again, so they put the oxygen on full slow, and then I was able to complete the mission. The next day, I was in the hospital; they were checking my lungs and so forth, and my original crew was shot down that day. So then, I checked out as a togglier/air gunner after that, and I flew out of the third gunner's pool until I was assigned to another crew. That's the reason I was with two different squadrons.

I was 17 and not quite 18 when I entered the service. I was originally an armor and a gunner, which took care of the bombs and things like that. And after I went back to flying again, I was a togglier gunner, where I dropped the bombs. Totally, I flew 19 missions.

Every mission, with nine people on the aircraft, they all had a different story. They all saw different things and experienced different emotions. So the most memorable mission, this would be an individual feeling. On the fifth mission, when my crew went down, our navigator was killed. They were prisoners of war. Some of them bailed out and the pilot, Harry T. Nylon, he crash-landed trying to save Frank. The strange thing was that every Sunday, Frank made us all go to church, regardless, and then we could do what we wanted, and he was the only one to get killed. So strange things happen.

It is questionable if I was ever wounded, but before I started flying again after I was on flying status, we checked my equipment, and we found flak in my oxygen mask. So I guess my oxygen mask came off due to enemy action, because when the antiaircraft shells exploded, some of the shrapnel hit the mask, took it off my face, and that's the reason I passed out.

My plane was never shot down. Any plane that I landed on, I flew with; the original crew was on the "Yankee Maid." She had completed a tour, and on the fifth mission, when I wasn't flying, she went down.

Gentlemen From Hell

One of my experiences, I was flying with Dick Allhouse as waist gunner. They needed an extra crew member. Our wing man was hit by flak between the third and fourth engine. We lost part of the wing. When he came down he took off our vertical stabilizer, trim tab. Dick Allhouse was a major pilot and he had to fly the plane back to the base on the engines. There were no controls because we lost part of it. After he took off our trim tab, he hit the plane on our right wing, about where the tail gunner would be. They went out of sight, and we don't know what happened to them. But that was an experience.

The pilot was Harry T. Nylon. He was a First Lieutenant. Bill Rip was a co-pilot. Frank Abbot, our navigator, was killed. In fact, in the American Museum in England, Doxler, his name is on the top of the list. It was alphabetical. So Frank Abbot, navigator. Johnny Claxton was our top gunner, and I just found out he's still alive and lives in Arizona. I talked to the pilot, Harry T. I had back surgery, and he was afraid to have back surgery, so I explained to him about my back surgery. He wasn't playing golf or walking or anything. Since I've been speaking with him, he's had his back surgery - he's playing golf again. He lives in Sacramento, California. Ray Litka was our tail gunner. He tells me the day they were shot down, he was able to shoot down two ME 109s from the tail position. Angelo Overoll was the radio operator. He was the one that brought the oxygen and saved my life and the one who explained to my wife - she said she'd get even with him for that.

Let's see, I was discharged in January of '46 in Florida, but I went into the service from Atlanta, Georgia, and I came out in Saint Petersburg. I lived in Atlanta for a while and worked with my father. I was looking for a rich widow, but I never found one, so I had to go to work. I came out of the service and worked with my father for a while. He was a house painter, a contractor, so I worked with him there. Moving to California, we owned a lumber and wrecking company - my father, my brother and myself.

I was married 42 years ago on Thanksgiving Day. The Flamingo Hotel in Las Vegas put on the wedding for us, and my wife, Joe, said it was a better wedding than her mother put on for us. My second wife, which was Joe, second marriage, she had three children, and I had three children from my former marriage. So together, we had six children; The Brady Bunch. Then we have eight grandchildren between us.

The first I heard about the 487th having reunions, I lived in Long Beach, California. They were having a reunion. My wife found it in the paper that they were having a reunion in Las Vegas. In Las Vegas was the first time we attended a reunion and since then we've been attending all the reunions. Occasionally, due to health, we'd miss one now and then. I have put on two stateside reunions and four overseas reunions for the 487th. We went to England and Scotland, but we always end up back at Lavenham, at the field. My wife and myself, we've hosted them. I'm proud to say that I was the one who founded and organized the auxiliary, the 487th Bomb Group Auxiliary, and without them, there's a lot of history we'd have missed. We've done an excellent job, and just recently, I was able to get some funding for the auxiliary. As long as there is an auxiliary, the 487th will be alive. Normally, they're at our reunions. I'm 76 now; I'm the youngest one in the group, so you can see that there are some of them that are old. But there will come a point where we'll have to turn the organization over to the auxiliary and the children of the people that flew with us, or ground crew with us. They brought up the history of it and they really are pushing it. They will take over one day, and the 487th Bomb Group will live.

Every mission is a story in itself - it could be a book in itself. And for everyone on the crew, it would be another book. It's what you experienced. On our mission to Berlin, I was flying as a spare togglier and gunner, which was right up on the front, the bombardier's position. I looked over to my right and I said to the navigator, "I'm glad we're not going over there, because look at the sky, it's black." And he said, "Don't be so happy, because that's where we're going." We'd come back several times without an engine. One time, we came back with 32 holes in the aircraft. So they were kind of accurate. When I was flying as a spare gunner, it seems like luck was with us because we did have some damage, but never had any casualties. In fact, Angelo told my wife, "When Roy didn't fly with us on that fifth mission, we lost our luck." So I was the youngest - they called me "The Kid." I was the youngest on the crew.

WILLIAM C. RICH

Major William C. Rich served three years in active service and twenty years in the reserves.

I'm not sure my story has much merit in your collection of stories, but I will at least respond with what little actual war service I did have.

I am William C. Rich, Major, retired in 1984. I spent approximately three years in active military service and the remainder of 20 years in the reserves. I actually entered service in Feb. 1943, and after all the training entered the 8th Air Force in Nov. of 1944. I arrived in England Feb. of 1945. My crew was assigned to the 838th squadron. At that time, I was 20 years old. We were assigned to a B-17 that had about 80 missions on it, so we felt comfortable to have survived that many missions. We were a full crew of 10 with a bombardier who had already served 35 missions in B-26s in Southern Europe and did not want to stay stateside after his tour and opted to return with our crew. He was immediately taken from our crew and was assigned to a "lead crew in training."

As first pilot, I flew one more mission than the rest of the crew because at that time it was procedure to give new pilots one mission with an experienced crew as a co-pilot to better understand the importance of close formation flying. At that stage of the war, our fighter cover was very good, so the gunners had little to do except to keep lookout. The one incident of a German fighter getting close to the formation was when a ME-262, a twin-engine jet came sliding past our formation after making just one pass at us. I believe no one was hit. Except for being hit with flak a couple of times, we suffered little damage. The hydraulic system ruptured one time, resulting in a "hairy landing" - no brakes. The crew flew a total of 14 missions before VE day.

One memorable experience after VE day was a mercy trip to the continent. A floor was put in the bomb bay, and boxes of food were loaded on board. We were instructed to fly to Linz, Austria, where the food was offloaded and about 20 French POWs - men, women and children - were loaded on to the airplane. We distributed them from the waist, radio room to the nose and took off from a rather short runway on a hot day in late June. With that kind of a load, the take-off was kind of exciting! We flew over the Black Forest at an altitude that resulted in a lot of thermals. Some got sick, and it was the only time in my flying career that I felt a little queasy! Anyway, we flew on to France and landed on a "steel mat" landing strip near Paris and off-loaded our passengers. We took off, circled the Eiffel Tower and flew back to England.

The trip home to the U.S. was memorable, in that we, the flight crew and ground crew, loaded up in early July and headed for Prestwick, Scotland. The next day, we took off for Iceland. We got almost to Iceland, ran into weather and had to return to Scotland! We then waited about 14 days, took off again and made an uneventful flight to Iceland; Gander, Nova Scotia; Presque Isle, Maine, where we said goodbye to our weary bird "Bashful Bessie." The name of the little girl painted on the nose of the aircraft.

We were all given a short leave, and I was given orders to report to Santa Anna, CA, for reassignment, probably for duty in the Pacific. VJ day came along while I was at the station, and they really didn't know what to do with all of us. I was at Santa Anna until I was separated in Oct. 1945.

With the help of the GI bill, I went back to Iowa State University to finish my education, getting married while I was in school. Our son, Bruce, was born about the time I graduated. I took a job teaching Vocation Agriculture in Clear Lake High School. I taught AG for 17 years, got my masters degree and went to North Iowa Community College as an administrator and was there for 19 years before retirement. A daughter, Victoria, was born while I was teaching in Clear Lake. Both my children are graduates of Iowa State. Bruce is an electrical engineer and Vick is an accomplished designer of commercial interiors. Bruce has two children, a boy and a girl, so, I have two grandchildren. Unfortunately, my wife died in January 2000.

The whole experience had been memorable, and I feel fortunate to have lived through it without battle scars.

CHUCK HASKETT

LEFT: *Haskett and his crew were shot down during the Battle of the Bulge on December 24, 1944.* RIGHT: *Two days after his plane was shot down, Haskett was recovering from wounds at an inn in Belgium when the owner of the inn and his daughter approached Haskett. After the 10/11-year-old girl asked Haskett if he had "killed any Bosch" (what they called Germans) and discovered that he had, she gave him a big hug and kiss. During a trip back to the area 57 years later, Haskett was re-introduced to the girl, Janine Gillett.*

"To Hell or to Glory." These words will live in my memory forever. They were given to my inquiry of "well, where do we go from here?" It was the answer given me by Jimmy Weber, from Texas, who was our engineer/gunner on the B-17 crew we were assigned to. We had just completed our training prior to going overseas to join the 8th U.S. Air Force in England. Their reputation was well known at this time as being a very risky organization to be a member of.

It had been almost two years of training for me. Shortly after Pearl Harbor - Pearl who? I had never heard of the place, but it didn't take long to realize that we were at war and the lives of all of us would be changed forever. All the young men of my hometown of Bedford, Indiana were eager to go into the service and kick the hell out of the Japanese. From most of the news at the time, it seemed the quickest way to do this was to join the Marine Corps. So two of my best buddies were accepted, but I was told to go home and get some dental work done.

Being very disappointed, I returned home and got a job working for the Navy at an ammunition depot at Crane, Indiana. My job there was load, transport and store high explosives. Very dangerous, but someone had to do it. I could get my dental work done with my pay from this and get into the service.

During the summer of 1942, I had an opportunity to try for enlistment in the Naval Air Corps as an Aviation Cadet V-5. It was a very tough service to get into, but they had recently lowered their standards to take in men who had no college, but good high school education. I passed with flying colors, and for the next 10 months and 19 days, I completed many hours of ground school and learned to fly a small plane to begin with, the complete pre-flight school at the University of Iowa. From there, it was the Naval Air Station at Ottumwa, Iowa. There, we flew Stearman bi-planes, and I had some dual time in an SNJ, Army designation, At-6. I fouled up early one morning and was going to be taken before a washout board for possible action. At the time I had enlisted, there was a clause in the papers that would allow us to resign from the service if we failed to complete flight service. I took this option and received a Special Order discharge under honorable conditions.

Returning home, I went back to work, and since everyone at that time had to go through the draft board, I asked to be shipped out with the next group. I had talked with an Army recruiter, and he told me that within a few weeks I could be flying an Army plane with all my experience in the Navy. I later learned that you can't believe everything you are told by some people in authority.

I was sent to Jefferson Barracks, Missouri for basic training, and after about three months of going through the very basics of how to wash pots and pans, clean latrines, learn how to salute anyone that moves and wear blisters on your feet from marching, I was finally declared fit to enter school to be a flying cadet. Mt. Union College at Alliance, Ohio was the place chosen to teach me all the things I had just learned in the Navy. Where are the planes?

After about two months of this an order came down that since they needed more gunners than pilots, our entire class would be sent to aerial gunner school at Kingman, Arizona. When a bomber is shot down, we lose a pilot and a co-pilot, but possibly five gunners. It doesn't take a mathematics genius to figure out the attrition rate for gunners is far above that for pilots. That should have been a warning enough for us.

After gunnery school, we were sent to Lincoln, Nebraska where we were assigned to crews. Our crew consisted of: Pilot, Kenneth Lang of New York; Co-pilot, Howard Miller of Washington; Bombardier, Howard Cox, Hometown unknown; Navigator, Samuel Alvine, Jr. New Jersey; Engineer/Top-Turret Gunner, James Weber, Texas; Radioman, Donald Huck, Montana; Armorer/Gunner: Donald Kausrud; Ball-Turret Gunner, Robert Yowan, Pennsylvania; Togglier/Waist Gunner, Donald Boland, Oklahoma; Tail Gunner, Charles "Chuck" Haskett, Indiana. An All-American crew in an all-out war.

We did our transitional training at Alexandria, Louisiana. There, we learned to work as a team. We became as brothers, knowing full well our lives depended on each other. We had no doubts as to what we were going up against.

After completing this part of our training, we returned to Lincoln, Nebraska. Here, we picked up a brand new B-17 and were told to head for "jolly old"

GENTLEMEN FROM HELL

England. We flew without incident to Wales by way of Labrador and Iceland. We were then sent to Stone, England for assignment to a bomb group. We knew we were being replacements for crews that were lost to combat or that had completed their quota of 25 missions. More likely the former reason. We hoped to be assigned to a good group with a good record and our luck held with us. We drew the 487th Bomb Group that had already been cited by the President for flying the shuttle missions to Russia and Africa. Also, they had the highest bombing accuracy in the Eighth Air Force at that time.

Our crew was assigned to the 838th squadron under the command of Major Francis C. Eberhart. As mentioned before, we were with the 487th Bomb Group at station 137, Lavenham, England. We were in the 3rd Air Division and the 4th Wing.

Our first mission was Bingen, Germany on November 27th, 1944. We had spent several weeks flying indoctrination missions to get us acquainted with the area and practice our skills at close formation flying. Also, the weather was a factor in any flying at that time of year in England. We spent many days on the ground "sweating it out." That first mission was a "milk run" - no flak (antiaircraft fire) or fighter attacks. I thought to myself, man, this is going to be easy. However, I saw the realization of war on the next mission.

It was probably one of the most dangerous targets in Germany at that time - Merseberg. Anyone who had that occasion to fly over there knows what I mean. It was our second mission on November 30, 1944. Being in the tail, it was impossible for me to see directly in front, but I could see from about two o'clock to ten o'clock, and that was plenty. The flak was so thick, it was hard to see through it. I could see planes going down in a spiral to their death, and some were dropping out of formation to be pounced on by the Luftwaffe. They loved to go after a crippled plane like a pack of hounds after a hamburger. We at least didn't have to worry about the fighters attacking us who were still in formation. They wouldn't fly into their own death trap. However, I'm keeping my eyes wide open just in case, and out of the corner of my left eye, something caught my attention. It was a huge flash, and I turned my head to see a large ball of fire that was beginning to fall away. I exclaimed, "what the hell kind of flak is that?" Jimmy Weber answered, "Flak hell, that was a B-17."

That was not the last plane I was to see go down, but being the first, it made me realize that a person could get hurt up there. We lost a lot of planes that day over that city. We had to go back there on the 6th of December, but it was a little easier. The first time the area was clear, not a cloud over the target, but the next time it was cloudy and the gunners on the ground had to use radar with the aid of some chaff (aluminum strips like icicles from a Christmas tree) dropped from our plane. That first mission was without a doubt the worst mission I was on during my tour of duty, except the one that I am about to tell about now on December 24, 1944 ... Christmas Eve.

It all began on December 16, 1944. We awoke that morning to look out and see a fog that was impossible to see through. No wonder we were not alerted for a mission. We normally were given rides to the mess hall by trucks, but this morning there was nothing moving, neither on wheels or in the air. Even the birds were walking. Visibility was zero.

For the next few days, it was the same. We heard stories about a huge offensive by the Germans in the Ardennes in Belgium. Our ground forces were caught off guard and were being overrun at all points. The Germans were not playing by the rules and were not taking many prisoners, and in some cases were shooting the ones who tried to surrender. We hated to hear this and were getting madder at each report. For the first time since we had arrived at the base, I saw the men really wanting to get in the air and help those men out. The weather lasted for a week. Finally, on the 23rd of December, it cleared. We were alerted for the 24th.

At briefing that morning, we were told of the situation in Belgium and that our targets would be the German fighter fields. We wanted to draw the Luftwaffe into the air and destroy them. We were also told that they would come up to meet us and that to be ready for a fight. And a fight we got! We were still climbing to our bombing attitude of 25,000 feet when we passed over Liege, Belgium. It was burning in many areas from, as we learned later, a massive attack by V-1 rockets. We were at about 22,000 feet. It was just about high noon.

From twelve o'clock high they came, ME109s, several of them. I couldn't see them from my tail position until they had passed by and could not get off a shot. I asked that someone let me know when they were coming so I could fire at them as they went by. However, they did a lot of damage as they went screaming through our formation. I'm sure our pilot, Kenneth Lang, was killed at this time and possibly two of our men in the waist. My first knowledge of a hit was within the plane, I saw fire coming from the wing. At this time, a group of Fock Wulf 190s had lined up behind us in what was known as a company front attack. They began firing their 20mm cannons at us. Again, I heard a loud whump and could feel the plane shudder. I was firing my guns at the plane I thought was coming at us, firing intermittently, one barrel at a time to keep from burning them up. When I saw the plane I was shooting at was still boring in, I said to myself, to hell with the barrels, and locked both triggers down. This brought results - the Focke-Wulf exploded. I cried out, "I got him!"

At about this time, I heard Bob Yowan, the ball-turret gunner, call out, "Kausrud, I'm hit." There was no reply from Kausrud - he may have been hit himself at that time. I could see a line of holes appear along the lower left side of the fuselage. The plastic window near the right side of my face shattered. It seemed like a dream - this could not be happening to me, it happens to other people. Jim Weber called out on the intercom, "hit the silk boys, she's burning like hell." I realized that something was wrong with the pilot since he should have been the one to give the order to abandon ship.

Just before I bailed out, I heard the co-pilot, Howard Miller, say "Chuck," that was all. He was still holding the plane under control, because it would have been in a spiral with both left engines out and the right side engines going full throttle. I tried to answer, but I had disconnected my system or it was shot out. I'll never know what Howie wanted. He never left the plane alive.

As soon as I left the plane, the prop wash grabbed me and turned me in a loop. My first thought was "oh hell, I forgot my chute." Somehow, in all that confusion, I must have grabbed my chute and snapped it on.

I made a delayed opening of my parachute and almost waited too long. I hit the ground very hard and broke my left ankle plus slammed into the frozen turf with my tail end and back. I left quite an impression in that Belgian soil. I was hurting very badly, and for the first time, fear was a factor. I had been well-trained as to what to do in the air, but on the ground in what I felt was enemy territory, I was confused. Expecting someone to show up and shoot me or at least take me prisoner, I crawled upon that big parachute that looked like a comfortable place to sit. I lit up a cigarette and calmly began to smoke it. After a while, I thought, they must not have seen me, so I'm going to head for home.

In lieu of my .45 caliber pistol we all had, I had a large Bowie-type knife. I cut a small tree and fashioned a crutch and went on my way. I headed west, avoiding all sounds of gunfire or any other sounds of civilization. While I was sitting on my chute, I had seen many parts of planes coming down and one parachute. All too far away for me to get to with only one leg to travel on.

It was the day after Christmas when I was found by four men from a Ranger battalion who, after some questions, determined that I was indeed an American and took care of me. They loaded me into a Jeep and gave me a rough and fast ride into a small Belgium town named Awaille. There was an American aid station here set up in an inn. They tried to make me as comfortable as possible.

After the medics checked me out and cleaned me up a little, a middle-aged gentleman and a little girl about 10 to 11 years old came to talk with me. The girl asked me something in French, and the medics that understood said she wanted to know if I had killed any "Bosch," which is what they called the Germans, and told her I had probably helped kill many of them with our bombs. She gave me a big hug and kiss.

That cheered me up, and since this was during the "Battle of the Bulge," they were out of pain medication and had to give me cognac. Believe me, it worked. I was sent from there to a temporary hospital in Verviers, Belgium. From there to Paris, then on to the port in Cherbourg, France. Crossing the English Channel on New Years Eve, we had a little party with some beer an English medic had given me prior to sailing.

I spent four months in various hospitals in England and finally returned to the 487th on April 23, 1944. By this time, the war in Europe was about over and I never flew another mission.

To summarize it all up, we lost four members of our crew on this one mission. Two, Lang and Miller, are buried in the Henri-Chapelle American cemetery in Belgium. Kausrud and Huck were returned to their homes to be buried there. Yowan received a severe wound with a 20mm cannon projectile through his hip. Alvine and Lang, the bombardier and no relation to the pilot, received leg injuries. Weber was unhurt and returned to the group to fly more missions until the war was over. I received severe leg and back injuries.

I was awarded the Purple Heart, the air medal, three campaign medals, the good conduct medal and various medals for proficiency with different weapons. I am presently with a service connected disability of 50 percent. I belong to the American Legion, the VFW, the DAV, The Military Order of the Purple Heart, the Mighty Eighth Historical Society and the Caterpillar Club, having saved my life by parachute.

I was reported as missing in action from December 24, 1944 to January 16, 1945. Discharged from active service October 12, 1945. Have been married to my wife, Wilma, for over 58 years. We have three children, nine grandchildren and 19 great-grandchildren.

And now, for the rest of my story. Early in the year of 2000, I read a copy of a New Year's greeting from Pol Walhain of Comblain-au-Pont, Belgium. Pol had met with several of our bomb group at an earlier reunion in Belgium. He is one of the many fine Belgian people who really appreciate what the Americans did in WWII. In his greeting, he stated that he had taken part with friends in a great exhibiting in Louveigne, Belgium where a large part of a B-17 wing from a Lt. Lang's plane could be seen. Seeing the Lang name, I got excited and started making inquiries. One correspondence led to another, and an exchange of information and pictures followed.

It wasn't long before we had established the fact that the wing was from the plane that my crew and I had been in on our last and fateful mission. The final I.D. being a picture of the tail section, taken on or near December 24, 1944 by a Willy Rousselle, a local resident. The I.D. #448192 being very visible in the photo.

During the summer of 2001, our oldest daughter, Janice, was traveling in Europe with part of the Royal family of Saudi Arabia. She is a governess for a Saudi princess. Upon learning of my contacts about the wing, she began an investigation of her own and decided to contact the people in Belgium to learn more about the details of that fateful day in 1944. It was decided that Wilma and I should go to Belgium and see the wing for ourselves and meet the people who had owned and cared for it all these years.

We flew to London in August, then took the high-speed train through the "Chunnel to Brussels, Belgium." In Liege we met with Marcel and Mathilde Schmetz of Thimister-Clermont and were taken to their beautiful home near the Henri-Chappelle cemetery. They took us to the cemetery that day, and we placed flowers and a flag on the graves of Lund and Miller. We also decorated the grave of General Fred Castle, who was also killed that day. He was awarded the Medal of Honor for his actions that day.

Gentlemen From Hell

The following morning, we received a huge surprise. On the pretext of going to see the wing, we went into the town of Louveigne. Our hosts wanted us to see the insides of a building they said had a connection with the war. As soon as we stepped inside, we were greeted by a large group of people that were applauding and cheering for us. I was totally embarrassed but very happy to finally meet the people I had been corresponding with for the past year. They had set this all up over a short length of time. What was so significant about Louveigne was the fact that seven of our bombers from the 487th had crashed and burned within a very short distance, and they knew all the names of the crews and their disposition. They have "adopted" those who are buried there and decorate their graves each Memorial Day.

The three days we spent there were unbelievable. We were treated like royalty. The Belgian people thought the Germans were going to overrun them again and they would be under their control. They had been there for four years and hated every minute of it. They referred to the Americans as their "Liberators," and they loved them for it. The "Battle of the Bulge" had them worried. And on the 24th of December, when we flew over and they witnessed one of the largest air armadas ever put into the air, they knew the end was near for the Nazis. We saw the wing that day and heard many eyewitness accounts of the air battles of Christmas Eve.

We were taken to many sites where monuments had been erected to the memory of our fallen. We visited the building where the inn I had been taken to in Awaille and had met the gent with the cognac and his daughter who had given me the kiss. Low and behold, these fine people had found this little girl, who was now a 67-year-old grandmother, and brought her to meet me. We still couldn't understand each other, but with the aid of Mathilde, we worked it out. She said she remembered me and the day they carried me out on stretchers. It was quite an occasion.

Then, they wanted to try to find the spot where I had landed with my parachute. Not having any luck by land, we were going to find someone with an airplane to help. We did that - except the pilot would take no compensation. He only wanted his picture taken with me. We found what we thought was the spot and had a volunteer to take us by a four-wheel drive vehicle. In fact, it was an old army Jeep. Sure enough, it was the place I had landed 57 years before. It was confirmed by several topographical features.

Before we left, the lady, Anne Marie Lamort, who owned the wing along with her husband, Willy Rousselle, who had taken the picture of the tail of our plane, said that if I wanted the wing and take it home with me, I could have it.

Returning home, I contacted Henry Hughey, a man who can get things done, and he began to pull strings, and before we knew it, the wing was sailing across the Atlantic on board a cargo ship bound for Savannah, Georgia, the home of the Mighty Eighth Air Force Museum. The 487th Bomb Group paid the freight. It is on display at the museum today.

838TH SQUADRON

I am proud to have been a part of the 487th Bomb Group and a friend to the men who served with it. These memories have been put together in May of 2004 using notes, audio tapes, from memorabilia kept by my mother and my wife, Wilma, and from the areas of my mind that will never forget some of these incidents.

MIKE QUERING

"When you see that flak bursting around you and you see these fighters coming in at you, and you can see the goddamn 20-mm shells bursting in front of you, you know, you say, "They're going to kill me. They're going to kill me."

My name is W.A. Mike Quering. I went into the service right after high school. I graduated the first part of May. The end of May I was down in Biloxi, Mississippi. I was born in Glasport, Pennsylvania, which is a suburb of Pittsburgh, Pennsylvania. When I joined up, I was scheduled to be drafted, but you had the option of applying and taking an examination to enter the Air Force, which I did. I was accepted into the aviation cadet program. We were sent down to Biloxi, Mississippi for basic training. We had 13 weeks of basic training down there, and then after that I was sent to Rome, Georgia and I attended Barry College through the aviation cadet program. While we were there, it was mostly studying and catching up on mathematics and education and things like that because I had just graduated from high school and I didn't go to college. So, we also had preflight training there. We also flew Pipercubs. After training there we were sent to Nashville, Tennessee. At that particular time the situation in Europe was very dire with regard to air crews. The class that I was in, unfortunately, instead of taking the examinations for pilot or bombardier or navigator, we were sent to gunnery school. We became gunners.

So, I became an armored gunner and was sent to Buckley Field in Denver, Colorado. There, I learned armored gunnery, or armament, and we were trained in machine guns, cannons, 75 mm cannons. We were also trained in 37 mm cannons and also synchronizing machine guns going through, firing through the propellers. From there we went down to Nevada for air to gunner training.

838th Squadron

While we were training there, we were being assigned to the 8th Air Force at that time, although I didn't know it at that time.

After gunnery training and you graduated both as an armor and as a gunner, you got your wings. From that point there, we were sent then to Alexandria, Louisiana. From Alexandria, Louisiana, we formed our crew, and that was our combat training. It was unfortunate at that time, things were very difficult and we didn't get any time off. We didn't get home. After our combat training in Alexandria, Louisiana, we flew back to Lincoln, Nebraska - or we took a train back to Lincoln, Nebraska, and while we were there we received our bomber. We received a bomber and were just waiting for orders. They issued us weapons and additional clothing and supplies. And from that point, once we received our orders to fly overseas, we took off, and the memorable thing about that was we had taken off and it so happened that we had a malfunction and we had to come in for landing. We returned back to Lincoln, Nebraska, and as we were coming in, while the tower was flashing all these seven four signals and lights and that, they finally got on the radio and said, "Lower your goddamn landing wheels." So they got that, and we landed. They corrected that, and we took off from there. From there, we went up to Bangor, Maine. Then, we went up to Newfoundland, and then from Newfoundland we flew over to Iceland. In Iceland, we stayed there overnight. We didn't get there till night, and one of the things that we had to do was cover up the engines. The wind was blowing. It was a terrible time because when we landed we got caught in our cross-wind and just ran off the runway - just ran off the runway and they had to tow us out. It was September of 1943. I was only 18 years old. God, it was only the first time I had been outside of Pennsylvania. You know, I had never been anywhere before. We spent the night there. When the weather cleared up, we took off and at that same time, then we knew that we didn't have a bombardier. The bombardier wasn't with us. We don't know what happened to him. So he wasn't with us - whatever happened to him, we never did find out.

So we took off from Reykjavik, Iceland, and we flew to Valley, Wales. Once we got to Valley, Wales, we had to park our aircraft, and once the aircraft was there, the pilot and the co-pilot signed off that they had received it there, we were sent to a replacement depot. I can't recall the name of that, maybe some of the other guys would. So we were there for a few days. I can't recall how many days we were there. And then, when we did get orders, we were sent to the 487th bomb group. So that was probably at the end of September or the first part of October then when we knew where we were going to go, and that was down to Lavenham. We arrived at Lavenham, and once we were there, we were assigned to the 838th squadron. Then, we noticed that the aircraft that we had flown over was assigned to our squadron also. It was aircraft #4388888. I remember that very distinctly. I still have the original orders for that, too. Anyway, I believe we flew one mission in that airplane and then it was transferred over to the 839th squadron. So, when we would start flying for combat missions, we would always take a look at briefings where that aircraft was in position and what squadron or what flight it was going to be in. So we always watched that. While we were there, we naturally had a lot of training missions we had to fly for the combat training. We flew our first combat mission on November 16, 1944. That was quite an experience.

My position in the crew was waist gunner, and of course, at that point then, we only had a nine-man crew. In our original crew, we didn't have a bombardier, and then it seems like after we had flown several missions, then George Johnson, who was our other waist gunner, was taken off the crew (and I don't know what happened to him from then on - see, I don't know what happened to him). When I was the armored gunner, my responsibility was the guns. I took care of those things like that. All in all, I flew 34 missions. The rest of the crew - well not all the crew, part of the original crew - flew 35 missions. Some only flew like 14 and 15 missions due to wounds.

When I reflect on what happened in all those, my memory gets a little clouded because there are a lot of things I try not to remember and don't then, you see. But reflecting after talking to our ball-turret gunner and our top-turret gunner, who was also the crew engineer, we had a total of eight wounded in our own original crew plus the replacements that we had. It got to the point where we had replacements we didn't even know their name. Fortunately, we didn't have anybody killed. I was one of the wounded of the original crew, and so was Joe Leboard, who was the radioman. I remember that mission there. That was a secondary target for us, and we were in the lead that day. We went to our secondary target, and when we were with the target, we were hit with antiaircraft fire and our radioman was very seriously wounded. The thing I remember about it is, because I was flying in the waist that day, and after we dropped our bombs, I was able to go into the radio room. At that time, I used to wear a big towel, must have been about six feet long, and I put it around my neck to keep my neck warm. So what I did is, I just took it off after we had (we all carried first aid kits on our parachute harness) - I just took my towel and just stuck it in his back because he was badly, badly wounded. But we gave him morphine and we limped back. We went back on three engines again and got back to the base. The thing of it is that then, we got a new radioman. Anyway, Joe Leboard was our radioman. He was wounded and we didn't get to see him till, I believe it was 1982, after all those years. He comes to the reunions. He's even come to this reunion here.

When you fly that many missions and you realize that there were so many ways that you could be killed or wounded, you became very, very aware of where you were and what you were doing. When you looked out the window and you saw anything, you were just on edge every damn minute of the time. And you really were. You weren't at ease. You were afraid. You weren't afraid. But what we would do, you would take in the morning, you would be awakened early in the morning depending on where the mission was going to be and you would get to breakfast. Those who wanted to see a chaplain or a rabbi had that opportunity. Then, we would go into briefing, and there we would see exactly what our target was going to be and where we were going to be and what our bomb load was and what our gas load was going to be. From there, we would load up in the jeeps or the trucks or the lorries, whatever they had, and they would take us down to the hard stands to our assigned aircraft. As we went along, we never had a plane or a bomber that we could put a name on. It just seems, so many times, it seems like we would fly a bomber one or two, three times and then it would be taken out of service because we were so badly damaged all the time. You know, it was just one of those things, I don't. I talk to many guys who flew combat, didn't have a scratch, nothing went wrong. But it just seemed like our crew, we didn't have bad karma or anything like that, but we always seemed to be in the thick of it. We always were. We took many damaging hits and made many trips. One trip in particular, we were missing in action because we just barely made it back.

Of course, the thing of it is, I can remember one mission in particular. We flew a low-level mission at either 10,000 or 12,000 feet, which was really low for a bomber group like that. The cut was Germany. At that time, they had these devices they put in the radio room, and they had these radar jammer guys. We were under attack both by fighters and flak, and this damn guy was cringing on the floor in the back in the radio room. At that time, we only had one waist gunner in the plane. I was throwing empty shells at him to get him up there, you know. I really complained about him when we finally got back. I don't know what ever happened to him again, but it was really something. The other thing our crew did was, we also flew camera ship. We were the camera ship. We would fly over after the bombs were dropped and had the hand held cameras. That was very exciting to watch all that going on and to film the actions that were going on. We also flew what we call chaff missions that we would throw out the chaff to disrupt the German radar signals. And, of course, they said, "You know this is the way you're supposed to do it. You drop one, then you count to 10. You drop the other one." Well, we designed our own rules. We just dumped out all the damn stuff out, just got it all out, you see.

To tell you how I really feel or how you feel going on a mission like that, you know, from the minute you reach 10,000 feet, you're on oxygen. That's another thing a lot of people don't realize. You're on oxygen at 10,000 feet and you don't get off oxygen until you come down to 10,000 feet after the mission is over. So we were on oxygen anywhere from six to 10 hours during a mission. And, of course, the weather, it was cold, really cold. We had, back in the waist positions there, we were flying between 35, 40 and 50 and 60 degrees below zero at that point there. Of course, we wore our long underwear, our uniforms, and on top of that you had your flight suit, your heated suits, and they were vital, especially if you took your gloves off (we used to wear nylon gloves underneath our heated gloves). If you had to repair or if you had a malfunction in your machine gun, you had to have those gloves on because your hands would just absolutely freeze out there.

The most memorable mission, of course, is December 24, 1944, when our bomb group led the 8th Air Force during the Battle of the Bulge. We were maybe just outside of Liege, Belgium, when 50-60 fighters hit us, and the first attack occurred head on - just head on. When they came through, unfortunately, our air lead at that time was General Castle, who was experiencing aircraft problems. He had an engine go off. They hit him, and he was one of the first ones to be shot down. I can remember at that time I wasn't flying in the waist, I was flying in the nose as a nose gunner on the B-17 along with the navigator up in the nose and the togglier at that time. The togglier would drop the bombs when the lead bombardier dropped his in. I can still see those planes coming in and a number of the fighters breaking off. You could just look out the nose window and just see, zooming up, you could see the black crosses on there. Well, we really didn't know how many airplanes we lost that day, but nine in the original attack and then the overall we dropped 13 bombers that day. Of course, our crew and the crew that was lost, we were both in the same points. Five of that crew were killed and four survived. They're not here today at this reunion here. That was a terrible, terrible mission. What we had been planning all that time, every time we'd go to London, somebody would pick up a bottle of whiskey or scotch, or something like that. We planned to have a big Christmas Eve, Christmas party. Well, it wasn't much of a Christmas. We did have a Christmas Eve party, but everybody drank - everybody drank, see. It was a sad, sad day, but we were up the next day and went on - we went on.

Our group did finally ... the mission was successful with regard to the targets we were after. We had, I think it was 62 bombers in that formation. So, the Germans had a field day. After you hear about the rest of the mission or the rest of the flights in the bomber screen, nobody else was hit like we were hit. We were the ones that really got it. So then, we went on and then, after that, we were on flak leave. We'd go to seven-day flak leave. We went down to the southeast coast of England. We were down there across from the Isle of Wight. We had civilian clothes, clean bed sheets, and it was warm. The bed sheets that we had were white, and we had solid mattresses. The mattresses we had were biscuits. They had three, they were like three big pillows. And, of course, everywhere you turned you rolled into the split end. Of course, it was cold. That was the coldest it had ever been in Europe for many, many years, and that's why we couldn't fly during the Battle of the Bulge, because the weather was so cold. But December 24, that was the first clear day in almost two weeks before the Air Force could really get up.

You know, there are many memorable missions that we can talk about, but I want to tell you about that bomber that we flew over in 1943, and it came to the 839th squadron then. We were on a mission on March 11, 1945, and it was in high squadron and it was shot down that day. It got a direct hit in the bomb bay even before the bombs were dropped, and it just blew up - it just blew up just like that. I signaled to everybody else, there goes 88, it went down. And then everybody was able to take a look at it. It went down and they were all killed. As a matter of fact, two of the enlisted men, two sergeants, are buried in Fort Logan, Colorado within 15 minutes where I live. And that is where my wife is buried, in Fort Logan Military Cemetery. They're two of the earliest spectrums from World War II to be buried there. They're in the roster there. But anyway, that was quite a shock that day because we had a special affection for that airplane.

Then, of course, on March 15, that was the day I was wounded. We were on a mission. That was a mission we were scheduled to fly. We were supposed to take off about seven o'clock in the morning after the briefing. We got to the heart stands, getting ready to load up and to prepare for take-off, and there was a delay in the mission because of the weather. Our mission that day was to go to Oranienburg, Germany, deep in Germany, which is just kind of northeast suburb of Berlin. We were told many, many fighters, but most of all, most of all were anti-aircraft guns. That was going to be the big, big problem there. Well, in the meantime during that week, I had been wearing a pair of OD trousers for 34 missions that were really dirty and greasy. So a couple of days before that, I decided, well, you ought to get these cleaned. So I washed them and cleaned them, but they weren't dry. I also felt those were my good-luck pants. I got on a different pair of OD trousers that day and didn't think anything of it till after. But anyway, we finally took off, it was probably about 10 o'clock in the morning. We took off and went to our targeted mission. We were under heavy fire deep in Germany, particularly when we were hit by fighters, and what they would do … the fighters would hit you and they would attack you, and then the antiaircraft guns would start firing. But, it so happened in March of that year, the fighters were so desperate, they even started flying through their own flak. They were coming in there. Well, we had just started on the IP, and we were hit just in the waist where I was standing - right there, right up through the floor. Of course, on the IP, nobody could come back. Nobody could do anything. You couldn't leave your position because of what was going on, and we were under fire at that time.

When I was hit, it blew me up and I slammed into the side of the waist and just laid there a bit. In the mean time, what happened was, my throat mike was disconnected and I lost my boots. I lost my boots at the same time. So then, I could hear them talking. They knew that we had gotten a big hit. So the pilot just said to anybody, hang on till we get out of here and drop our bombs. Well, after the bombs were dropped, why then somebody came back, either the radioman or our crew engineer or the tail gunner, and gave me first aid. But the funny thing was, I was out. I was out like a light. I finally came to and was really cold. I was really cold, and fortunately, my oxygen mask didn't break off because the tube must have been eight or nine feet long. So I was okay that way. Then, I said my feet are really cold and I'm cold. I didn't bleed because everything froze. I had numerous body wounds and leg wounds. But I'll tell you, it was funny when I woke. The thought in my mind was, "I'm going home. I'm going home." I just kind of spaced everything out. I wasn't in any pain because they doped me up with morphine.

I knew I was going to go home, but I just have to tell you, I could remember on those missions, under fighter attack especially, you would pray and you would swear in the same breath. You perspired, you overheated, just from the adrenaline running through your body. I can recall something else. At the time I was wounded, we got back on three engines that day. We got back on three engines and that just became so damn normal for us to come back on aircraft that was so badly damaged that we just took it for granted. We didn't worry about it anymore. We got back or we didn't get back. Our crew never aborted a mission unless the whole group was aborted, but we never did. But one time we almost said we got to get out of this thing because they had a fire in the electrical system of the nose terminal. Well, I was flying in the nose with our navigator, Chick Caledar, and that nose term you sit on like a bicycle bench, but at the same time, that is fastened down on some plywood onto some armor plate. We couldn't get the fire extinguisher to those motors underneath there. So Chick and I grabbed that plywood. We tore the plywood off and we bent the armor plate. We bent the armor plate to get in there and were able to extinguish the fire. But, of course, we didn't have any nose guns, either. But at the same time, we didn't abort. When we got back to the base, Chick and I said, let's bend this thing back down. We couldn't touch it - we couldn't move it. It just was that surge of adrenaline at that point that we bent that armor plate back to get in there, and we did put the fire out.

But you know, when I was wounded (when anybody else was wounded), they always fired off flares, and you had first right to come into land. Of course, when they took me off, they gave me a big shot of rye whiskey - it was the worst thing they gave me. They took me to one of the hospitals. I forget what general hospital that was there. I was either in a general hospital or a station hospital. I can't remember right now. When they were operating on me I said to them, "You know, I'm going to throw up." They said, "Go ahead and throw up." But anyway, I could hear them, especially with the shrapnel in my leg. I could hear them with a hammer. It sounded like they were chiseling it out, but that's beside the point.

One of the difficult things of explaining to somebody what it's like in combat is to really get you to feel what it's like without embellishing or anything like that, but just to tell how it is. I say to you that it's hard to do if you haven't experienced it. But let me just say this: you feel like you're going to jump out of your damn body and your skin. You're either overheating or you're freezing or you're sweating or you're perspiring. When you see that flak bursting around you and you see these fighters coming in at you, and you can see the goddamn

20mm shells bursting in front of you, you know, you say, "They're going to kill me. They're going to kill me." It just ... you know, I can remember being under another bomber and the guns are firing from that bomber up there and the damn shell cases come down and smash right through the nose - right through the nose. Just things like that. What else could go wrong? The other problem you had is, you had an oxygen check every three or four minutes because that's all it took. If you're off the oxygen at an altitude of 25,000 or 27,000 thousand feet, you're a dead man. That was one of the serious malfunctions we had with our oxygen systems during that period. They would have malfunctions and you wouldn't know it. The navigator would usually call for an oxygen check, and everybody absolutely had to answer. If they did not answer, somebody had to absolutely go back and check on them.

Another problem you had when you dropped the bombs and you had a damn bomb stuck in the bomb bay. It was either the armor's position or his job to get that damn thing out with the crew chief. The crew engineer would get you a hand or something like that. And here you are with the bomb bay open, and you're up there with whatever size bomb it was, and you had to get that damn thing out - and we did. There were many times when you did where they would get hung up, and these bombs were all armed at that time. Because once they dropped, then we had an army wire and that army wire, when the bomb dropped, it would pull out and then the propellers would start on the bomb when it was dropping down. So that happened, but you were on oxygen. You had an emergency oxygen bottle. When you had to do that there were several times when you had to crank the bomb bay doors closed. You had to crank the landing gear down or the landing gear up. Talk about strenuous work. I'll tell you that. Just think about it. I mean, here you are. You're at altitude trying to close those doors, and it's not in a convenient position, and it's just an old damn hand crank. You just crank and crank and crank to get it up.

November 13, 2002 - additional information sent by Mike Quering
Just two days ago, Nov. 11th, Veterans Day, I participated in the Veteran's Day ceremonies at Fort Logan National Cemetary; also visited my wife's grave, four other comrades, and the graves of S/Sgt. Eldon A. Mau and S/Sgt. Clyde L. Yaegle, KIA on March 11, 1945. These two comrades were flying in the bomber S/N 43-38888. Our original crew flew this bomber from Lincoln, Nebraska to Wales, and it was transferred to our bomb group and our 838th squadron, then to the 839th squadron. We watched it as it was blown out of the formation by intense flak. This made me realize that I do not remember it so clearly after all. Your mind refuses to unlock memories of such intensity, and there are many black holes in your memory. I will try to relate my combat missions and training for combat. One thing about basic training I remember is that sleep devoured boredom and enabled you to put up with the "Chicken Shit" of the Army K.P., canceled passes, verbal humiliation or chewing out, spit and polish, this had

nothing to do with winning the war. This was just a way of making us long for combat, and when you went to combat crew training, it made it easier for you to have a frame of mind and commitment to the easy comradeship with your crew, to the exclusion of any one else. You sacrificed yourself and became a combat team, no matter what your position was on the bomber.

Cannot remember where we stopped in Omaha. I was just 18, graduated from high school in May 1943. By the end of May, I was in Biloxi, Mississippi for basic training. I had applied for Cadet training and sent to Berry College, Rome, Georgia and college training detachment. Went to classification, received notice, the need for gunners far exceeded pilots, etc.; without prejudices, started training as armor gunner.

Combat training, crew formation, Alexandria, LA, orders to pickup bomber 43-38888 in Lincoln, Nebraska. Flew this bomber to the northern route, loaded with supplies, but no oxygen. We could have used it! Assigned to 487th Bomb Group, Lavenham, England. Our bomber was soon to follow. We flew one mission in it, and then it was transferred to the 839th squadron. I always kept a lookout for it when we flew the same mission.

Looking back and thinking about all 34 missions I flew, one thing I remember was the state of constant anxiety, for there were so many ways you could be killed or wounded out of combat and in combat. We flew hours on a mission, no pressurized cabins, no heat, on oxygen, only with heated suits and oxygen masks, the cold was always 50 degrees below zero. Most all missions were flown at high altitude, and this is also one time your crew had to be on alert for every member. With oxygen checks, it seemed like we never had a mission that someone wasn't suffering from lack of oxygen, due to malfunctioning equipment.

When General Doolittle assumed command of the Eight Air Force, he ordered a new offensive against the German Luftwaffe, meaning our fighter cover was to go after the Luftwaffe, no longer provided cover for the bombers, but to destroy the enemy. We became the bait for the Germans and we paid the price, but this tactic was the beginning of the defeat and destruction of the Luftwaffe.

Recalling from memory and visiting with crew members about some of our missions is at best, like the difference between a fairy tale and a war story. A fairy tale begins with, "Once upon a time." A war story begins with, "No shit, you ain't going to believe this." We never had a bomber that we could call our own, for it seemed no matter what mission we flew, we had battle damage or wounded on board. Many combat crews survived their tour of duty without a scratch. Our crew suffered a total of eight wounded, that included myself and Joe LaBorde, our radio man. I have not listed the other six wounded crew members, for they were replacements and I never did know their names.

On a mission to Hamm rail yards, we aborted the formation because of engine trouble. The group had already bombed the target; beginning at the point of no return, the pilot asked, "Should we try anyway?" If we turned back, we would get no mission credit. After two passes, we finally dropped our bombs with the flak guns all around, then the flak guns shot color burst to let the German fighters know it was clear for them to attack. Evasive action and cloud cover, along with P-51s, saved our skin. We struggled back to our base, found out later, we were listed missing action and received a real ass-chewing. Our bomber was out of action for several days for repairs. While on a mission to Magdeburg synthetic oil refineries, the high-squadron lead aborted, and we assumed the lead as deputy lead. We had to make sure this target was hit, for if you did not, you were coming back the next day. The oil refineries were a prime target, and on November 30, 1944, our mission was to Merseburg (deadly place). The lead ship aborted at the beginning of the bomb run and we took over lead position. All groups bombed short of the target. We suffered major battle damage, and that day, the Eighth Air Force had lost 56 bombers and 31 fighters. The mission to Mainz marshaling yards was a success. Fighter cover kept the Luftwaffe from us, but the huge problem was the head winds of 140 knots, reduced our ground speed to 64 knots. We were like sitting ducks to flak and enemy fighters, but our P-51s were there and gave excellent cover, although the Germans were near by. The December 6 mission to Luxendorf was diverted to Merseburg again. Flak and fighters were worse than ever. I recall a replacement bombardier wounded and a radioman lost consciousness because of a lack of oxygen. I revived him. Weather always played a part in our missions, either in England or over Germany. We had bombed targets at Darmstadt and had a wind shift, so that pilot was going to land in France, but we all elected to try for our home base. We did get back with about 50 gallons of fuel left in the tanks. Lavenham was in the soup with a 200' ceiling.

December 24, 1944, our Christmas Eve mission, the first time the Eighth Air Force was able to take to the air to help stop the Germans and the Battle of the Bulge. It was so cold in England and in Europe, I remember sleeping under eight blankets and in my OD uniform, with the helmet liner cap on. We had very little coal for that measly stove we had in the Quonset Huts. Our group led the Eighth Air Force that day and the group leader was Brig. General Frederick Castle, who just had been promoted the day before to general. Our crew flew No. 8 in the lead squadron, and about 15 miles west of Liege, we were attacked by enemy fighters, ME-109s and FW-190s. We were attacked from a direct frontal with 50 or 60 fighters. I can remember this, for I was in the nose as togglier/nose gunner. You could actually see the 20mm cannon shells bursting in front of you, and as they broke off, they flew directly over you to the side. I actually saw the pilots in two of the fighters. At that time, I was sweating, praying and cursing, because I did not think I hit any one of them. The first plane to go down was with the lead ship with General Castle and his crew. Subject to correction, many say we lost 11 or 13 bombers that day. One of the worst losses our group suffered. Most of the losses were in the low-low squadron that day, for our fighter cover was late arriving and the Germans just shot us out of the sky.

A crew in our Quonset lost five members, and we thought they were all lost. We did not know that four gunners survived until weeks later. During this time, our navigator was losing consciousness from lack of oxygen. We revived him and tried to survey the losses and went on to bomb our target, Babenhausen, with good results. A few days later on a mission to Aschaffenburg, we lost an engine to flak, our nose-turret was shot out, and a fire started. The navigator and I put out the fire, but not before we bent the armor plate under the seat to get to the fire. We could not bend it back when we landed. The surprise on this mission is the appearance of the German jet, M-262k; we had seen one in November. Fortunately, our P-51s were able to protect our formation.

On January 14, 1945, we were on a mission, again to Magdeburg. The high lead aborted, and we assumed the lead of the squadron. The target was covered with smoke, and there were terriffic air battles going on high above us. Confusion supreme, squadrons became separated from the formation, and you could see one flying in the wrong direction. The target was obscure, and with the confusion, the pilot asked the navigator, Chick Coletta, to select a target of opportunity. He had recalled at briefing that at the marshalling yards at Osaanbruck, a large troop concentration was preparing to board trains for the front in Belgium. The pilot led the squadron there, and we bombed successfully. The ball-turret gunner, Bucky Buxtion, reported to the pilot that fighters were coming up from the airfields below. So the squadron took evasive action and headed home without any losses. The group commander gave our squadron a pat on the back.

February 14, 1945, Dulmen, a secondary target, turned out not to be a milk run. It was a terrifying mission. It was reported to be lightly defended, but on the bomb run we were hit with a flak barrage. Our radioman was hit with a blast from the side and tossed to the other side of the radio room. I wasn't able to get to him until we were off the target. He received wounds to his back and shoulder. I gave him first aid, took the long towel I used around my neck, after dosing him with morphine, and stuffed the towel into his wounds. We got back to our base with major battle damage and took Joe to the waiting ambulance. Joe survived his wounds. I did not see him until 1982, along with the rest of the surviving crew at a group reunion.

The next day, we flew to Cottbus, Czechoslovakia to support Russian troops. This was the beginning of many 10 and 11-hour missions. In February, we bombed marshaling yards in Nuremberg with bad weather. We flew a mission to Ansbach at 12,000 feet and received minor battle damage. We went to marshaling yards at Neumarkt at 10,000 feet. The flak was very heavy. Then, we went to Berlin and returned with battle damage and glad to get back to base. Then, on March 11, 1945, our mission was to Hamburg-Wilhelmsburg oil refineries. Our old bomber (S/N 43-38888) received a direct flak hit and was blown out of the formation, one survivor. The entire crew was just stupefied seeing it go down, and the bond we had with that plane. I always visit the gravesite of Mau and Yaegle at Ft. Logan and think of them and our flying the bomber.

March 15, 1945 was the end of the war for me. Our mission was to Oranienburg marshaling yards and also a secret plant working on heavy water and the atomic bomb. The weather was bad in England. We formed up over France and then on to the target. This target was defended with over 150 flak batteries. We were hit with flak and fighters, and on the bomb run, we were hit with a blast that wounded me. I was flying in the waist position. I was knocked out and lost my boots and my heated suit connection, but my oxygen was still connected. No one could get back to me, for we were still on the bomb run. After the bombs dropped, someone came back to help me. I received numerous wounds and frozen feet. We had major battle damage, and pilot Lt. Hal Roberts said, "Don't worry, we are going to get back," and we did. Three engines and my combat tour was over. I was in the hospital till after the Germans surrendered. However, a side note, when I was released from the hospital, I went back to Lavenham to pick up my personal possessions and Squadron Headquarters said the group was scheduled to go to the Pacific Theater, and do I want to go. I said, "No way. I have a Zone of Interior order in my hand and I'm going home."

Remembering those days, you realize you did not have the time to mourn the dead or the wounded, but just went on. Even at the time of crisis, the routine of war still ruled us all. We did not see each other after you were wounded, did not have the time or the chance to visit in the hospital. We just hoped that they and you would survive and get back safely.

WALTER W. MOORE

To put the insignificance of one flyboy soldier and the significance of the Eighth Air Force in perspective, I was just one of a crew of nine on our B-17 Flying Fortress. We were identified as the Kohr crew. The Kohr crew was one of nine in the 838th Squadron. The 838th was one of four Squadrons when flying in a diamond formation with the 836th, 837th and the 839th Squadrons. The four Squadrons made up the 487th Bombardment Group. The 487th was one of 46 Bomb Groups in the heavy division of the Eighth Air Force. The Eighth was one of several Air Forces in the US Army Air Force, now the US Air Force. In a maximum effort day on December 24, 1944, the Mighty Eighth sent over Germany 2,034 B-17s and B-24s and 936 fighters, the greatest single force of airplanes ever dispatched in history. The Eighth Air Force was the largest military unit in World War II: 350,000 served in the Eighth, 26,000 lost their lives and another 28,000 became prisoners of war.

To put the significance of the Mighty Eighth Air Force in perspective, our job was to help Allied troops defeat a highly effective German military machine that was under the control of the Nazi regime who had conquered 27 countries one by one over a number of years. The Germans had advanced to the outskirts of Moscow and were attacking England with fighter and bomber airplanes and with V-1 robot buzz bombs and V-2 rockets. Submarines were attacking USA shipping. Wherever they went, the Germans were reputed to be ruthless killers with little regard for human life.

America was mobilizing a big plan, part of which was to dominate the sky with air power and to devastate the German military infrastructure from the inside. The Eighth became the largest air armada ever assembled, henceforth and forevermore to be known as the Mighty Eighth Air Force. We were made to be mighty because we had a mighty job to do. Major targets included the Luftwaffe and their airports, oil refineries and storage facilities, transportation facilities such as railroad marshalling yards, locomotives and bridges, factories that produced war equipment such as ball-bearing plants and engines, and submarine pens. The heavies of the Eighth Air Force operated out of England and attacked during daylight hours with 46 Bomb Groups of 36 planes each, usually, but as many as 54 per Group. The 15th Air Force, based in Italy, also attacked during daylight hours. The British Royal Air Force attacked during the night with individual plane sorties. 'Round the clock, the Germans only respite was weather too bad for flying.

I was the co-pilot on a B-17 Flying Fortress. We were on our 31st mission over Nazi controlled Germany. Four more missions and our tour of duty in the European Theater would be completed, and we would be rotated back to the States for possible re-assignment to the Pacific Theater. Seventy-five percent of the air crews in the Eighth completed their mission assignments, so we had our fingers crossed.

Our crew had been assigned a brand new B-17G that had never been flown on a mission. We took off at daybreak from Lavenham, England (near Bury St. Edmonds) on a 10-hour mission across Germany to provide tactical support to the Russians. The target was an oil refinery near Ruhland, Germany. Our navigator, Bill Crow, said the target was only nine minutes from the Russian front line. We were flying in our regular formation position off the left wing of the 838th Squadron leader. As always, we flew a zigzag course over Germany to avoid areas of known or suspected anti-aircraft artillery. We encountered no enemy opposition on our way to Ruhland. The mission appeared to be a "milk run" until we reached the Initial Point (point from which we started the bomb run). The formation always flew in a straight line from the Initial Point to the target to allow time for the bombardier in the lead squadron to aim his Norden bombsight at the target. This is the time when we were the most vulnerable to their anti-aircraft artillery because they knew we would not deviate from the course. Bomb runs usually lasted 10 to 15 minutes. During this time, we usually saw lots of black puffs of exploding artillery called flak. When under attack, your mind and body are on high alert. There is no time to think about being scared, but you do realize that the next burst, any second now, may have your name on it. Then there's no "you" anymore. There are no evasive choices; you must stay in formation. The Infantry has foxholes and they say there are no atheists in foxholes. There are no foxholes in the sky, and there are no atheists on a bomb run either. So you think a little prayer, "Oh Lord, please protect us if it be thy will." You can be scared later when it's all over, but by then, it is not scary anymore. The flak was moderate to intense on this mission. Much of it was below us because preceding groups had dropped Christmas tree tinsel made from aluminum foil, called chaff, which had descended and fooled the German radar.

After bombs away, we were cruising along on a clear sunny day at an altitude of 25,000 feet. The mission was essentially over because we rarely encountered enemy activity on return flights. It was pure pleasure to be flying in formation with a bunch of magnificent four-engine flying machines. They were good war birds that could take a lot of punishment from flak and enemy fighters and still bring their crew home. This is not to imply that there were zero problems with various conditions external to the quality of the plane. For example, sometimes the outside temperature at 25,000 to 27,000 feet was 50 degrees below zero. In the unheated models that we flew earlier, the temperature in the cockpit was so cold that our skin would freeze to the metal throttles if we were not wearing gloves. The moisture from our breath would freeze on the exhale ports of our oxygen masks and form an ice beard that would extend down to our chests. On descents, frost would form on the windshield so quickly it was difficult to keep it scraped off fast enough to maintain outside visibility. We wore electrically heated underwear to cope with the cold. They looked like a jumpsuit made from green satin cloth with veins of electric cords running throughout. It also had snap-on electric booties. Toes get very cold without the booties.

On a previous mission, after hitting the target, our B-17 could not keep up with the formation and we had to fly unescorted across Germany to Brussels. Two engines had been knocked out by flak. We feathered one propeller, the other was wind-milling. We had to make a forced landing at Brussels because we were losing altitude too fast to make it back across the English Channel. After landing, our bombardier, Herb Stoltz, counted 26 shrapnel holes in our B-17 caused by the flak. The date was December 18, 1944. The Battle of the Bulge was underway and although the Germans were making good progress, Brussels was not endangered, or so we thought. However, many of the Brussels citizens thought otherwise and were already flying the Swastika flag out of their windows. That was the time the weather closed in and we were unable to depart Brussels until December 23. When we returned to our base at Lavenham, we were told that the entire Eighth had been grounded by the same weather that prevented our return to England and had delayed the Eighth from supporting the Allied troops at the German breakthrough in the Battle of the Bulge. We also learned that the flight schedule for the next day had been filled. Another crew was scheduled to fly in our regular formation position. Thus, we were going to miss flying in the largest air armada ever to fly over Germany. That day, the 487th led the entire Eighth Air Force across the English Channel. An estimated 50 fighters from the Luftwaffe met them over Belgium before our "Little Friends," the fighter plane escort, arrived. We lost nine of 36 planes, including General Castle. I still wonder if one of the nine losses was the crew filling in for us in our regular position off the left wing of the 838th Squadron leader.

I didn't know it then, but as good as it was after the bomb run over Ruhland, my time as a B-17 pilot was about to end forever. The time was about 12:20 P.M., about 30 minutes after bombs away over the oil refinery. A single black puff of flak appeared in front of us at eye level, and then another - the third was directly under us. The plane lurched up about five feet from the blast. From the cockpit, we could see torch-like flames spouting up from a hole in the No. 2 inboard engine nacelle on our left. Radio operator Dick Sprock called on the intercom to report that the waist and bomb bay were flooded with orange colored smoke. Ball-turret gunner John Atkinson reported flames trailing 10 to 20 feet behind the wing, almost back to the ball-turret. We pulled the fire extinguisher cord, but the fire was behind the firewall and the extinguishers don't work there. Next, we dove 1,000 feet or so to increase the airflow, hoping to blow out the fire, but this did not work either. By now, it was two or three minutes after being hit. It was a tough decision but Ted conferred with Flight Engineer Tom Emerson and me, and then gave the order on the intercom for every body to bail out. (A review of Missing Air Craft Reports shows that B-17s on fire often explode within the first 30 seconds after a hit).

838th Squadron

My thinking about Guardian Angels is that they don't work full time, but they are always there when you really need them. I believe one or more of mine were on duty this day. Remember, the fire was spouting from the number two engine nacelle about eight feet to the left of the cockpit. Our regular position in the formation was off the left wing of the squadron lead plane. This made it much easier to fly in formation from the right seat because visibility from the left seat across the cockpit is more restricted. I flew the right seat and had an excellent view of the plane on our right. We were encouraged to fly a tight formation for two good reasons: It concentrates firepower and it discourages pilots from drifting and thus becoming isolated targets for enemy fighters. One of our Generals always encouraged us to fly a tight formation and to "stick the wing in the tail gunner's face." This is safer and easier to do when there is little or no turbulence. There was no turbulence at our altitude. I was flying and the wing tip was almost touching the tail gunner position - I mean within an inch or two of touching the plane. I enjoyed doing this on return flights with no bomb load and no turbulence. If I had been flying in turbulence, or if Ted had been flying from his position across the cockpit, the plane would have been about 10 feet to the left and the explosion would have been in or directly under the cockpit. It was a perfectly aimed shot. We just were not in the position the Germans expected when they fired their 88mm anti-aircraft gun.

Bailed out over Czechoslovakia. We were never trained for parachute jumps, but it becomes natural when you think the plane may explode any second. In our haste to get out, I forgot the small emergency bottle of oxygen and my jacket. That was a stupid thing to do because as I was freefalling, I became increasingly concerned about whether or not the parachute would open. So I committed another stupid thing by pulling the ripcord at an estimated 20,000 feet. There is not much oxygen at that level. It felt like running out of breath after a 400-yard dash and then getting no oxygen for relief. Without the emergency oxygen bottle, I almost asphyxiated, and without my jacket, I almost froze. I was breathing as fast and deep as I possibly could. I found that by pulling on the right or left shroud lines that the chute would partially collapse, dump some air and possibly descend faster. I overdid it once and the chute almost collapsed. The expected relief at the 10,000 foot level where we always went on or off oxygen when climbing or descending did not occur, probably because I was so oxygen depleted.

At a lower altitude where it was a little warmer, I realized that I was experiencing a rare and wonderful event. It was so very quiet, and the view from beneath the parachute looking across the North Bohemian countryside was so beautiful. It was a euphoric situation as though I were an eagle, or even a buzzard, just sailing along in soundless space. I imagined that in post-war years, high-altitude parachute jumps could possibly take the place of merry-go-rounds at the carnival.

The heavy gasping for more oxygen continued almost to ground level. In addition, pain from sitting on the narrow seat straps was becoming almost unbearable. The parachute drifted over a forest. As it neared the treetops it became apparent that the wind was moving the chute at 20 to 25 miles per hour and that I was going to land in a forest of tall trees. I prepared for the collision by turning the chute so I was facing downwind, doubled up my knees and covered my eyes and face with my arms. I don't recall the moment of contact with the treetops, except that it was quick. I was suspended in the parachute harness about five feet below a large limb and about eight feet from the tree trunk, and a long way to the ground. The parachute was caught in the top tree branches. My guess is that the opened parachute was about 25 feet deep from top to bottom. I don't know how tall a tall tree grows, but it was a long way to the ground. The pain from the narrow seat straps was becoming unbearable and my legs were getting numb. Something had to be done now. I realized it was too far to drop without causing some kind of injury to myself, but there was no other choice. I unhooked the straps, let go of the harness, landed feet first and fell over backward. Fortunately, a layer of dead leaves that covered the ground helped cushion the landing. Nothing broke, but my lower back and left leg were numbed. It got worse when the adrenalin wore off.

The first thing I saw after hitting the ground was a huge white rabbit. It was perhaps 20 times the size of an American cottontail rabbit (It was an albino Hose, or Hare, grown for food, but the meat is tough). Next, a teen-age boy's head appeared from behind a large tree trunk. He called, and a bunch of civilian men armed with rifles, shotguns, sticks, whatever, arrived. They were excited, nervous and maybe a bit scared because they had captured an enemy soldier that had bombed their country and maybe some of their relatives or friends. There is a long list of Eighth Air Force personnel who were shot down over Germany who have never been found. They probably thought I was armed. (As a matter of fact, the Air Force issued all combat flyers a .45 caliber pistol, but we had heard you are usually better off without them, so we all were unarmed). They led me through the forest to a clearing off the side of a narrow paved road. A man in a uniform that I thought was Gestapo or German SS faced me from about 20 feet away. He held a P-38 pistol in his hand and shouted an order. There were 15 or 20 people lined up on my left and another 15 or 20 on my right; none stood in the line of fire behind me. I did nothing but stand still with my arms raised because I did not understand his language. He shouted the order again, then walked forward pointing his pistol at me. Cautiously, he began frisking. He seemed very nervous and unaccustomed to the task. He felt something in my shirt pocket, jumped back and shouted something again that I did not understand. I continued to stand still. He cocked his pistol and held it next to my head. Then, he cautiously reached inside my left shirt pocket, retrieved something, looked at it and flung it to the ground. Some of those in the crowd laughed when they saw it was a fountain pen that had fallen sideways in my shirt pocket. My thinking now is that the brute was just trying to act like the Gestapo. Nevertheless, it was a dangerous situation. I remained calm throughout the ordeal because I had a feeling of being protected by an invisible shield all over my body. I also think I was mentally numb about recognizing the seriousness of the situation.

Next, I was put in the back seat of a Volkswagen and driven to a nearby town named Komotau. (Now Chomutov). The entire crew was captured and assembled within two hours after bailing out. We all survived the jump. Bill (Red) Crow, our navigator and an Irish Catholic, said St. Patrick let us down gently, this being March 17, his duty day. Some of us had been injured by the strong wind while landing in rough terrain or treetops. Medical attention was not offered, probably because we all appeared to be okay. We would have refused anyway because no one was hurt badly enough to leave the security we expected by staying together. The nine of us were transported by rail about 10 miles from Komotau to Saaz (now Zatec) and spent the night in a small stinking jail. The lidless toilet had a full accumulation from previous occupants; it reeked and could not be flushed.

Our first food in 36 hours was brought in the next morning. It was just foul tasting ersatz coffee and a slice of black bread. It was called black bread, but it was more brown than black.* The taste was so bad that we could only eat it off and on during the day. Later in the week as we grew hungrier, we began to like it. Dinner was a small bowl of thin soup. Supper was another slice of black bread and a piece of cheese that had the color and texture of axle grease. Even in our hungry condition, we could not stand the odor. To eat it was impossible. (It may have been old Limburger that had putrified).

There were no contacts with us all day except for the food servers. We had heard a lot about German atrocities. The suspense of being in a jail, waiting and not knowing what they were going to do with a captured bomber crew caused us a lot of anxiety. John Atkinson, our ball-turret gunner, had a pocketknife so, for good luck, we cut memento scarves from the parachutes that some were still carrying. My chute was left on top of a tree. Some of the crew broke out into a popular song in America at the time called "Heil Heil Right in der Fueher's Face."

*The following recipe for black bread comes from the official record from the Food Providing Ministry published in Berlin 24.XI 1941 and the Director in Ministry Herr Mansfeld and Herr Moritz. It was agreed that the best mixture to bake black bread was:

50% bruised rye grain   20% tree flour (saw dust)
20% sliced sugar beets   10% minced leaves and straw

Published in the Ex-POW Bulletin, May 1997

About 4:00 A.M. on the third day, we were given some ersatz coffee and black bread, and walked to a nearby train station in Saaz for a 40-mile ride to a large train station in Pilsen. We attracted a crowd in our flight clothing as we moved through the station and out to a street corner where we waited for transportation. At times, some would point at us and yell, "Flieger, Flieger" (meaning flyer). No one threatened us physically because we had three armed guards, but we were not sure the crowd would do nothing.

The guards commandeered a streetcar. By that, I mean they boarded the streetcar, forced the passengers off, ordered us aboard and directed the conductor to proceed with no more pickups. The streetcar took us most of the way to what appeared to be a Luftwaffe training base. It was common talk around our home base in England that if shot down, hope you are turned over to the Luftwaffe and not the Gestapo or German SS. In this case, we were luckier than we realized at the time. They gave us two bowls of soup and bunked us in a well-constructed barrack containing over 100 military-neat bunks on the second floor. We shared the room with about two-dozen uniformed soldiers believed to be aviation cadets. There was a heater at one end of the room, and they gave us the bunks close to it.

After a few hours, we were roused and given rations for what they thought would be a two to three-day trip (three loaves of bread and two feet of sausage for the nine of us). Left the Luftwaffe base by 10:00 P.M. and spent most of night in a bomb shelter at a large train station. Obviously, the trains did not run on schedule. There was a lot of waiting for trains wherever we went. Three armed guards were assigned to escort us to a destination unknown by us. The guards were neither friendly nor unfriendly, just doing their job. The language barrier was a deterrent to establishing a friendlier relationship during the next five days as we traveled on catch-as-catch-can trains from Bohemia in Czechoslovakia to Bavaria in the southern part of Germany, almost to the western front near the American Army. In retrospect, I have often wondered if returning us toward the American front was an act of kindness. I sensed that these people did not want to be captured by the Russians.

Departed Pilsen early in the morning and arrived in Nurnberg just before sunset. We walked from one train station, through Nurnberg, to a second train station. The streets were filled with debris 12 to 15 feet high from toppled buildings. There was a 10-foot wide path down the middle. We passed by a marshaling yard containing hundreds of wrecked train cars and locomotives. Some were still upright on abandoned rails while others were stacked in a huge pile. Our crew had been over Nurnberg a month earlier with the 487th Bomb Group on our 23rd mission. The marshaling yards were close to downtown and bombardiers are not that accurate when aiming through clouds. The city was devastated. Glad we had the guards with us for protection as we passed through.

Also glad we did not bail out close to any major target areas such as this. We boarded a second train at Furst and traveled all night and the next day with frequent stops and delays. Along the way, when air alarms sounded, the trains would stop and the passengers, including our guards, would dash off the train and leave us locked in the car. We were concerned because we could see bullet damage from previous strafing.

We arrived at Lohr about sunset on day five and had another miserable night cramped in a cold jail. The journey was taking longer than expected, and our rations were long gone. We had no food for two different 24-hour periods. There was not much to eat even then, just what the guards could forage and were willing to share.

More of the same for the next two days - a little food and cold local jail.

On the seventh day, all nine of us shared a parlor car with our three guards and traveled stop and go all night. Arrived early morning at a large platform, not a regular station, where a Company of German infantry was waiting for the same next train we were to take. There were about 300 of them. Some were walking wounded with bandages, all were solemn, and they appeared very tired. So did their uniforms. They were neither friendly nor unfriendly, just there. Apparently they were heading for the Western Front, the same direction we were heading. We felt at ease standing among them, almost like we were all fellow soldiers. One was very friendly. He had a bottle containing something that he said was like Coca-Cola. He insisted on sharing it with us. It tasted like weak cool aid. We did not disillusion him. When the train arrived, our guards commandeered another parlor. The aisle was full of standing German soldiers, several with bandages.

We arrived at Ludwigsburg about 10:00 A.M. and were delivered by our three guards to a Luftwaffe interrogation station. We never saw the guards again. We were placed in solitary confinement. The cells were made of stone walls, steel bar doors, a wooden bench and a window near the top of one wall that was too narrow for a person to escape. It may have been sound-proofed because we could hear no sound whatsoever, just eerie silence.

Solitary confinement was, to me, the most nerve-wracking experience we encountered. This was the time when I most realized my freedom was being violated. I was totally helpless. There was nothing I could do but wonder what's next and what's happening to the others. Left alone like this, my imagination tended to gravitate to the worst that might happen, even the possibility of a torture chamber. I had resolved to give only the information required by the Geneva Convention: name, rank and serial number. Later, we were interrogated one-by-one and relieved of our "good luck" parachute scarves. At this stage of the war, the Germans were not trying to force information from us. They already knew our bomb group number and the name of our home base. As I was being interrogated, the interviewing officer, who spoke broken but understandable English, asked for my name, rank and serial number, which I provided, and then about my parents name and address, which I refused to answer. He politely explained that he needed this information so he could tell the Swiss Army to notify my parents that I had survived. I reasoned that knowledge of my parent's name and address could not possibly harm the war effort at this stage, and that it would relieve a lot of anxiety if they knew, so I consented. They were never notified. The interrogation ended, but the officer motioned me over to a window where we watched a real-time combat show in progress. Two P-51 Mustangs were strafing a high bridge over a deep valley between two mountains. I believe he said the bridge was on the road to Heidelberg, or Heilbronn. As the air show was going on, he talked about how useless war is, that we are all nice people and should strive for Utopia conditions where we all can get along together in peace. He said Sir Thomas More was one of his favorite authors and asked if I might be related to him. "Perhaps, but not to my knowledge," I said. (Sir Thomas More was a great prose writer of the last half of the Romance Period. He wrote a romance called Utopia, which describes life in an ideal commonwealth, where men have freedom in religion and just social and industrial conditions. In this, More makes public his dream of happiness for the human race). My impression of the interrogator was that he was an officer, a gentleman and a well-educated, friendly person with excellent morals.

About sunset, we were transferred to a POW camp and locked up overnight in a small barren room with a cold concrete floor and no windows. The toilet, like all the others we encountered, was a large coal bucket reeking with accumulated filth. It was another miserable night. (This was Dulag Luft 15, later changed to Stalag V-A).

On the morning of Day 9, we were released from this "Hell Hole" into an adjoining compound that was encircled with barbed wire and elevated guard stations. There were about 1,000 American soldiers, including 27 American officers, in our section of the compound. Other sections included 400 Indians from the British Army plus about 300 French, Russians and a small bunch of British. Several 10 to 12 year old boys were in the Russian group. There were 1700 POWs in total. These numbers are from a letter dated Feb 2, 1988 from John Young, a U. S. Army Sergeant who spoke Deutsch and English fluently and was in charge of the American compound. He worked very well with the 27 American officers in dealing with the Germans.

The Stalag guards fed us a thin watery soup and a slice of black bread twice daily, except on Sunday and Tuesday. The soup was made from dehydrated spinach and was gritty. The black bread tasted better with some kind of liquid greasy stuff smeared on it and then toasting it on the side of a potbelly stove when charcoal was available. Our best food came from the American Red Cross parcels that were delivered by the Swiss Army. We were supposed to get one parcel per man per week, but we were lucky if we got one parcel for three men per week.

The bunk mattresses were straw sacks; some had lice and bed bugs. They were uncomfortable, but we considered them to be very comfortable in comparison with our first week of sleeping on concrete and wooden floors.

We figured we must be in or close to a war zone. Fighter planes, obviously from the Eighth Air Force, were constantly strafing and bombing nearby targets.

We could hear them but not see them. This boosted our morale because it made us think liberation was near. There were lots of rumors and some news brought in by newly captured men.

Life in the prison camp during the next six days was the same boring routine day after day. Our daily schedule was to arise in time for assembly and a head count, eat something if available, talk to somebody about something and hit the sack for another nap and another dream about food. The sounds of war became increasingly closer. Our fighter planes continued to bomb and strafe nearby targets. Then, the sound of heavy artillery could be heard during the day and the bloom from firings could be seen on the horizon at night. There were many rumors of Allied victories. Freedom was expected soon.

Late in the afternoon of the 17th day, we were alerted for evacuation and departed from the compound near Ludwigsburg soon after dark. We marched an estimated 10 kilometers and bivouacked in a field near a lumberyard. Our spirits were high as the bloom of artillery flashes seemed to be coming from three sides. The guards were outnumbered by a wide margin, but they had the guns. Nevertheless, it was dark and the lumber yard provided a safe-looking hideout. It appeared to be a good opportunity to escape. We decided not to attempt it because we expected to be liberated soon and it was not worth taking a chance of being shot. The next morning, however, we found out that during the night our flight engineer/top-turret gunner, Tom Emerson, had slipped into the nearby lumber yard and escaped. He told us at a reunion of the 487th Bomb Group Historical Society in Orlando that was the worst 30 days of his life. He had to hide during the day, be wary during the night and exist with almost no food.

From our observations traveling across Germany, it was obvious that the Jerry's could provide neither shelter nor adequate food for so many on a march, and we were not properly dressed nor outfitted for rain, sleet and cold wind. What made it worse was that both Ted and I had jumped out of a warm cockpit and forgot our hat and jacket and the emergency oxygen bottle. We made do by cutting our fleece-lined flight pants to fit over our shoulders.

By the Geneva Convention rules, Prisoners of War are not allowed to return to combat. If you ponder about why we had to go on a march, a possible explanation is that to just leave us in the compound and do nothing might be construed by superior officers as a sign of weakness during times of war. I was totally impressed with the resiliency of the German people and wonder why and how they managed to hang on when the conditions we experienced and observed indicated their country was vastly depleted. Another possibility may be important logistically. War is about killing or capturing the enemy, and combat troops are the hard core of an army. For example, the US had 15 million in uniform during WWII, but only 1.5 million were involved in actual combat. That's a ratio of 10 supportive personnel to one combatant. That means 90 percent of our armed forces are needed to support the 10 percent who are combat soldiers. So, logistically thinking, if one prisoner is worth 10 other supporting soldiers, the Germans should retain all prisoners as long as possible because one equals 10. In an arguable way of thinking, if a combat soldier is worth 10 others, why weren't we paid ten times more?

On April 3, 1945 (Day 18 of our captivity), the column moved out from our first encampment in rain. The Russians were at the head of the column, followed by the American enlisted men, the 27 American officers, the British, the Indians and the French. Everybody in the entire column of 1,700 just ambled along, except the British officers forced their men to march in cadence and in formation. Typically British, old chap, wouldn't you say?

It became increasingly evident that the German guards did not like the Russians. They didn't care much for the French either, but there were not so many of them in the column. The Russians were not under the Red Cross program and received no parcels of food whatsoever. They were at the head of the column, and many of them passed out beside the road. An English doctor with us examined a few and said most of them will die in a short time. Rumor was that if you fell out, you were shot. This may have been true because we did hear one or two rifle or pistol shots coming from the rear on various occasions.

This day's march ended at Schorndorf. It rained off and on all night to make a miserable condition more miserable.

On day 19, we observed a P-47 strafing Lorch as we approached it. It was just another real-time war show.

I was unable to eat anything on Day 20 because of stomach problems: Dysentery, I guess. We called it "the GIs." What? No toilet paper? (Note: GI stood for anything issued by the Government and included soldiers, clothing and even diarrhea.)

Departed about 6:00 P.M. It rained all night while we were marching. Arrived at bivouac area about 4:00 A.M. and slept on wet muddy ground.

Stayed day 21 here in a trampled, rain soaked, muddy field. As usual, Ted, Red and I slept side-by-side for added warmth. Our high-top GI shoes were put in our bags and used for pillows. We lived full time in the same clothing and never had an opportunity to wash the clothing, nor ourselves. The sky was covered with beautiful bright stars on clear nights. Navigator Bill Crow knew something about astronomy and taught us to recognize various constellations such as Orion the Hunter, Cassiopeia, and the Seven Sisters.

Sleeting on day 22. It was good to be on the road again and out of the mud. The Russians and French were left behind. Arrived at Unterkoch just out of Aalen. Slept on hillside. Our blankets, which were still wet, froze during night.

On day 23, April 8, we headed southeast on an old clay road. I heard some talk about an "Old Roman Highway." I think the word was that this was a part that has been preserved through the centuries. The Romans in their day built roads to England, Greece and other places. Now I understood the old saying, "All roads lead to Rome." There is now a modern expressway that passes near Augsburg, and where we were that is called "The Old Roman Highway." That night, we camped near a small town named Unterriffiaen. Somehow, we managed to boil two large rutabagas for the three of us.

The Indians in our column were interesting people. There were five tribes. I only recall the Muslims, Punjabs, Brahmins and the Gherkas names. They all were friendly, but each tribe had uniquely different customs. For example, almost everybody was addicted to cigarettes in those days. They were high priority for bartering. One of the tribes would not allow tobacco to touch their lips. So, they held two fingers parallel to their lips and drew the smoke through their fingers in such a way that the tobacco would not touch their lips. The Brahmins were dedicated to body cleanliness. Each morning, if any water was available, they would strip and bathe no matter how cold the weather. Some would even pour a bucket of cold water over their heads to rinse off. This day, we had camped by a stream feeding into the Danube. One Indian from the Brahmin tribe swam to the other side while taking his bath. A guard yelled for him to get back. He was almost all the way back when the guard shot him.

The next day, the Indians built a pyre according to their custom and cremated their friend. I have a letter that John Young, our friendly Sergeant in charge, wrote in response to a letter I sent to him: "I was a Sgt. in charge of the camp, and I lived in the small shack in the center of the compound. I recall the incident about the Indian that was shot. That was brutal, and the Germans knew it. We got the Germans to postpone the march for one day so that he could be cremated. If you saw that, I was the one who represented the Americans and placed flowers at the base of the pyre. The Indian had been a prisoner for three years. After we were liberated, the Indians picked out the German guard and shot him." The pyre was in an outdoor area. The smoke had an odor of a steak cookout.

This was a clear and sunny day. While the funeral service was underway, I began to hear a low droning sound. I looked in the direction of the sound and saw some speckled dots in the distant sky. The drone got louder and the specks got larger. It was a group of B-17s on a mission. It was an awesome sight. I thought that could be the 487th Bomb Group and, except for our misfortune, I could be up there flying a B-17 in our regular position off the left wing of the 838th Squadron leader. And maybe it would be our 35th and final mission before being rotated back to the States. Ernie Pyle, a famous war correspondent during WW II better expresses the feeling on page 434 in his book "Brave Men" and repeated on page 332 of his book "Ernie's War." The comments are in reference to the "Break-Through" at Saint-Lo following the Normandy invasion. A reference to these comments by Ernie Pyle was made in the May 1989 issue of a newsletter published by the Florida Chapter of the Eighth Air Force Historical Society. Pyle is referring to the Mighty Eighth Air Force.

"The first planes of the mass onslaught came a little before 10 A.M. They were the fighters and dive-bombers ... The air was full of sharp and distinct sounds of cracking bombs and the heavy rips of the planes machine guns and the splitting screams of diving wings. It was all fast and furious, yet distinct.

And then a new sound gradually droned into our ears, a sound deep and all encompassing with no note to it just a gigantic faraway surge of doom-like sound. It was the heavies. They came from directly behind us. At first they were the merest dots in the sky. We could see clots of them against the far heavens, too tiny to count individually. They came on with a terrible slowness. They came in flights of 12, three flights to a group, and in groups stretched out across the sky. They came in families of about 70 planes each. Maybe those gigantic waves were two miles apart, maybe they were 10 miles apart. I don't know. But I do know that they came on in a constant procession, and I thought it would never end. What the Germans must have thought is beyond comprehension.

The flight across the sky was slow and studied. I've never known such a storm, or a machine, or any resolve of man that had about it the aura of such a ghastly relentlessness. I had the feeling that even had God appeared beseechingly before them in the sky, with palms outstretched to persuade them back, they would not have had it within their power to turn from their irresistible course."

Day 25 was a nice warm spring day in Bavaria. We camped in an open field about 5:00 P.M. for the night. Again, water was not provided. There was a drainage ditch nearby with running water but two high-ranking German officers who appeared at the scene barred us from using it for sanitation purposes. We did anyway but did not drink it. We had to have some water to boil some rutabagas or else go to bed without supper.

On day 26, we marched to Whittingen and camped at a ball park. Civilians were allowed to mingle with us. We traded soap and brushes (from Red Cross parcels) and other personal stuff such as watches and rings for bread and potatoes. Everybody was hungry on the limited Jerry rations. Many were falling out on the march. More rain during the night.

We stayed another day at the ballpark. There were several rain showers during the morning. Hunger pains and thoughts of food occupied our minds most of the time. Another major concern was about the folks back home. I correctly thought the War Department would send a telegram to the folks telling them that I was missing in action (MIA). I worried about the anguish this would cause, especially for Mom, who was already worried about both of her combat sons, brother Bill in Italy and I in England. I also correctly thought the Germans would not notify the Swiss Army. I wished so much that I could somehow communicate to the folks that we were okay, so I tried mental telepathy. To my knowledge, it did not work, but the War Department MIA telegram was delivered.

Home was a farm in the Popash school district east of Wauchula, Florida. We grew lots of oranges and had a small herd of cattle. Almost everybody knew almost everybody. The MIA message affected a lot of people in various parts of the county and town and all the relatives where ever they were. Mom told me later that people came to our house in droves to offer sympathy and to pray for my safe return.

On day 28, we left the ball park about 10:00 A.M. as the rain continued. The Indians were separated from our part of the column at Dillingen. Sergeant Young arranged for the 27 officers to sleep in a hay barn just past Dillingen. This was our first night under shelter since leaving Ludwigsburg. I felt guilty because it was a cold rainy night and the men had to sleep on the ground in an open field.

On day 29, the officers spent the day in the barnyard. The men were on an open field. Our food supply was almost depleted. Red Cross rations arrived late in the day. The farmer helped by giving each of us about 10 boiled potatoes.

Day 30, April 15, through Day 34, April 19, was spent in barnyard. Apparently the urge to keep moving was now considered unnecessary. However, there was nothing to do nor that we could do. It was boring. In fact, about 80 percent of the time in captivity was boring, the rest of the time was just plain miserable. We received two French Red Cross parcels during this period. These parcels contained noodles, beans, lentils, crackers, chocolate, cigarettes, coffee and sardines.

On April 20th, day 35 of our captivity we departed on the road to Augsburg. Along the way, a low-flying P-47 appeared suddenly. We dove for the ditch and lay still. Any movement attracts the pilot's eye. For a moment we sensed the terror of being strafed by a fighter plane. It was a chilling feeling. The pilot circled, recognized who we were, dipped his wing, then flew on and strafed a bridge over the Danube River, or something near the bridge. Stayed the night in an open field. I was sick that night. My feet got so cold that I dreamed I was opening big blisters on them.

On day 36, we marched about 16 kilometers in intermittent showers. A cold front with a driving rain arrived about camping time. The enlisted men slept in an open field. According to RHIP (Rank Has Its Privilege), Sergeant Young again arranged for the 27 officers to sleep in the farmer's hay barn. What a privilege that was with cold wind and showers lasting all night. The rain sounds on the roof were very comforting. We were in Hammen – just before Augsburg.

The cold, driving rain continued the next day as we marched through the edge of Augsburg to a camping spot. Augsburg had been hit hard by the Eighth Air Force. Jerry rations for this day consisted of one can of beef for 11 men and a loaf of bread for five. We slept on cold ground under a large tent that kept the cold wind and rain out. Not bad under the circumstances, but not nearly as good as a hay barn.

On the morning of day 38, April 23, we received one Belgian Red Cross parcel plus one American Red Cross parcel packed for invalids for each two men. The food situation was getting better, but the weather was still cold and raining.

On day 39, the American enlisted men, including our crew, were split off in Augsburg and marched on the road to Munich. From a beginning column of 1,700, we were now down to 27 American Officers. The smaller number made it much easier for the Sergeant to arrange more suitable accommodations.

The 27 of us continued through Augsburg on the road to Regensburg (Route 300). Marched a few kilometers and stopped at a large dairy farm for the night.

Gentlemen From Hell

Fresh milk and potatoes were available. This was luxury compared with the previous weeks. Rather than sleeping outside in the weather, we chose to sleep in the cow barn with the cows. There was clean hay on the floor, and the cows did not step on us.

Stayed day 40 on the farm. Ate well from what remained of the Red Cross parcels.

Left the farm on day 41 (April 26) and marched to another nearby dairy farm where we waited for liberation. Sergeant Young got the farmer to butcher a calf, and we ate beef stew.

Nothing happened on day 42. We had adequate food and a good appetite, but our stomachs had shrunk.

About mid-afternoon on day 43 (April 28), artillery shells began whistling overhead. We divided into groups of eight and waited inside a concrete cow barn for protection in case of gunfire. It had a strong bovine odor, but it was warm and there was clean hay on the floor.

Not much activity on the morning of day 44 (April 29). We heard a few bursts of machine gun fire and constant mooing by the cows as though they sensed something was about to happen. Toward noon I lay down for a nap and was awakened by someone shouting, "They are here!" We all rushed out to meet our liberators. A hundred or more American soldiers on tank destroyers and loaded with snacks, sodas and cigarettes. What a day!!! Forty-four days of captivity, and suddenly we are free again. Troops from the 3rd Infantry Division (Mechanized) of the U. S. Seventh Army liberated us, and then drove us back to Augsburg, where we spent the night in a factory office.

On Day 45, we moved into the Kaiserhoff Hotel in Augsburg and began our wait for transportation back to the States. For us, the war was over.

During our six-week tour we saw lots of things inside Germany as we traveled by train from Pilsen, Czechoslovakia to Ludwigsburg and on the march from there to a place east of Augsburg on the road to Regensburg named Erasburg (too small to find on recent maps).Their country's infrastructure was virtually wiped out. In a way it was impressive that the Germans still had some fight in them and had not yet capitulated from all the things they had to cope with. Their air force, army, transportation, fuel and food were almost depleted. Some of the autos we saw had large furnaces on the rear to generate steam power. We saw autos parked along the road while the occupants chopped wood for their car's steam furnace. Trucks having gas would tow as many as three other trucks without gas. Horse drawn autos were sometimes seen, but auto traffic was almost non-existent. They were harassed by the constant threat of bombers and fighter planes from the Mighty Eighth Air Force in England and France, plus the 15th Air Force in Italy and the Royal Air Force.

On May 1, Day 46, we were still waiting for transportation. and we were restless from what you might call a boredom hangover. The beds in this hotel were fair, but there were no bed sheets, no glass in the windows, no doors and no maid service. The food provided by the Army was good. Lots of chicken and steak, things we had not tasted for a long time. We had good appetites, but our stomachs had shrunk.

No word from Army the next day, so we hitched a ride in an army jeep going to Mannheim. The driver was with the 94th Engineer Corp. We drove thru Stuttgart on the Autobahn and spent the night near Pforziem in a farmhouse commandeered by the driver. He picked out a nice house on a country hillside, knocked on the door and told the elderly husband and wife that we are staying for the night and want beds and hot food for four. Apparently, conqueror soldiers do such things routinely. The owners were very gracious. They prepared a great dinner and their beds were clean and comfortable.

Left Pforziem for Mannheim on Day 48 and hitched a ride in a C-47 cargo plane to Paris. The pilot flew low over Mannheim as we departed, and we observed the bomb and artillery results - KAPUTT. The city was virtually leveled, but many church steeples were still standing in isolation.

Circled low over Paris and got an aerial view of the city and the Eiffel Tower. We got a courtesy room at the Hotel Francia. It was about three blocks from the Champs Elysee's in downtown Paris and not far from the Eiffel Tower.

Paris: Ted, Bill and I stayed at the Francia Hotel for five days until May 8th. We were issued new clothing and visited the Eiffel Tower, the Seine River and various parts of downtown Paris. It was not a lively place at the time. First, we sent telegrams back home telling the folks we were liberated and safe. On the eighth of May, we boarded a train going to a deportation center named Camp Lucky Strike near Le Havre, France. This was VE day: We missed the celebration in Paris.

We were at Camp Lucky Strike for a week or so. I weighed in at about eight pounds less than my normal weight of 163 to 165. Funny thing about it was that our legs were fatter. We wondered why and how many more pounds we would have lost otherwise.

When the war was over, the 487th Bomb Group had 48 combat losses. When "all causes" are counted, the 8th Air Force lost 4,754 B-17s and 2,122 B-24s.

General Jimmy Doolittle tells us to be proud that you were a member of the 8th Air Force. "Whether a mechanic, cook in the mess hall, sitting at a desk or a member of an air crew, you were part of the largest military unit in World War II. 350,000 served in the 8th, 26,000 of your comrades lost their lives (more than the Navy in both the Pacific and the Atlantic) and another 28,000 became prisoners of war. That is a terrible price to pay, but, at that time, the job had to be done.

In air battles during 1944, fighter pilots and bomber crews destroyed over 6,000 enemy aircraft ... strafing attacks by our fighters accounted for 1,900 more.

In precision attacks on enemy airfields and factories, our heavies damaged or destroyed an additional 2,630 Nazi aircraft.

Gentlemen From Hell

Fighters also knocked out 3,652 locomotives, 5,702 freight cars, 3,436 trucks and significant numbers of tank cars, ammunition dumps and similar ground targets."

In my post-war work-a-day world, I had access to a smart marketing consultant. His name was Milton and he was from Detroit. I recall a statement that he attributed to his Jewish mother. "There is nothing so good that there is not some bad associated with it, and there is nothing so bad that there is not some good associated with it." With respect to the widely-known wisdom of Jewish mothers, I have temporarily re-phrased my viewpoint to express what a lawyer for the defense might say is the good part of the bad part of my POW experiences.

PAUL WHITE

What was supposed to be a 10-12 hour mission for White's crew - their longest to that point - ended up taking much longer. They were away from the base for nine days and returned to find their belongings packed away.

Fifty-five years later, it's easy to say that what happened to us on number 25 was a standout. It wasn't our last mission; we still had 10 more to go.

This story is from my point of view as a 21-year old co-pilot. You may ask how come I was a co-pilot on a heavy bomber. Not by choice; I wanted B-25s or 26s, but the Air Corps needed bomber pilots, period.

I'll give you some background on our crew. 487th Bomb Group, 3rd Division, B-17's, Square P on the tail, based in Lavenham, England, about 60 miles north of London. Pilot Ed Clarry, New York, New York; Co-Pilot Paul White, Ontario, California; Navigator John Phillips, Falon, Nevada; Engineer Lee Britton, Miami, Florida; Radio Operator Tony Humick, New York City; Ball-Turret Sylvester Materovitch, Pennsylvania; Tail Gunner Jack Harless, Layfayette, Indiana; Togglier Norman Westbrook, Alabama; and various Waist Gunners.

The mission was to Nurenberg, Germany on February 20, 1945. We knew it would be a long mission, 10 to 12 hours, our deepest mission.

We were in the high squadron at 25,000 feet, 20 minutes to I.P. I looked up and could see 155s and 105s bursting directly overhead. We knew the shells had to go by us to get there.

Number three engine was hit, and both Clarry and I tried to feather it, but it ran away. We pulled out of formation, smoking badly. The engine finally froze and the prop broke loose, just windmilling free. We had lost a couple of thousand feet by then. We dropped our bombs in train, trying to tear up as many cabbage patches as we could.

Gentlemen from Hell

We stabilized the plane, and the pilot asked the navigator for a heading to Switzerland so we could bail out. Number three was smoking badly. Two prop was spinning and getting hotter. We leveled out and slowed down to 115 indicated to keep the vibration as low as possible.

We lost altitude slowly. At about 10,000 feet, we knew we were sitting ducks; no clouds to hide in and still deep in Germany.

It was a beautiful clear morning as we headed for Switzerland, hoping to make France.

We were chugging along, Alps to the left, and the navigator was pointing out various lakes and the town of Berne. Suddenly, four ME-109s flying in combat formation came in to check us out. We were relieved to see white crosses on their tails, but did not know if they would attack or not. We were apprehensive, making sure all our turrets were flashing in the sun as we tracked them.

They finally got tired of stalking us and moved on. We chugged along at slow speed, enjoying the scenery and thinking we had an outside chance of making it to France. We tried different speeds, but if we sped up too much the vibration on number 3 was too great.

We flew out of Swiss territory, ran into some turbulence, and number 3 prop dropped straight down, leaving a big smoking hole in the engine. Some French farmer got a surprise present from us.

We spotted a fighter base and headed in. No radio contact since we had no frequency information. We landed downwind, praying the plane would hold together. Our host was a P-38 base at St. Disia Merville, France.

The fighter base personnel took us under their wing, and we stayed at a chalet for about three days.

They had their own mess with stacks of Wesson oil for trading material with other bases and the infantry.

The fighter group had come up from Africa. While we were with them, they switched over from 38s to P-47s. They were tactical close support outfit. I really felt sorry for the pilots; they were given five hours in their new planes and began flying combat.

We waited around for a repaired 17, since ours was going to need a new engine flown in. Soon, there was a bloody 100th ship ready to go and we were scheduled to fly it up to Belgium. While we waited, we had a chance to chow down with the infantry, and they introduced us to Calvadose (White Lightning) that took our breadth away.

We took the bloody 100th ship up to Belgium late in the afternoon. We had not colors of the day, a real screw up. There we were in a beat up airplane; the only radio that worked was a liaison set our radio operator could use. At night we worried about German night fighters, and the field in Belgium would not turn on the field lights for us. I can still remember that our call sign was Blundish Blue Baker and the field was Martini.

What a screw up! We finally got in. I'm sure the Russians could hear the liaison set we had to use.

We had to hang around in Belgium for a few days, and finally, 22 of us got in a B-24 and headed for England. We arrived back at Lavenham nine days after we left. We found all our clothes and personal items were stuffed in barracks bags and B-4 bags, candy bars and all; bedding all gone. What a greeting!

We went up to headquarters to be debriefed and were welcomed with a chorus by another available crew, reading our epitaph on the bulletin board: Last seen No. 3 smoking and pulling out of formation.

Our group had not heard about us until we walked in. We finished our missions March 30 by going to Hamburg.

Don't think we didn't sweat that last mission. While we were on "flak leave," another crew had taken our regular plane to Hamburg and got shot down.

You had to be good, and you had to be lucky.

839th Squadron Introduction

The 839th Squadron begins with the story, sent to me by Kay Voss, who was also quoted in Tom Brokaw's book, *The Greatest Generation Speaks*. He tells of a certain day that he says will, "Live on in my memory forever," and how after he landed, "the pilot, Vince, and I just sat there too exhausted to move." Walter Baker is the second chapter in this squadron, and his story is a very emotional personal interview I did with him in Memphis, Tennessee. Read his description of flying French people out of labor camps and how they were so desperate for food that they "pounced on the K-rations like a pack of hungry dogs." Toward the end of his interview, he got choked up and we had to stop several times, as I had to do with quite a few of the veterans that I have interviewed.

Don Kilburg is the next story, and he tells of his most memorable mission while he was deputy group lead bombardier December 24, 1944 on his 18th bombing mission. He ends his story with, "Yet, our regular brushes with the horrors of war, the loss of friends and comrades, the uncertainty and danger of each mission, are things that marked us for life." Al Rasof's chapter is that of a radio-gunner on the B-17 "Gravel Gertie." On a personal note, Al sent me a silk scarf that he purchased in London after the war was over, before coming home. I've framed it and placed it in the office where I've written this book, and will treasure it forever.

Gerald Obrecht's chapter tells of his most memorable times. Walter Wise tells his recollection of the December 24, 1944 mission, which was to "help change the Battle of the Bulge." Bobby Heard is the final story in this squadron. He says, "My story is one that represents the experiences of thousands of average American men and women who had courage thrust upon them, to face their deaths, for their country. It is a story of heroism - an American story that needs to be told again and again." He goes on to say, "However, those two years of fighting in the war made a tremendous impact on my life. To this day, I carry the spirit of the American mindset from 60 years ago and treasure American freedom." Bobby Heard's words ring true for many of the soldiers in this book.

Kay Voss

It is one thing to read some of the history of WWII, but it was entirely different to have lived in those historic times. The magnitude of the task which lie before the nation in the 1940s was almost beyond comprehension, but once the serviceman donned the uniform, there was one resolve - to be victorious. Not only the servicemen and women, but the entire nation was behind the total effort. From food and gasoline rationing to collecting and saving grease from cooking to collecting scrap metals and old newspapers and going without many of the ordinary things of life they were used to, there was no complaining. They just did it, because the "boys" needed it!

I enlisted in the Army Air Force while attending the University of Michigan in 1942 and was called up in February of 1943. After graduation from Flight School and Transition Training, I was assigned to the 8th Air Force and arrived in England in December of 1944. Our first introduction to England was in a fog so dense you could not see across the road. I can remember my first thoughts, "We are going to fly in this stuff?" And that kind of weather was exactly what we flew in most of our time there. Many a morning we took off when you could not see the end of the runway. You just timed the plane in front of you and hoped and prayed that they were out of the way before opening your throttles.

There were times after take-off, while still in the "soup," you would see bright flashes in the clouds and knew that some of your buddies were not coming home that night. Some days, we fought and feared the weather as much as we did the enemy. Our crew flew December, January, February and March - without a doubt the worst time of year in England as far as weather was concerned.

The air fields were built on farm land, consequently they were still farming as much of the land as they could between and at the end of the runways, right up to the barracks areas - every place that was not needed to make the airfield operational. The weather was a big problem, not only in the air, but on the ground, as well. It never got cold enough to freeze, consequently. There was mud to contend with almost all of the time until May. It was a long walk to the Mess Hall or Headquarters if you walked the roads; consequently, everybody took short cuts across the muddy fields. What a mess!

The blackout was a new experience for all of us, also. With an overcast all of the time and no reflected light anywhere, it was black, black, black! All of the vehicles had hoods over the headlights, with about an inch slit to let light shine through. The trains ran without lights of any kind. It was quite an experience to stand at the train station and hear the engine coming and not know where it was. I remember one night, we were moving from our base to another by truck (for

839TH SQUADRON

some reason long forgotten), when it was so dark and foggy, we took turns walking along side of the trucks so the drivers could watch us and stay on the road. It seemed like it took forever to go just about 10 or so miles.

We lived in Quonset huts made of pre-shaped-ribbed steel. They were cold and damp most of the time. Our heat came from a steel oil drum fashioned at the flight line shop into a stove. For fuel, we burned whatever we could find. The bombs came packed with two heavy cardboard rings coated with paraffin. Needless to say, there were "tons" of these around the area. When these were cut up and stuffed into the stove, that little sucker turned rosy red. There was one problem, however. They did not last very long.

Each barracks held four crews of three officers each, making 12 officers in each barracks. On one of our rare days off, we borrowed a truck from the motor pool and went looking for some wood. We found a sawmill that had piles of slab wood. We loaded the truck with every piece we could and headed home. We piled the wood outside of our barracks and proceeded to build ourselves a real fire. That worked fine until our wood began to disappear. Our "friends" in the neighboring barracks had themselves a fire also. We ended up piling all of it inside the barracks anywhere we could find to put it - behind the beds, under the beds, stacked against the walls. We had a mess, but at least we had a warm mess.

We had a fire mostly on our down days. When we were flying, we came home to a cold, damp barracks. Being made of all steel, the walls would get wet from the condensation. The water would run down the inside and be almost as wet as the outside; consequently, we had cold, damp floors most of the winter.

A lot of our flying came at the Battle of the Bulge and shortly after. The Allies were trying to make a maximum effort, so we were called on to stretch ourselves to the max. There was one stretch when we flew seven missions in as many days. They all started at three or four in the morning. By the time you had breakfast, dressed into flying clothes, had briefing, preflight and the plane, warmed it up for 45 minutes, flew the mission of six or seven hours or longer, landed, took care of your equipment, had debriefing and supper, you finally got to go to bed for some uneasy sleep. There were times I would climb into bed, clothes and all. Everyone was exhausted. Then, you were aroused out of bed the next morning at three or four to start it all over again.

We did have a few down days when crews were rotated for a day off. Once in a while we had a weekend to ourselves. As I remember, we made a couple of trips to London. Our base was about 50 miles north of London, with about a four or five-hour train ride to get there. It stopped at every little town and crossing along the way. I think we made the trip a couple of times.

The most pleasant experience undoubtedly, was the "flak leave." After 20 missions, we were given a week of R&R. We went to an old English Mansion away out in the country side. It had been taken over by the Army Air Force and made into a rest home, and that is what we did a lot of - rest! We were there to enjoy ourselves and forget about the war. There was nothing to do but rest, eat and have fun. And that is just what we did to the max! There were civilian clothes to wear, softball, volleyball, basketball, tennis, ping pong, billiards, horseback riding, movies and good old home grown, honest to goodness, American girls! I don't know how many fellows were there, but there must have been 35 to 40 of us, and the girls remembered everyone's name by the second day! How they were able to do that, I don't know, but it certainly made you feel at home. The leave came just in time for each of us, as we were exhausted both physically and mentally.

The most horrible experience, of course, was the bomb run itself. The first time I saw the flak, it dawned on me, "This is the real thing." No more practice missions. Those were real shells and rockets I was seeing bursting out there and there was no turning back!! When the flak got so close it could be heard bursting over the roar of the engines, and you saw some of your buddies go down ... you came home with dirty underwear more than once!

I tried to keep a diary of the missions, but they came so close together and were so long that fatigue and weariness set in and one seemed to run into another. At the time, sleep was the biggest priority on one's mind rather than pages filled in a diary. I can recall some of the things that happened, but exactly which mission or date I wouldn't remember now, perhaps except for one. I remember because it was the Ides of March (March 15, 1945). The date in my pilot's log states only that it was my 21st mission and that it was to Oranienburg, Germany, and that we hit uncharted flak on the way home. Very intense! Our maps of Germany included "flak maps," which outlined the known areas where the enemy had installed their anti-aircraft batteries. Through intelligence and past experience, the maps were usually pretty accurate and reliable. The Germans always seemed to have one more trick up their sleeves, however.

On this particular mission, we had been briefed to drop down from our bombing altitude, which was usually 20,000 to 25,000 ft, to about 12,000 ft., after bombs away. The route home was to be over a remote wooded area which showed no flak on the map. The enemy, however, had moved in "flak trains" and were waiting for us. They blasted the "Hell" out of us. We lost some planes; I don't recall how many, but everyone came back with battle damage. We wondered long and hard about how they knew where we were going to be ... was it dumb luck on their part, or were they tipped off? We never knew.

The German Air Force was pretty well defeated by early 1945. The P-51s were able to stay with us all the way to the target and back. Some of them would drop down to ground level and shoot up any target they could find. Any target of opportunity was fair game. We occasionally were warned of "bandits" (enemy fighters) in the area, but the P-51s usually took care of them long before they could do any damage to the bomber formations. We were hit one day by a German Jet fighter that flew right through our formation. Their jets were much faster than our P-51s. There was one flaw, however ... they ran out of fuel rather quickly. Our fighter pilots would box them in until they ran dry and then nail them.

839TH SQUADRON

Having been pretty well defeated in the air, the enemy concentrated on anti-aircraft guns and rockets to protect their targets. They had learned how to improve the accuracy and technique. Probably Frankfurt, in western Germany, was one of the worst targets for picking up flak damage. They had figured out that if they coordinated every gun battery in the city and fired them all at the same time, setting them at varying altitudes (approximately at which we were flying), they would have a better chance of hitting their target. Now let me tell you, they were right! If you were one of the lucky ones you might come out of there without battle damage. We were very happy they never did the same with every target.

On one of our missions to Berlin area, we carried time delayed 500 lb bombs, set to go off one hour to 72 hours later. Only the Lord knows the terrifying effect this must have had on the civilians below, with those things going off constantly for three days around the clock. I think about that now, but at the time, I'm sure it made no difference to me.

There is another day that will live on in my memory forever. We had engine damage and had to leave formation before getting to the target. Both number three and number four engines lost oil pressure. Oil was streaming out of the rear of each engine cowling. We feathered number three, but number four had lost all the oil from the hub and could not be feathered. It just windmilled and acted as a break. It was all both of us could do to keep from turning to the right and flying in circles. With all the trim rolled in and with both of us having two feet on the left rudder and full aileron, we headed back toward England. Somewhere over the North Sea, we jettisoned our bombs, guns, ammo and anything else we could find to lighten the load. We brought everyone from the rear to the radio room to help with the trim. We flew this way for an hour or so. The Air Corps had built a runway on the coast of East Angela, the furthest point east in England. The runway was two miles long with a two mile over-run. It was built especially for crews who had problems making it all the way back to their own Home Base. It may very well have saved our lives, and I'm sure many others as well. It was a welcome sight.

After we landed, we cut engines and both the pilot, Vince and I, just sat there too exhausted to move. I remember Vince and I could hardly walk when we finally got to solid ground. While at the field we inspected a lot of planes that had landed there with battle damage. When you stood there and looked at how badly damaged some of them were, you just marveled that they made it back at all. One had its rudder completely gone along with only about half of the tail fin left. Another had number three engine burned almost completely out with about six feet of wing behind the engine gone. The only thing holding the wing was the main spar. There were many untold stories that went along with the planes that were there. The B-17 was a great airplane, and many a bomber crew owed their lives to the way it was built and performed under the most extreme circumstances imaginable!

Gentlemen From Hell

When I made the decision to enlist in the Army Air Corps, there were several things that helped me to make up my mind. Probably the foremost was a movie short advertising the Army Air Corps narrated by Jimmy Stewart. I saw that movie short on a trip to Detroit to check out the recruiting possibilities. I stopped in one of the theaters just to kill some time waiting for my ride back to school at the University of Michigan. The movie short came on just before the main picture (I have no idea what it was). I was so impressed with what Jimmy Stewart said about the Air Corps and being a cadet that I enlisted with a traveling recruiting unit back at Ann Arbor shortly after. It was kind of ironic that Jimmy Stewart was a General in the Eighth Air Force and flew missions right along with the rest of us. He was a great regular guy that understood the common GI and was loved by all who served under him. He was on the Queen Elizabeth coming home from England at the same time I was.

There are a few "stand-out" moments that are still in my memory yet today. A few are worth writing about here. There were several while in cadet training. The very first occurred after we arrived in Miami for basic training. We had spent three days on the train going down to Miami from Detroit. The old train cars had been in storage for a long, long time and were never cleaned before we climbed aboard. After about the second day, we looked like coal miners just out of the mine. The cars soon ran out of water, so we could not wash.

When we arrived in Miami, we were bussed to Miami Beach where all the hotels are. We sat on the lawn of several hotels waiting for orders. We waited from about noon to late afternoon for someone to tell us where to go. We finally got supper, but still no hotel to go to. Some time after dark we were taken to a small hotel called the Indian Queen, just off of the main street of Miami Beach. There were not enough cots or beds for us, so many of us slept on the floor.

After about a week, still in the clothes we left Detroit in, we were taken to a Hotel on the Main Street and issued uniforms. We found out later that we were not supposed to have arrived until a week later.

There were something like 100,000 recruits in Miami Beach living in the hotels on the beach ... six or more to a room. You can imagine the plumbing problems that developed with that many toilets being flushed all over the area. And besides that, there was a toilet paper shortage. So, what did we use? Anything we could find. Any old piece of newspaper would do, if you could find some. I'll leave the rest to the reader's imagination. It was a mess!

I took my primary training in Jackson, Mississippi. I had an excellent instructor. The small field we were at had been a flying school before the war, and they kept many of the instructors on when the Army Air Corps took over. Many of them were older men that had years of experience instructing flying. I was one of the first ones to solo. I know it was because of my instructor. He was a great teacher, firm but kind and understanding. By the second month, we were learning some acrobatic maneuvers - spins, loops, slow rolls, snap rolls, lazy eight's and more. I got to where I could handle the plane pretty well and I was

839TH SQUADRON

allowed to go into the practice area and do some acrobatics solo. I had been up for most of my period when I decided to do a loop. When I got almost to the top of the loop, I decided to roll out on top. I began to feel light in my seat. I looked down. No seatbelt! That scared me so that I flew straight and level the rest of my period. That was a good lesson, however. It taught me not to get too "cocky" and always fasten your seat belt and think, think, think, while in the cockpit. That stood me in good stead later on.

I took my basic training in Greenville, Mississippi. We had been there about a month when a terrible accident happened. We had been flying in the morning session and it was about noon, time for all of us to be in from the practice area. Most of us were on the flight line watching the last ones come in. The wind had shifted and the tower changed the runway to compensate for the change. One cadet was on his final approach when the call came in to change runways. Instead of pulling up and going around again, he racked it around and tired to make the other runway. He spun in right on the end of the runway. We all stood there in stunned silence and watched it all happen. He was a cadet from the same barracks as mine and was in the room right next to me. I helped pack up his belongings to be sent home. That was another lesson learned. You must think, think, think while in the cockpit.

Advanced training found me at twin engine school at George Field, Illinois just across the Wabash River from Vincennes, Indiana. We took our training in the AT-10. Most of the cadets found it a rather difficult plane to land. It was our first experience with two engines, and it did not behave like the single-engine plane we had been used to. It was pretty difficult to keep on the runway once you were on the ground. It was in the spring of the year and the ground was still wet and very soft. All along the runway there were "ground loop" marks where cadets had gone off of the runway and gotten stuck. I added my "signature" to the rest on one landing. I had to be pulled out. It was always embarrassing when that happened. One consolation was, you weren't the only one. Sometimes, even the instructors had difficulty.

The last landing I made in advanced training was the best I ever made there, and it was with a check pilot on my last check flight. I came in as smooth as silk. I never felt the runway when we touched down. I kept waiting for the usual bounce. It never happened. I looked at my check pilot and he just smiled. I knew before he told me. I had passed my test. I felt warm and satisfied all over … a great feeling!

The greatest feeling of satisfaction in training came on Graduation Day. My parents were there to see it all. What a feeling of satisfaction and relief, to know you had come though all of those difficult days and now were a commissioned officer in the United States Army Air Corps.

After the war in Europe was over, we all expected to be sent back to the States for more training and then be moved to the Asian Theater. I was assigned for training in B-29s, having been checked out as first pilot on the B-17 after the

Gentlemen From Hell

war in Europe ended. I was on schedule to be assigned to McDill Field in Tampa, Florida.

On July 20, 1945, we were moved from our base at Lavenham to a holding camp to await our ride back to the States by boat. We soon learned that many men at the Processing Base had been waiting for three to four weeks for their shipping orders. We learned later the reason being they wanted to get the POWs back first, which was as it should be. Every morning, everyone gathered around the bulletin board looking for their name. That was a very popular spot. In the meantime, there was the waiting. There were plenty of books to read, and I remember reading four ... including *The Tale of Two Cities* ... anything to occupy your mind. There was the usual floating card game going. I played a lot of solitaire, also.

While we were there, the news of Japan's surrender came. It didn't take long before celebrating broke out. A huge bonfire was started with anything and everything that would burn tossed in. This had been an English Naval Base at one time and at the entrance gate was an old relic of an ancient sailing ship. That was soon dismantled and tossed in to the flames. Things had really gotten out of control. Everybody scattered when some "joker" tossed in a handful of 45 ammo and a hand grenade. Luckily, no one was hurt. It sure would have been a tragedy to have something happen that late in the game!

I don't recall the date we boarded the Queen Elizabeth to come home, because my letters had stopped and no entry was made in my diary. There were about 18,000 of us on board. Ced, our navigator, had long since left us to navigate for some "Brass" going back to the States by plane. There were so many on board the ship that we were served just two meals a day. The mess halls were going from 0400 until 2000 or 2100 hours.

The crossing took just five days ... good weather all the way. We entered New York Harbor to a tumultuous welcome. There were hundreds of boats of all description, loaded down with well-wishers. Fire boats were filling the air with their spray. The blasts from so many ships' horns were deafening. When the Statue of Liberty came into view, everyone on board began to shed lots of tears ... myself included! It was a thrilling, emotional and rewarding experience that I remember like it was yesterday.

As we disembarked, the Red Cross met us with truckloads of milk! We all had been so starved for it for so long that we really soaked it up ... chocolate or white. All you wanted!

We boarded trains and headed out as fast as they could handle us. We headed to Union Town, Pennsylvania for a one-night stay. From there we had to find our own way home. We said our farewells and were on our individual ways. What a glorious, happy day! That terrible, horrible yearning was finally satisfied! I arrived home on Labor Day with a 45-day leave before reporting to Randolph Field, Houston, Texas for my discharge. Home again by the middle of December for good!

WALTER BAKER

LEFT: Baker, pictured during the Oxford Circus in London in April 1945. RIGHT: Baker was present at a May 1995 ceremony in Lavenham to place a wreath.

My name is Walter N. Baker. I was discharged as a Tech Sergeant in November 3, 1945. I entered the service in September of 1943. I arrived in England in early February of 1945. I was in the 839th squadron. I was 19.

I was assigned as a radio operator on a combat crew. On a lot of missions, you didn't actually do any radio operating. You would dispense chaff through a chute on the side of the fuselage out of the radio operator's department. You had several boxes like this and before you reached areas where you had high concentration of anti-aircraft, or flak, you would throw this out, which would jam or interfere with the radar signal from German ground forces. If you had an emergency or for some reason you did not stay with the group and you needed info back in England for weather or whatever, you could operate the radio. But normally, you did very little radio operating. The radio operator on the lead aircraft transmitted strike reports and info back to the base during the mission. In effect, a lot of the time you didn't really operate the radio at all. You might listen and monitor a frequency, but as far as transmitting, you would do very little of that.

I was not on a lead crew. The lead crew was given special training, and they didn't fly every mission that the group or squadron would fly. You would have two or three lead crews in the squadron. They would alternate on missions, which in effect, if you were assigned on a lead crew that required special training after you arrived in England, it would take you considerably longer to fly tour of combat, as opposed to just an ordinary crew, who is flying many more missions in a given time frame that they could fly. I flew 26 missions.

We had the navigator sustain one superficial injury from flak. He was not required to be hospitalized. It was a superficial wound. We had a waist gunner that took a piece of flak in his back. He had on a flak suit, which prevented any injury. He had a bruise, but nothing serious. Those were the only two incidents we had of personal injuries.

We had one mission, I don't recall the target, but we took a direct hit from probably an 88 or a 125mm. We took a direct hit underneath the right wing and through the fuel tank and out the top of the wing. It didn't explode. It almost inverted the aircraft and we lost all the fuel out of this tank that we took the hit through. I recall one of the men on the intercom stating that we had a lot of fuel coming out over number three turbo. We were concerned about the airplane exploding. It was kind of frightening when you get back, and you could stand on the ground on the stool and put your head up in this fuel tank. Then, we did sustain numerous flak damage from nose to tail. The aircraft, I recall was not available for flying for about a week because we had a lot of patchwork to do on it. That was the most damage we sustained. We sustained superficial damage, as well as other aircraft, on different missions. Some missions you didn't sustain any damage at all, but that was the closest call I guess you could say as far as something becoming catastrophic.

As I stated earlier, most of those missions were considered routine missions. On some missions we would have flak damage. I know we were attacked by ME-262s on a couple of occasions. I didn't see these aircraft. In other words, if you weren't looking for those aircraft, you wouldn't see them because they were that fast. They'd make a pass and they were gone.

I don't recall the targets. I do recall going to Berlin on one or two missions, which really, I guess at that stage of the war, was no big deal as far as a lot of flak - no fighters. I don't recall any fighters at all. I do recall two missions that we flew down in Southern France, around the Royan area. On one of those missions, we carried napalm. I had never heard of napalm. We couldn't smoke cigarettes until the napalm was dropped. I thought that was a rather scary thing to walk in the radio operator's department and open the bomb bay doors and smell that napalm. That was, needless to say, a little different mission. The other men on the crew, I'm sure they were aware, because we had been briefed very explicitly about not smoking. This was something that was different from carrying an iron bomb. This was the one and only time that we carried napalm. There was a pocket of resistance down there that had not surrendered. They had been by-passed during, I guess the invasion of southern France. They were holding out down there and we just proceeded to hose them down, if you want to call it that, with some napalm and some RDX. I know the one mission we carried RDX bombs and one mission we carried the napalm.

On one occasion, we were flying in marginal conditions. Usually, you were in formation and had visibility among the squadrons and groups. On this one occasion, we had flown inadvertently into some weather, low visibility. When we came out of it, our group was gone. We couldn't find it anymore. To make a long story short, we ended up alone, and we tacked on to another group. I recall the pilot asking for the signal light that you could send morse code with; we called it blinkers. He said get back in the waist with your authentication sheet and let these people know who we are. Everywhere you looked, there was a gun pointed toward you. Out of every aircraft that could bear on you, they were there. The reason for that being, prior to this time, on one or more occasions, the Germans had B-17s that they had captured intact, probably much earlier than this. They had tagged on to a group and flown all the way back to England and their intelligence people knew what was happening. The gunners were taking their guns out over the English Channel inbound, and they were getting all their gear together so they could get out and get away from the thing. Apparently, they were aware of this and they tagged on to this group, and they didn't do anything until everyone was in a traffic pattern. This is when all hell broke loose. They started firing. They shot down several B-17s right in the traffic pattern. So from that time on, if you tacked on to another group you were going to be challenged to determine whether you were friend or foe. I'm back in the waist with the signal lamp, and I'm being challenged by another radio operator. I have got to give him the proper response, which we used from our authentication sheet which, incidentally, was printed on rice paper. You were supposed to swallow this before you bail out. To make a long story short, after the proper authentication, then everything was okay. So we stayed with the group all the way back to England.

I do recall one mission. It was on our 20th mission. I believe the target was Brandenburg, I don't recall the target. But anyway, the word was that there would be very light flak, but it seems that the Germans had moved some flak in on Tae River, but they had brought some flak guns in on boats. They had said the weather is going to be nice. There's no flak, so you can go at 17,000-18,000 feet, which was really several thousand feet below your normal bombing altitude, which would be like 25 or 27. We got eaten up with a lot of flak. I recall sitting there, I didn't have anything to do. I'm just sitting there watching the show, and you kept smelling this cordite from flying through the flak bursts. Even with an oxygen mask on, you're going to get a certain amount of air from the area - this odor, this cordite from the flak bursts. I sat there and watched a B-17 that got hit, and they could not stay up. They pulled off on one side of the formation and the guys started bailing out. I guess, probably, all except maybe two, probably it would be the pilot and co-pilot, but anyway, the thing exploded - just a huge ball. I looked around and I saw another B-17 that was being attacked by 109, and I was fascinated. The fact that I was sitting there, and I'm getting at this stage because we hadn't been used to seeing this sort of thing, but the 109 shot down this B-17. It appears that the tail gunner got some hits on the 109 because after he broke off, he started smoking and then went out of sight. But I sat there and watched that B-17 go down. None of those guys got out because once those aircraft start spinning, the centrifugal force is just too much. You can't move.

You can't get out. You sit there and you watch. I watched the thing all the way down, and no one ever came out. It's kind of unnerving to sit there and you know what's about to happen.

We came back one day and apparently had the right main hydraulic line from the brakes shot in two. Fluid leaked out, and when we touched down, the pilot hit the brakes - he had the brakes on the left side, but he didn't have any on the right side - and we're off the runway. We stopped with minor damage, but it does get your attention. You expect a normal landing and you end up out in the grass off the runway.

You could fly several missions, and a lot of the flak was very alive, but you never saw any fighters because the German Air Force at that time was very small, except on a special occasion. In other words, what I'm saying here, compared to what I was flying at that stage, as opposed to what it was like in 1943 or '44, was entirely different. The mission was in April, late April. Incidentally, we flew our first mission on the first of March of '45 and our 26th mission on the 20 of April, which we're approaching a tour of combat here in short order. In a month and 20 days, you fly 26 missions and you're hard at work. As I said, most of those missions were what guys referred to as milk runs.

The first three missions we flew we didn't sustain any damage at all. I'm beginning to think, "what's this all about?" I'm sitting there on the fourth mission - the fourth mission was to Frankfurt - and I'm sitting there looking out over the left wing from the radio operator's position and all at once I see several holes appear at the top of the wing, out toward the tip of the wing. I felt just a little bit of vibration from the aircraft, and I began to realize that this isn't fun anymore. It was something different. But as I said, as far as being a radio operator, I didn't man a gun because we had at that time extra gunners that were trying to get their tours completed. At the beginning, they had a machine gun at the top of the radio operator's compartment, which was taken out. Then later on, the radio operator, if you were under attack, was supposed to man one of the waist guns. But at this stage of the war, we didn't lack for personnel. As I said, most of the time, I just sat there and tossed out chaff and enjoyed the scenery, if you can call it enjoying scenery. But that 20th mission was really the one that got my attention, even though I don't recall that we sustained any flak damage on that particular mission, but the fact that I'm sitting there watching other people that had problems is what really got my attention. I think that's a normal reaction when you watch this and realize that this could be you.

I had not trained with this crew and the crew that I trained with was shot down, I believe, on their sixth mission. But this crew that I flew combat with, I didn't train with them. I was assigned to that crew at the time we were going overseas.

We left New York in January of '45, and we flew the aircraft back in July of '45. I believe we arrived back at Bradley Field, Hartford, Connecticut around the 8th of July of 1945.

Myself and two or three others are the only people that are still around. The pilot is deceased, and I'm sure the co-pilot is. I haven't heard from him in several years. The navigator is deceased. The ball-turret gunner is deceased. I'm sure the flight engineer, the last I heard, he had terminal cancer. I don't know about the details. The togglier is still living. He lives in Cheyenne, Wyoming. At one time, I tried to get the crew together for one of the bomb group reunions, and the only guy I could get was the togglier from Cheyenne. This was Cincinnati back in the early '90s.

After we had finished 26 missions, shortly after the 20th of April, we were sent on flak leave, which is a rest period for a week. We were at Henley-on-Thames on flak leave when the war was over. We immediately got a call from the base to report back to the base. Since we assumed that we were going home it was good news. We left Henley-on-Thames and caught a train in to London. This was when the celebration was going on - VE Day - and London was just a mad house. We got out of London and got back to base, and it was also a mad house. Guys were celebrating all over, but we thought we were going home. This was in early May, and we didn't leave until July - certainly after the first of July before we left, bringing the aircraft back to the USA. After the war was over, we didn't do a great deal of flying, I don't recall. I do recall one incident. Some of our aircraft were assigned to fly down to Linz, Austria and fly some French people back who had been down there in labor camp. This was a rather distressing thing. They told us before we left that there'd be no mess facilities there, and if we wanted anything to eat, we'd have to take it with us, which consisted of K-rations. We had a pilot and a co-pilot and a radio operator; that was the crew. We arrived at Linz at 11 o'clock in the morning and they had assigned these people that we would fly back to Paris in groups of 20. These people came out and they were in terrible condition. You could see that they had missed a few meals. They also told us that we would have to use DDT powder. In other words, we had to douse them with DDT powder. They placed planks in the bomb bays and before we loaded these people, we were waiting for whatever reason, and I broke out one of these K-rations and sat down underneath the plane. It was a nice warm day. I was going to have lunch with these K-rations and these people who were standing there were like animals. I got up and walked away and they pounced on that like a pack of hungry dogs.

We got airborne and it really got bad. It was warm and all this DDT powder was on these guys, and they started getting airsick. We had people in the nose, we had people in the bomb bays, I had five in the radio operator's compartment, we had them in the waist. They hadn't had a bath in who knows when. And I'm telling you, I was glad that when we arrived in France, those people were absolutely ecstatic. You wouldn't believe the animation when they found out that they were going home. Since they were speaking French, I had no idea what they were discussing, but it was obvious that they were well pleased. I knew a lot of other crews flew these missions, too. At the time, being young, I was not really impressed about the situation these people had been faced with. When you get older, you realize what they had been through and the fact that they were going home. It was just very emotional. I don't recall how many trips were made. I know other groups did the same thing, and talking with people later on, they'd say they remembered going down to Linz. We flew them back to Paris. I have no idea of how many plane loads. I'm sure that there are records that would indicate how many of those flights were made, but I know there were several in our group. I don't recall how many. I know there were numerous flights made getting these victims back to France.

Regarding the celebrations, it was bad enough in London, and we got back to the base and just about everybody I could see was either drunk, trying to get that way or getting over. Someone said that before we had arrived back, they had stolen a lot of flares out of the aircraft and they were using those for fireworks. They cleaned out a hangar, and they brought in several barrels of beer, and they had an orchestra. All the girls were invited. Obvious to say, it was quite a party. I know it took the MPs a couple of days to get those girls off the base. It got a little bit raunchy. I guess they thought one incident of that would be enough. But I do recall they dropped softballs out of a single-engine two-seater. They're going to drop these softballs out in this open area. If you get one of these softballs, you could exchange it for a bottle of scotch. Well, we're out there thinking you're going to catch a softball coming out of an aircraft traveling 75 or 80 miles per hour. That doesn't sound so easy, and one guy, there's always one, he tried to catch a softball out of this aircraft. It put him down on the ground. So the guys said to let the darn thing bounce first. Let it hit the ground first, and then it's everyone for themselves. Can you believe a bunch of kids out in an open field fighting over a softball to get a fifth of scotch? It's kind of like a football with everybody just piling on. I thought, I don't need this. I don't like scotch anyway, but it was fun to watch them fight.

Being a 19 year old, this was probably the biggest emotional roller coaster of my life. Some of it you just forget over a period of time. But I thought it was interesting, in thinking back. I was over there in '95 and out to the base at Lavenham. I'm walking to the different places; of course, most of the buildings were gone. Some of the people with this tour were somewhat confused, and it struck me as odd. I recall where the combat crew mess was located and the squadron area, and they were gone. I talked to some English people there that have taken some of the people around that were stationed there during war, and this one fellow said it was amazing. A lot of people come back, and they can't even remember where their squadron area was. I thought that it was strange that I remembered that. I could still go back today and find exactly where the squadron area was and mess halls, etc.

I did mention that the crew I trained with was shot down. I was taken off the crew in Gulf Port, Mississippi and assigned to this crew. The crew that I began training with was shot down. I don't know what group they were in, but I met some people in Iceland on the way back that knew them. They said that they were shot down on their sixth mission. They didn't survive. Then, I had an incident during the Korean War when I lost a crew that I didn't happen to be with. So I figured, maybe I better get out of this darn business.

Very briefly, I was discharged in early November of '45 at McDill Field. I was home for a while and decided that I wanted to stay in the Air Force. I re-enlisted and stayed through the Korean involvement. After that, I absolutely decided that I didn't need anymore of that. I had nine years of Air Force time and got out. I went to school for a couple of years with TVA in Power Production. I spent 33 years in the Department of Power Production with TVA and retired in March of '87. I was married for the first time in July of '54. My wife passed away in '95. I remarried a couple of years ago. I married a retired schoolteacher. I presently live in Bethel Springs, Tennessee. I have no children.

Through Henry Hughey's encouragement, I started the Tennessee State Chapter of the 8th Air Force Historical Society. I'm still involved in that. We presently have about 140 members. We have some good memories. A lot of our people are now at the stage where they can't travel. They don't come to the meetings, but we're still active.

I had mentioned earlier about lead crews. I had stated the fact that the lead crew took longer to complete a tour. Well, we had one in our hut, a lead crew gunners, flight engineers, radio operators, all in our hut, along with about three or four other crews. This flight engineer on this lead crew was quite a comedian. He slept on the top bunk and he had a flashlight that you squeeze the handle; it's a little DC generator, and it makes a whirring noise. We get a new crew in and they'd set this thing up to see what kind of reaction we would get. Of course, we would help this crew, this lead crew had been over quite a while, but watch this guy on the top bunk. He's a little bit of a flak head. We get this thing set up, and we go to bed and turn the lights out and this guy lets out a blood-curdling scream. He comes out of the top bunk with this flashlight, this hand-operated flashlight, and he's running up and down the aisle and he's squeezing this thing and it's making this whirring noise. He's looking under all the bunks and then he stops and he jumps back up in his bed, and there's silence. The guys the next day say, "What is wrong with that guy?" They said not to worry about it. He's been over here a long time; he's seen a lot of combat. He's all right, just don't bother him. These guys, they looked at him and thought, "I don't know about him." It was fun. It was fun in a way, but it was a cruel thing to do really, when you reflect on it, to get these guys all upset over something so silly.

DONALD KILBURG

Kilburg, on the effects of the war: "... our regular brushes with the horrors of war, the loss of friends and comrades, the uncertainty and danger of each mission, are things that marked us for life."

After all these years, it is difficult to put the events of my war years experience into an organized format. As I recall events, a flood of additional memories begin to flow. It was a simple decision on my part to volunteer for the Air Force, because as a much younger boy, I was enamored with flying and reading many books and watching movies of World War I dogfights. After Pearl Harbor, everyone that I knew was flocking to the Service of their choice. I was not going to sit around and wait to get drafted and become a possible "gravel agitator."

I passed the physical and mental tests early in 1942 and was allowed to stay home as a Private Unassigned waiting for Cadet schools to open up. Finally, in June of '42, I was sent to Ground School at Kelly Field in San Antonio, Texas for some open cockpit flight training. With that fresh in my mind, I was off to Ellington Field near Houston, Texas for Navigator and Bombardier Ground School, and then finally to San Angelo, Texas for Bombardier training.

On March 31, 1943, my high school sweetheart, Carole Hafner, came down from Chicago and we were married in the base chapel. We left the ceremony under an arch of bombs held aloft by my training classmates. Relatives in Chicago saw our "wedding photos" on the movie house newsreels. The next day, I was commissioned a 2nd Lieutenant and received my wings.

My training qualification was high enough to hold me at San Angelo as an Instructor until November 1943, when I was sent to Harlington, Texas to Aerial Gunnery School. Immediately following, I was moved on to Salt Lake City, Utah to await assignment to a B-17 crew-training center, which eventually be-

839TH SQUADRON

came Rapid City, South Dakota. Carole came right along with me, and we were able to be together until I and my crew were ready to fly to Europe in June of 1944. She returned to Chicago for the duration of the war.

Our crew picked up a brand new B-17 "Flying Fortress" at Kearney, Nebraska and flew to England with stops in New Hampshire; Goose Bay, Labrador; Thule, Greenland; and Reykjavik, Iceland along the way. We arrived in England in early July and were assigned to the 487th Bomb Group at Lavenham, England as a replacement crew. After additional training and familiarization flights, we were ready to go into combat - scared as hell.

We were all "green." On one of our first take-offs, the pilot sheered the trees at the end of the runway, and we flew the entire 10-hour mission to Czechoslovakia with tree branches hanging out of the engine nacelle. After a few more missions, our crew that had been together since Rapid City was broken up, and I and my Navigator were assigned to a lead crew and additional training.

A mission group consisted of three squadrons of 13 planes, each flying high, low, or middle in the form of a diamond. This was done for optimal bomb pattern on the ground and mutual protection in the event of a fighter attack. Each squadron had a lead crew and deputy lead crew flying on his right wing. The lead crew in the first squadron was the mission group leader. The group leader would do all of the target sighting, and then all of the planes in the group would drop their bombs simultaneously.

Some missions did not go as intended. Once on a mission to Hamburg, I incurred the ire of my commanding officer by dropping our entire squadron's load in the North Sea on way back to England. That day, when we arrived at the target, the cross winds were so strong (over 100 miles per hour) and from a completely different direction than presented in our pre-flight briefing that we slid over the target sideways, unable to release the bombs with any accuracy at all. We were then to find a "target of opportunity" on the way back out of Germany. Groups were flying in every direction.

At 30,000 feet, I finally picked out what looked like a small town with a railroad. As we came closer to the bomb run, I saw that what I was sighting on was a large church in the center of a small town. I told myself I couldn't do this and instructed the rest of the planes to close their bomb bay doors. We wouldn't be bombing today. Since there wasn't any space left on the northern border of Germany to search for another target, we dumped the bombs in the ocean. I've always felt good about listening to my conscience on this one. I'm certain those people in that little town had no idea how close they came to being obliterated. After my irate Colonel finished chewing me out for dumping the mission and listened to my explanation, he understood.

My most memorable mission of the Second World War was as deputy group lead bombardier, December 24, 1944. It was my 18th bombing mission and certainly not the way I had hoped to spend Christmas Eve. We hadn't been able to fly for a week previous because of the clouds, snow and generally bad weather.

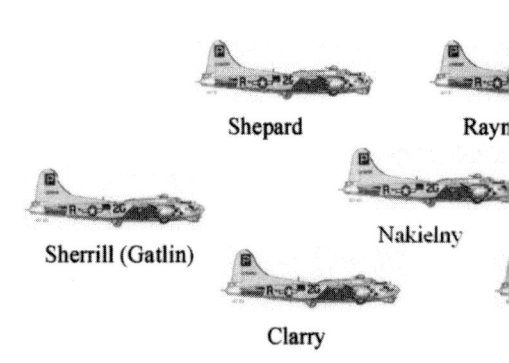

Shepard   Rayr

Sherrill (Gatlin)

Nakielny

Clarry

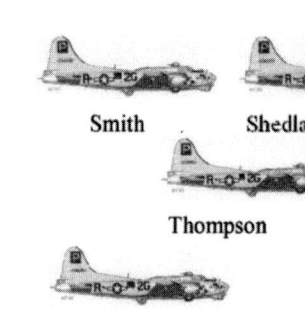

Smith   Shedl

Thompson

Pennedson

Kilburg said his crew's pilot, John Edwards (lower level of Lead aircraft), flipped a coin with Robert Harriman (middle Lead), another lead pilot, to see who would fly with General Frederick Castle during the Battle of the Bulge. Edwards lost the toss, and it was Harriman's crew that was flying with Castle when their plane was shot down.

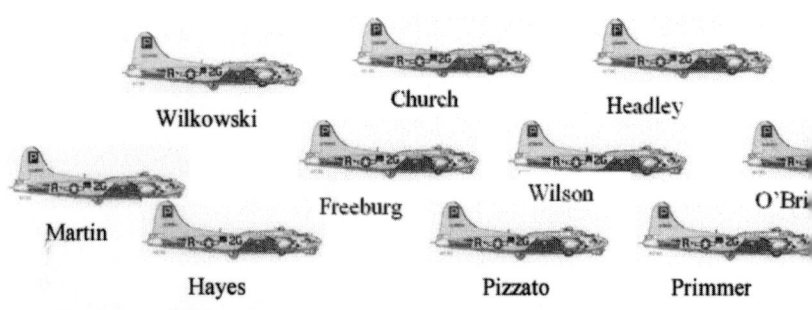

Wilkowski   Church   Headley

Martin   Freeburg   Wilson   O'Bri

Hayes   Pizzato   Primmer

The Low formation was part of a composite that also included planes piloted by: Reed/Nash, Densmore, Lester, Kulp, Curtis, Ball, Crockett, Waldron, Pittsley, Perrot, Allard, Lang, and Turnquist.

839th Squadron

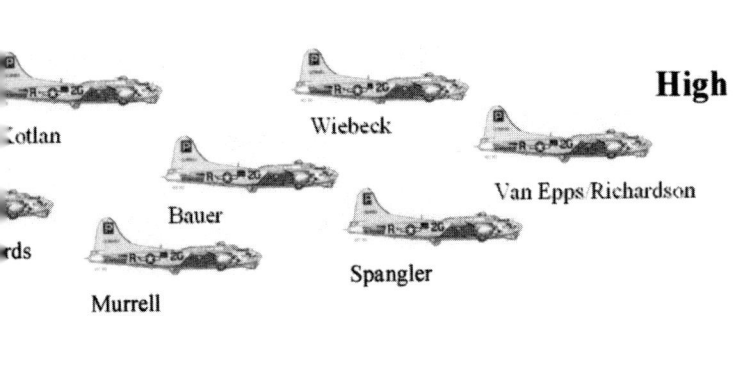

High

Kotlan
Wiebeck
Bauer
Van Epps/Richardson
rds
Spangler
Murrell

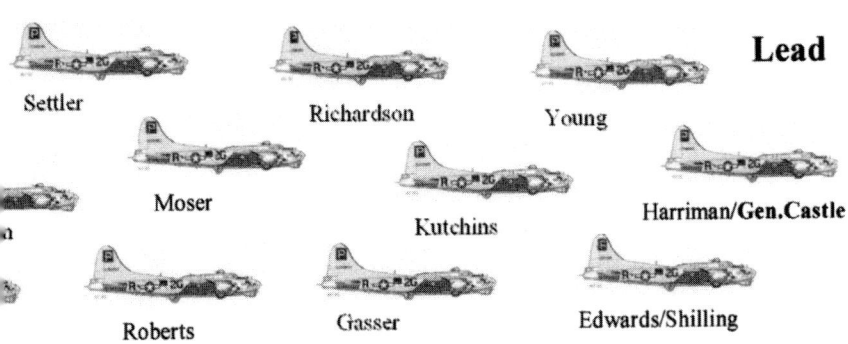

Lead

Settler
Richardson
Young
Moser
Harriman/Gen. Castle
Kutchins
Roberts
Gasser
Edwards/Shilling

Low

Kraker/Robertson

Pilot and Position
8th Air Force Bombing Raid
December 24, 1944

Gentlemen From Hell

The assigned target was Babenhausen Airfield just southeast of Frankfurt a Main. The 487th Bomb Group led the entire 8th Air Force that day - an armada of 2,032 B-17 Flying Fortresses. Because we were to lead the 8th, the 3rd Division sent Brigadier General Frederick Castle, commander of the 4th Combat Wing, to fly in the lead plane. My pilot, John Edwards, told me that he and the other lead pilot, Robert Harriman, flipped a coin to determine who would fly with the General. We lost the toss, luckily, as proved by later events.

Harriman, with General Castle in the right seat, led the formation, with our plane flying off their right wing and the remaining 2,000-plus planes of the mission behind and below us. While en route across Europe, we encountered flak over what we thought to be friendly territory, never realizing at the time that the Battle of the Bulge and the German Ardennes offensive was in full swing beneath us. Shortly after that, things took a turn for the worse. Our P-51 fighter cover, delayed by snow and ice, failed to meet up with us at the appointed time.

As we crossed from the skies over Belgium into Germany, 50 aircraft of Hitler's Luftwaffe ferociously attacked us. Before our own fighter cover arrived, the Germans were all over us. They got the group leader on the first pass, blowing up the General's lead plane right next to us. They also destroyed most of our low squadron. In all, our group lost 10 planes before our fighter support finally arrived and drove off the German attackers. Our plane and others in the formation sustained severe damage in the chaos of the attack, but we were able to assume the lead and reform the scattered group. We continued on to our assigned target at Babenhausen despite the enemy resistance. I was able to sight our target, and with precision accuracy, we leveled the airstrip and disabled the aircraft that remained on the ground. We made it back to Lavenham, where we counted more than 150 bullet and flak holes in the shell of our plane and thanked God that we were alive. Later historians have described this mission, with its protection of 800 fighters, as the greatest armada ever attempted.

My pilot, John Edwards, and I each received the Distinguished Flying Cross for our efforts that day. We went on to fly a total of 30 missions, 18 of those in the lead position. Luck was with us throughout our campaign. Though our plane was hit repeatedly and sustained serious damage on a number of occasions, it always brought us home safely to our base in Lavenham, England. Though our navigator was critically injured on one mission, the rest of the crew survived the war without a scratch. Yet, our regular brushes with the horrors of war, the loss of friends and comrades, the uncertainty and danger of each mission, are things that marked us for life.

AL RASOF

LEFT: *Rasof, pictured while on furlough at home.* RIGHT: *Rasof and his wife Betty married during furlough on July 29, 1945. Rasof said, "VJ Day was our wedding gift from the World."*

My name is Al Rasof. I was a Staff Sergeant, the radio gunner on the B-17, "Gravel Gertie," AC Serial #43-39188, more commonly known as #188, assigned to the 839th Bomb Squadron; the serial number can identify the date built (1943) and factory. We were the last regular crew assigned to the 487th and were involved in seven of the last eight missions flown by the 487th. The last mission for the 487th was on April 21; the 8th did fly some after that date but not over Germany. Because the war was just about over and we never encountered any enemy action, we were known as "The Milk Run Kids."

I went into the service on May 27, 1943 at age 18. I went overseas and into the 8th in England on March 17, 1945, and returned to the States on July 14, 1945. I was honorably discharged on January 5, 1946.

The 8th was due to take part in the November assault on the main Japanese Islands and our crew, not having completed its tour, was to be included. We were given a 33-day rest and recuperation furlough, going from the base in Lavenham to Drew Field (Tampa, Florida) for whatever was needed (same plane, different crews? Who knows…). I married my Betty during the furlough on July 29, 1945. VJ Day was our wedding gift from the World. (Please know that the war with Japan would NOT have ended without the A-bomb, or at least an additional 100,000 American deaths and millions of Japanese deaths, notwithstanding what revisionists not involved with the possibility of dying may say…). By the way, ours was a pretty typical wartime romance and marriage. I met my Betty in 1942 on the beach in South Haven, Michigan. I was from Chicago, and like many teenagers waiting to go in the service was doing something to aid the so-called war effort. I worked on a farm in Wisconsin. Pitching those darned early morning dew-covered peas pulled something in my back, and the farm doctor put a plaster of sorts on my back. When I finally got home, the plaster had generated an infected back, and my doctor at home recommended sitting in the sun. And, so, I went to South Haven, at that time a Lake Michigan shore resort of sorts. There, I met my Betty. She was from Wyandotte, Michigan. We corresponded for over two years. I saw her the second time when she came to Lincoln before I shipped out. We were married the third time I saw her. That was over 57 years ago. No, we don't have any children, only each other. As my mother was one to ask, "what do you do for aggravation?"

Betty stayed with me at Drew until I was discharged. The first "home" we had was a room in some lady's house in Tampa. Just a room. I'll never forget how, me with my bride of a few weeks, she said to us that the slop bucket was under the bed ...

We couldn't find a place to live after Tampa and finally ended up living with Betty's sister in Detroit, Michigan, sharing their small apartment with her husband, son and a Murphy bed. Except for two years in New York, we have lived in Michigan.

I should have gone to school, as most GIs did, but opted instead to work.

I've been lucky, having two careers. First, I worked in retail for a chain of women's clothing stores, even as a buyer for them in New York. Retailing women's clothes really wasn't for me, and so, after 13 years, I went back to school (at age 34). I eventually earned a Ph. D. and directed programs for the Detroit Board of Education until I retired in 1983, as well as taught night school for Wayne State University (in Detroit).

War is a young mans' game. And, of course, the definition of "game" depends on what happened. The first years of the 8th were pure horror. And, yet, everyone suffered, at one time or another, one way or another. Just being in and near those gasoline-loaded, bomb-carrying, ladies could be a fright. I estimate that 10 percent of all casualties were either by stupidity or error (are they different?). We had bombs hung up. Once, Gil, the flight engineer, laid on the catwalk (without his chute, there wasn't enough room for both) trying to free up a bomb hanging by one shackle so it could be jettisoned over the English Channel, while I, weighing a good 20 pounds less, tried to steady him by kneeling at the edge of the catwalk, holding him by the chute straps - had he fallen, it would have been sure death.

And then, there was the last mission of the 487th, April 21, when we lost the 8th Air Force. Our Group went into a cloud bank, and when we came out, everybody was over there and our plane was over here. It wasn't safe to join up a Group (the Germans were known to have joined up Groups in captured 8th planes and shoot down adjoining planes before taking off) and so we followed the rest of the 8th at a distance. We were so sure, all alone, sitting targets that we were, that we'd not make it back, but we did. There is a wonderful book, *Wings of Morning*, by Thomas Childers, the nephew of the ROM on the last 8th plane lost over Germany, also on that date, April 21, 1945. I encourage you to read this book. You will find a "kinship" in Childers.

As for the most memorable moment and event, it's gotta be the fact that the experienced pilot on our first mission (SOP to have an experienced pilot fly as first officer on the first mission to break in the new pilot and crew) was Phil Becker, a boy I grew up with and from the same neighborhood in Chicago, Albany Park, and the same high school, von Steuben. When we were over the target, he called me on the intercom; I was busy setting a new record in throwing out the "chaff" (the tinsel that sometimes deflected the radar-directed flak). "Al," he said, "It's a long way from von Steuben."

Since the war, I've been in touch with Gil and his wife, "Tex" (a nickname we set on her while she stayed with Gil during our training as a crew in Rapid City, South Dakota). Gil passed away five years ago and I still stay in touch with Tex. I also hear from Gerald Obrecht, a fellow ROM who lives in southern Illinois. I haven't seen Gerald since Lavenham, but hear from him via email and Christmas family letters.

GERALD OBRECHT

As a member of a replacement crew who arrived on the scene fairly late and got to fly only a few missions, some of my most memorable moments were not of the combative kinds, but more the human interest type. So naturally we were there when the war ended in Europe and awaited flying back home on the plane that we inherited upon our arrival at the 487th. But after V-E Day, I was privileged to fly one more mission, which was the most memorable one of all.

During the war, the Germans had captured a lot of the French civilians and put them to work for them as French slave laborers. They worked on farms or wherever there was need for a job to be done. I have no idea as to what all they all had to do, but we found out that we were going to have the opportunity to fly over to the continent and pick up these people and take them back to France. Of course, the 487th was not the only bomb group involved, and not every crew got to go, but I believe there was an effort to involve as many as possible, as our group did this in two days. But our crew was one of the many that did, and we got to fly the second day.

A few preparations had to be made to convert our plane into a "passenger" plane that could haul the most people while keeping the load balanced at the same time. This included putting a floor in the bomb bay, and we even took along large metal containers, probably large coffee cans, anticipating the well-known needs for those who may become airsick. And that proved to be very successful, thanks to someone's careful and thoughtful foresight.

Our turn to fly arrived; we took off early that morning. Our destination was Linz, Austria. The flight was uneventful, and we anxiously awaited arrival. After we landed, it did not seem too awfully long before passengers were boarding our plane. They were distributed fairly evenly throughout the plane so as to keep the plane balanced - some in the bomb bay, some in the radio room, which was my station, some in the waist. I can't recall, but there may have been a couple up in the nose of the plane - I cannot verify that. There were men and women and even smaller children, some being born after their parents were captured as slave laborers. So a lot of different ages were represented. There was somewhere between 20 and 24 persons in each of their groups, which were apparently pre-decided before boarding. They had few belongings, because they probably weren't allowed to own anything except what they wore and a few personal items. There were about a half-dozen or so in the radio room with me - whatever it could, not comfortably but reasonably, hold.

We took off and were on our way back to France. After we gained altitude and were on course, I offered those in my station candy from my candy rations, which they were so delighted to get. Since the radio room was always the smoking room, I gave cigarettes to those who wanted to smoke, and some did. What a treat. I could read their expressions. My main handicap was that I could not speak a word of French. I remember one fellow who smoked his cigarette down to where it was so short the ashes had to be falling behind his teeth.

From where I sat at my station, there was the small window that one could see out. I enjoyed having them to take turns coming up and looking out the window to see what they could see below. They were so anxious to get home. When we would fly over a large city, they would gesture to me, wanting to know what city it was. I would then call Lt. McLean, our navigator, and ask him. Then I would write it down on a piece of paper. There being enough similarity in the spelling of a name, regardless of language, anyone can tell what it is. Then they would smile and nod their heads, and inform the others and they would all again take a turn looking. This routine continued throughout our journey. There was this little man, perhaps 45 years old, who caught my attention. He was so excited to go home, and a little more emotional than the others, if that is possible. It was almost summertime, and he was wearing shorts with suspenders. His cap reminded me of the caps we made when we were children. We would take one of our mother's old Sunday hats made of felt and cut it down to where it fit just the top half of our head, coming down to about the top of our ears or a little above. We'd turn up the bottom edge and decorate them. There is probably a name for that kind of cap. We didn't have baseball caps to wear at home during the depression. His cap reminded me of those, and he wore a feather as part of the décor in his cap. Anyway, he was very interesting to observe.

I kept looking out, watching for the Eiffel Tower. And, finally, I spotted it. My first reaction was to call this little man over to the window, and I pointed for him to look out of it. He quickly leaned over and put his head near the window. His eyes opened wide, as if he couldn't see enough of what he was seeing, his mouth opened wide, and immediately he grabbed one of the others to come up for a look. There was a chain reaction of each taking a turn. There was shouting, laughing, crying, hugging, jumping up and down, and I know Lieutenants Ellis and Cline, our pilot and co-pilot, and our engineer, Sgt. Foy, had to feel the jarring from all this excitement. And there I was being fortunate enough to share this unusual homecoming, fighting back the tears and laughing with them.

We soon landed at an airfield just outside Paris. Our passengers were extremely anxious to debark and again touch the ground of their precious homeland, from which they had been taken years before. We said goodbye to them, and our "Bonnie Lassie" was soon airborne, and it was so quiet all of a sudden. All I could hear was the roar of the four engines of our B-17. What a memorable day. God, with the help of the 487th Bomb Group and many other bomb groups, had delivered so many people safely back to their homeland.

WALTER WISE

Your request for "war stories" has probed my fading memory, but what follows are a few, but nowhere near the number of pages you suggested.

One memory that Rusty Smith and I remember was on a mission to Hamburg. Most journeys to Europe in those days were greeted along the way with areas of flak. Most flak was from .88 mm guns and was black blooms. Hamburg had some bigger guns that were .105 mm and had near white blooms. We made our bomb run amidst heavy flak, and as Rusty's voice announced "bombs away," a huge white bloom covered us. I can't remember now the words Rusty said, but if we'd been a split second ahead, I wouldn't be writing this. A few moments passed before a rumble of activity developed in the nose section. A piece of shrapnel came through and hit the navigators' helmet (denting it) and went down his back. It was hot and I think Rusty helped get it out. I don't remember the navigator's name, but he was from Lancaster, PA.

The 487th led the 8th Air Force in a maximum effort on December 24. We had been grounded by terrible weather for several days, but this day we could go help change the "Battle of the Bulge." This was my second mission. I was replacing an ailing crew member on Captain Shepard's crew. I would be in the ball-turret. Many details have escaped me but I got into the turret (and I think I took the crew with me). Just south of Liege we began to get attacks from ME 109s. They came in from various directions, but I couldn't find a target until I found a gaggle of three rows at six o'clock level. This was a company front attack that I had read about. It was out of range. I entered the wingspan into the computing sperry gun sight and began firing when the target filled the sight. One gun quit after a few bursts, but I kept on with short bursts with the other gun. The recoil jerked the turret, making it hard to keep on the target. These German aircraft were FW 190's. My target began smoking and was not after us, so I looked around for another but didn't see any, and I cleared the malfunctioning gun at this point.

I have always wondered what happened to all those other planes that were in that company front. I remember them looking like they were getting bounced around as they approached us and thinking at the time that they were not skilled flyers. But they would be getting a rough ride in our wake.

I flew 19 missions - five as a spare and 14 as the engineer gunner on Capt. Liebert's crew. He was returning to the 839th for a second tour.

Many of the events remembered were not combat related. We flew a lot of practice bombing runs. We were a lead crew. A radar dome on lead ships replaced the ball-turret, and we practiced with that as well as visual runs. All this was done in England.

839TH SQUADRON

On one of these missions, we had just put on oxygen masks at 10,000 ft. and entered an overcast. At 13,000 ft., all the instruments went crazy. Manifold pressure dropped, RPMs dropped, the automatic horizon flipped up and both pilots were fighting the yoke with nothing happening. Then a sudden "whump;" we bottomed out at 3,000 ft. and everything returned to normal. I was standing between both pilots and had trouble keeping from folding up. We had flown into one of those storm clouds and hit the down draft. Now, that was scary! I loved to fly, and after that was over, I developed more respect for the adventure.

Other local flying was testing the instruments after an engine change. It was known as "slow time." I joined the 487th, 839th Squadron as a Buck Sergeant and left as a Tech Sergeant, thanks to Captain Rusty Smith, for whom I am very grateful.

BOBBY WAYNE HEARD

LEFT: Heard, who flew "Lucky Joe," "Lucky Lady" and "Lucky U.S.A.," said his 31 successful bombing missions were "just part of what had to be done." RIGHT: After the war, Heard spent 41 years with Allstate Insurance Company.

Sixty years ago, I was doing what most other young men at my age were doing - fighting for freedom in France. Today, with much humility and dignity, my participation in World War II was just part of what had to be done. And until the most recent celebration of the 60th anniversary of D-Day, I had the Distinguished Flying Cross, Air Medal with three oak leaf clusters, a Bronze Battle Star and other service metals stored away.

With the D-Day celebrations in full swing earlier this month, I got those medals out again with the memories they told. My story is one that represents the experiences of thousands of average American men and women who had courage thrust upon them to face their deaths for their country. It's a story of heroism - an American story that needs to be told again and again.

I was born on September 25th, 1923 in Erick, Oklahoma to Arlie and Winona McGowen Heard. After graduation from high school there in 1941, I started studying at the University of Oklahoma, but a friend convinced me to give up college, and we took jobs with Douglas Aircraft in Tulsa. I was trained in drafting for Douglas Aircraft and was part of a team making B-24 bombers. Ironically, I would later be a crewmember on one of these bombers during service in the war.

On January 13, 1943, I was called up in the draft. I reported to Fort Sill in Lawton Oklahoma, where I was assigned to the U.S. Army Air Force. I was then sent to Amarillo, Texas for engineering school, and then to Kingman, Arizona for gunnery school.

839th Squadron

One of my favorite memories is impressing Bob Hope with a demonstration of a soldier's ability to take apart and put back together a .50 caliber machine gun, blindfolded. The purpose of the skill was to prepare the men to continue their job shooting their weapons should they be blinded while at war. I was enjoying a meal at the Dallas Athletic Club when I recognized Mr. Hope's voice. I went up to the entertainment superstar and introduced myself as the man who performed that blindfold demonstration in Kingman, Arizona. He remembered me with a smile and a genuine laugh.

Life in the military got serious. Service overseas was inevitable and after receiving all my gear, I was sent as a member of the 8th Air Force to England. For those who have seen Memphis Belle, the movie accurately depicts, in my opinion, what life was like for me and the other bomber crewman who tried to shut down the German offensive.

I completed 31 successful bombing missions, six more than the required 25 at the time. I flew "Lucky Joe," "Lucky Lady" and "Lucky U.S.A." After I completed 25 runs, the military asked me to complete five more - I agreed. The Air Force then asked for one more - I reluctantly went. Finally when they asked me to go up for the 32nd time, I asked to see the general and was allowed to go home.

The bomb runs were terrifying. Because of the time of the year, the planes endured bad weather as well as anti-aircraft fire and German planes.

The worst thing was when a crew wouldn't return. It was hard to look at empty bunks on the base that had been filled the night before.

I was very jumpy. It took about 15 flights before I was comfortable.

We unloaded bombs over Frankfurt, Munich and Berlin, among other "enemy towns." My last three missions were over Normandy and Omaha Beach in the Allied effort to dislodge the German military, which had invaded and were entrenched in France in mid-1944.

On one of those missions, our plane had been damaged enough that after the bombs were dropped, the pilot felt it probably would not make it back over the English Channel to safety. So, we made an emergency landing and scattered into haystacks on a French field for cover. The men had to be completely silent as German soldiers jammed their bayonets through the hay. One of them hit me. I did not think much of it at the time; it seemed like just a scratch, but I was left with a long, thin scar on my left knee. We were not discovered and were rescued within a day.

I was injured another time in the air when I went to help a colleague, a waist gunner, who had been hit by an anti-aircraft fire that ripped through the plane's belly. In assisting him, a machine gun fell, injuring my left leg. Although, I was able to continue my missions, upon returning to the United States, I was treated at a military hospital in Santa Anna, California.

I recall that on various leaves in London, where American soldiers tried to get some "R & R," life was still consumed by the war, with German bombs frequently hitting the streets in the evenings. Piccadilly Square became a popular meeting place. I ran into a hometown friend there on one of my leaves from duty.

Gentlemen From Hell

Although I cannot remember celebrating D-Day in 1944, I definitely celebrated at the end of the war. When I was on my way to Chanute Field near Chicago, I heard the announcement on the radio. Upon arrival in the area, I decided to stop and share a few drinks with my friends. After having a little much to drink, we were late getting to the airfield. When we arrived after being AWOL (Absent without Leave), we told the commanding officer about our small celebration. He apparently understood and we were not punished.

I was discharged from the military service at Randolph Field in Texas on September 26, 1945. I went to Dallas, Texas where my aunt lived on Wycliff Avenue and bought some civilian clothes at James K. Wilson in Highland Park Village. I then returned to college in Tulsa, Oklahoma, where I proposed to JoAnn Hayden, a woman I had met at the University of Tulsa.

After college, I took a position as a sales executive for Allstate Insurance Company, and retired in 1990 after 41 years with the company. We moved to University Park, a Dallas suburb, in 1944 and raised three children - Robert, Sally, and Ann. We also have four granddaughters and one grandson - Leigh Heard, Sarah Heard, Frank Davies IV and Anna Davies.

I remain active. I am a member of St. Michael and All Angles Episcopal Church and work as a business psychologist for insurance companies. My office is on McKinney Avenue in Dallas. I enjoy playing tennis and being involved in civic activities, such as charter membership in the Park Cities Exchange Club, which is working to prevent child abuse. I am president of the Heard Foundation and a member of the Heard Natural Science Museum and Wildlife Sanctuary in McKinney, Texas. My third cousin, Bessie Heard, founded the museum. I also aid children through my work with the Scottish Rite Hospital.

I am a life member of the Veterans of Foreign Wars, the Disabled American Veterans and the American Legion. Former Texas Governor Bill Clemets commissioned me as an admiral in Texas in 1983.

As a World War II veteran, my name will be among those tens of thousands of American soldiers, sailors and airmen on the new Wall of Liberty in Normandy. It is the first memorial to honor all servicemen who participated in the European Theater of Operation in World War II. I was invited to the recent 60th Anniversary ceremonies in France, but was unable to attend. My name will also go on a new plaque in the American Air Museum in England.

However, those two years of fighting in the war made a tremendous impact on my life. To this day, I carry the spirit of the American mindset from 60 years ago and treasure American freedom. I also carry respect for the military, which I think will have to grow again to address the struggles the world is now experiencing in hot spots around the world.

I think that every man and woman who wants to should serve in the military for a short time. Even in times without war, it builds character that will benefit them for their entire lives.

669th Aero-Engineering Squadron Introduction

William Michaels, although not a member of any squadron, was a mechanic that moved through all four squadrons in the 487th. You'll read about the Christmas party he was a part of for displaced kids while overseas, how he flew in the Berlin Airlift, and his tours of duty when he made a career in the military.

There's one incident that I must tell you regarding Bill Michaels. He and I rode to the airport together after the Omaha Reunion. I jumped out of the shuttle before Bill and asked the "sky-cap" if he could get my bags and my friend Bill's bags. Bill was behind me about six car lengths, and I told the sky-cap that Bill and I had just attended the 487th Bomb Group Reunion. Our driver yelled through the crowd at the top of his lungs, "Hey Bill," and when Bill turned around, the sky-cap was standing at attention saluting Bill. There must have been at least 75 people hustling to and from the airport, but they all turned and looked at the man saluting the veteran. I told the man I wanted to have his name and address so I could let him know when my book was finished, so he gave it to me and said to me, "You'll never remember," but I assured him I would! His name was Grady and he had been a marine in Vietnam. He and Bill exchanged words about their tour of duty. Both men had spent time in Danang, and they talked about their experiences.

When I called Bill, he said he wouldn't be at the reunion in Washington D.C. because his leukemia had slowed him down, but he and I reminisced about that day at the airport, and Bill said, "He really honored me, and he even gave me a big bear hug. That meant so much to me."

WILLIAM MICHAELS

MEMBER OF 669TH AERO-ENGINEERING SQUADRON

LEFT: Bill Pecourcey and William Michaels. As an aero-engineer, Michaels serviced planes for each squadron of the 487th Bomb Group. RIGHT: Bill Michaels recent photo.

I'm William Michaels. I usually go by the name of Bill. I was born in Youngstown, Ohio, in March of 1922. The rank I had in England was Staff Sergeant, but I spent 30 years in the Air Force and retired with Senior Master Sergeant, E8. I was drafted on December 3, 1942. I was working experimental at Patterson Field, Ohio. We were doing experimental work, and I was accepted by the Air Force as a Staff Sergeant having previous experience in aircraft maintenance. But I had to get clearance from the draft board. I went to the draft board and they said, "Well, you'll never get called. You're doing experimental work. This is tough stuff. So you don't need us." Well, I was registered for the draft in Youngstown, Ohio, Mahoning County. The draft board that I saw was in Yellow Springs County, and about two weeks after they said I couldn't be called, I received a letter, "Greetings" ... and I was drafted into the infantry.

In 1942, I was 20 years old. I was drafted into the infantry and finished infantry training. I was working fighting floods on the Ohio River when I was told that the commander wanted to see me. When I got to the office, he was very upset. He said, "You've got three years aviation mechanic experience. The Air Force needs mechanics. What are you doing in the infantry?" And that same day, I was on my way to Florida to the Air Force. I went through B-24 training at Keesler Field, Mississippi. Naturally, my first assignment out of school was with B-17s, Fortresses, even though I had gone to school on 24s. I entered the 8th Air Force when I arrived in England, which was in November of '43, with a B-24 outfit at North Pickenham near Kings Lynn - it's on the Wash, the northern part of the southern part of England. I was with the group in North Pickenham when they selected 15 men who had experience - more experience than others I guess, or the most experience - to repair ground power equipment and get a base ready for U.S. Air Force in Lavenham, England. I was one of the first fifteen to arrive there as maintenance people. There were, of course, construction people and truck drivers there ahead of us, but we were the first ones to set up the base. They just looked through the records, I guess. If you had three years already and were one of the oldest people, then you were going.

I was not even in the 836, 37, 38, or 39th squadron. I was with a sub-depot, which was a 669th Aero-Engineering Squadron. We performed all of the heavy maintenance that the flight line or the squadrons could not perform, whether due to manpower, time constraints or equipment. I was a member of a team, even though I was assigned as an aircraft instrument specialist. Due to my background, I was assigned to anything and just about everything - wing changes, engine changes, sheet metal work, electrical work, anything they had to have done if they needed a body, I was with it. We wanted good stuff for the pilots to fly.

We had some very innovative procedures that we started. One aircraft, it was in the bluebook in the book for 487th, shows the side of the airplane blown out right below the left waist window. Cannon fire had hit the armor plate below the window and blasted about 40 square feet of skin out. My team was assigned to that, us sheet metal people and everybody else. Anyhow, the sheet metal chief assigned a crew to clean up the damaged section. The interior of the aircraft is divided into stations or sections - station so-and-so to station so-and-so. We get there and in the meantime he assigned another crew to go to the salvage yard in Cambridge to locate a B-17 with the same type - in other words, B-17 G with the same block number (block number meaning they should have been identical, they were the same run). [They were] to cut out a piece of station three to station six, plus one foot all the way around. By the time the team got back from Cambridge, the aircraft was cleaned up and they just put this piece in, riveted everything up armor was installed. I talked to the navigator at one of our reunions, and he asked how we fixed it, and I told him and he said, "You SOBs. We thought we were going to have a three day pass in London. We were assigned in the next mission." So that's the kind of work that was done.

I mentioned that the B-17s were in a salvage yard in Cambridge. If you can picture this: a huge field, a square, let's say - well, an inverted U - and on the left side there were B-17 fuselages, the bodies piled like cordwood. It probably went 10 or 15 high. On the right side were B-24 hulks. At the far end were the twin engine bombers in piles, and in the center were burned out aircraft. It was just a heap of burnt metal. We couldn't use burnt materials. Once it's exposed to heat, you can't use it. All this would be supported or more or less fenced in by wings, damaged wings that were standing on end that were barricades for this. So you have to root through the equipment to find what you needed and get it. But it saved a lot of money, and it saved a lot of time.

I was going to say I was at the sub-depot, and we did this heavy maintenance as if we were the ground crew. As I said, my basic job was aircraft instrument technician. Whenever we had a compass swinging, calibration of the aircraft compass on the lead airplanes, I would be sent out to do the compass swing. I would go out in the field the crew chief would run the engines on, and the B-24s, we tried to do it with bombs in the airplane because of the magnetic attraction. In the B-17, we didn't need it because the main master compass source was out in the wing, away from the rest of the steel. We had an RAF sighting compass on a tripod, and I would take reference points on the airplane until the crew chief had to taxi to his specific heading. I said we usually started off with North. So he taxied the airplane heading north and I would check with my compass, which did not have any magnets in it for corrections. It was just a straight compass and I would mark my readings. He'd mark his and I'd mark mine. Then we'd go East and do the same thing, South same, West the same. After that was over we had a formal meeting. They'd tell us what the corrections would be on North, South, East and West and we'd make them all on the airplane. Following that they'd fly the airplane and the navigator would, as we say, air-swing the compass, usually following a road or something that they knew the exact heading. I did that, or the other times I flew with the airplane were instrument calibration, airspeed calibrations.

We had a trailing static bomb. If you could picture a chrome-plated bomb shaped figure, it looks just like a little bomb with a steel cable attached, attaching it to the aircraft and a flexible tube to the aircraft. We wanted to read undisturbed air, air that was not disturbed by the airplane. The airplane had a PITO source, which means pressure, and a static source, which is the least disturbed part on the airplane. The airspeed is calibrated, it's just a barometer and it would expand or contract due to the difference in force between the PITO and static. Well, by getting the trailing static bomb 50 feet below the airplane on a cable, and it had static line (just the air reading), you would have undisturbed air, and so you would measure the pressure to the PITO tube as related to the static air and the trailing bomb. So any turbulence that you might read without this correction would be eliminated. We had correction cards that we put beside the airspeed indicators. These are mostly lead airplanes. We put this correction card and it would say, if you were flying 150 mph indicated, your true airspeed is actually 148. So you should fly 152 to maintain 150. That was interesting.

We lost our bomb one day flying home from Wales. We'd gone over there across England over Wales and all of a sudden the cable became slack, and you could see the silver bomb just arching toward the ground. There was a small building down there and it looked like it was going to impact. I don't know where it hit, but we all swore that we had a dead hit on that target. We had no complaints, so apparently it didn't hurt anything. We flew back to our base, and I was sitting in the right waist window holding on to the machine gun, and the pilot hedge hopped all the way back at about 50 feet. He hopped up over the power lines and over the trees and the taller buildings-a lot of fun going back.

487TH BOMB GROUP

One time, I waved to a farmer who was plowing uphill. We were below him, and I waved to him. I remember that well. We went over a girl's school, and they had laundry out, and as we went over the pilot pulled the nose up suddenly and straw and dirt and everything else just went over these clothes hanging in the yard - terrible. But, boys will be boys.

An airplane might come back with wing damage or antiaircraft damage - or, in one case, we had a wing damaged by four bombs falling on it from an airplane above it -five hundred pound bombs. We started at the wing tip, the outermost part of the wing (this is the left wing), so the outermost part. The top and bottom skin of that wing was almost touching. It was dented in where the bomb hit it and bounced off. Several feet inboard of that was another big dent and so on to the fourth bomb. The nose just cut a little wedge shaped piece out of the trailing edge of the wing. You can't repair anything like that. Outboard of the engines was a separation point for the wings. In the wings, we also had what we called Tokyo Tanks, additional bladder fuel tanks that would extend the range of the bombers. After we had the fairing and access to the bolts and everything in place, we could change a wing in a day. No special tools.

Well, we had a wrecker. AC2 wrecker is what we called it. It was like an auto wrecker with an extended crane. We'd use a big hemp rope and we'd lash it around certain points on the wing. Our C2 wrecker driver was so good he could position this within an eight of an inch of where you needed it. He was good. He could not read or write, but he was good. He knew how to drive his truck. The wings were held on with taper pins instead of straight bolts. They were a bolt without a head with a tapered body. The attachment points were milled, heat-treated aluminum - these pins went into them and you "torqued" them down to a certain amount to make them tight. You lined up your wing, you used a taper reamer, you smoothed everything out, then you put the taper pin in and just tightened it down. We didn't get these out according to the manuals. We just used a hammer and drove them out. Of course, you got them spoiled, but you drive these pins out. Well, we were running short of pins, so one of our people had the idea that we'll make a hydraulics remover. He went to Cambridge and took a tail-wheel retraction cylinder from a P-51 Mustang Fighter - it was just right there.

The machinist made a C-type clamp device where the piston of the retraction cylinder would push against a small part of the taper pin. We just had a hand pump and we just cranked this thing until all of a sudden, POP, and there goes the pin. We could reuse it. It was good.

As an idea of how old people were for example, when I was 22, in 1944, I was put in charge of a hut with 16 men including myself. I was the old man. I was "Pop."

One of the things I wanted to say about when I was a hut chief, my hut made up a little medal for me. A multi-pointed star like the air medal stars. They put "Hut Mother" and "Hut Number" and a ribbon, of course. It had a cluster, but instead of an oak leaf cluster they had a beer bottle cap cluster.

Another special decoration we had, it was a fellow in the outfit that worked with trucks mostly, he was not the C2 wrecker driver. He drove the truck under the wing of the B-17 and scraped the wing. It had to be repaired. I was running up an engine on a Thunder-Bolt that we'd maintained, we'd repaired, and he backed into the tail of this airplane. So we had another repair to do. He did this with five different airplanes. So one day in front of the sub-depot hanger, "Pop" Courtney, our chief inspector, he had 30 years of service December 7, 1941, and of course he couldn't be released. But Bob had us in ranks in front of the hanger when he called this guy out - I won't mention the guy's name. He called this fellow out - let's say "Joe Blow" - front and center. Joe came out and "Pop" had an ornate scroll in his hand and he said, "By the order of the Fuhrer and the Commanding General of the Luftwaffe, I hereby make you a knight of the iron cross first order." And he presented this guy with an iron cross, about a foot across, Maltese Cross, just like the German decoration, but about a foot on each measurement but with a silver and black ribbon. He had to wear it around his neck for the rest of the week. He got the point.

There was some humor there at times. I might be in bed late at night and someone will shake me and it was usually Corporal Baker. I would open my eyes and he would say, "Sarge, I got this for you - fish and chips, ice cold fish and greasy chips." He's bringing his old Sarge some fish and chips.

I went overseas in November of '43. I was at Lavenham before the first airplanes arrived. They arrived in April of '44. I don't think I finished that story where the 15 of us were down in Lavenham and we saw the first airplane land. I was there until after the last airplane left. I was there until August of '45. Our outfit, 400 men, were put aboard a Liberty ship, the 32nd hull built by Kaiser. It had been on the Murmansk Grain Run into Russia. It was the first time they ever carried troops, but there were oats growing in the scuppers. We were on our way through the English Channel, still in sight of land, we could see the lizard at land's end, and the skipper, who was a regular Navy Lieutenant Commander, come up on the bridge with a bullhorn and said, "Now hear this, now hear this. The war's over. We're going home." That was August 15, 1945. He said that we were headed for India to work on B-29s. We had plenty of fresh water, so each man could have a fresh water shower a day. The galley would be open 24 hours a day for coffee and sandwiches. We would have three meals a day, had no duties, and while he's talking, his crew had a team painting the after bulkhead of the bridge white and he said, "Weather permitting, we'll have movies on the after deck every night." It took 15 days to get back to the states from there. We were supposed to land in Boston, but they had no space. We couldn't get in; there was nothing there. So we ended up in Staten Island. It was a very pleasurable trip.

One of our fellows was a medical hypnotist. He was trained as a therapist in hypnosis. That wasn't his job over there in England, but he had that ability. He put on little shows now and then. He'd tell a fellow, put him under and ask him a few questions. He'd go through this stage routine and then he'd say, "When I snap my fingers," or whatever, "and you come out of it, you will walk to the bow of the ship and a bee will sting you. You'll slap it." We're in the middle of the Atlantic. There are no bees there. But he'd bring the fellow out, the guy would go up to the bow, and all of a sudden, just a few seconds he'd let out a scream, and he's slap his thigh or whatever - the bee got him!

In that same vein, this is interesting, we had a party for our squadron commander. The squadron commander was on his second tour of duty, second combat tour, and after several missions he could start the engines fine, but he'd start taxiing out, and he'd begin to shake. He was suffering combat fatigue. Since he was still a trained pilot, they made him the commander of our organization, and he would fly the administer flights-test flights, administrative. That was okay. But as long as he had bombs aboard, he just couldn't handle it. But we were going to have a party for him when he got his silver leaves. He became a Lieutenant Colonel, and he was going to be assigned back to the States and go to War College. This hypnotist was going to put on a little show during the party. Our guests were some WAAFS, some British Air Force gals and he had this one girl that went under real well. After going through the preliminaries, name and all that stuff, he said, "You are six years old. It's your birthday and you're having a party." And that little girls voice, "Yes, we're having party. Who's there? Well give me so and so and whatever." The posthypnotic suggestion was that "when you leave the stage, you go to the commander, throw your arms around him and give him a big kiss." She's a leading aircraftsman, which is about the same as a PFC, and he's a Colonel, and she did that, although she was so flustered, because the British - you just don't do that to officers!

One other party, I don't remember the month, but it was before Christmas in 1944. Several months before we decided we would host a party for children who were displaced. They came from the larger cities to the countryside from foster homes while their cities were in danger, you know. And also the local kids and orphans, what have you. So we had boxes set up around the PX and the squadron area where we get rations and throw some of our candy bars and different things in this barrel for the party. The parachute shop - well, we found out approximately how many girls there were going to be and how many boys - so for the girls, the parachute shop made Raggedy Anne dolls. And for the boys, the woodworking shop made a pony cart with a silhouette pony. The paint shop, of course, painted this all up. The Colonel took a B-17 to Scotland for a nice tree - a nice Christmas tree, a big one. He flew it back in this bomber. He also went to Portugal and got some bananas and oranges, something the kids had never seen. He brought that for the party. We decorated the Christmas tree - the lights were kind of boring because all we had were red, green and white lights. We took them from airplanes - these are the navigation lights from airplanes that were down due to maintenance. They decorated the tree, and when the party was over, of course, the lights went back to the airplane. The icicles on the tree were chaff, these radar deflecting strips of foil that they drop from airplanes. We weren't supposed to have that, but if you took them from an airplane waiting maintenance, there are going to be more put in there when they're ready to fly a mission. So, we decorated that and the Christmas tree ornaments, such as the angels and the various things, we saved our soft drink and beer cans, and the sheet metal shop cut out silhouette pennons to hang from the trees. As hosts, assigned people were going to be an uncle to a boy and a girl. I was chosen to be an uncle and I was very upset about that. I didn't want any part of that thing. But once the party began, I was glad I was there.

During a reunion in England several people said, "You know, there's a man I want you to meet." They brought this English fellow back. This fellow, I cannot confirm this, but he said, I can confirm what he said, but I can't confirm the event, he said, "You were my uncle at this party." He said, "I got a baseball in my pony cart." He said, "There are no instructions. I don't know what to do with it, but I got it in the box on the mantle piece." And at the last reunion we had in England, he had passed away in the mean time. The last reunion, his wife was my hostess for the day that the local people would take us where we wanted to go. She took me to her home and met her daughter and son-in-law. Her husband was no more than 10 years old [at the time] I'd say. But he had a stroke or a heart attack or something like that. But he remembered that party.

One of the children got sick, of course, because we had ice cream for them and the mess hall made some cakes. We had a fellow that could do wonders with powdered milk. He made ice cream out of it.

I said at the beginning that I was there until the last airplane left. We were cleaning up the base and some farmers across the fence shouted to us, you know, "Come here," and they said, "Have you heard about the anatomic bomb that the U.S. dropped on Japan?" Anatomic - I got a big kick out of that.

So anyhow, after appearing in the States and not going to India, I was discharged on December 3, 1945. I wanted to go to school, but there were no openings because the earlier dischargees had taken all the spots. So, I re-enlisted. I re-enlisted after three months out and I stayed in the service for 30 years. For 13 years, I was a technical instructor at Chanute AFB, Rantoul, Illinois, and Shepherd Air Force Base, Texas. In between these - well, let me back up just a minute. Before I became an instructor, the Berlin Airlift was on, and at that time, I was a flight chief for a single-engine flight, 15 airplanes, the 19 T-Gs and six P-51 Mustangs. It was getting pretty boring doing nothing. I was also flying test flights as a maintenance man on all the multi-engine airplanes. A message came out asking if anybody was interested in flying in the Berlin Airlift. I put in my name and was accepted. I went to Great Falls, Montana, for a six-week transition course. It was the only air base I was on that I saw the hanger roofs were held down with cables, hammered into the ground because the wind was so strong. At Great Falls, Montana we'd go to town and if we had change, silver dollar change, there were no one dollar bills, after you broke a ten you were loaded down. But we had training there, and around Thanksgiving of '48, I was in Wiesbaden and flew the first mission on the Airlift there. We flew mostly coal and flour, industrial coal. Our base was RAF station, Celle, near Hanover. I flew 174 missions into Berlin, out of Celle as a flight engineer. After that, I became an instructor of propulsion, piston engines at Rantoul.

I went back to Germany to get married. I met a girl during the airlift and I was the first person from the air training command to request a leave to go overseas to get married. We didn't know what we needed as far as paper work was concerned, so I went to the authority library and I had copies made of everything I thought I'd need. It was a good thing I did, too, because before I returned from the airlift my wife had an accident. Her leg was smashed and she was in a full body cast when I went back to get married. She came to the states on the Fourth of July 1950. I had two children, two boys. One was born in Rantoul, Illinois. The other one was Offenbach, Germany, because after the duty at Rantoul, Illinois, I was sent overseas for four years. I was a Propulsion Chief at Rhein-Main Air Base for military aircraft. After that, we were sent to Shepherd Air Force Base where I was again an instructor. My total instructor time was 13 years. In the meantime, I was part instruction duty and part mobile training, which meant we had mobile training detachments to go to various reserve and National Guard bases to give continual training to these guardsmen that were using our type of equipment. In our case, it was the C-119 G aircraft. I was the instructor on engines for that airplane.

Also, when President Johnson decided to have a Vietnamization Program, where the Vietnamese would have their own schools and instructors, I was named noncommissioned officer in charge of that program at Shepherd. We got the better qualified Vietnamese students; we taught them the material and then sent them to instructor training school. This was in Texas. We went to Ohio in the wintertime, and the students had never seen snow. They had their hands-on training in Ohio. The following April, I went to Vietnam and had to be with them until they had two classes graduate of their own people. I had already been to Vietnam in '66. I helped them set up their school at Bien Hoa and had to wait till two graduations. Then I came back home and went back to Vietnam in '70 as an advisor to the first Vietnamese Air Division in propulsion - very interesting duty. It was a beautiful country. The people are so nice, too - except for the VC.

That's what I did. I retired from the Air Force in July 1974, 30-year service. Our boys were away at that time. They were away at school. I went out to Shepherd Air Force Base, contract maintenance and got a job as an engine mechanic. I didn't want any supervisor position, just a mechanic. My wife was a diabetic and had other problems, so I chose the evening shift from four o'clock to midnight. That way we could make sure that she had her breakfast, had her proper lunch, had her insulin shot, and then she'd be awake watching TV when I got home at midnight. And so she might have a snack then, too. She usually forgot her supper, so that worked out all right. But after she passed away, I had eye surgery and realized that there was no sense of me working anymore. There was no sense of me working if I had to get someone else to check my work because I wasn't sure because of my sight.

I heard that there was a B-25 Mitchell bomber privately owned at the local airports. That same day, I got my toolbox out of the car and I started working on the B-25. I spent the next eight years flying all over the country with the air shows. So, I stayed with aviation all the time until he sold the airplane.

As I said, I was married overseas. My wife was in a full body cast wearing a blue nightgown. Since we got married, she said when she passed away, she wanted to be buried in a blue nightgown. It's so strange - I'm very forgetful - but years before she died, she said the blue nightgown would be in a certain place in the house. When she passed away, the mortician asked me if there were any special wishes. I said she wanted a blue nightgown, and I went right to the spot she told me and got it.

I had two boys as I mentioned, George and Robert. Now, they are both PhDs. One is a physicist working for a lab in Newport News, Virginia. The other one is an archeologist working at the University of California-Santa Barbara. But they're both into computers now, even though they didn't have any training. The one in Virginia is in charge of a multimillion-dollar computer system where he reads out the effects of particle acceleration - whatever that means, I have no idea. George, the one in California, has been field director on several trips down in Central America and Mexico, the Mayan culture. He's considered an expert in stone tools. They're all good boys. Rob, the physicist, graduated from Texas A&M Summa Cum Laude in physics.

Epilogue

I wrote this book and compiled these personal interviews of the men of the 487th Bomb Group in the hopes of keeping their stories alive for future generations. It was over two years ago that I said to Jim Erskine that I'd like to write a book of interviews of these veterans in their own words. He first looked seriously into my eyes and said, "Well, stop talking about it and just do it, Cindy!" Thank you, Jim! And to all of you who have taken the time for a personal interview and those of you who have written your own stories and sent them to me, many thanks to you also. It's been an honor and the privilege of a lifetime to have gotten to know each of you who contributed to my book, as well as your families.

When my dad passed away in 1998, I had never attended a 487th Reunion, but my mom and dad loved attending these events during the last years of his life. In April of 1999, my husband, daughter, mother and I went to Savannah Ga. to the Mighty Eighth Air Force Heritage Museum for the first time after my father died. Still missing him tremendously, there standing beside us were Henry and Jean Hughey at the Wing Commander's Circle.

Words could never begin to express how thoughtful and compassionate Henry and Jean have been to our family. They literally took us under their "wings." My dad practically raised my son and daughter, and it was especially tough for them after he died. Henry and Jean drove seven hours to attend my sons wedding. They presented a plaque with a piece of the runway from Lavenham to him at the rehearsal dinner. Henry told a little about the war and the Men of the 487th. He said he didn't want Tommy, my son, to forget, or the world to forget the sacrifices that were made for our freedom! My 28-year-old son wiped the tears from his eyes, as everyone else was doing, as he jumped up to hug Henry. When he wrote Henry and Jean their thank you note, he said, "I used to think my grandfather was the greatest man to walk the face of the earth, but now that I know the Men of the 487th, I know there were a lot of you." My daughter Sherry won the lottery of the 487th stain glass raffle item in Savannah, in January, at the 60th Anniversary. She said, "That's a sign for me to be involved with the 8th Air Force." This is a story of the difference one veteran can make in the lives of the other children and grandchildren of the members of their group.

In October 1999, my husband, mother, son and I attended the 8th Air Force Historical Society reunion in Savannah. My son wanted to walk through the inside of the museum at his own pace, and apparently a few veterans stopped to look at exhibits alongside him. That evening, he was so enthusiastic telling us stories that veterans had taken the time to stop and tell him.

Gentlemen From Hell

My Dad's pilot, at one point during the war was Walter McCarty, and when their plane went down in the English Channel, my dad was actually in the hospital recuperating from severe shrapnel wounds in his arm, for which he received the Purple Heart. I never got to speak with Fred Sweeney from my Dad's crew, but I spoke with Richard Atkins before he died, who was on that flight and knew my Dad. We had a great talk. He talked to me like I was the only person in the world he cared about talking to that day. His wife even told him that he had to get off the phone so his doctor could call him with his test results. With that, he told her, "I can get my test results anytime this afternoon – this is important!" These are some of my remembrances since I've come to know the men of the 487th.

All of the veterans in my book have been so helpful regarding my journey with this book. Your letters, e-mails and stories for your chapters brought tears to my eyes, joy to my heart and laughter to my soul. I never dreamed I would have such an overwhelming response.

One of my biggest sources of information was in Omaha, Nebraska. In Omaha, I personally interviewed Henry Hughey, Art Silva, Roy Levy, Jim Erskine, Jack Kohl, Leonard Davis, Mike Quering, Bob Densmore, William Michaels, Jim Bradford, and Roy Hon. In August 2002, I interviewed Richard Atkins over the telephone with my tape recorder running, and his enthusiasm during this interview was unbelievable, considering how very ill he was at that time, but he was determined to do the interview. Sixteen days after that interview, his wife called to tell me that he had passed away and was going to be buried on November 1. Richard was the last living member of my father's original crew, and November 1 happened to be the very day that my father was buried also! A few weeks after his death, I received another package of information that he had told his wife to send to me.

Just to tell you a little more about how my book progressed, on November 12, I interviewed Stanley Rolfes by phone. Pete Riegel prepared a tape, with the help of Mel and Patty at their home, and mailed it to me, as did Jim Wandless.

On February 21, I drove to Henry and Jean Hughey's house, spent the night, and the next day, Henry and I were off to Memphis, Tennessee, where we stayed with Henry's tail gunner, Jimmy Spurlock. After I interviewed Spurlock, Walter Baker came over for his interview, and then we went on to Francis Eberhart's house. Upon leaving Memphis, we headed for Maxwell Air Force Base in Birmingham, Alabama, where Amy Lawley, wife of Congressional Medal of Honor recipient Bill Lawley, met us to help us get through "tight security" to get to the base library to do research on my Dad's records. Upon returning from there, my husband and I drove to Benson, N.C., outside of Raleigh, to interview Paul Tomney.

Never in my whole life have I felt such passion for anything that I have undertaken. Raising my daughter and son to become honest, caring and independent adults has been the greatest accomplishment of my lifetime, and when this book is finished, it will be a very close second!

In my travels, the veterans who have told me their memories and opened their hearts to me, and the dealings I've had with all their family members, opening their homes to me, will be forever in my mind. The laughter telling me their young war years as well as the tears will be a part of me until the day I die.

The tears and emotions of these men of the 487th telling their stories to me are what kept me on track with this book and gave me the determination to see the book to its completion. If you have a relationship with a veteran of World War II, treasure it; and remember any time you see a veteran that it's because of him that you enjoy the blanket of freedom that you sleep under each night.

Index

A

Abbot, Frank - 201, 202
Adams, Richard D. - 192
Alcar, Max - 93
Alford, Sibyl - 124
Allhouse, Dick - 202
Alvine, Samuel, Jr. - 207, 211
Arce, Johanna P. Zmud - 123
Armstrong, Fred H. - 120
Arnold - 5, 13
Atkins, Richard - 149, 153, 156, 159, 161, 162, 163, 292
Atkinson, John - 228, 231
Austad, Jake - *vii*

B

Baker - 284
Baker, Walter - 247, 255, 292
Ball, Ira L. - 21
Ballman, Bob - 176
Bane, James - 182
Barrow, Klay - 160
Barrow, Sherry - *vii*, 160
Battschinger - 80
Battschinger, Bob - 107
Battschinger, George - 91, 106, 107
Bavender, Bruce - 173
Becker, Cuno V. - 21
Becker, Phil - 269
Beckman, Robert W. - 120
Beeson, Betty - 119
Beeson, John - 115, 119
Belt, Dave - 194
Belt, Fred - 192, 193, 194, 196
Berg, Chet - 83

Besson, John - 91
Biri, Paul - 5, 29, 30, 31, 172
Blackie - 12
Blaha, Henry - 153, 154, 155, 156
Blair - 108, 109
Blake, Henry - 159
Bodsky - 168
Boland, Donald - 207
Bon, Lester Paul C. - 120
Boss, Larry - 169
Bowers, William - 150, 191, 192
Bradford, Jim - 5, 29, 292
Brennen, George - 71, 77
Britton, Lee - 243
Broadbent, Don - 83, 84
Brodsky, Ed - 159, 165, 166, 167
Brokaw, Tom - 247
Brooks, Claudia - 93
Brooks, Hugh - 83, 84
Brooks, Jim - 2, 91, 92, 93
Broom, Elizabeth - 24
Broom, Jeanne Michelle - 24
Broom, John - 5, 19
Broom, John William, II - 24
Bross, Larry - 173
Brown, Neil E. - 19
Browning, Robert - 32, 33
Burrage, Gene T. - 176
Buxtion, Bucky - 224
Byrnes, Alferd J. - 66

C

Caledar, Chick - 220
Callaghan - 66
Callaghan, Frank J. - 65
Campbell, Blair - 107

Carey, Dennis - 93
Carpenter, Jeff - *vii*
Casillas, Ruperto - 83
Castle, Frederick - 12, 17, 18, 21, 22,
    29, 31, 54, 66, 86, 125, 126, 132,
    137, 138, 146, 171, 172, 194, 195,
    211, 218, 223, 228, 264, 266
Ceder, Dick - 53, 54, 55, 56
Chatterton - 54
Chavez, Paul - 128
Cherry, David - 173
Childers, Thomas - 269
Churchill - 114
Ciserano, Anthony - 173
Clarry, Ed - 243
Claxton, Johnny - 202
Clemets, Bill - 276
Cline - 271
Coles, Keith - 153, 154, 156, 159
Coletta, Chick - 224
Collings, Buford E. - 37, 38
Collins, Thomas W. - 65
Cooke, Rodney T. - 164
Cornery, John J. - 21
Cox, Howard - 207
Craig, Louise - *vii*, 160
Craig, Thomas - *v*, 2, 149, 153, 154,
    155, 156, 157, 158, 159, 160, 162,
    163
Cromwell - 195
Crosby, Bing - 70
Crow, Bill - 227, 231, 236
Curtis - 12
Curtiss, Willard J. - 59, 60, 65, 66

D

Dahlberg, David - 91, 141
Davies, Anna - 276
Davies, Frank, IV - 276
Davis, Jim - 152
Davis, Leonard - 2, 91, 102, 292

Densmore, Bob - 5, 11, 12, 13, 15,
    29, 292
Densmore, Jeanne - 29
Dickinson, Hewitt J. - 19
Dolin, Leon - 115, 119
Doolittle, Jimmy - 222, 241
Dorsey, Tommy - 80
Doty, Richard A. - 37, 39
Dougherty, Ann Marie Zmud - 123
Drake, Virgil - 93
Drinnon, Kenny - 192, 194, 196
Drury, Brendan - *vii*
Duane Kaiser - 47
Duffy - 12
Dumler, Fred - 29
Dumler, Smitty - 29

E

Eads, Patty Riegel - 180
Eberhart, Francis - 150, 169, 192,
    198, 208, 292
Edmonds, Betty - 10
Edmonds, Roger - 10
Edwards, John - 264, 266
Eisenhower - 5, 13, 101, 188
Eleanor, Matz - 58
Elliot, Robert - 83
Ellis - 271
Emerson, Tom - 228, 235
Erskine, Cynthia - 33
Erskine, Diane - 33
Erskine, Jane - 33
Erskine, Jim - 5, 32, 291, 292
Erskine, Joe Ann - 32, 33
Erskine, Michael - 33
Erskine, Scott - 33
Erskine, Timothy - 33
Etters, Peter - *vii*

F

Foote, Chuck - 152
Foster, Jonathan - *vii*
Freeman, Roger - 85
Fuchs, Robert - 192, 193, 196
Fuller, Edgar Lee - 19
Furr, Wilburn E. - 19

G

Gabresky, Francis - 172
Gaffney, Jane - 83
Gaffney, Jim - 83
Gaffney, Joe - 6, 83
Galand, Adolph - 172
Gasser, Robert J. - 192, 193, 194
Gaudin, Duffy J. - 21
George, Willard - 153, 154, 155, 159
Gervassi, Gori - 83
Ghezzi, Edward M. - 65
Gillett, Janine - 206
Goodenough, Robert L. - 97
Gossell, Junior - 5, 25
Graham, George - 107, 109
Graves, Hudie E. - 19, 20
Green, Willard A. - 19
Gregory - 54

H

Harless, Jack - 243
Harriman, Robert - 5, 9, 10, 11, 12, 13, 29, 30, 264, 266
Haskett, Chuck - 150, 206, 207
Haskett, Janice - 211
Haskett, Wilma - 211, 213
Hatfield, Roger - 29
Hawkins, Jack - 192, 193
Hayes, Grayson - 164
Headley, Julian - 91, 124, 126

Headley, Sibyl Alford - 124
Heard, Ann - 276
Heard, Arlie - 274
Heard, Bessie - 276
Heard, Bobby Wayne - 247, 274
Heard, Leigh - 276
Heard, Robert - 276
Heard, Sally - 276
Heard, Sarah - 276
Heard, Winona McGowen - 274
Herberger, William - 37
Hernley, Frederick E. - 19
Hiser, William J. - 66
Hitler, Adolph - 187
Hoelscher, Melva - 164
Hollifield, Glen - 164
Hon, Ron, Sr. - 149, 175, 177, 185, 292
Honey, Kate Miller - 160
Honey, Thomas Anthony - *vii*, 160
Hope, Bob - 275
Hopkin, Reese - 115, 118, 119
Horan, Frank E. - 37
Hoyle - 199
Huck, Donald - 207, 211
Hudson - 9, 13
Huff - 176
Hughey, Jean - 32, 291, 292
Hughey, William Henry - 32, 149, 169, 173, 174, 212, 261, 291, 292
Hughey, William Henry, III - 172
Humick, Tony - 243
Hyland, Jim - 2, 6, 85

I

Isaacson, Joel - 181

J

Jackson, John - 83

Jeffers - 9, 10, 13
Johnson, Bob - 172
Johnson, Lee - 165, 167, 168
Johnson, Lyndon - 287
Johnston, Lee - 166

K

Kaiser, Duane - 6, 49
Kandler, Karl, Jr. - 6, 59, 61
Karn, Susie - *vii*
Katz, Harry - 192
Kausrud, Donald - 207, 209, 211
Kersten, Helen - 86
Kersten, Lloyd - 85
Kilburg, Donald - 247, 262, 264
Kleinman - 53, 54, 56
Kneeley, Bill - 70, 78
Kohl, Jack - 5, 33, 34, 35, 292
Kohl, Judy - 33
Kraft, Marvin - 37, 39
Kulik - 167
Kulik, Steve - 164

L

LaBorde, Joe - 222
Lacy - 176
Lamort, Anne Marie - 212
Lang, Kenneth - 207, 209, 210, 211
Lank - 108, 109
Lankiewicz, Stanley - 107
Lawley, Amy - 292
Lawley, Bill - 292
Lay, Bernie, Jr. - 1, 36, 37, 159, 165, 167, 168, 186, 187
Leboard, Joe - 216
Leon, Jack - 115, 119
Lerner, Isadore - 149, 183, 188
Levy, Roy - 150, 201, 292
Lewis - 80

Liebert - 272
Lindbergh, Charles Augustus - 36
Litka, Ray - 202
Lloyd - 134
Lorre, Peter - 70
Lull, Robert H. - 21
Lund - 211
Luther, Jean Ann - 172

M

MacHauer, Dave - 53, 54, 56, 57
Marino, Leonard - 115, 118, 119
Marquez, Cosme P. - 176
Marthaler, Johnny - 93
Martin - 13
Martin, Robert - 107
Massey, Arthur - 19
Materovitch, Sylvester - 243
Matz, Neil F. - 6, 51
Mau, Eldon A. - 221
Mazzole, Albert - 97
McCarthy, Harold J., Jr. - 47
McCarty - 10, 13, 153, 154, 157, 159, 165, 166, 167, 168, 292
McCleary - 38, 159, 165, 167, 168
McGill, Justin - *vii*
McKee, John - 173
McLean - 271
McLeary - 184
Meier, Bob - 93
Meredith - 10, 12, 13
Merritt, James K. - 65
Messerly, Earl - 157
Messerly, Howard - 157
Messerly, Julian - 2, 149, 151, 153, 154, 155, 156, 157, 159, 160, 162
Messerly, Ron - 151, 157
Messerly, Russell - 157
Michaels, George - 288
Michaels, Robert - 288

Michaels, William - 1, 279, 280, 292
Miller, Glen - 73
Miller, Howard - 207, 209, 210, 211
Milton - 242
Mixon, Mattie - 112
Moore, Paul - 119
Moore, Ralph - 115, 119
Moore, Walter - 2, 150, 226
More, Sir Thomas - 234
Moser, Alvin, Jr. - 197
Mount, William C. - 37, 39
Mulhollon, Jack - 50
Mullins - 120, 121
Murray, Don - 83, 84

N

Nash, Lloyd - 18, 29
Neal, Cynthia Craig - 158, 160, 167, 172, 291
Neal, Larry - *vii*, 160
Nolan, Barney - 37
Nylon, Harry T. - 201, 202

O

Oaks - 76
Obrecht, Gerald - 247, 269, 270
Osieki, Lucien - 115, 116
Overoll, Angelo - 202
Owens, Harold - 165, 167

P

Parks, Warren H. - 21
Partain, Donald Frantz - 5, 36, 37
Partridge - 13
Patrick, Harold, - 83
Patridge - 5
Patterson, Pru - *vii*

Patton - 45, 87
Patton, George - 81
Pecourcey, Bill - 280
Pete, James - 164
Peterson, Howard (Pete) M. - 91, 130, 141
Peyton, Jim - 93
Pezzato, Leno - 107
Pflieger, Clifford - 93
Phillips, George - 2, 91, 96
Phillips, John - 243
Pittis, Robert - 107
Polen, Robert - 115, 119
Porsche - 182
Porsche, Robert - 182
Price, Charlotte Broom - 24
Pyle, Ernie - 237

Q

Quering, Mike - 150, 214, 221, 292

R

Rasmussen, Charles - 164, 165
Rasof, Al - 247, 267
Rasof, Betty - 267, 268
Raymer, Candy - *vii*
Reed, Lloyd - 18, 29
Rich, Bruce - 205
Rich, Victoria - 205
Rich, William - 150, 204
Richards, Ned - 29
Richman, Laura - 149, 151, 156
Riegel, Cynthia - 167
Riegel, John - 167
Riegel, Mark - 167
Riegel, Marsha - 165, 167
Riegel, Melva - *vii*, 164, 165, 180, 292
Riegel, Patricia - 167

Riegel, Pete - 149, 159, 164, 167, 169, 180, 292
Rip, Bill - 202
Roberts, Hal - 225
Roberts, John - 182
Robertson, Hugh - 41
Rogers - 176
Rolfes, Stanley - 5, 41, 43, 44, 292
Rommel - 98
Roosevelt - 88, 188
Rousselle, Willy - 211, 212
Rowe - 9, 12

S

Sam - 12
Saporito - 66
Satterfield, Veston - 120
Schooner, Larry - 83
Schoonover, Larry - 84
Shanks, Arka M. - 37
Shaw, Robert - 115, 119
Shepard - 272
Shields, Craig - 93
Shorty - 12
Silva, Art - 149, 176, 177, 180, 292
Simmons, Ed - 164
Slusarczyk, Stan - 166
Smith - 108, 132
Smith, Fred L. - 120, 121
Smith, Rusty - 272, 273
Snider, Billy - 93
Spaatz - 13
Spatz - 5
Sperber, Harold P. - 21, 22
Spoerl, Raymond - 153, 159, 161
Sprock, Dick - 228
Spurlock, James - 171, 173, 292
Stanton - 54
Steck - 13
Stephens, Roscoe J. - 66
Stewart, Jimmy - 252

Stoltz, Herb - 228
Sunberg, John - 115, 118, 119
Swain - 9, 12
Swarzon - 65
Sweeney, Fred - 153, 155, 157, 159, 292
Sweet, John W. - 120, 121

T

Tepper, Claude - 29
Testa - 182
Tigh, Charles E. - 19
Tomeo, Gordon R. - 21
Tomney, Paul - 5, 7, 292
Tuel, Dean - 152
Turnquist - 53

V

Valentine, Tom - 127
Van Dyke, Joe - 38, 39
Voss, Kay - 247, 248
Vratney, Frank - 159
Vratny - 154
Vratny, Frank - 168

W

Walton, Herb - 107
Wandless, Jim - 6, 67, 292
Warner - 113
Warren, Lisa Broom - 24
Watson, Robert D. - 66
Webber - 176
Weber, James - 206, 207, 208
Welko, John - 169, 173
Westbrook, Norman - 243
Wheasler, Alan H. - 91, 136
White, Frank - 164

White, Paul - 150, 243
William - 9, 10
Williams, Jim - 41
Williams, Robert - 153, 155, 156, 159
Williams, Sam M. - 120
Willis, Joseph - 166
Wisdom, Bob - 193
Wise, Walter - 247, 272
Wood, Robert - 107

Y

Yaegle, Clyde L. - 221
Yakobsky, Julia Ann Hughey - 172
Yocum, Clark - 91, 104, 111
Yocum, Esther - 112
Young, John - 234, 237, 239, 240
Young, Richmond - 169, 173
Yowan, Robert - 207, 209, 211

Z

Zaletski, William J. - 37
Zee, Zeider - 195
Zeidman, Elmer - 192, 193, 194, 196
Zmud, John Peter - 123
Zmud, Robert W. - 123
Zmud, Walter - 91, 120